ART IS
LIFE

ART IS LIFE

Icons & Iconoclasts,
Visionaries & Vigilantes,
& Flashes of
Hope in the Night

JERRY SALTZ

Riverhead Books · New York · 2022

RIVERHEAD BOOKS
An imprint of Penguin Random House LLC
penguinrandomhouse.com

With the exception of "The *Medusa* and the *Pequod*" and "Basquiat Painting Becomes Priciest Work Ever Sold by a U.S. Artist," the essays in this book have previously appeared, in slightly different form, in *The Village Voice* and *New York* magazine.

Grateful acknowledgment is made for permission to reprint "Basquiat Painting Becomes Priciest Work Ever Sold by a U.S. Artist" © 2017 National Public Radio, Inc. The news report by this title was originally broadcast on NPR's *Weekend Edition Sunday* on May 21, 2017, and is used with the permission of NPR. Any unauthorized duplication is strictly prohibited.

Page 20: © Carol Diehl. Used by permission.
Pages 32–33: Jeff Koons, *Puppy*, 1992 © Jeff Koons. Photo by Bart Barlow. On view from June 6 to September 5, 2000. Organized by Public Art Fund in association with Rockefeller Center
Pages 50–51: Photo © Alessia Pierdomenico/Reuters Pictures
Pages 94–95: Photo © Grotte de Niaux—R. Kann
Pages 198–99: Photo by Jeenah Moon/The New York Times/Redux.
© 2022 Estate of Pablo Picasso/Artists Rights Society (ARS), New York. © 2022 Faith Ringgold/ Artists Rights Society (ARS), New York, Courtesy ACA Galleries, New York

Riverhead and the R colophon are registered trademarks of Penguin Random House LLC.

Library of Congress Cataloging-in-Publication Data

Names: Saltz, Jerry, 1951– author.
Title: Art is life : icons and iconoclasts, visionaries and vigilantes, and flashes of hope in the night / Jerry Saltz.
Description: New York : Riverhead Books, 2022. | Includes index.
Identifiers: LCCN 2022006448 (print) | LCCN 2022006449 (ebook) | ISBN 9780593086490 (hardcover) | ISBN 9780593086506 (ebook)
Subjects: LCSH: Art and society.
Classification: LCC N72.S6 S248 2022 (print) | LCC N72.S6 (ebook) | DDC 701/.03—dc23/eng/20220216
LC record available at https://lccn.loc.gov/2022006448
LC ebook record available at https://lccn.loc.gov/2022006449

Printed in the United States of America
4th Printing

BOOK DESIGN BY LUCIA BERNARD

For Art
and to Roberta for saving my life

To all my readers:
I can't write if writing is without you.

Contents

TOWARD A RECKONING: 2009–2016

THE LONG AMERICAN NIGHT: 2016–2021

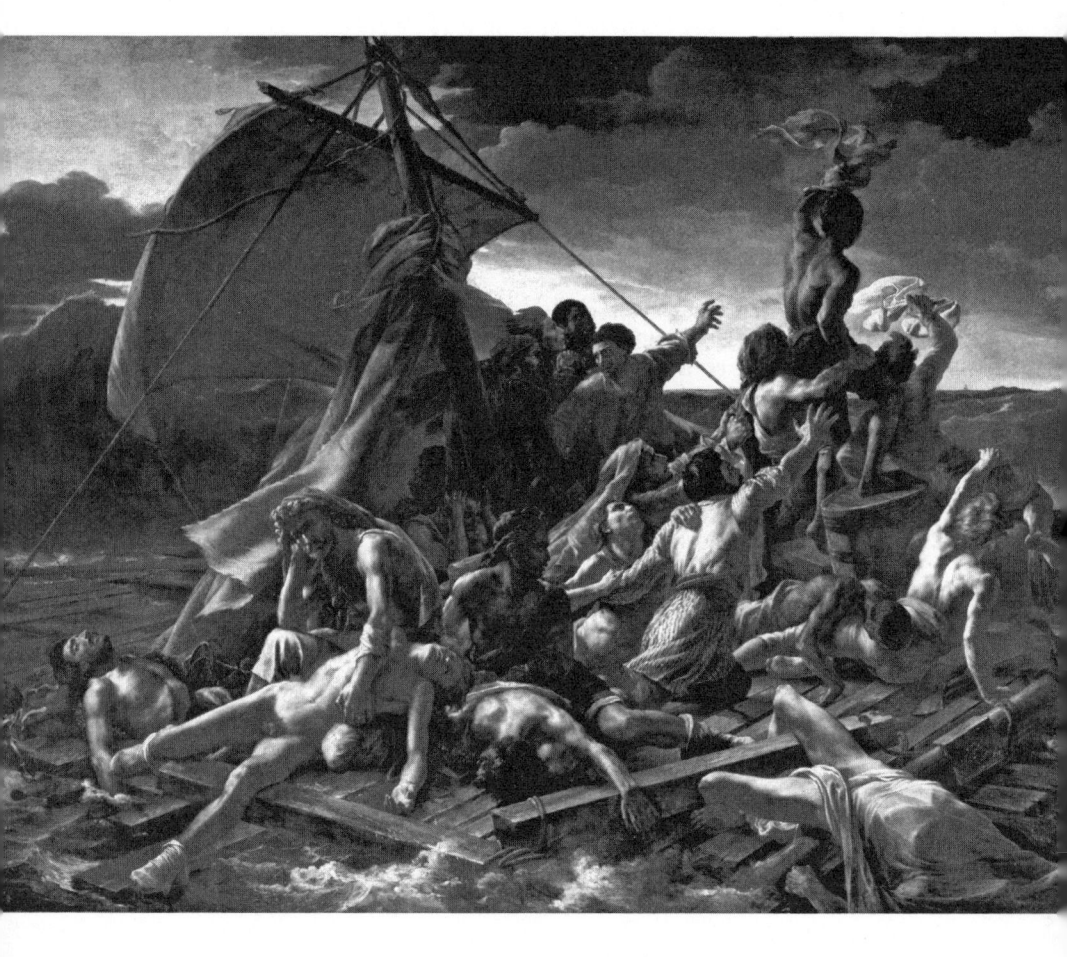

INTRODUCTION

The *Medusa* and the *Pequod*

ART, AND LIFE, IN OUR TIME

T he first time the power of art pulled the rug out from under me, I was
nineteen years old.

It was the early 1970s. I was in Europe for the first time, on my way
through Paris to Warsaw with my Polish girlfriend, on a bizarre quest to
sell blue jeans behind the Iron Curtain. On that day, during my first pilgrimage to the Louvre, I laid eyes on a painting that seemed the sum of all
things. It was a cosmographic perpetual motion machine, a purgatorial
charnel house—as far from the warmth of any human sun as anything I'd
ever beheld. The moment I saw it, something like Krakatoa went off within
me. That painting was Théodore Géricault's *The Raft of the Medusa*. Standing before it, I felt the gravitational field of my life shift forever.

The Raft of the Medusa is massive in scale, yet its subject matter is as
simple as cows in a field, bathers by a river, or a birth in a manger. We see
a large raft bearing a crowd of male figures, at the mercy of heaving seas.
Their poses suggest a classical frieze, like Elgin marbles from hell—a collective ash heap of individually vivisected souls stripped bare of humanity.

Each of the men is marked by a distinct, unforgettable gesture. Some are reckoning with their wounds; others seem to be coming to terms with death; some seem closer to damnation than to life. Every one of them appears hopeless. Our eyes are compelled by shafts of flickering phosphorescent light that rake at angles across the figures in the painting's foreground, tracing its dark pyramidal structure. It's a vision of jagged complexity and somehow also of profound grandeur.

That day, as I contemplated the *Medusa*, I felt the shattering heartbreak of a long-forgotten memory. My mind carried me back to a moment when I was ten years old, left by my mother to wander alone in the Art Institute of Chicago, scared and confused, until a small colorful diptych by Giovanni di Paolo beckoned to me from across a gallery. A portal opened.

A month later, my mother committed suicide. The portal slammed shut.

I never looked at art again. Until I did.

EVERY WORK OF ART tells a story: From hands on a cave wall to figures arrayed along a table for a Last Supper. From gleaners in a field to luncheons on the grass. From romping Greek gods to a Sunday in the park to the cutout silhouette of a white man beating a slave. As Marcel Proust wrote, "Every reader, as he reads, is actually the reader of himself." The subject matter of Michelangelo's *David* is a biblical tale told in marble. But the deep content of this five-hundred-year-old sculpture—its aesthetic substructure, its crux and lifeblood—includes ideas about sensuality, beauty, majesty, pathos, the power of the self, the potentiality of movement, the inchoate softness of marble, even the awareness of recently rediscovered classical Roman statuary so radical that it almost gave Michelangelo a nervous breakdown. Goya's *Saturn Devouring His Son*, like Toni Morrison's *The Bluest Eye*, Aleksandr Solzhenitsyn's *One Day in the Life of Ivan Denisovich*, Nina Simone singing "Strange Fruit," or Francis Ford Coppola's *Apocalypse Now*, makes you experience alienation, rage, horror, revulsion, love, grace, ugliness, absurdity, hopelessness, bloodlust, bleakness, the memories of meetings and partings, nightmares, phantoms, cultural dysmorphia, shapeless inner shadows, the shattering collapse of moral order, and the decay of the soul—*all at the same time.*

The painting I saw that day at the Louvre had its origins in a real-life story of the transatlantic slave trade. In June 1816, the French frigate *Medusa* and three other ships were dispatched to Senegal to reestablish operations and resume the trade, which had been interrupted by the Napoleonic Wars. The *Medusa*'s captain was Hugues Duroy de Chaumareys, a fifty-two-year-old royalist who hadn't been to sea in decades and had never piloted a ship. The passengers, more than four hundred in all, were a mix of monarchists, left-wing crew members, families, merchants, mercenaries, and convicts. The ship was inadequately outfitted, carrying outdated maps and too few lifeboats. On his first day at sea, Chaumareys disobeyed orders and sped ahead of the rest of the fleet, hoping to impress superiors. Soon he was sailing alone. After a series of miscalculations, including the failure to retrieve a man overboard, others began issuing orders.

By July, the *Medusa* was approaching the deadly Arguin Bank, an expanse of shallow water more than forty miles off the coast of West Africa that had wrecked numerous ships. The crew knew the maneuvers to steer around this grave danger, but Chaumareys ignored them; finally, fatally, he mistook one crucial landmark for another, and on July 5 the *Medusa* headed directly into the bank. The color of the ocean changed from deep blue to lighter green, then turned clear altogether. Dread came over the crew; the ship fell into hushed terror. Then, with a great scraping sound, the *Medusa* shuddered, shook, and ran aground.

The crew scrambled to free the boat. The ship was far too heavy to pull out using lifeboats, and Chaumareys refused to jettison its fourteen heavy bronze cannons to make it lighter, fearing the wrath of his superiors. Panic set in; recriminations flew; fighting broke out among factions reflecting the ship's political divide. Finally, Chaumareys ordered the construction of a very large raft to be pulled to shore by the six lifeboats. As the raft was being built, the captain, along with his officers and their families and friends, boarded the half-full lifeboats and prepared to cast off.

With that, everything fell apart. Violence erupted; the panicked hordes filled themselves on wine, water, and food and threw the remainder over-board. People jumped off the ship to claim the best spots on the raft. One hundred forty-seven people, including one woman and a twelve-year-old boy, crowded onto the unsteady raft, which sat two feet deep in the water. Many had to stand; others lashed themselves to whatever they could find. In the light of early morning, the lifeboats started rigging lines to the raft. When the ropes were pulled, the raft barely moved. After six hours of strug-gling unsuccessfully to tow the raft, at eleven o'clock in the morning came the fateful order: An axe was taken to the lines. The raft was cast adrift. Chaumareys and his privileged companions sailed off.

The raft had no maps, steering device, sail, or navigational instru-ments. On the first day, several threw themselves overboard. That night, a storm wracked the raft. By morning, twelve were dead and many others grievously injured. The next day brought two suicides. Then came hallu-cinations, hunger, thirst, fights, and another gale. Some ate their belts and hats for the oil in the leather. Next came the violence. People were beaten, stabbed, trampled, hacked with hatchets, had their eyes gouged out, were bayoneted, were pushed into the sea. Political factions slaughtered one an-other. By dawn, another sixty were dead. On the third day the cannibal-ism began. Those deemed too weak to survive were sacrificed for food. Their dead flesh was hung from ropes to dry. Some survivors ate directly from corpses. Fourteen days passed this way.

On the morning of July 17, a tiny white speck was spotted on the hori-zon: a sail. Pandemonium broke out, as survivors gestured wildly for help. Then the sail disappeared. This is the *exact* moment Géricault gives us in *The Raft of the Medusa*, the one survivors said was darkest of all: a tableau of souls being cast into hell. This is the deep content of the painting—the moment when all hope is lost.

The calamity of the *Medusa* is a story of abject human failure. Although the sail eventually reappeared on the horizon, and the fifteen surviving passengers were rescued, five of them died within days of reaching land. As the survivors' stories of malfeasance, cruelty, betrayal, and barbarism poured into France, the wreck of the *Medusa* became a national scandal, a

symbol of a country torn apart. At the subsequent court-martial, Chaumareys blamed the crew, bad maps, and faulty equipment for the disaster, taking no responsibility himself; he never mentioned the raft. He was found
innocent of capital crimes and sentenced to three years for simple negligence. No one else was found guilty of anything. None of the survivors were
compensated for their losses.

THERE HAD NEVER BEEN a painting that looked like Géricault's *Raft of the
Medusa*. While its geometric composition, figurative skill, and virtuosity
recall the Neoclassicist art that immediately preceded it, the *Medusa* is fundamentally different. The surface feels alive and molten, like sluicing
paint; its tone is darker, its imagery more graphically dramatic and aggressively convulsive, as if Géricault were approaching some new fiery sublime. He began work in a moment when the qualities of eighteenth-century
Neoclassicism—its enervated smooth surfaces, silky perfections, rote lion-
izations of male strength and idealization of history, myth, revolution, and
war—had come to seem insipid and irrelevant. By 1815, when Napoleon
was defeated at Waterloo, as many as three million people had been killed
in a decade and a half of European wars. The continent was decimated.
Great Britain and Russia were ascendant. France was annihilated, its population saddled with rampant unemployment, its national coffers destitute,
its society in chaos. It was a nation in mourning, and at war with itself. Yet
after all that, less than a month after Waterloo, the guillotined king's
younger brother was named king. Soon he began reinstating many of the
failed figures of the *ancien régime*—aristocrats, generals, bureaucrats, min-
isters, and lackeys. This, too, is part of the deep content of *The Raft of the
Medusa*: It marks the dying of one epoch and the start of another, one not
so different from our own.

   Géricault was twenty-seven in 1818, a good-looking, well-off artist
who'd just returned from Rome after an ill-fated affair with his uncle's
wife. The Paris he returned to was seething with rage at its leaders over a
slate of new censorship laws, and over the fate of the *Medusa*. Galvanized

by the survivors' stories, Géricault resolved to capture the catastrophic implications of the wreck. Before setting down his vision, he interviewed the authors of the bestselling account of the wreck and met with as many of the other survivors as he could. He sailed the English Channel to study waves, examined J. M. W. Turner's paintings of skies and water, even retrieved cadaver parts from a nearby hospital to his studio to better capture the appearance of dead flesh. He made scores of preparatory sketches and studies and constructed a full-size replica of the raft in a studio he'd rented just to make this picture. He shaved his head, withdrew from society, and worked alone in complete silence for months, sleeping in the studio, seeing only the single assistant who brought him meals and supplies. By July 1819, three years after the wreck, the painting was done. In August it was delivered to that year's Paris Salon.

At first the painting was mounted high on a wall, but before the show opened, Géricault persuaded the organizers of the Salon to install the painting more prominently. It was presented under the generic title of *Shipwreck Scene*, in order to circumvent government censorship, but everyone who saw it recognized what they were looking at: the raft, the faces, the flesh, the horror. Some reviewers lambasted the scene as a "pile of corpses." Many were disturbed by its gruesome imagery and dark implications. But the wisest of Géricault's contemporaries understood what one French observer wrote: that "our whole society is aboard the raft of the *Medusa*."

THE RAFT OF THE MEDUSA became the most famous painting in France. It was awarded one of the Salon's gold medals that year, but the government declined to acquire the work. This devastated Géricault, who removed the canvas from its stretcher, rolled it up, and stored it in a friend's studio. The painting was purchased by the Louvre not long after Géricault died at thirty-two of spinal tuberculosis. At the time of his death, he was preparing another gigantic work—this one on the annihilating atrocities of slavery.

At the apex of the *Medusa*, its protagonist and focal point, is Jean-Charles, one of three black figures in the work. Many of the other figures on the raft surround, hold on to, stretch toward, and support him; he is their avatar and savior. Here were three black men pictured as people, not property. Other faces depict actual individuals on the raft, including survivors Alexandre Corréard and Henri Savigny, who penned the book that led to the scandal. The model for the figure at center foreground, lying face-down with one arm outstretched, was the young Eugène Delacroix, who found the painting's effect so "terrifying" that after posing for it he "broke into a run and kept running like a fool all the way" back to his studio. On the right we see the mangled body of a drowning man and the remains of a tattered French flag. On the left, an old man stares into space as he cradles the iridescent dead body of his twelve-year-old son. He is a pietà for a modern age.

The Raft of the Medusa helped initiate the new movement called Romanticism. In it we find the birth of the modern consciousness, with its new anxieties: the individual on their own, homesick for other times and places; the violence of war; the end of rationality and idealism; an interest in mysticism, fairy tale, and the occult; a turning away from God; the worship of youth and innocence; and an ecstasy in sublime states of mind and nature, even as the natural world was on the verge of destruction. It was an age that saw countless institutions collapse. This psychic shattering is reflected in the creations of five other artists working in the same historical moment as Géricault: Mary Shelley's *Frankenstein* (1818); Percy Bysshe Shelley's "colossal Wreck" of "Ozymandias" (1818); the Black Paintings of Francisco Goya (1819–1823); the cryptic visions of William Blake (from 1788 to his death in 1827); and Beethoven's Ninth Symphony (1822–1824).

The elemental power and poetry of Géricault's *Medusa* changed me forever. It told me things that I've known and lived by ever since. To encounter a work of art for the first time is to confront, for an instant, something you've never seen in your life. You are reminded that what you're looking at was once (or perhaps still is) contemporary art, in direct conversation with its own time. All art is a kind of exorcism. This is what gives art its power to change the conditions of our life.

Art not only saved my life in very real ways (of which you'll read more in this book); it also exerts an ancient force that gives me access to a place where things are more than the sums of their parts, where—in violation of all natural law—objects give off more energy than went into their making.

ART IS THE GREATEST OPERATING SYSTEM our species has ever invented, a means of exploring consciousness, seen and unseen worlds. It is an instrument, medium, matrix, or miracle that transforms old impressions into new thoughts; that makes a thousand insignificant details light up and draw you out. For many of us, it is another country, a new home. The artist is a sort of Dr. Frankenstein, transmuting the rules of nature and the material world, memory, influence, culture, and tradition, trying to bring something new and unknown to life. Its soul might be instinct. Art is two parts agency and one part inner heat. The artist loves going down rabbit holes, working toward and against something at the same time, translating sensory and extrasensory impressions that all have their own sovereignty or joy, each of them on a journey to bring something back from a personal underworld, to build a new body out of disparate parts and materials. In this way, art is something like an undoing of death.

Art allows us to ask big questions, to think in languages beyond words. It makes us reckon with uncomfortable things, compels us to look for difference, to glean the pressures of necessity, and to notice the monumental in details: how a girl's pearl earring can become the center of the world, or how the image of a famous face, rendered in Day-Glo silkscreen, might become an avatar of the damned. Art can be talisman or comfort, used to heal or to make people kill. At the same time, art cannot be understood in terms of *purpose*. As the sculptor Charles Ray has said, art is "for absolutely nothing." To make, or experience, art is to enter a kind of free zone; it slows us down, places us in some epistemological estuary, takes us into the wild. We make art from our flaws, fragilities, perversities, from our need to communicate or be entertained or stave off death, to create our own mating dances, to deliver our own children, to mourn. Art is bigger than mere subject matter. It is as big as life.

ART IS LIFE is a kind of real-time chronicle of the astounding changes that have overtaken the art world in the twenty-first century. It's a period that has seen dramatic disturbances in the art world. Massive trees have fallen. The center is not merely holding but continually expanding, multiplying, superheating and cooling over and over again, threatening to atomize or collapse, but then ever re-forming.

Since 1999, the furioso world I call home has been waist-deep in excess but also passion, punctuated by tremors of ambivalence, finally attaining a new equilibrium of contradiction. It has been a time of stratospheric prices, of alpha dogs and megacollectors trying to buy credibility by amassing cookie-cutter collections. It's the century that saw the birth of the megagalleries—corporations with behemoth spaces in multiple cities, run by massive staffs who pull the strings of even more wide-ranging PR networks, publishing in-house magazines that employ critics and curators who claim to be against just this sort of late capitalism. Some of these behemoths are great; others are a mess. Many of the online art magazines have gone along for the ride, devoting much of their space to these bull elephants, posting nearly all positive reviews and endless features and listicles on "Hot Artists," "Last Night's Parties," "Best Art Fair Booths," "Price Indexes," and the like.

All of this has happened against the backdrop of the collapse of one of the longest-lasting movements in art history: Modernism.

Modernism was the most visually and intellectually consequential Western art movement since the Renaissance. It was the spawn of the mid-nineteenth century, when the five-hundred-year hegemony of pictorial realism—representational art aided by the illusion of perspectival space—had grown so universal, so *known*, that it became an empty vessel and finally a prison. For a half century, artists including Gustave Courbet, Édouard Manet, Claude Monet, Georges Seurat, Vincent van Gogh, and finally Paul Cézanne went about breaking up space, demolishing optical hierarchy to make every part of a work important, while foregrounding process and materials, allowing us to see how a painting is made. What made their work revolutionary was its brilliance in finding new ways to portray old subject matter. That hadn't happened since Giotto painted the Scrovegni Chapel in Padua in 1305.

It is impossible to overestimate the effects of Modernism as an international style. Everyone reading this book knows these effects in their bones. Modernism is in the air we breathe, the furniture we sit on, the buildings we live in; it's in our ideas about time, material, form, newness, and progress. Modernism is part of the deep content of everyday life.

Modern art has changed my life many times. It still does. By the turn of the millennium, however, Modernism had become lost in its own myth. What had begun as a disparate set of individual instincts, impulses, and values had hardened into an ideology—a bizarre teleological catechism that maintained that the causes and designs of modern art had an end goal that was embedded in the movement's very nature. Modernism became isolationist and protectionist; it conceived of art as the exclusive province of its own chosen geniuses and excluded anything outside their realm. It became a mad race for some illusive purity, with artists generating work that was about nothing more than its own conditions, forswearing figuration and illusionistic space in favor of monochrome abstraction. The Modernist canon had the unyielding determinism of a biblical family tree: he begat him, who begat him, who begat the next him, who wanted to fuck, marry, or kill the last white Western him. By the mid-1960s the movement's reflexes were shot, and an even longer, more oedipal movement kicked in: Post-Modernism. Art became a way for artists to prove what was already known, gaslighting anyone outside the club with catchphrases and novel-length wall texts. By the start of the period covered in this book, Modernism meant aesthetic apartheid.

How bad did it get? In 2004, the brakes of Modernism screeched to a halt. That year, New York's Museum of Modern Art—the mother ship and

Garden of Eden of the movement—revealed a new curation of its vaunted permanent collection. On two floors of its shiny new half-billion-dollar building, women made up only 4 percent of the artists included. The percentage of work by artists of color was near zero. Outrage spread across the art world. MoMA had run aground.

The big museums knew they needed to change, but not yet how. Many chose quantity over quality. Size mattered, not programming. Museums worldwide turned themselves into Modernist theme parks and "architectural destinations," most with massive atriums that needed filling with mediocrities. The three worst institutional mishaps of the century occurred in New York. In 2008, after nearly bankrupting the Guggenheim Museum, its mad-expansionist director, Thomas Krens, finally stepped down. The Guggenheim is still in recovery. In 2010, several years after director Michael Govan decided to discontinue the Dia Art Foundation's massive, essential exhibition space in Chelsea, the building was finally closed to art for good. In 2001, starchitects Tod Williams and Billie Tsien created a new handsome totally useless-for-art museum for the American Folk Art Museum. In 2014, the building was torn down for MoMA's next expansion. For a moment, it looked as though the great museums of the Modernist era might not survive the death of that movement.

The elephant in this big room, obviously, is context. In America, the twenty-first century began with the contested election of 2000, followed shortly thereafter by the terrorist attacks of September 11, 2001. From there came the wars in Iraq and Afghanistan, the financial collapse of 2008, the lightning-rod election of the first black president, the rise of anti-democratic authoritarianism at the hands of his successor, and finally a second contested election and a worldwide pandemic that saw the death of one million Americans. All of which is to say: None of the art made in this period happened under "normal" conditions. All of it was produced amid shattering structures. We must acknowledge that the art of these years happened within a context of insanity, hopelessness, frustration; a continual state of emergency; a fear that the things that made our world great, or even tolerable, could be lost.

Inevitably, then, much of the art of this period has been political. But the strongest art of this time has not been obvious, not merely an expression of outrage. The most moving art, as always, deals in ambiguity, unexpected surprises, undermined expectations, complexity, interior drama. Its visionaries are driven by a new and very different set of values. This work reminds us that the contemporary museum, long revered as an elite sanctuary, now beckons as a new commons: a town square, a venue for community building, even an agent of change. A major factor in this is the influence of social media—especially Instagram—with its effect of sidestepping gatekeepers and fostering ardent fandom, debate, cross-pollination, societal change, and a new kind of citizenship. The result has been a great opening, a time of schism and volatility, a feeling of dams bursting everywhere. Everyone felt they had a stake in whatever the future might hold. The art of these decades has shown us that the world didn't begin long ago, but rather that each of us creates the world anew every day.

One sign of change was that doors of galleries and museums started to open to artists who'd long been ignored by these institutions: artists of color, trans and nonbinary artists, self-taught and disabled creators, artists from indigenous cultures, street artists, older artists, even long-overlooked deceased artists. Ceramics, tapestry, and other mediums long considered "crafts"—and even the nonmaterial material of digital files—assumed equal footing with painting, sculpture, and the like. Without this new openness, we might never have been treated to retrospectives featuring artists like Martín Ramírez—one of the greatest so-called outsiders who ever lived—or Bill Traylor, or Joseph Yoakum, or Beauford Delaney. The walls of the sexy Frieze art fair would not have been graced with the "ledger drawings" of the Cheyenne artist Bear's Heart, work made in a U.S. Army fort—more like a concentration camp—in the late 1800s. We might know little of the African American quiltmaker and fiber artist Rosie Lee Tompkins, whose work was granted a full-scale retrospective at the UC Berkeley Art Museum in 2020. Space was cleared for works that needed space to achieve their grandeur. The Whitney Museum might not have devoted a room to Kevin Beasley's monument to slavery, a wildly whirring old cotton gin encased in a room of glass, as alien and silencing as the room at the end of Kubrick's *2001*, leaving humanity in limbo. We almost certainly would have missed the revelatory self-portraits of the disabled body of Robert Andy Coombs. And think of the loss if we had failed to recognize the work of Kerry James Marshall and Arthur Jafa, two of America's greatest artists, who both worked quietly for decades before their genius received widespread attention. It has been an era of riches.

Along the way, this new ecumenicism also left the door open for certain interlopers. Illustrator Norman Rockwell was granted a retrospective at the Guggenheim. The wildly successful merchant of American sentimentalism, Thomas Kinkade, shared mindspace with the destructive gremlin on the wing of America, George W. Bush, whose deeply squirrely paintings—of Vladimir Putin, of his own father, of himself naked in the bathroom—were somehow both fascinating and vacant. The protest art of Ai Weiwei and graffiti of Banksy made them perhaps the most famous artists alive, though not the best. Christie's pawned off a fishy Leonardo for $450 million. Maurizio Cattelan's golden toilet was installed in a bathroom at the Guggenheim in 2016; in 2019 he taped a banana to the wall at an art fair in Miami Beach. Each of these stunts made headlines; the banana was a rare example of a bad work of art that nevertheless made the entire world think anew about what a work of art was. The same could be said of the NFT by Beeple that sold, in 2021, for $69 million.

My lesson from all this is: Take things as they come, case by case. Bad art can tell you as much as good art, sometimes more. In my twenties I embraced Shunryu Suzuki's idea of maintaining a "beginner's mind," the attitude of staying open. This has allowed me to entertain the possibility that the vast variety of other people's ideas might be right, helping me to process the contradictions of our time without becoming cynical.

Two moments illustrate the tectonic shift that distinguishes our time. The first is the appearance of *Puppy*, Jeff Koons's enormous sculpture of a terrier, installed in front of the GE Building on Fifth Avenue in the summer of 2000—the moment before *Bush v. Gore*, the last time America allowed itself to feel optimistic, or at least a little silly. An arrangement of seventy thousand living plants, each meticulously placed by Koons, *Puppy* is the greatest control-freak sculpture ever created. One night, Koons asked if I'd like to place one flower in the sculpture. I did. He looked at it and said, "Perfect, Jerry. But I think it should go here," and moved it half an inch. *Puppy* was an all-welcoming Jeffersonian object, a kind of huge hood ornament that combined Ronald Reagan's 1950s optimism, Warhol's edgy embrace of American culture, and an almost spiritual hope that the American Experiment might redeem all who came to it.

The second, very different moment came courtesy of the artist Kara Walker, whose work I first saw in 1994, when she was still a student at RISD. Even then, her work was already incendiary—it seemed to whisper "After me, the deluge"—and I wrote about her powerful, discomfiting work as early as 1996. In 2014, in an old Brooklyn sugar factory, Walker installed a gigantic sculpture: thirty-five feet tall, seventy-five feet long, a naked sphinx with the features of a black mammy. Part alien, part parade float, and destroyer of worlds, *A Subtlety* was a new Melvillian symbol for slavery and the continued nightmare of race in America. In its blank, snowy figure I thought I saw misery, winter, excess, fate, and some glistening midnight.

As dissimilar as these two masterpieces seem, they both work a similar kind of magic. They stop people in their tracks; cast spells; quell insider conversation about high and low art. They inject a powerful retinal-emotional-philosophical dose of art directly into the public cerebral cortex. Works like these, and others, account for some of the deepest moments of transcendence in these decades.

The work of three other artists suggests how these twenty-first-century counterforces overlap with one another. In *Love Hotel and Other Stories*, her mysterious 2005 show, the Japanese-born artist Laurel Nakadate featured photographs and videos of herself engaging with that species of white heterosexual men who seem to lack the ability to seduce or be loved by women, but who try to lure women to them in awkward, halting ways—men who would later become known as incels. Nakadate reversed the polarities of such interactions, using tropes of control, vulnerability, sluttiness, and voyeurism to create situations where these men hit on her, only to have her respond by springing her photographic trapdoor, revealing them acting out sexless renditions of just the kind of sexual fantasies they had in mind for her.

In 2007, the painter Carroll Dunham offered *Square Mule,* an image of a man bending over to insert a gun into his rectum, like a baboon sexually presenting before he blows himself and the viewer to bits. This figure, at once ridiculous and insolent, appeared in many of Dunham's paintings of the period, sometimes sporting a fedora, other times adorned in archaic tribal tattoos and dreadlocks.

By 2018, the residents of Flint, Michigan, had spent four years subjected to lethal amounts of lead in their drinking water, due to the mismanagement and negligence of government. That year saw a devastating exhibition of photography by LaToya Ruby Frazier, whose own family's health was directly affected by environmental toxins in Braddock, Pennsylvania, the steel town where she grew up. Frazier created a shockingly intimate portrait of environmental, physiological, economic, medical, and emotional systemic racism in those two cities, and of how such forces undermine the lives of poor and middle-class families around the country.

Where Nakadate was enacting the disaster of prescribed sexual roles in the years that culminated in #MeToo, and Dunham's work evoked the bloodlust folly of American machismo in the peak years of two parallel wars, Frazier showed us America turning on itself, throwing bodies into the maw of death. All three offered windows onto the killing machine of the modern social order, echoing Nietzsche's dictum "One must still have chaos in oneself." The vision of these artists captured an array of subtle, subsurface emotions: the feeble masculinity common to Nakadate's and Dunham's work; the casual malice and indifferent violence portrayed by Dunham and Frazier; and the defiance and hope shown by all three artists in the very act of making and presenting this work. In all three I see the incubus spirits of America: lone gunmen, wounded bystanders sleepwalking in a failing state on a way to nowhere. All three are reminders that looking only forward makes a culture blind.

Today, artists are living by Seneca's notion that sometimes we need to look backward to see forward. Rather than trying to kill the past, to make everything make sense—like their Modernist predecessors—artists are choosing their own forebears inside and outside the canon. They are *collaborating with* history: drawing on it, adding to it, extending and re-forming it. Artists are archaeologists and astronauts of the present-day world, storytellers who both witness history and change it in the ways they portray it. What might seem fantastical or unbelievable in their work might actually be the reality of the people pictured. Art is rising from its own ashes. Modernism's arrow of continuity has finally been scrapped, replaced by a new model of evolution that is more like an ever-changing cloud formation, expanding, condensing, never predictable.

Yet Seneca's credo has hidden fissures; history is treacherous territory. I fell into one of those fissures in 2015, during Obama's second term, when it felt like the future might actually be arcing toward justice. Several years before, the Whitney Museum had commissioned a work from one of America's best sculptors, Charles Ray, to be placed in the plaza in front of the museum's new building in downtown Manhattan. Ray responded with a standing sculpture titled *Huck and Jim*—a large, monochrome vision of Mark Twain's lead characters, naked and resting on their flight through the South en route to Ohio. But in 2015 it was revealed that the Whitney had declined the figure, not wanting to "offend non-museumgoing visitors." At the time, I wrote that this decision showed a lack of nerve on the Whitney's part, that the sculpture embodied "so much of America's past and current struggles." In an excess of enthusiasm that makes me wince today, I claimed it would be "a beacon, a lightning rod, a second Statue of Liberty." I wasn't wrong about the work itself, which is still tremendous. I was wrong that it should be placed there. It was not the time to devote another prominent position to work by a white man, about such a charged subject, when any number of talented contemporary artists of color might have had something very different and pressing to say on the same topic. It's a mistake that reminds me of the importance of listening to other voices, communities, and experiences. This has nothing to do with censorship; it's about empathy, compassion, and solidarity.

One thrilling manifestation of this is a new generation's radical embrace of a genre that many had left behind: portraiture. A generation of artists including Njideka Akunyili Crosby, Lynette Yiadom-Boakye, Mickalene Thomas, Nina Chanel Abney, Henry Taylor, Jordan Casteel, Jonathan Lyndon Chase, Amy Sherald, and many others are investing this dormant genre with unprecedented meaning. They are doing it, as well, through the medium that has always been at the center of art history: painting. These artists are actively excavating the intrinsic intelligence, narrative potential, formal implications, and semiotics of portraiture. The number and variety of black lives we are seeing, through the faces and figures of modern portraiture, amounts to an almost epistemological renaissance. These artists are making art in the first person, not from outside but from within, defining culture rather than being defined by it.

There is a potent antimatter built into this work. We are conditioned, from childhood, to believe stories. Yet the narrators creating the stories in these portraits are authentic and at the same time intentionally unreliable. In their work, not everything is known; references, signs, symbols, signifiers, costumes, histories, and body language are not always easily readable. This decenters the viewer, undermining expectations; the result is to make a simple painting of people at a barbecue as radical-looking as anything you've seen. Such works are simultaneously private statements and public addresses. Rather than imploring you to understand the experience of others, they allow you to witness the experience of others. They invite you simply to wonder.

Many of the formal aspects of this new portraiture—its new ideas about color, geometry, shape, surface, composition, space, material, tools, and more—suggest an overdue act of reparation. Artists are taking art back from Cubism and Modernism, revisiting and reinventing cultural norms enforced by five hundred years of colonialism. Museumgoers are seeing lives and faces that have never appeared in museums before. This is one way that artists can change the way we understand the world.

THERE IS, HOWEVER, one almost insanely incongruous paradox afloat in all this. Much of the money fueling this storming of the gates is coming from the very titans behind the system that makes the lives of so many a living hell. MoMA's former chairman, the billionaire investor Leon Black, donated heavily to Republican PACs and senators Mitch McConnell, Lindsey Graham, and Tom Cotton, and also paid a rumored $158 million to Jeffrey Epstein. MoMA also received $50 million from trustee Steve Cohen, who donated $1 million to Trump's inauguration and served as vice chairman of that event. Art Institute of Chicago trustee Ken Griffin gave MoMA $40 million and contributed $46 million to Republicans. James Murdoch, son of Fox News' Rupert Murdoch, is a co-owner of Art Basel. *But he's the good Murdoch*, the art world insists, just as it accepted *the good Sackler* before that.

Today, industrialists, investors, oligarchs, oil barons, and other villains of the world economy use art to enhance their social standing, signal virtue, or store money, by very publicly paying high prices for works of art by women and artists from underrepresented communities. Whether this is slumming or sincere, cultural tourism or actual activism, the art world is collectively willing to dance with these devils. Money and art have always had sex together in public. They're just doing so now more than ever. The credo seems to be Laurie Anderson's "O Superman": "This is the hand; the hand that takes." It's a risky strategy. I have doubts, although such deep pockets can obviously have a transformative effect on the careers of emerging artists.

Whatever the case, the results have been dramatic. We will never again see the all-male, all-white museum shows that were the norm at the start of this century. In 2018, the official portraits of the first black president and first lady in American history were painted by young black artists. The 2022 Venice Biennale was 90 percent non-male—and art didn't die. MoMA is getting its act together, as are many other museums. Maybe the Met will one day install Egypt in the African galleries, where it belongs.

AT THE BEGINNING of the pandemic shutdown of 2020, amid fears that the art world might be lost altogether, gallerist Mike Egan wrote something to me that has stayed on my mind: "Art will not survive as some dull thing, some social good that we must support out of consensual responsibility. . . . Art will explode with the desires of the people to see action play out, with tears, screams, harmonies, and some death. How to survive? Passion. Obsession. Desire." Egan is right. Art is never neutral. Whatever is happening among the power brokers of the art world—or the greater systems that support them—one senses that artists themselves are impatient, and that something tremendous is blossoming in the paradox.

Art Is Life concludes with a profile of Jasper Johns, who in 1955 dreamed that he'd painted the American flag, followed that dream, and did it. This initiated what we call contemporary art. It's probably safe to say that Johns will be the last artist who will ever be called "the greatest artist in the world." Such categories are no longer part of our vocabulary. In his recent full-career retrospective, however, I felt a reconnection with the earliest reservoirs and inner architectures that drew me to art. I saw an artist investing everything into *how* a thing is made, trying to embed his deepest self in something as basic as paint. I recalled how Giovanni di Paolo demonstrated the narrative power of a static image, how Géricault embedded his art with history and time and the fragility of life itself. I saw the breathtaking power, archaic wisdom, mysteries, and infinity of art.

In his celebrated essay on *Moby-Dick*, D. H. Lawrence recognized that Melville's epic tale of the white whale, Ahab's crippling obsession, was really the story of "the deepest blood-being of the white race." It was a story of intimations: "Something seems to whisper it in the very dark trees of America," he wrote, the "doom of our white day." After decades of wars over territory, oil, and culture, contested elections, black leadership and white grievance, our times have felt like one long American night. Yet perhaps here, on our own *Raft of the Pequod*, the artists of this new day may look upon the bravery and cowardice and cracks in the world that still control our fate—and transform them into a lasting vision of human possibility.

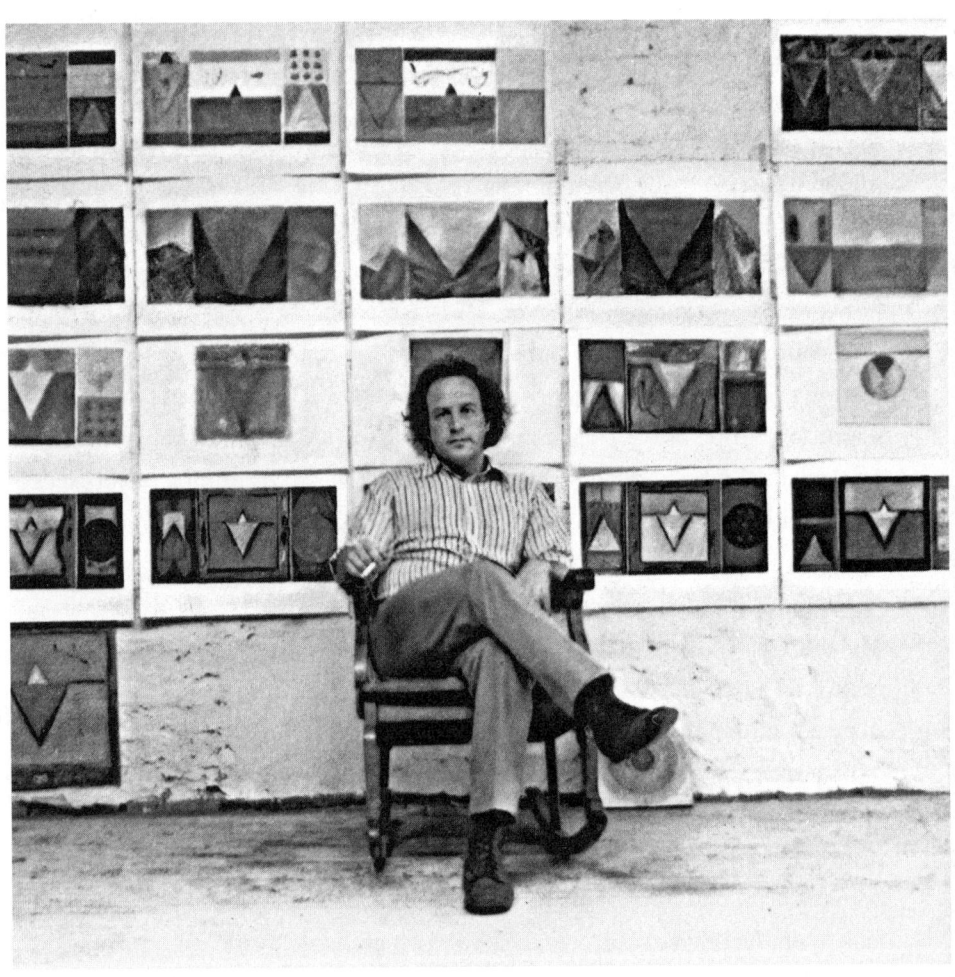

My Life as a Failed Artist

It pains me to say it, but I am a failed artist. "Pains me" because nothing in my life has given me the boundless psychic bliss of making art for hours at a stretch, as I did every day in my twenties and thirties—always thinking about it, looking for a voice to fit my own time, imagining scenarios of success and failure, feeling my imagined world and the external one merging in things that I was actually making.

Now I live on the other side of the critical screen, and all that language beyond words—all that doctor-shamanism of color, structure, and the mysteries of beauty—is gone. With time, I've come to consider myself fully and purely a critic, working through the same problems of expression from the other side. Yet I miss making art—miss it terribly. I've never really talked about my work to anyone. In my writing, I have occasionally mentioned the bygone years when I was an artist, usually laughingly. When I think of that time, I feel stabs of regret. But once I quit, I quit. I never made art again.

Of course, I often think that everyone who isn't making art is a failed artist, even those who never tried. I did try. More than try. *I was an artist.* At times, I even thought I was a great one.

I wasn't totally deluded. But I *was* a lazy smart aleck who felt sorry for myself, resented anyone with money, and felt the world owed me a living. For a few years, I attended classes at the School of the Art Institute of Chicago, although I didn't always pay tuition and got no degree. But I did meet artists there, and I learned that staying up late with one another is how artists learn everything—developing new languages, communing, trading ideas.

In 1973, I was twenty-two, full of myself, and frustrated that I wasn't already recognized for my work. I walked into my roommate Barry Holden's room in our apartment, three hundred feet from Wrigley Field, and said, "Let's start an artist-run gallery. The two of us and our friends." He said okay—and we did it. For lack of a better name, we called it N.A.M.E.

It was great! People took notice; articles were written. I was interviewed by Peter Schjeldahl, the bigwig New York art critic. I met hundreds of artists and felt part of a huge community. I lived across the street from the gallery, in a huge sixth-floor unheated cold-water walk-up loft for which I paid $150 a month. The place had previously been a storage facility for Jerry Lewis's muscular dystrophy foundation, and my furniture was mostly what had been abandoned there: a wooden bench for a couch, a huge drafting table in the center of the space, a hot plate, buckets on the floor to catch the leaks from the ceiling, a pail to fill for pouring down the toilet to make it work, and a mattress on the floor. I was an artist.

By 1978, I'd had two solo shows at N.A.M.E. Both shows were part of a gigantic project I had begun the day before Good Friday in 1975. I was illustrating the entirety of Dante's *Divine Comedy*, starting with *Inferno*. Both exhibitions sold out. Museums bought my work. I was reviewed favorably in *Artforum* and the Chicago papers. My work was shown by the great Rhona Hoffman in Chicago and at the proto–Barbara Gladstone gallery in New York. I was delirious. Mice were still crawling on me at night; I was still showering at other people's houses. I didn't care. I had everything I needed. I even got a grant from the National Endowment for the Arts, for the huge sum of $3,000—which, along with the help of an artist girlfriend, enabled me to move to New York.

But then I looked back, into the abyss of self-doubt. I erupted with fear, self-loathing, dark thoughts about how bad my work was, how pointless, unoriginal, ridiculous. "You don't know how to draw," I told myself. "You never went to school. Your work has nothing to do with anything. Your art is irrelevant. You don't know art history. You can't paint. You only draw and work small because you're too afraid to paint and work big. You aren't a good schmoozer. You're too poor. You don't have enough time to make your work. You're a fake. You're not a real artist."

Every artist does battle, every day, with doubts like these. I lost the battle. It doomed me. But it also made me the critic I am today.

I STILL WONDER, *Was it my upbringing that sealed my fate?* Art certainly wasn't in my life in the Chicago suburb where I grew up, unless you count the cheesy reproductions of French-ish Impressionists in our rec room.

When I began as an artist, my main spiritual home wasn't the Art Institute—even though I spent hours there, spellbound. It was Chicago's Field Museum of natural history. I loved that the work there wasn't freighted with art history; I felt freer fantasizing about it. More important, I loved that the ancient artwork at the Field Museum was for more than just looking at. It was meant to cast spells, to heal, to protect villages from invaders, to prevent or foster pregnancy, to guide one through the afterlife. I was devoted to art from the Northwest Coast, the Plains, the Southwest, and South and Central America. My favorite schools of abstract art were Navajo sand painting, Oceanic art, and the newly revealed work of Swedish visionary Hilma af Klint. All this work felt driven by innate spiritualism and inner necessity, a far cry from the abstraction coming out of New York.

What did the contemporary art world look like to me then? There were plenty of artists whose work I loved: Nancy Graves's sculptures of camels, Eva Hesse's gnarly materials in space, Lynda Benglis's giant poured-paint blobs coming off the gallery wall, Jennifer Bartlett's process dot paintings. And the work of my friends. At the time, I imagined that our nonrepresentational, process- or performance-based, and conceptual art would save

Chicago from a group of artists I now love: the figurative surrealists—Jim Nutt, Roger Brown, Christina Ramberg, Gladys Nilsson, and Jeff Koons's teacher Ed Paschke—who became known as Chicago Imagists.

But art history was more important to me. I adored the Byzantine, the medieval, early Sienese painting, Native American art, Tibetan mandalas, Japanese prints, all of the Baroque, everything from the Northern and Southern Renaissance. I especially loved the cryptic illustrations, charts, and diagrams dealing with magic, mysticism, and visual mnemonic systems made by medieval and Renaissance-era alchemist-metaphysician-philosopher-artists most people have never heard of: Robert Fludd, Athanasius Kircher, Giordano Bruno, Ramon Llull, Giulio Camillo. By the time I was twenty-one, I was making hard-edged geometric drawings and paintings based on the I Ching, which looked a lot like Southwest Native American art and pre-Columbian Peruvian feather art. I thought, or hoped, they could tell the future.

Another regional strain coursed through me, too: Chicago's powerful connection to self-taught and outsider artists. I saw and loved the great outsider Lee Godie selling her drawings on the steps of the Art Institute; I admired the work of the self-taught Joseph Yoakum, who was promoted by many of the Chicago Imagists. The work of two outsider masters was discovered and embraced by Chicago in the 1970s: Martín Ramírez in 1973 and Henry Darger in 1977. I was a guard at Chicago's Museum of Contemporary Art during its show of Adolf Wölfli. I even worked at the New York gallery of Phyllis Kind, the Chicago dealer who showed many of these Imagists and outsiders. I wanted to be an outsider worm in the bowels of the insider hyena.

I BEGAN MY *INFERNO* PROJECT just before dawn on the Thursday before Easter 1975, because Maundy Thursday is when Dante's story begins in the poem—lost in "the dark wood of error," having strayed from the "true way." I planned to finish on Easter, the same day Dante finished his own journey in 1300. I would finish in the year 2000, by which time I would have made one hundred opening-and-closing altarpieces for each of the hundred cantos of *The Divine Comedy*. The ten thousand finished altarpieces would represent an idea of the infinite—and a way to set myself free.

Why Dante? Especially considering that I barely read at all and didn't believe in God? I think because *The Divine Comedy*, which is a gigantic organized allegorical system where every evil deed is punished in accord with the law of equal retribution and divine love, supplied me with the formulated structure I craved. The highly established internal architectonics, the almost primitive definitiveness, what Beckett called the "neatness of identification," offered me what seemed like both psychological shelter and weapons of revenge. A way to right my own world, to grasp an order like that in the Bible: "all things by measure and number and weight." Most of all, it was a vision of justice—the good being rewarded and the bad getting their punishments.

All of this seemed like a powerful counter to the chaos of my childhood. My mother had committed suicide when I was ten; my father remarried shortly thereafter, to a Polish Catholic woman with two sons—one of whom was my age, so that I felt I had to go to war with a twin. My step-twin brought drug use into our house; I committed petty crimes and got caught by the police. This was in our otherwise stately suburban home, where the children and the parents had absolutely no overlap—right down to the separate entrances and dining rooms, which came to feel almost like compartments. Or hell.

Dante's world was also compartmentalized, but it was enormous—the most systemized megacosm I'd ever seen. It was a galaxy of good and evil, catharsis, sin, injured spirits, saints, battle scenes in heaven, a fallen world, those waiting for redemption, monsters, yearning, shame, Satan, and rising again. I did not believe, in the conventional sense of the word, but Dante's metaphysical, moral architecture got me through my twenties, at a time when I had no internal structure whatsoever. (Or perhaps I had one that was already collapsing under the weight of repressed pain, rage, loss, self-pity, and fear.) Dante is a paradigmatic figure of the canon—therefore a perfect picture of the dream of artistic canonization—but he's also a weirdo Boschian fantasist; as such, he satisfied my obsession with hermetic traditions, indexes, myth, archaic cultures, and mystics and visionaries like William Blake. This late-medieval universe freed me from making choices; the story and structure told me exactly what to do, what to draw, where to draw it, what came next, what shape things should be, everything—even sometimes governing colors, making Virgil blue and Dante red according to past art. Without knowing it, but in desperate need, I'd contrived a machine that allowed me to make things that I couldn't predict, which is one of the first jobs of any artist.

I made art obsessively. I'd wake up and go down to the local diner at the corner for coffee and breakfast, smoking, reading the sports section. After breakfast, I'd stand at my desk all day and work while smoking and listening to my music—1970s rock and disco—on an old tube radio that had no covering, just the guts. Lunch was at the same place; dinner at one of two nearby local bars, where I was a pinball champion. I also won a local pool tournament. Other times I'd nurse beers and talk to artists, or go to Chicago's great jazz and blues clubs, which were so underattended that I met a pantheon of living gods simply by showing up.

I worked on paper because I didn't have a choice. I had no carpentry skills; I had tried to make stretchers, but I failed miserably, so canvas was out. So were wood or Masonite panels: too heavy, expensive, large, and I didn't know how to cut them. My medium was pastel, charcoal, and colored pencil. I was too much of a smarty-pants to ever learn to paint. After all, painting was dead and only losers did it. So I would use my hands and rub, drawing over, making ruler lines, scratching and blurring this supersaturated pastel. Every minute or two, I'd take a huge breath and blow the colored dust off the drawing. (The space around my desk looked like a coal mine.) To this day I'm convinced that my susceptibility to upper respiratory infections comes from years of breathing all that dust at close quarters.

I didn't know what I was doing. I was delusional. But I knew how to do it, and I had the feeling that I was doing it to save my life.

My process was as structured as the rest of the project. I made paper and cardboard templates so that every drawing could have the same size and layout. Since I knew I couldn't really draw, I turned to drafting tools. I had none of the technical skills you were supposed to be taught in school (what an asshole I must have been), so the tools helped immensely: They were cheap, small, easy to use, and fun to misuse. They let me measure everything and be able to make the same thing over and over again. This meant that my symbolism, shapes, and system were all semi-geometric. (It never occurred to me that I was making geometric abstraction. The thought would have horrified me.) I devised my own pictorial language for everything: hell, Dante, Virgil, boats, dead souls, the whole thing. For the funnel cone of the Inferno that Dante and Virgil descend into—seeing ever more evil sinners and increasingly hideous punishments—I used an upside-down triangle. Above it, always, was a small upward-facing triangle, a symbol of the Mount of Joy that Dante tried unsuccessfully to climb to avoid hell.

ON THE OUTSIDE, things were great. On the inside I was in agony. I was terrified of failing, anxious about what to do next and how to do it. I started not working for longer and longer periods. Hiding it. Then not hiding it. Until all I had left was calling myself an artist.

At twenty-seven, I had what I think of as a yearlong walking nervous breakdown. It was shattering. I began having panic attacks; couldn't be around people even though I was dying to be around them; got insomnia; took five-hour walks to wear myself down; was filled with bitter envy for everyone and everything. In this state of self-deprecating deprivation, I wanted what others had. I hated anyone who had more space, time, money, education, a better career. To this day, I tell all young artists: *Make an enemy of envy, or it will eat you alive.* Like it did me.

When I arrived in New York in 1980, to become part of that art world, I didn't know what hit me. I was so out of step. I had no idea how much of the deep content in my art was a product of Chicago, my own naivete, and isolation. The Chicago art world I'd left behind was still preoccupied with 1970s conceptualism, straight photography, regional ideas of hard-edged abstraction, process art, and pluralism. Things in New York were so different: The city was exploding in Neo-Expressionism, the Pictures movement, and graffiti art. The first of these was out of my painterly and scale reach; the second out of my intellectual depth; the last was nothing I was involved with. And I could never stay up late enough or do enough drugs to participate in clubbing.

I was in shock, unable to muster the kinds of inner resources that real artists use to fortify themselves when faced with such a challenge. When I teach today, I often judge young artists' chances of survival based on whether they seem to have the character necessary to solve the inevitable problems in their work. I didn't. I also didn't understand how to respond to an outer world that was out of step with my inner life without retreating into total despair. Oscar Wilde said, "Without the critical faculty, there is no artistic creation at all." Artists have to be self-critical enough not to just attack everything they do. I had self-doubt but no real self-critical facility; instead I indiscriminately loved or hated everything I did.

Instead of gearing up and fighting back, I gave in and got out.

But I learned so much about being a critic.

Artists often complain that critics are animated by resentment. Most of the time I don't think they are, but having been an artist, I understand the feeling. Which is why, whatever my flaws as a critic, I have always tried to be as generous toward the people making the work as I would have wanted anyone to be toward my own. I want my criticism to reflect the hell I went through as an artist—to look, even with work I do not appreciate at first blush, for the sign of the soul yelping at me from within or behind. I believe that every artist means everything they're doing, that no one is making art just to make money or pull the wool over people's eyes. All artists may want to make money and be loved, but at base they're still serious about their art. That's why I hate the cynicism of the art world: All the money and glamour can make it hard to see, and sometimes even harder to believe, that artists mean everything they do as powerfully as anything they've ever meant in their entire lives. Jeff Koons is as earnest, in his *Howdy Doody*–Teletubby way, as Francesca Woodman and Francis Bacon. His willingness to fail flamboyantly is part of what makes his great work great.

Outsiders often see the art world as a fashionable never-ending party, buffered from reality by money. I see it very differently. I see it as a great broken beautiful family of misfits, searching and yearning and in pain— and, under pressure, doing what they have to do to survive. I refuse to believe that this spirit has left the art world, even though I recognize that this exquisite internal essence can be buried under loads of external bullshit. I know that almost every artist wakes up at three a.m. in a cold sweat thinking that the bottom has fallen out of their work. That each of us is self-taught and some kind of outsider. I want to celebrate, examine, describe, and judge this otherness, outsiderness, and try to see if an artist's vision is singular, surprising, and energized in its own original way. My vision wasn't—at least, not in a way I was able to realize in the ten or twelve years I spent trying. I didn't have the ability, or the fortitude. That's why I always look for it in others—root for it in others—even when the work is ugly or idiotic. I want every artist, good and bad, to clear away the kinds of demons that stopped me, to feel empowered, and to be able to make their own work so we can see the "real" them. It's why I look hard at every artist, at the rich and well-known but also at the late bloomers, bottom-feeders, outsiders, and eccentrics. Since it's nearly a miracle that I finally ended up in the art world as a critic—something I never wanted to be—I want every artist to have a shot, to see that the power, access, and agency are in their hands. It's why, in all writing about art, I value clarity and accessibility over jargon. I want critics to be as radically vulnerable in their work as I know artists are in theirs.

Being an artist also made me realize that I wasn't built for the loneliness of the artist's life. Art is slow, physical, resistant, material; it involves an ongoing commitment to doing the same thing differently over and over again. Criticism involves constant change, drama, information coming in from the outside, processing it in the moment in front of everyone, always being in the here and now while also trying to access history and experience. Every week. I love and live for that jolt. As my wife, Roberta Smith, co–chief art critic at *The New York Times*, has said many times, "Being a weekly critic is like performing live onstage." That's what I want, what I need, who I am.

HOW DEEP IS my lack of artistic character? Pretty deep, it turns out. Recently, after I hadn't seen my art for thirty years—I'd assumed it was gone for good—three portfolios of my work surfaced. No altarpieces. Somehow, though, around seven hundred drawings survived. And within one extraordinary day, three weeks ago, I relived a perfect repeat of my entire artistic journey. I went through these newly discovered portfolios. One by one. Drawing by drawing. I studied them all. I knew almost every one by heart; I knew what every move and mark meant. The few I didn't remember were like revelations. My breath was taken away. I fell madly in love with my work. I was astonished at how beautiful much of it was. How much sense it all made. *I was a great artist*, I thought. There were tears of joy in my eyes.

Soon, I went to tell Roberta the news. She came into my office and started looking. For a long time. Longer than I had. Studying, not saying a word. After a while she turned to me.

"They're okay."

"*Okay?*" I said. "What do you mean, *okay*? They're beautiful. Aren't they?"

She turned back to the drawings, looked a little longer. "They're generic," she finally said. "They're . . . *impersonal*. No one would know what these are about. And what's with the triangles? Are they supposed to be women?"

"No!" I shot back. "They're hell!"

"Many artists never get better than their first work," she said. And just like that, I was right back to where I was when I quit: crushed, panicked, frozen. In crisis.

Looking at the work now, I understand Roberta's reaction. A number of other ideas from Oscar Wilde apply here. Art that's too obvious, that we "know too quickly," that is "too intelligible," he wrote, is doomed to fail. "The one thing not worth looking at is the obvious." My work had the opposite problem. It was arcane and therefore obsolete. Only I could decipher it.

Wilde also wrote that "the vague is always repellent." Roberta was right: My work was generic, impersonal, because of the ideas I brought to it—ideas that were mired in the Post-Minimalism of the 1970s. I wanted to transcend memories, to achieve an accessible complexity, to enter history from the side. I used to tell myself that I wanted every decision that I made in my work to be about beauty. Instead, even when it produced flashes of beauty, the work couldn't gain emotional traction; it failed to create depth and density, or to evoke mystery, to impart its secrets, ironies, drama, to cross the threshold of history. I was blinded by the rules I made.

Wilde got this, too. "It is with the best intentions," he wrote, "that the worst work is done."

(2017)

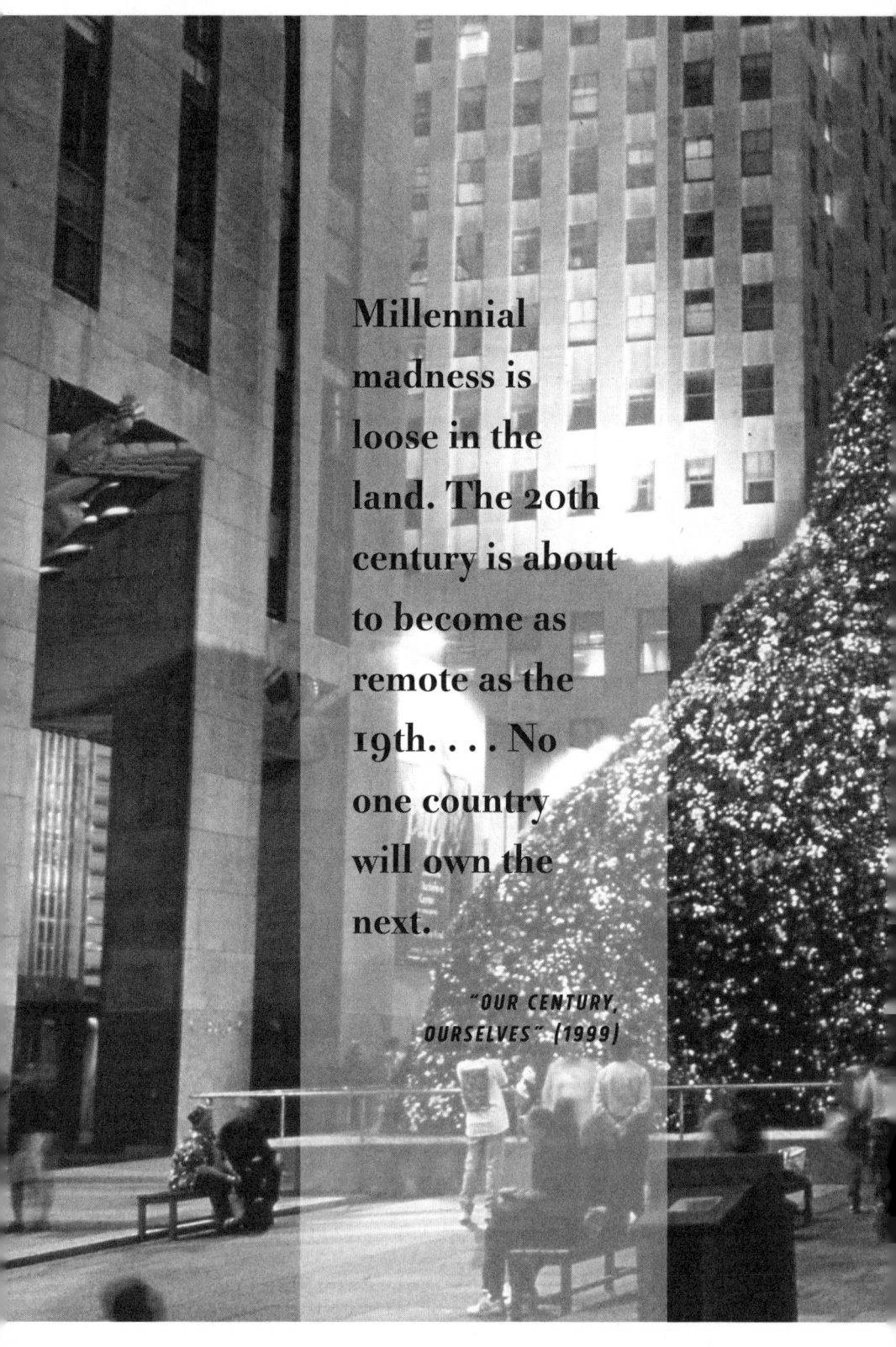

Millennial madness is loose in the land. The 20th century is about to become as remote as the 19th. . . . No one country will own the next.

"OUR CENTURY, OURSELVES" (1999)

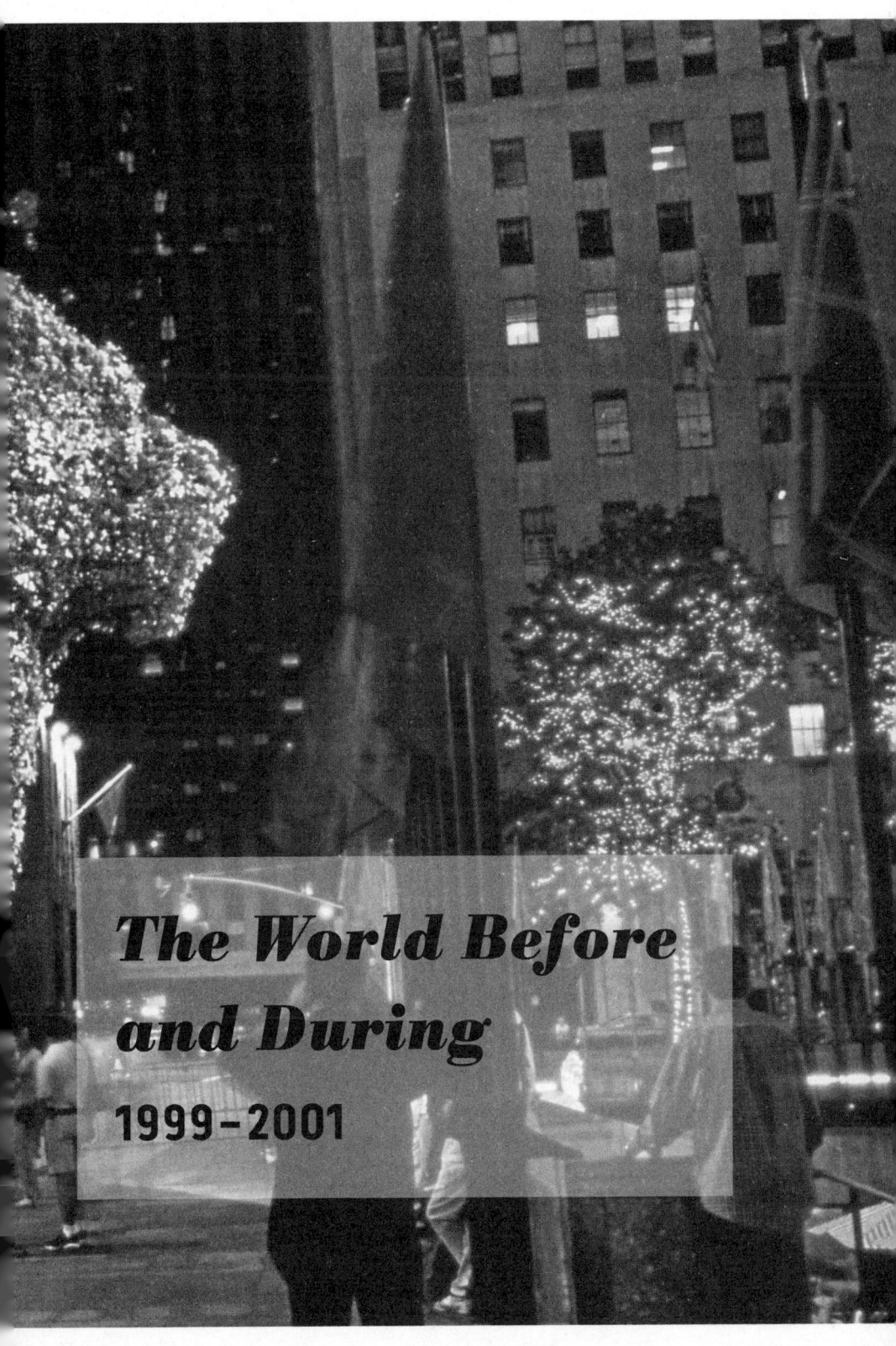

The World Before and During

1999–2001

Living Large

I love museums. It's museum curators I sometimes wonder about. Maybe I'm just jealous about how little traveling a New York trench critic gets to do. These days, curators seem to have all the fun. They're the frequent-flying freelancers and salaried professionals. They stay up late, drink together in hotel lobbies, see one another's shows. Always talking, taking meetings, being on panels, or organizing exhibitions, curators are themselves art stars—power brokers and precinct captains.

That's why I was feeling testy recently as I walked into "Curating Now: Imaginative Practice/Public Responsibility," a two-day symposium organized by the Philadelphia Exhibitions Initiative under the directorship of Paula Marincola. Turns out I wasn't alone in my skepticism. Before the proceedings even began, a well-known critic whispered to me, "I'm hoping to get enough incriminating quotes to hold over these people for years." It was all very A-list. Participants included Nicholas Serota, director of the Tate; MoMA's Robert Storr; Paul Schimmel from L.A. MOCA; Kathy Halbreich, director of the Walker Art Center; Thelma Golden, deputy director of the Studio Museum; Philadelphia Museum director Anne d'Harnoncourt; the peripatetic international curating machine and Antonin Artaud look-alike Hans Ulrich Obrist; and Dave Hickey, who wears his curator's hat with the same rebel abandon with which he wears his critic's hat.

A lot was said. My favorite moment came after one speaker spouted a bunch of familiar nonsense about curators as "agents of change," "teachers," and "producers of theory." When she repeated the old standby, "As many people go to museums as go to sporting events," a pregnant pause followed, as though the room was about to slit its collective wrist—until another panelist, Paul Schimmel, wondered aloud, "What does that mean?"

In the afternoon, Halbreich delivered a rousing Clintonesque speech about the Walker's outreach programs and educational initiatives, with lots of talk about "interactivity" and "hyperlinks." Her main point, however, posed an interesting quandary for the symposium, drawing a line in the sand. "The museum," she said, "should be a town square, *not* a temple." If I'm not mistaken, an air of disdain shrouded the word *temple*.

And that's where she lost me. In many parts of the world, *town square* and *temple* are the same thing. Today, the entire city is a town square; metropolises are busy, noisy places; they sustain us. But we go to museums for a different reason: to get *away from* the crowd and tap into the collective unconscious. In those halls, we step outside of time and into something almost primitive or unknowable. I'm not saying art is sacred, only that it does something somewhat indefinable. In a sense, the museum is an ecstasy machine: a building filled with wormholes and time warps, extrasensory switching stations and ecto-transporters, psycho-circuits and invisible diving bells. Museums are strange places where people stand in front of inanimate objects, talk to themselves, and experience rapture.

I left the symposium after the first day, but in my time there, the pressing questions of academicism and institutional scale never came up. Beset by a desire to please, beleaguered by "educational initiatives," a pious virus of expansion is spreading unchecked within the art world. Museums are building bigger buildings and erecting huge impersonal additions to house uneven collections. Trustees, millionaires, and board members pick architects; they help lay out loading docks. Museums are becoming architectural attractions in and of themselves. But is bigger better? Is more

more? The credo has become "To expand is to grow." MoMA's expanding, the New Museum's moving, and the Guggenheim just got the go-ahead to erect a 575,000-square-foot Frank Gehry building on the East River—that's ten times the size of their Fifth Avenue flagship. I'm sure Gehry's swooping structure will end up on hats and T-shirts. But when it comes to programming, expansion often brings dissipation—or, worse, stupidity. Gigantic edifices are built, then filled with junk.

Museums can't be all things to all people. Every temple can't be St. Peter's. What about smaller congregations, the humble parish church, the basement chapel, meeting halls, or the small but exquisite shrine? How about museum as nightclub, lounge, or honky-tonk? Just as a pot by George Ohr can vie for greatness with the Sistine ceiling, a small museum can be as exalted as a big one. In London, where millions of people live and work, the new Tate makes sense. In smaller cities, building a giant museum is like plopping down a shopping mall in a small neighborhood. More people come, but for what? I remember standing six-deep at a Monet show in Chicago, while the upstairs Impressionist wing, containing several top-notch works by the artist, was nearly empty.

Museums are great. The problem is, too many curators have started to believe what they're doing isn't just good, but *necessary*. They want to teach or preach to us; some are more interested in being do-gooders than in letting the art do its own good. As Gilbert & George put it, "To be with art is all we ask."

(2000)

Jeffersonian Koons

I t's finally here. Eight years after its debut in Germany, after a stint in Sydney, an installation outside the Guggenheim in Bilbao, where Basque guerrillas threatened to blow it up, a recent spider fumigation by

Australian shippers, and who knows how many false starts and delays caused by its creator's perfectionism, one of the two versions of *Puppy*, Jeff Koons's inflorescent topiary masterpiece, has reached Manhattan. And it's the cutest, most purely pleasurable public sculpture I've ever seen.

Puppy does what movies do: wows people, makes them stare at one thing for a long time and experience wonder. It sneaks in under their radar, disarming fears of art. In some quintessentially Jeffersonian way, *Puppy* renders all who see it equal. It is the rare work of art that laymen can talk about with the same confidence and authority as those in the art world.

Puppy is a forty-three-foot-high, forty-four-ton West Highland terrier constructed out of stainless steel, swathed in nearly seventy thousand petunias, marigolds, begonias, impatiens, and lobelia, which are potted in twenty-three tons of soil and kept alive by an internal irrigation system. It sits in front of the GE Building—where the Christmas tree usually stands—like a watchdog, or a pooch waiting for a walk. Initially, I thought it looked too small for its site, but then I realized its location is part of the magic. *Puppy* fits right in with Rockefeller Center; it's just as classic, utopian, sincere, and silly. *Puppy* is the landmark's best friend.

It's also a monument to us. The main emotional hit you get from *Puppy* is joy—oddly, an emotion we Americans give off when we're insecure. You can see this especially abroad, where we wear joy on our sleeves, probably as a way to avoid judgment or to offset nervousness. Outfitted in fanny packs, we're the annoying, noisy, worried ones: the terriers of tourists. Strangers tend to misread this joy as friendliness, but we don't really want to get to know anyone; we just want people to like us, like doggies.

Sitting in the midst of Rockefeller Center, *Puppy* is like a new Statue of Liberty. It receives and redeems. It should stay right where it is.

(2000)

Auntie Hero: Alice Neel

The way Alice Neel rides the edge of something primitive in her work, the physicalness of her process, her alternately agitated and mangy surfaces, her breathtaking brushstrokes and the hypersensitive obsessiveness of her portraits: All these factors and more suggest that Neel ranks among the greatest American painters of the twentieth century.

Neel's rise and fall and rise isn't a classic story; the highs aren't as high as the lows are low. Born in 1900 to a middle-class Philadelphia family, Neel studied art, married the Cuban painter Carlos Enríquez, and moved to New York in 1927 with him and their infant daughter, Santillana. You can see them in what might be the last purely innocent image she would execute for thirty-five years: a 1927 watercolor in which a topless Neel sweetly diapers the baby, who sprawls in Carlos's lap.

Then the bottom fell out: Santillana died of diphtheria. Neel gave birth to another daughter, Isabetta, eleven months later, but the child was immediately taken away to Cuba by Carlos. Finally, in 1930, Neel had a breakdown and attempted suicide; she was institutionalized on and off throughout the following year. "I died every day," she said. But, in a quality that would serve her well, Neel willed herself to paint. She took four lovers in seven years (including a sailor named Kenneth Doolittle, who burned hundreds of Neel's works in 1934), and gave birth to two more children by different fathers.

Neel had an up-and-down career as an artist, but the beginning was almost all up. At the press preview, a critic cracked, "She's like Soutine lite." Not true. Chaïm Soutine was an expressionist head to toe; Neel adulterates her expressionism with heavy doses of reality, visionary flights of fancy, and something like fractured consciousness. In a way, her work is the opposite of Alex Katz's: Where his art is angular, cool, lean, and lanky, Neel's is saggy, roiled, weird, and rumpled. Her early paintings and watercolors here, done in a naive-expressionist-meets-social-realist style—especially those of Carlos, her children, lovers, and a swarthy friend named Nadya—are among the most convincing of her career. Several of these, including an intimate postcoital watercolor of herself and John Rothschild (from 1935) and a portrait of the Village character Joe Gould as a satyr, complete with three penises, rate among the century's strangest and most original pictures of sex in the city.

In 1960, at the behest or at least nudging of her therapist, Neel asked the poet-critic-curator Frank O'Hara to sit for a portrait. After one very tortured version, she generated a looser one that launched her next great period. From this gutsy moment—born, I think, of desperation, ambition, and the fear that she had stayed too long outside the art world—Neel reinvents herself and retrieves some of the rawness that had been lost. Over the next twenty-four years, in that same loose style, she painted a plethora of art world movers and shakers, strangers and misfits. While uptowners were making their way downtown to have their portraits painted by Warhol, downtowners were going up to 107th Street to sit for this bohemian auntie.

Some of the results are amazing—especially her portrait of Warhol as a wounded, introverted angel, in which Neel meticulously renders his scars like some modern Saint Thomas. We're treated to some scary fashion moments: The artist Louise Lieber wears a blue minidress and a purple macramé hat; the art critic Gregory Battcock dons yellow bikini briefs and red socks while, next to him, fellow critic David Bourdon sports a pair of Beatles boots. Henry Geldzahler, curator at the Metropolitan Museum, looks indifferent, if skeptical. During their sitting, Neel asked to be included in a show Geldzahler was curating. "Oh," he replied frostily, "so you want to be a *professional?*"

By the time she died in 1984, Neel—who saw herself passed over by many of her own sitters—was celebrated as a symbol of what expanding the canon could do. She even wound up on the Johnny Carson show, twice. Today, who she is as a painter is more important than who she was as an icon.

(2000)

The Anger Artist: David Wojnarowicz

David Wojnarowicz was angry enough to become a murderer, but instead he became an artist. Again and again, in his writings, he imagines himself committing savage acts: "tipping amazonian blowdarts in 'infected blood' and spitting them at the exposed necklines of certain politicians or nazi-preachers," or "blast[ing] through the gates of the white house" to dump the corpses of AIDS victims on the front steps. You can still feel Wojnarowicz's searing, well-aimed rage, the ranting clarity, and the pressured urgency as you walk through the retrospective of his multimedia art at the New Museum.

Wojnarowicz's story is romantic, but his work is not. His bio reads like Malcolm Lowry on a Dante jag: abused, abandoned, kidnapped; orphanage, prostitution, heroin, hustling; Paris, San Francisco, NYC; finally AIDS, and his death at thirty-eight. His work was choppy—he was unstoppable when he was on, rough and weak when he wasn't—but at its best his art was undeniable. In this retrospective, curator Dan Cameron traces how this artist pushed himself until he found some metaphysical escape hatch, some sphere where suffering, incredulity, vulnerability, and queer love merge into an enraptured lamentation, where rage transforms into a love that has the power to change the world.

Wojnarowicz was a pound-of-flesh vigilante; an activist, painter, photographer, printmaker, performer, musician, writer—a whatever-it-takes kind of artist. As a gay man whose whole existence was deemed unnatural by society, Wojnarowicz developed a highly charged feel for nature, science, and archaeology. He lived the life of an outsider, but in his work he is something of an insider. His art brings together the three dominant strains of the 1980s—Neo-Expressionism, photo appropriation, and graffiti—as tempered by the intensely sexual, almost classical, no-nonsense photography of his friend, mentor, and lover Peter Hujar. But first and last he is a witness.

One of the first things you'll see in this show is a hauntingly funny series of black-and-white photographs titled *Arthur Rimbaud in New York* (1978–1979). A lanky man wearing a Rimbaud mask stands in various New York locations: Coney Island, Forty-Second Street, the gay piers. The series reveals Wojnarowicz's aching, youthful identification with this figure—a gay icon and rebel, a ghost watching over the outlaw edges of the city— and a penchant for disjointed, mystical slippage. It's simultaneously ridiculous and compelling.

Next, Wojnarowicz paints and stencils over supermarket posters. In one, a buff, bare-chested soldier is shot; in another, a man sits up in a bed, startled by a rumbling at the door. Here sex, death, and cartoons mingle freely. By the mid-eighties, he is making installations and sculpture, and painting on pig skulls, tree trunks, and garbage can lids. His expressionism is rawer and more personal than his peers', his "graffiti" more pointed and less arty. In 1987, a quartet of paintings based on the four elements raised his art to a new level, depicting a world under attack. And then his world changed.

On January 3, 1987, Peter Hujar was diagnosed as suffering from pneumocystis pneumonia and AIDS. By November 26, he was dead. A few months after that, Wojnarowicz himself tested positive for HIV. *Untitled (Hujar Dead)* (1988–1989) is a painting of this crucial moment in Wojnarowicz's life, and in a way, of all his remaining moments.

In the painting, a block of text is superimposed over a delicate, collaged border of cut-up money, broken words, maps in the shape of spermatozoa, and nine black-and-white photographs of Hujar taken just after his death by Wojnarowicz. Anyone who has experienced the enormity, the earth-stopping stillness, of the moment when the life force leaves a body will recognize the profound reverence and implacable sadness of these images. Wojnarowicz lingers over Hujar's face, feet, hands, and body one last time; he caresses him with the camera—loves him, heals him, weeps for him, says goodbye to him. He seems to say, *Everything is over; everything has just begun.*

The text—the longest Wojnarowicz had ever incorporated into his work—leads the viewer through a psychological door few of us have ever opened. It is a powerful confession filled with bloodthirsty, kamikaze scorn; a political manifesto; and a warning that "as each T cell disappears from my body it's replaced by ten pounds of pressure ten pounds of rage." It is a declaration of indignation, retaliation, and endless anger.

Wojnarowicz got caught in a cross fire of denial and ignorance. "As a society we had to endure the media spectacle surrounding the polyps in Ronald Reagan's asshole," he wrote, "and yet for the eight years during his presidency, he was completely silent about the AIDS epidemic." After the silence ended, the geopolitical buck-passing began; when evidence suggested that AIDS came from Africa, Rwandans and Zambians blamed Zaire, and Uganda blamed Tanzania. The Soviet Union called the disease a "foreign problem," and France blamed Morocco. Meanwhile, back in America, the same folks who poured their hearts out for Jerry's Kids on Labor Day burned down the houses of children diagnosed with AIDS. As Camus said, "Each one of us has the plague within us."

After *Untitled (Hujar Dead)*, Wojnarowicz must have decided that painting could no longer satisfy his artistic goals. Anxious to work faster and reach the widest possible audience, he turned to photography, writing, and performance. Now Wojnarowicz's courage, humiliation, and eye-for-an-eye fury comes into full focus; as he acts as a witness to his own dying, the love born of rage turns to terror. Recordings of Wojnarowicz's final readings and performances are potent and painful; you can feel him dying. It is in these performances that he is the most totally angry, the most totally beautiful. If it is possible to free the spirit with incantatory rage and howling passion, then Wojnarowicz does this, and it's devastating.

On July 22, 1992, David Wojnarowicz died. More than thirty years after Allen Ginsberg wrote *Howl*, Wojnarowicz lived it. Both these visionaries sing a song of America and otherness, and the last line of *Howl* feels written for Wojnarowicz: "in my dreams you walk dripping from a seajourney on the highway across America in tears to the door of my cottage in the Western night."

(1999)

Babylon Now

"Things fall apart; the center cannot hold." Turn it around, and Yeats's famous verse fits the contemporary art world: *Things run together; the center only grows.*

Not only is the art world bigger than it's ever been, its workings are better known. Efficiency has replaced disorder. Chaos is on the wane. The mood is self-congratulatory and the password is professionalism. As Barbara Kruger put it in a recent ad, "Another artist. Another exhibition. Another gallery. Another magazine. Another review. Another career. Another life."

The avant-garde won and took no prisoners; there's no place left to trespass. Shock is a passé tactic, and "irony," as the L.A. novelist Vanessa Place wrote, "is a dead man's game." The art world is like a conference call, a strip city run by a student government, an insider's game everyone is in on. The way some people talk about its humanitarianism, you'd think it was a Sting song. We may not understand ourselves but we understand our system. And although this system undoubtedly affects the kinds of art that receive attention—making it harder for the smaller gesture, the slower take, or anyone over thirty-five—the system *runs*, which is what people want it to do.

As mainstream culture usurps countercultures, and youth has its lifestyle sold back to it as catchphrases, subcultures are merging with one another. Just as skateboarders in Moscow are aware of their counterparts in Los Angeles, artists in London and Tokyo know what's going on in Berlin and Buenos Aires. This means hierarchies are breaking down. The art world is decentralizing. Demographics are changing, and smaller nodes may soon supplant the center. Nonetheless, for now, the pecking orders persist, alpha males (and some alpha females) continue to roam, cliques are common, and an establishment mentality is the norm.

In any case, these are challenging times. The art world is among the most idealistic spheres on earth, but as its mechanisms accelerate to absurd rates and business permeates everything, finding a zone where things seem not commercially but aesthetically driven grows harder. A coterie of educated professionals, enterprising aficionados, and appreciative fans—all of whom think art is in the answering business, not the questioning one—seem determined to make art safe for everyone. I adore museums and galleries, but both have become more corporate. Museum directors function like CEOs; curators act like superstars; critics are perceived as (and often behave like) PR agents; auction houses ape museums; and museums exhibit fashion designers who make huge donations. The art world has never suffered from too many rules, but even what rules there were have changed.

These changes have produced glitches—art world equivalents of Bizarro World, an inverted domain where box office receipts count as critical consensus. Here a few young artists—who don't make waves but ride them—are having the ends of their careers without ever having had the beginnings. Instead of being buoyed by grassroots energy, these artists are already surrounded by boldfaced names, socialites, and yes-people. Their openings look like those of aging art stars, teeming with Hollywood types, stylists, models, dot-commers, and publicists busy shuttling micro-celebrities between interviewers and paparazzi.

Bizarro World also flourishes in the auction houses, which have started touting their four-day sales as bona fide equivalents of museum exhibitions—instead of what they are, which is a way for people to make money. They're producing lavish catalogues with essays by art critics and dabbling in the emerging artist market. They enlist the artists to install their own work and participate in publicity. Like real estate firms that issue glitzy brochures on deluxe properties, Sotheby's published an entire volume promoting the sale of Jeff Koons's sculpture *Michael Jackson and Bubbles*, which eventually sold for $5.6 million.

As alienating as all this is, none of it is cause for alarm. If the Bizarro boats float, all who cruise on them will sail away happy. If the ships sink, everyone on board will go down with them. Those who insist that art is in trouble mistake all this background noise of money and ambition for art. But art is resilient and crafty. It's been around for 25,000 years; it knows how to take care of itself. As categories blend and definitions blur, as art absorbs aspects of visual culture and new technologies (and vice versa), art and our ideas about it will change. For now, the weirdness in the system means we have to be that much more conscious of the system. We have to try not to resolve ambiguities, to remember that for many the art experience is a series of lowercase, low-definition encounters. The system, as Shaw said of fashion, is essentially an "induced epidemic." What happened with the internet may happen here: As more people come to know the art world, those without preconceptions about its uses will use it in new ways.

In the meantime, just because we are ambitious, it doesn't mean we have to *act* ambitious. Maybe if art were more like getting dressed—something we do almost unconsciously, yet with passionate attention to what makes us feel or look good—then the art world might become a place where the weather suits our clothes, not a place where uniforms are worn. In a moment when so many people are still stuck on autopilot, behaving like establishmentarians, pursuing the named instead of the nameless, there's no better time to do things your own way.

(September 5, 2001)

Keeping the Faith

Everything is different in America, and everybody knows it. We don't know how, only that it is.

All bets are off. Old arguments are out the window. American history has leaped off the tracks. This is what a paradigm shift feels like. Lives have been changed. Ideas will be tested. Art will be altered. We don't know what it all means, only that it's happening. Complacency was buried in the rubble; narcissism went up in smoke.

Like a pet snake that has escaped its terrarium, something familiar—terrorism—has turned truly terrifying. In the art world, the rush for money and fame will continue; careers will be spun, self-absorption will persist, and there will be art that is adolescent and petty. But all this, and the art world of the recent past, will soon seem dated.

Many say, "How can you think about art at a time like this?" Art can appear so insignificant when the world gets crazy. But the world has always been crazy, even if it hasn't been as horrifying. Art's been around a long time. It knows how to handle good times and bad. And it's never really been insignificant. Theodor Adorno famously wrote, "Poetry after Auschwitz . . . has become impossible." But weren't his very words poetic?

Most art is superficial. However, the aesthetic experience (that tinny, off-putting term), the enigmatic interior place we go when we make or look at art, is still what it's always been: complex, rich, rewarding, meaningful, and moving. It is a place we will always return to. A place, presumably, we all come from. A place, moreover, that tells us things we didn't know we needed to know until we knew them.

We should keep in mind that this place is also old, deep, and probably hardwired. In his immensely influential 1980 essay *Within the Context of No Context*, George W. S. Trow claimed that ours is a world without differentiation, where all distances have faded into one continuous blur—a world where dissimilarity has been replaced by similarity. This is an absurdity, especially now. America's context and the world's have just collided.

Whatever happened, we should never again allow ourselves the illusion that everything that happens is happening to everybody, everywhere, at the same time. The pragmatists were right. Everything that happens to everyone is understood differently by everyone. That globalist hum people thought they were listening to turns out to have been background noise to a cacophony of conflicting contexts.

Now we know we are nothing but context, and that context changes everything. When it comes to art, this means that things made at one time, under one circumstance, will look different in another time or circumstance. Who thinks about flatness when they think about Rothko? Who thinks about German Neo-Expressionists like Rainer Fetting at all? The Sistine Chapel doesn't rouse the passions it did during the Counter-Reformation. Cubism isn't shocking. Fauvism isn't ugly.

On September 11, context changed again. This month's terrorist fashion feature in *The Face* doesn't look so imaginary anymore. Camouflage designs are more ominous. The titles of current movies—*Training Day, The Glass House, Soul Survivors*—take on new meanings. Suddenly, *Beau Monde*—the title of Dave Hickey's SITE Santa Fe exhibition—seems a little off, while Robert Gober's installation in the American pavilion in Venice, with its glowing, redemptive light shining through cracks in a cellar storm door, takes on new relevance. At Friedrich Petzel Gallery, Richard Phillips's big, gray-toned portrait of George W. Bush really looks different. Gazing at our leader's sly expression is more disconcerting than ever. Before he was just a nebbish. Now he's a nebbish at the helm of a country in danger. Perhaps this image will turn out to have predicted a catastrophe for America; perhaps it will one day register an entirely different range of emotions.

IN THE WAKE OF CATACLYSM, how will masculinity, violence, and government be represented in the near future? What will become of our taste for celebrity and glamour? Has the audience for art changed? All these questions hang in the air. Nevertheless, although contexts change, people sometimes stay the same. That's why some are resorting to shooting the messenger.

Already, an old American puritanical streak has resurfaced. Some of the very people who have raked it in for the last ten years are calling for art to "clean up its act." Others are condemning the art of the nineties as shallow or trivial—as if Jeff Koons and Karen Kilimnik are responsible for pissing off the Arabs; as if the art world were the Great Satan. Others claim that formalism and self-involved art are now gratuitous. We may be in for a wave of preachy art, mawkish performance pieces, all manner of castigation, and insipid social realism. As surely as patriotism engenders kitsch, guilt walks hand in hand with hypocrisy.

Those who look back in anger at the art of the recent past are exploiting the circumstances to attack things they either never liked or felt ashamed of. It's an old song in a new time. We don't know what is to come, any better than they do. All we can say to them is, when it comes to art, have a little more faith.

(September 26, 2001)

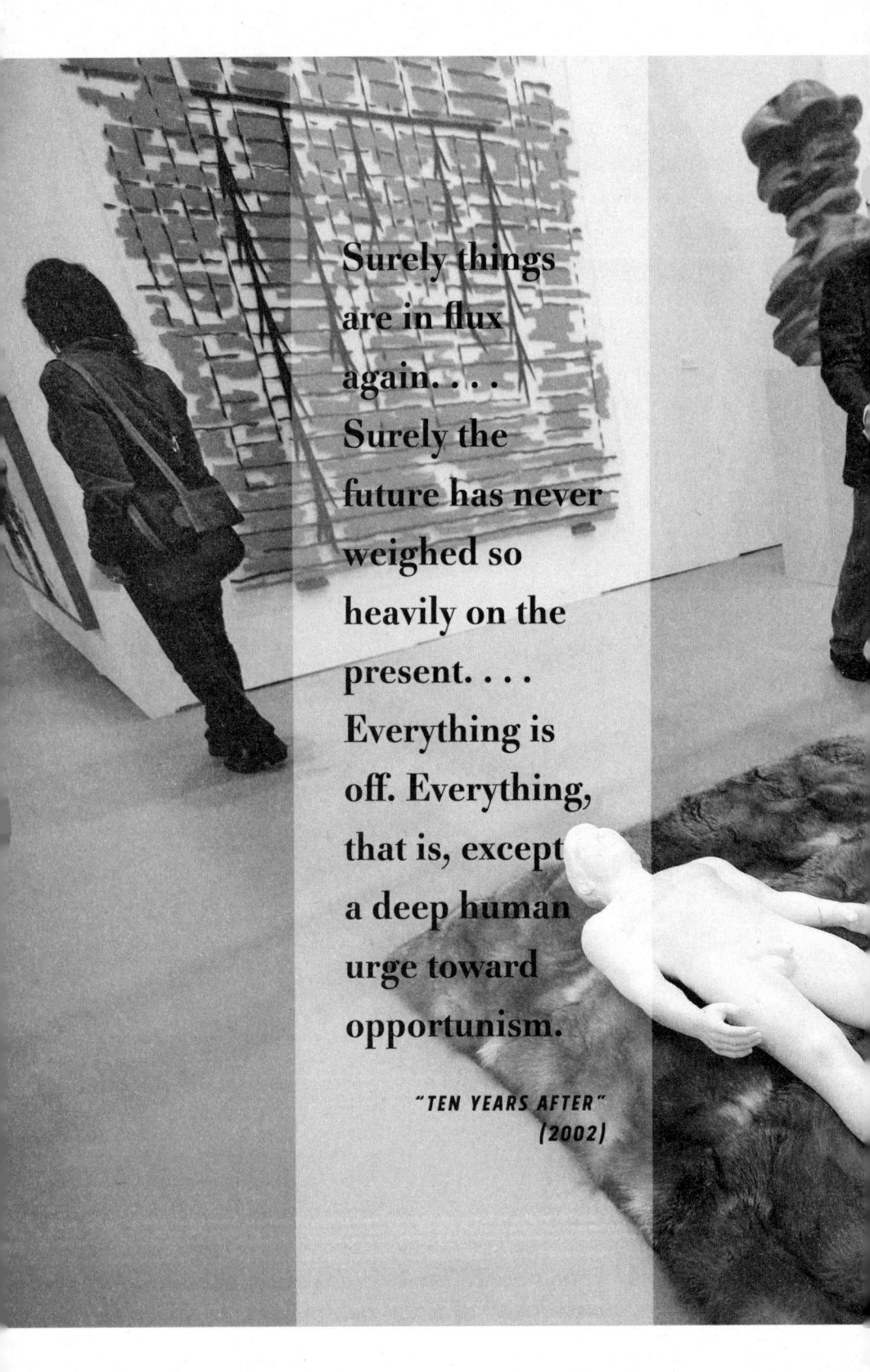

Surely things are in flux again. . . . Surely the future has never weighed so heavily on the present. . . . Everything is off. Everything, that is, except a deep human urge toward opportunism.

"TEN YEARS AFTER"
(2002)

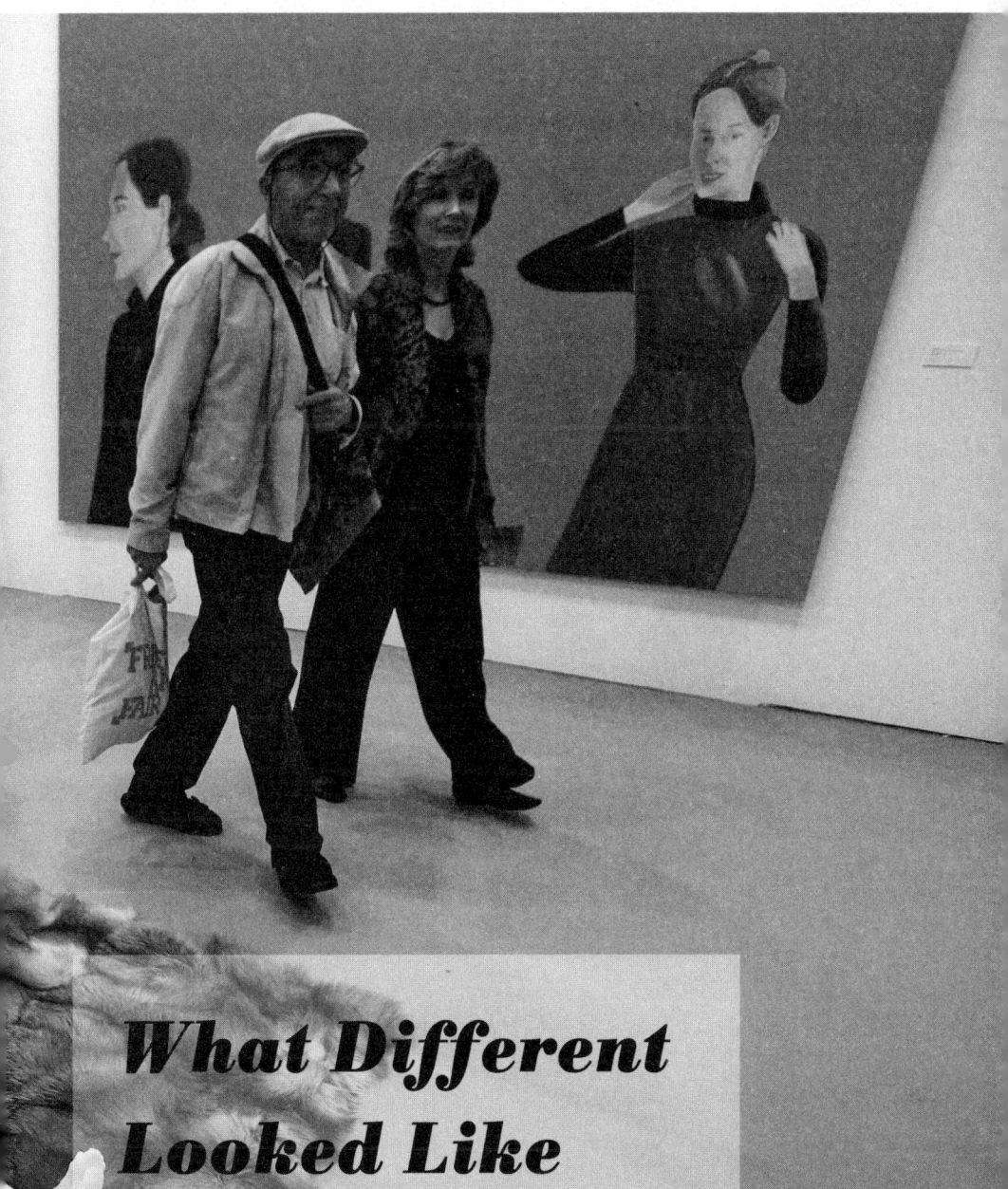

What Different Looked Like

2001–2008

Middle Americana: Norman Rockwell

When it comes to the claims being made for Norman Rockwell, my advice is *just say no*. A cadre of museum directors, curators, national critics, art historians, and suddenly populist art theorists want you to love him. Rockwell is hip. He's a big moneymaker and crowd-pleaser, an everyman artist everyone can understand. He's also a postmodern fad.

To love Rockwell is to shun complexity. To equate him with Vermeer is not to have really looked at either of their pictures. In person, Rockwell's paintings are pretty dead. They are mechanical, washed out; they have little space, limited color, and no surface. As the artist Carroll Dunham said, "You are not in the presence of artful thought." Instead, Rockwell exhibits a canny sense of caricature, costume, props, and narrative—what Robert Hughes calls giving "every hair of every mutt its share of picturesque completeness." Rockwell is a picture maker, not a painter. It's not surprising to learn that many of the companies that commissioned work from him tossed the originals once they were reproduced. His work was never meant to be seen in the flesh; it was meant for reproduction. As Rockwell said, "I never painted pictures to be seen. They were painted for a camera."

Rockwell didn't think like an artist, but he certainly was tormented like one. When asked if he liked being an illustrator, he snapped, "I hate it." When ranked with his favorite artist, Rembrandt, Rockwell muttered, "I'm sure he's turning over in his grave." He often said, "People tell me, 'I don't know anything about art, but I love your stuff.' I wish they'd say the opposite, 'I know a lot about art, and I love your stuff.'" It's no wonder people want to rescue him.

The problem is, Rockwell is no longer in need of rescuing. Overstating his case only isolates him once again. Nowadays, Rockwell is treated not as a pariah, but as a major talent at one end of the spectrum. Even the critic Clement Greenberg—who lambasted Rockwell's *Saturday Evening Post* covers—could allow that "it's entirely possible to like a Rockwell more than a Raphael." Many of Rockwell's illustrations—including *Day in the Life of a Little Girl* (1952), *Marriage License* (1955), *The Runaway* (1958), *Coming and Going* (1947), and *After the Prom* (1957)—can turn you into a quivering ball of mush. Nonetheless, I doubt even his most ardent supporter would rather live with the best Rockwell than a middling Raphael. Much is made of Rockwell's popularity, his "virtue," his ability to create a world. But an exhibition devoted to *The Simpsons* would be less sentimental, more visual, and have twice the actual virtue of a Rockwell exhibition. And an empty room with piped-in music by Hank Williams and Sonny Boy Williamson—both Rockwell's contemporaries—would take you deeper and tell you more about America.

(2001)

Harlem on His Mind: Jacob Lawrence

It is sad but not surprising that the tastemakers currently touting Norman Rockwell as "a master of narrative" and "an artist who speaks to all people" ignore a contemporary of Rockwell's whose work better embodies these qualities. That artist is Jacob Lawrence (1917–2000), now the subject of a probing, occasionally soaring, retrospective at the Whitney.

To understand why Lawrence is richer than Rockwell, you need only spend time in the gallery containing his great narrative masterpiece: the sixty-panel *Migration of the Negro*, which tells a story with real implications for all Americans.

Step by step—in alternately bright and dull tempera colors, angular compositions, tilting perspectives, blocky Cubistic forms, and flat shapes—Lawrence delineates the largest, most consequential exodus in our history. His subject is the nation-changing flight that took place in the first decades of the twentieth century, the journey of more than a million black Americans (many the children of slaves, many former slaves themselves) from South to North—from what was understood to be the scene of the crime to a hoped-for Promised Land. This mass movement marked the transition from rural to urban, agrarian to industrial, and a people's search for America itself.

Migration tells that desperate story movingly and with a vivacious, almost levitating pictorial flair. Lawrence's colors are flat-footed yet brassy; he loves deploying patches of bright yellow and off-orange across his surfaces, and interspersing these with murky, muddy greens and browns. The look of his work is at once crude and deft. None of the individual paintings in *Migration* is much bigger than a clipboard, yet the whole has an emotional resonance akin to that of "The Battle Hymn of the Republic," and is the equal of John Steinbeck's *The Grapes of Wrath* in its depiction of oppression, misery, and hope.

All you need to know about the making of *Migration*, other than that Lawrence worked on all the panels simultaneously and completed them at the precocious age of twenty-three, is that the artist lived it. By the time he was thirteen, when his Virginia-born mother moved him and his family to West 143rd Street, Lawrence had lived in three cities. When he completed *Migration* in 1941, he'd already executed multipanel paintings depicting the lives of Harriet Tubman, Frederick Douglass, and Toussaint Louverture. His early work, painted between 1936 and 1938, combines the veracity of street photography with the imagination of great storytelling. None of his subjects is heroicized, yet the pictures exude a sense of the heroism of everyday life in Harlem. We see peddlers, beggars, and brothels, a haughty black couple hurrying past a funeral, a mother greeted on tenement stairs by her jubilant children, and a prostitute beckoning to a nervous white customer. *Migration* is one of those rare, mature-on-arrival showpieces, a bit like Jasper Johns's first flag painting, completed when he was only twenty-five. Like Johns and *Flag*, Lawrence and *Migration* arrived with a bang. In 1942, the Museum of Modern Art, and the Phillips Collection in Washington, D.C., each bought thirty panels (for a total cost of $2,000). Lawrence became the first black artist represented by a prestigious New York gallery—the Downtown Gallery, which also exhibited Stuart Davis and Charles Sheeler—and *Migration* was sent on a fifteen-city national tour.

The first panel of *Migration* is a harbinger. A throng crowds through three open rail-station gates marked Chicago, New York, and St. Louis. The scene is all tumult. No faces are discernible, suggesting that this migration also marks the beginning of the journey from being isolated individuals to becoming a people. As LeRoi Jones (now Amiri Baraka) put it in *Blues People*, "The Negro as slave is one thing. The Negro as American is quite another."

The second panel, depicting a bulldozer and a crane, shows what the migrants came for: jobs. The third returns to the migration itself. We see another crowd, many with duffel bags and suitcases, all hurrying under a streaky sky. Even the birds in this picture seem to flee. A few panels on, Lawrence paints a locomotive hurtling through the night. The next image shows a passenger car crammed with migrants. Lawrence lays out his indictment of the South: sun-scorched fields, ravaged crops, flooded farms, shotgun shacks and crushing poverty, prisoners in handcuffs, a fat white judge staring down two blacks, and finally, a hangman's noose. An understated caption begins, "Although the Negro was used to lynching, he found this an opportune time to leave." "Opportune," indeed.

In panel 31, a starkly minimal picture of three tenement buildings, Lawrence turns to life in the North. Then he abruptly returns to a scene of a crowded Southern railroad station. This is followed by a gut-wrenching picture of a woman reading a letter in bed while a child cries. Lawrence captures the chasm that had opened up between the old and the so-called New Negro, between those who stayed behind and those who went north. (In later works Lawrence would confront the "disgust and aloofness" shown by Northern blacks toward Southern blacks.)

Migration's final eleven panels deal with what was encountered in the North. In addition to scenes of a new life and jobs, there are images of discrimination, segregation, riots, bombings, and child labor. The series ends as it began, with a picture of a crowded railway station, with the caption "And the migrants kept coming."

The inventive way Jacob Lawrence responded to Cubism—simplifying it, making it less formal and more accessible—coupled with the way he employed this sophisticated style to paint his own life and render the progress of a people, makes him the American Chagall. Both artists were giants, especially early on. Both were storytellers. Chagall painted his Jewish roots; Lawrence, the agony of the past and of building a future. Most of all, Lawrence gives form to the fathomless suffering and beauty James Baldwin wrote about in *The Fire Next Time*: "The Negro's past, of rope, fire, torture, castration, infanticide, rape; death and humiliation; fear by day and night, fear as deep as the marrow of the bone; doubt that he was worthy of life. . . . This endless struggle to achieve and reveal and confirm a human identity, human authority, yet contains, for all its horror, something very beautiful." Lawrence delivers this beauty whole.

(2001)

Poor Memorial

The worst show of the year, by far, is the display currently on view at the Winter Garden of the eight models for memorials to those killed in the attacks on the World Trade Center. Unless the jurors halt the process, or public outcry overwhelms it, one of these models—all of which resemble waiting rooms, food courts, corporate parks, underground malls, or airport architecture—will be built. The day that happens will be a sad one.

It's not that all the proposals are horrible; a few have poetic details. One, an affecting cemetery in a forest, features trees planted in rows in the buildings' footprints. Among the trees are 2,982 "memorial columns," each with the name of a victim and details of his or her life. Another plan has two evocative underground waterfalls. But none of the finalists, winnowed down from 5,201 entries by the thirteen jurors of the Lower Manhattan Development Corporation, captures the imagination. All are deeply derivative of Minimalism and generic installation art; none offers a significant form. There are waterfalls, gardens, trees, and lights and New Agey names: *Garden of Lights, Inversion of Light, Votives in Suspension, Suspending Memory, Dual Memory.* How could something so important and sensitive, something so in need of an inspired touch, go so wrong, so quickly?

To answer this, we need to look back to a month after September 11, when the air was still acrid with the smell of the smoldering wreckage—and the managerial mindset that brought us to this point surfaced. At a packed assembly of architects in Cooper Union's Great Hall, professionals from around the world met and spoke about the tragedy in ways I hadn't heard before or, thankfully, since. I love contemporary architecture, but I was appalled by the breathtaking opinion, expressed by many in attendance, that architects were the only ones who understood the site "in the deepest sense." Several exclaimed that "only Frank Gehry could build here," or extolled the vision of Zaha Hadid or Richard Meier. I admire all these people's work, but it seemed both premature and callous for this forum to turn its focus so quickly from the victims to the names of star architects vying for the commission. One expert brandished a bolt he had swiped from the site; another griped that he hadn't been allowed to conduct his own "structural analysis." This would have been amusing had it not been so contemptible. These puffed-up professionals and autocratic academics believed they were the ones who could set things right. Many referred to the site with a word I'd never heard invoked to describe hell: *opportunity.*

Which brings us to why none of these proposals can work: None of them diverts us from the humdrum buildings designed for the site by Daniel Libeskind, the celebrity architect who eventually won the architectural competition. These buildings are so nondescript that it's almost impossible to conjure a mental image of them. They are a cluster of angular masses, a collection of ungainly Citibank Building clones, one jutting higher than the rest. In the end, Libeskind's design is mostly a number: the so-called Freedom Tower is designed to reach 1,776 feet. The date is great and the height is fine, but tall is all this tower will be. Beyond that, these will be nothing more than slick structures on a burial mound.

(2003)

Babylon Rising

Times are strange. Not so long ago everything was extroverted, all about scandals and shock tactics. Now we don't know if Saddam is dead or alive, or if it's Osama on the tape. Deceitful politicians who have lost all sense of nuance act otherwise, but the line from *Harry Potter* is right: "The world isn't split into good people and Death Eaters." Today, things are ambiguous and cryptic. No one knows which way the wind blows. Certainty is suspect, even scary. This upheaval is causing tremors in the art world. There's no paradigm shift; no major fractures have appeared. But change is in the air. Batons are being passed.

Much of this is just a hunch, none of it's about big names, and as always in New York, money could quash things overnight. There's also the curator problem. Russians say, "If you see a Bulgarian on the street, beat him. He'll know why." Because they've damaged so many art institutions, this saying applies to many of our academicized curators as well. The Whitney is in dire straits, the Grey Art Gallery is missing in action, PS1 and the New Museum reel between excellence and awfulness, the Guggenheim is struggling to make good on its Matthew Barney moment.

Nonetheless, something promising feels afoot. Thrillingly, for the first time in a while, art seems more important than the system. The professionalism of the recent past, the thing that made the late-nineties art world seem corporate and unsafe, is morphing into something less predictable, more homespun. The fringes feel frisky, good new artists and galleries are appearing, hype and fashionableness matter less, those capacious Chelsea galleries don't seem as off-putting, and art is becoming the focus again. Art has brashly thrown itself over the pluralistic edge and into an amazing blender—one that siphons off moralizing and doesn't dilute the mediums but actually gives them solidity, specificity. At the same time, form is stepping out of subject matter's shadow. The way things look, how they're made, and what they're about are starting to coalesce.

Why is all this happening? Maybe because history isn't viewed as cynically as it was before September 11. The fundamentalist philosophers of Post-Modernist theory were locked in a grudge match with history—they had an adversarial, endgame relationship to it. History was a graveyard to them, a snake pit. Now artists are beginning to mesh history with lived reality. They're attuned to the sadness, the terror, and the ecstasy of history. They understand that the present is history, and that *all* art is contemporary art.

Most conspicuously, a new generation of gay artists has appeared. Excellent out gay artists have exhibited over the last ten years, but they were mostly confronting the culture wars and AIDS. Many artists died in those years, including scores we'll never know, and the aesthetic cloth was torn. Now it's mending. These days, galleries are filled with pictures of cute guys collaged onto pretty patterns (something an artist named Andy once did). A lot of this art is Pop-y, adolescent stuff. What's intriguing about it, the best of it, is that it's not preachy but visually ballsy.

Then there are what might be called New Modernists: artists who present odd or outlandish arrangements of found or made objects, whose work is imbued not with irony or nostalgia but with a belief in materials and the desire to meld them with subject matter. These artists aren't anti-modern or post-anything. They're probing Modernism and linking it with modern life. This connects them to a number of graphic whizzes, some of whom are taking cues from renegades like R. Crumb, Chris Johanson, and Barry McGee, as well as from street prophets and tattooists. All these artists are trying to fuse life, myth, narrative, and spirituality with form— the very things the early Modernists wanted to do.

Elsewhere, painters like Dana Schutz and Jules de Balincourt, who owe much to thrift store and folk art, are sifting through diverse, often devalued aesthetic currencies and coming up with fresh results. If their work turns mannered, it'll wither. Abstraction, spliced with fantasy, science, architecture, or whatever, is gathering steam. Meanwhile, videomakers are making dark rooms enjoyable again. Photographers and video artists like Katy Grannan, Daniela Rossell, Trisha Donnelly, and Francis Alÿs are finding ways around the arty discourse; collage and collectivism are ubiquitous; color is coming on like gangbusters; and all of it is happily happening across generational lines.

None of this guarantees good art. But people are realizing more than ever that the rules are dead, deader than they were under pluralism, and that we are all gypsies. In the end it comes down to what it always comes down to: vision and visionaries.

(2003)

Worlds Apart: Amar Kanwar

Initially, the antipathy between India and Pakistan captured in *A Season Outside,* Amar Kanwar's intensely affecting thirty-minute documentary-style film/political treatise/lament/love poem, seems wholly foreign, even ludicrous to us. After a while, however, a queasy feeling arises: You realize that our own red-state, blue-state separation is almost as noxious. Watching Kanwar's 1997 film, you wonder if the two Americas aren't only a decade or so from coming apart or coming to blows.

At the beginning of *A Season Outside*, Kanwar pictures a ritual that is at once gripping, pitiful, terrifying, and absurd. It is sunset at the Wagah-Attari border in the disputed Kashmir territory between India and Pakistan. A metal gate separates two large crowds. On the Indian side, hundreds of Hindu nationalists gather; on the Pakistani side, an equal number of their Muslim counterparts. So much violence has passed between these two warring nation-states that passage between them is now strictly regulated. The groups mill about, glare across the border at one another, or simply stare. Friction and listlessness fill the air.

Before long, soldiers appear on both sides of the barrier. Outfitted in multicolored bandannas and elaborate feathered headgear, festooned with ribbons and metals, and armed with swords and looks that could kill, they have the demeanor of agitated exotic birds. One by one, in a rigid, intimidating fashion, each soldier swiftly high-steps the twenty feet or so to the metal gate. With each stride, the foot is kicked above the head; the boot comes crashing to the ground; the soldier then jerks his head and lets out a grimacing huff. This insane display of alpha male behavior is riveting, menacing, and comical. This ritual unfolds on both sides of the fence. It's a performance from hell—history played out by grim-faced, resplendent demons.

Kanwar was born and lives in New Delhi. He has a poet's way of rhyming images, so that each interlude conspires with and reinforces every other. We're shown men releasing rams at one another; the head of each animal is painted either red or blue. Elsewhere, Kanwar lingers over a puppy being preyed upon by a conspiracy of ravens. In one extended sequence, shot in a Tibetan refugee camp not far from the border, Kanwar shows us one boy mauling another, bored young men pacing the street, and blank-looking old ones squatting outside a shop called Dreamland. In each episode, a psychic window opens onto a world of emptiness, separation, loss, and pain.

With *A Season Outside*, Kanwar joins a generation of artists who are making films and videos that manage to escape their own pedantic weight, occupying a lyrical realm where politics, poetry, passion, and form meld— a psycho-visual place where propaganda bleeds into consciousness and opinion becomes tangible.

(2004)

Mourning Glory: Steve McQueen

Turner Prize winner Steve McQueen's steamy video *Girls, Tricky* (2001) shows the creative act unfolding. I melted while watching it. On-screen we see the musician-producer Tricky (Adrian Thaws) deliver several takes of a manic song in a darkened London sound studio. McQueen's camera circles Tricky as he puts himself through a kind of psychic avalanche, performing a frenetic hymn, coaxing supernatural sounds from himself while smoking what looks like a giant spliff. Over the course of fifteen minutes, we watch as lived experience, thought, and desire are transformed into sonic matter. *Girls, Tricky* lets you see how controlled this moment of losing control is and how ultra-conscious tapping into the subconscious is. At one point, just when you think Tricky is in another universe, he stops, opens his eyes, and calmly says, "That was good; let's do it again."

De Kooning famously said, "Content is a glimpse." *Girls, Tricky* provides a glimpse of something I've heard in the voices of Howlin' Wolf and Billie Holiday, Kurt Cobain, and Dolly Parton on "Jolene." I saw it in Muhammad Ali just after he knocked out George Foreman, in Marlon Brando in *Apocalypse Now*, in Jimi Hendrix's "Voodoo Child," in the way the lead singer on "Louie, Louie" barks, "Let's give it to 'em right now!" and now in Tricky's possessed song. It's the sight or sound of someone turning himself inside out, so that one of the selves inside can momentarily appear. When someone renders something this raw this well, it begins a journey into forever.

McQueen is a very serious artist. His vision is grand and symphonic. His work is sumptuous but laced with bittersweet mourning and the feeling that he's engaging with history both as a participant and as an outsider. Forever and the limits of identity are places McQueen is interested in—a limbo where self and culture intermingle, where fiction and reality blend into history. This intermingling is rampant in *Once Upon a Time* (2003), a majestic seventy-minute video in which 116 of the images that were launched into space by NASA aboard the *Voyager 2* space probe in 1977 are projected in Marian Goodman's darkened main gallery. These pictures were meant to represent us to aliens. Here, each one is screened for a minute before it slowly fades into the next. Few viewers will likely see the entire work in one sitting.

Which may be the point. At this speed, the images are tyrannically oppressive. Kitschy, pious, and ragingly anal, all are universalizing representations of humankind. We see babies being born, benevolent old folks, diligent factory workers, and decent farmers. Children play; animals walk in splendor; an astronaut floats in space. But there is no death or disease, no bad blood or sorrow. It's an after-school special by way of *The Family of Man*. Roland Barthes lambasted such depictions as "amply moralized and sentimentalized." Homi Bhabha notes "the position of social authority" that images like these assume. Susan Sontag asserts that pictures of this type "deny the determining weight of history." McQueen, who says they're about "our so-called knowledge," allows us to see all of them as a single picture—a portrayal not of who we are but of how we want to be seen. It's an American version of Leni Riefenstahl's *Olympia*, a sort of psychological black box that provides evidence of our attempt to manage images and deny death. This gigantic fake self-portrait clarifies why Post-Modernism, and its ideas about pictures being biased, took shape at around the time

Voyager was launched. The soundtrack of *Once*, featuring people speaking in tongues, highlights the aspirational side of these pictures, the hope that we're not alone in the universe.

In the rear gallery, the riveting *7th Nov.* (2001) evokes another kind of speaking in tongues: the language of trauma and repentance. Projected for twenty-four minutes is the solitary image of a black man on his back, seen from the crown of his head. A pronounced scar runs across the top of his skull. On the soundtrack, McQueen's cousin Marcus recounts how he accidentally shot and killed his brother. It's a terrible story, told with sorrow, insight, and verve. The stillness and stateliness of this black body—which contrasts with the horror of the story—recalls Mantegna's dead Christ and surrealist photos of truncated bodies. Here, the head is a black planet, an empty eye or an abstract phallus. It is Rembrandtesque, mysterious and somber. The killing of a brother, together with the scar, suggest the mark of Cain. Rosalind Krauss has written about "images that do not decorate but rather *structure* the basic mechanisms of thought." That's what this image and soundtrack do. McQueen's *7th Nov.* is a contemporary history painting, a modern-day *Death of Marat*. It is a requiem and a confession, a cautionary tale about being human and being black, and an allegory for white society's discomfort with blackness.

(2005)

Whatever Laurel Wants

On the planet Heterosexual there is a race of men who lack the ability to seduce women and whom women never attempt to seduce. Their numbers are unknown, although, in some metaphysical way, all males may carry their recessive gene. These men make feeble, sometimes touching, often offensive, but always failed attempts to lure women—typically, women much younger than they are.

Enter artist Laurel Nakadate, the half-Japanese twenty-nine-year-old Yale photography MFA and standout in the *Greater New York* exhibition at PS1. In her exhibition *Love Hotel and Other Stories*, Nakadate puts herself into a position to encounter these men, allowing herself to be partially drawn into the webs they hope to weave. They hit on her; then she strikes like a trapdoor spider, responding with her own counterproposal. Arranging to go to their apartments or elsewhere, she arrives with a video camera and convinces them to enact strangely suggestive but asexual scenarios with her.

In the video *Lessons 110* (2001), Nakadate poses braless in a tank top and pink short shorts atop a table as one of these men draws her. As he looks at her, she—the "object of the male gaze"—looks directly at the camera, letting us know that she knows what's going on. It's all incredibly twisted. She turns from a baby doll into an avenging angel and a wolf in baby doll's clothing. Nakadate has staged birthday parties in which men sing "Happy Birthday" to her while she feigns delight. On some cosmic level, Nakadate is always "faking it." Sometimes she'll play dead while they snap pictures of her, other times she has them place a stethoscope to her chest or trace the curves of her absent body in midair. There's always a gaping hole in the center of Nakadate's world, something that echoes the disaster of prescribed sexual roles.

Voyeurism, exhibitionism, and hostility merge with gullibility, cunning, and folly in Nakadate's work. Not only is this creepy, it's confusing and complicated. The roles of hunter and hunted are blurred. Nakadate turns the tables on these men and also on herself. No one comes out of these Lolita-complex revenge fantasies unscathed.

The centerpiece of this exhibition is a three-channel video. Nakadate's work hasn't changed much since her first exhibition, in 2002; if anything, it is simply more focused and impudent, even sometimes annoying. As in a horror film, you sporadically want to yell, "Get out of there, you idiot"— both to the men and to her. In one section of the video, Nakadate toys with these would-be lotharios in their own lairs, having them either crouch in cages or crawl on the floor like dogs while she imitates a cat. The men are always off-balance in these wicked games, careful not to transgress, but visibly tempted to go further. Nakadate is off-balance, too, but in different ways. She's *always* in control, a kind of aggressive Olympia presence, artificial, at risk, and at the same time dangerous.

Nakadate is melding disparate bits of artistic DNA to crackerjack effect. On a visual level she seizes the force of Barbara Kruger's use of pronouns like *you* and *we* by getting us to think about *her* and *them*. She crosses this with the way Louise Lawler's photographs sneer to us, "Look at the way *they* hang *their* art in *their* museums," then introduces the socially constructed sexual roles of Cindy Sherman's *Untitled Film Stills*. Nakadate combines these hard-core feminist photographic essences with the taboo gutter love of Robert Melee and the anti-feminism of Vanessa Beecroft's complicated and compelling art. To this Nakadate adds her own back-alley eroticism, her vulnerability, insight, and isolation.

On the Heterosexual planet men rule through a combination of upper-body strength, institutionalized discrimination, sheer arrogance, and hogwash. Women are always in danger. Nakadate isn't, at least not in her work. She clearly chooses her subjects as carefully as they choose her. She could never do this with "normal" predators. If a young male artist preyed on women this way he'd risk being kicked out of the art world. But Nakadate exploits female sexuality as ruthlessly as any man.

In *Where You'll Find Me*, she acts out suicide scenarios, presenting herself as a dead figure in a range of locales. Here, Nakadate represents primal neediness—that fantasy that whispers, *They'll know how much they love me when I'm gone*. Then, out of nowhere, she suddenly comes close to the camera, looks from side to side, pulls her shorts to the left, stands, and pees while looking directly at you. It's weird and very feral. In *Love Hotel*, a similarly narcissistic and conflicted caprice unfolds as Nakadate writhes, near-naked, on a series of beds. Here, as alone and pitiable as the men, she's seeing what she would look like *if* she could actually be with a real person. It's onanistic exhibitionism—peculiar, devoid of obvious feeling, and disquieting.

That seeming absence of feeling is a touchstone of Nakadate's art. In the chilling, tear-jerking video *We Are All Made of Stars,* Nakadate appears on her roof dressed as a Girl Scout as the World Trade Center smolders behind her. She stands, stares at the camera, teary-eyed, and says nothing. Nothing needs to be said. It's uncanny to think about an artist making art that morning about that morning. Nakadate is a damaged unit and a loose cannon, clever, arresting, and slightly mad—a very promising combination.

(2005)

Hammered

I've got a little—no, a big—problem with contemporary art auctions. Last fall I set out to investigate it further. Beginning November 3, the day after the presidential election, I went to as many sales during New York's big fall auction week as I could stomach. This turned out to be a half-dozen spread out among the major auction houses—Christie's, Sotheby's, and Phillips. I learned a lot, but the problem only grew.

Contemporary art auctions are bizarre combinations of meat market, trading floor, theater, and brothel. They are rarefied entertainments where speculation, spin, and trophy hunting merge as an insular caste enacts a highly structured ritual in which the codes of consumption and peerage are manipulated in plain sight. Everyone says auctions are about "quality." In fact, they are altars to the disconnect between the inner life of art and the outer life of consumption, places where artists are cut off from their art. Auctions have nothing to do with quality. At auctions, new values are assigned and desire is fetishized. Consumption becomes a sort of sacrament, with art playing the role of sacrificial lamb as the Ponzi scheme surrounding it all rolls on.

Like a striptease, an auction relies on people being enticed by what's just out of reach. The auctioneer announces the lot number, the crowd stirs, and a turntable revolves to reveal the forlorn-looking work, which is frequently guarded by one of the few black people in the room. Completing this antebellum nightmare, petite blond women sit nearby in pretty dresses; they're there to spot bids but rarely actually do anything. Occasionally, a handsome swain—presumably another staffer—approaches from behind to whisper something into an ear. This lends a certain kinkiness to the proceedings. Of the hundreds, sometimes thousands of people in these rooms, only a tiny handful actually bid. The rest are there for kicks, networking, tracking values, and who knows what else. Meanwhile the ghostly "phone bidders" buy their art in public and private at the same time.

In my season at the auctions I saw seas of white people captivated by ruby-throated auctioneers—all European, all insanely artificial in their mannerisms. These showmen gesticulate and croon their odious, melodious, mathematical songs: "I have four million. Do I hear five million?" I looked on as three-quarters of a billion dollars changed hands, silently bidding farewell to works of art that will probably not be seen again in public in my lifetime. I saw a Mondrian, a Modigliani, and a Gauguin bring $21 million, $31 million, and $39 million, respectively. A Johns drawing fetched $11 million, a Warhol *Race Riot* $15 million, and a Maurizio Cattelan $3 million. I felt faint when a Matthew Barney photo in an edition of ten, which I'd seen in his studio years before, went for $200,000, then felt fainter as a restaurateur from a canceled reality show bid up a photograph while a stunning blonde ground her pelvis against his groin every time he waved his paddle. I was dumbfounded as a third-rate painting by Marlene Dumas broke the million-dollar mark, bought by one of her dealers. Numbers didn't matter any longer, as the crowd carried on and the tote board tallied the prices in international currencies. Suddenly, Bush's election victory seemed quaint.

What's out of whack at the auctions, however, isn't just the monetary values of the art, it's the values of the people who are buying and selling it. Wealthy collectors and their spawn tell everyone that they love the art they own. Then—instead of selling the top several works and being set for life, perhaps giving the rest to a museum and changing the course of that museum forever (while receiving a tax benefit for themselves)—they sell their collections at auction and everyone applauds. These collectors have no clue about what it means to own art. Like the auction houses, they're interested only in money and publicity.

The cupidity of many of the people who buy and sell their art at auctions has created what I call the parallel market: artists whose auction prices far exceed what their work costs in galleries. Christie's international co-head of postwar contemporary art, Amy Cappellazzo, ruefully admits, "Some people prefer to spend $500,000 at auction on something they could buy privately for $50,000." She calls these people "traders." Auction houses rely on the likelihood that their buyers don't know much about art, will buy almost anything if it has the right name on it, or just don't care. So much for "quality." Recently, *The New York Times* ran an article titled "The X Factor," about why art by women doesn't bring the same auction prices as art by men. Among the examples cited was an Elizabeth Peyton painting that sold for "only" $300,000, while works by John Currin and Luc Tuymans fetched more than a million. What the article and all of us should ask is why any of them, good or bad, should sell for much more than, say, $100,000. Art worlders grouse about the skyrocketing prices, yet too many of them are making too much money off the system as it is to step away.

(2005)

The Battle for Babylon

This time last year, I wrote that the art world had passed into what I called a superparadigm period, by which I meant a phase of continual growth. That's still true. The art world has never been so flush with money.

There are almost three hundred galleries in Chelsea, with more than thirty expanding or relocating there this season. A twenty-story "gallery condo" is under construction; Matthew Marks is opening a fourth gallery space, Perry Rubenstein a third, Pace a second; Marianne Boesky is building her own building. No one's closing. Plus, there are hundreds of contemporary galleries outside Chelsea. So New York truly is Art City. Or is it?

Even with all the buzz, we're in a predicament. Partly, this is because while this hyperdriven phase allows more artists to show quickly, it reduces art to its exchange value. Popularity and market viability are measures of quality; things are considered successful if they sell; selling means selling big. The system is making people offers they can't refuse, when it should be making them offers they can't understand.

Flush or not, people are frustrated. In private, many say most of the shows they see are safe or conservative. Yet most reviews are enthusiastic or merely descriptive. Too many critics act like cheerleaders, reporters, or hip metaphysicians. Amid art fair frenzy, auction madness, money lust, and market hype—between galleries turning into selling machines, gossip passing as criticism, and art becoming a good job—the system, while efficient, feels faulty, even false.

Perhaps it was ever thus, but today it seems more thus than ever. Now the system regularly replicates conditions it's familiar with, defaulting to known positions, producing pathogens of itself. It knows that art is a good investment—and traditionally made by men—so more men show and sell, while fewer women show at all. The ratio of one-woman shows in New York galleries between now and Christmas is deplorable, less than 20 percent. The discourse is being driven from a place that suppresses difference. This system needs to be starved into submission or changed.

Many people seem ready to do something about this situation, but much more needs to happen. Artists should be curating shows, writing about them, making their own publications. The agenda needs to be set by artists, not the market. Supply-and-demand thinking has to shift to production-and-experience thinking. Small communities or cells of artists, curators, and critics should band together, stake out positions, and present cogent arguments. If their positions are hostile to one another, fine; art isn't about getting along. Disagreement and criticism are ways of showing art respect.

If we're living in a time of genuinely new content, as everyone seems to maintain, new forms should be developed to house this content. We need to reimagine what a gallery is. Galleries shouldn't be seen primarily as shops or salesrooms, but as test sites and arks. Few gallerists are flesh-eating zombies who only want to sell art; most want to shape culture. Many are disgruntled with only being managers of the trading floor. Galleries should have attitude. There are signs of movement: After losing his lease, Andrew Kreps has opened a three-floor temporary space in which much of the programming is being carried out by artists. In Chelsea, the Kitchen has sprung to life under Debra Singer. The dynamic director of White Columns, Matthew Higgs, has fired a shot across everyone's bow, declaring, "I want to change the New York art world in twenty-four months." That's attitude. As is the bravado of gallerist Michelle Macca-rone, who begins her latest press release, "Maccarone is fuckin' psyched to announce its Anthony Burdin exhibition."

The New York art world is filled with extraordinary people. The infra-structure is here to do amazing things. I think those things are starting to happen; the Battle for Babylon is about to begin.

(2005)

Mr. System and Dr. Death: Luc Tuymans

Luc Tuymans's work can be romantic and repetitious. His enthrall-ment with hot-button subjects can make him seem opportunistic. Some of his latest paintings lack ambiguity. Even so, Tuymans deserves tremendous credit for a farsighted decision he made twenty-five years ago that not only changed his art but altered the way painting looks and is talked about today. Taking a cue from that brooding Dr. Death, Gerhard Richter—who claimed he was "indifferent" to his subjects and once wrote that "art is a wretched, cynical, stupid, helpless, confusing mirror image of our spiritual impoverishment"—Tuymans paints in systems. This allows him to render everything in the world, from pillows to dictators and gas chambers, through the same shadowy scrim. Painting heavy things in a light, Whistlerian way, he gets gravity, memory, and beauty to do a hypnotic dance of life and death.

In *Proper*, Tuymans turns his attention to the end of empire. It has been said that civilizations often crumble from spending themselves to death, and from spates of bad luck. As the theoretician Manuel DeLanda has observed, the downfall of the Ottoman Empire began with massive overspending, incurred from maintaining far-flung territories, and ended with "thirteen bad sultans in a row." The United States is now nearly $8 trillion in debt. It is also in the midst of having thirteen bad sultans in a row: The Vietnam-scarred sultanate of Johnson, two Nixons, one Ford, a Carter, two Reagans, the first Bush, the two horny sultanates of Clinton, and now Bush twice. That's twelve. In thirty-six months the United States could elect its thirteenth bad sultan.

The exhibition is bracketed by two commanding paintings. *Secretary of State* is a likeness of Condoleezza Rice; those in the Bush administration might deem it earnest and complimentary, while those opposed to it would find it ironic and ominous. It's a modern *Mona Lisa*—a picture of a cipher. The canvas is small, but Rice's head is massive within it. She looks simultaneously imposing, pinched, irritated, and isolated. Full-size, she'd be a monster. Brackish shades of ocher and mauve dance across her cheeks and jaw. The composition and the psychology are askew. The left side of Rice's face seems outer-directed, the right side oddly introspective. But while the subject of this jarring painting is explicit, its content is willpower, race, constriction, and solitude, as well as the thing holding two worldviews in tension: paradox.

This divergence seethes in *Demolition*, one of the best paintings Tuymans has ever made. The image—a viscous vision of billowing smoke—recalls the luminescent tactility of Brice Marden's early monochromes as well as the ravishing physicality of Manet and Degas that inspired Marden. *Demolition* might only be an image of a construction site, but its one discernible feature—a tiny lamppost in a corner of the painting—may cause many to flash to September 11. It's a reminder that all clouds contain traces of what we saw that morning: a glimpse of the end.

In ten years, the painting of Rice might seem as dated as an Oliver North portrait would today. Nevertheless, *Secretary of State* and *Demolition* are utterly public paintings that should be installed together in an American museum, allowing viewers to glimpse what D. H. Lawrence meant when he wrote, "There are terrible spirits, ghosts, in the air of America."

(2005)

Killing Fields: Thomas Hirschhorn

Thomas Hirschhorn's latest exhibition is a walk-in manifesto, a book of the dead about the psychic place where mysticism, Modernism, mayhem, and terror collapse into one another. Many will find this show revolting. Not because it's bad or resembles a parade float from perdition, or weakens on repeated visits, but because of Hirschhorn's use—and, some charge, his aestheticizing—of violent imagery. David Cohen of *The New York Sun* has already lambasted the show as an "adolescent crapfest" that evinces "a puerile addiction to the macabre and the scatological." This reaction is too easy. It's also fishy, considering that horrific images—from lynching pictures to gangland murders—have been seen and produced in America for more than a century.

Superficial Engagement is composed of four large makeshift platforms.

Viewers move between them along narrow corridors; everything is in your face. In addition to the gruesome images, each platform has a number of repeating elements, including quasi-primitive wooden effigies with thousands of nails driven into them, mannequins covered in nails à la acupuncture needles or the pinheads in Clive Barker's *Hellraiser,* along with facsimiles of the works of the visionary Swiss healer-painter Emma Kunz. The display includes hundreds of astonishingly gory color images, gleaned from the internet and specialty magazines, of mainly Arabs in Iraq and Afghanistan who have been blown to bits, bodies utterly destroyed— "bodies," as Hirschhorn hauntingly puts it, "in abstraction." You see riven flesh, severed limbs, decapitated heads. It's like a mass crucifixion, a *Massacre of the Innocents,* or Hirschhorn's version of *Guernica,* replete with disfigured, tortured bodies and the agonies of death. The pictures repulse, mesmerize, and anesthetize simultaneously; Hirschhorn steers art to shores beyond pornography. At the show I've heard people ask, "How can we look at images like this, let alone in an art gallery?" Hirschhorn's answers seem to be: "How can we not?" and "America is the only country in the world not looking at these images."

The exhibition is titled *Superficial Engagement* because, Hirschhorn maintains, "to go deep I must take the surface seriously." (Another obvious interpretation is that Americans are only superficially engaged with the carnage pictured.) Formally, Hirschhorn relies on bright lights, amplification, proliferation, and multiplication. His individual objects aren't anything special; he's more an assemblagist than a sculptor. The effect is like a jungle or junkyard crossed with a supermarket—a homemade temple of the martyrs and Goya's *Disasters of War.* Its roots are in punk graphics, Surrealism, Joseph Beuys, Kurt Schwitters, Edward Kienholz, and Warhol's razzmatazz.

Hirschhorn combines three worldviews: primitive religion, Modernist utopianism, and state-of-the-art militarism, displayed within four architectural archetypes—the mosque, the morgue, the museum, and the monument. The entire exhibition transforms into a contemporary *Merzbau.* The bodies are often paired with a Kunz abstraction, as if Hirschhorn wants the painting to heal them. Indeed, he's written that *Superficial*

Engagement is "an attempt to heal war and violence through art." This kind of magical thinking is apparent in the use of nails, meant to ward off evil but also familiar as tools of the suicide bomber.

Hirschhorn is a no-nonsense character who talks about moral responsibility, justice, and "art's power to change reality." He's desperately earnest and doesn't shy away from big pronouncements: "I don't make political art, I make art politically." "I fight hierarchy and demagogy." "Nothing is impossible with art." "I am an artist, a worker and a soldier." He scorns political correctness as "a sophisticated American invention to dissuade small-minded and fearful European artists from addressing the real questions in art." All this connects him to true believers of the Modernist faith: people like Mondrian, who called for the "abolition of every hierarchy"; Kazimir Malevich, who talked about "the beauty of speed" and "the zero of form"; Naum Gabo, who asserted "the active is beautiful; quality is garbage"; and Robert Smithson, who wrote, "The rat of politics always gnaws at the cheese of art." These artists wanted to ignite a cosmic revolution. Hirschhorn is unequivocal, but he doesn't want to burn the house down. What he wants is to unleash the explosive power of art—to remove boundaries, conjure the continuum of culture, create a constellation of meanings, and reveal that the fires burning now have been burning a long time.

(2006)

The Seventh Circle: Nan Goldin

Perhaps the most pitiable image in all of Dante's *Inferno* is the wood of suicides. Here, in hell's seventh circle, between a river of boiling blood and a desert of burning sand, is a dense, pathless forest where the souls of suicides are trapped among gnarled trees and fruitless bushes. Odious Harpies—monstrous birds with female faces—nest in the trees, racing from limb to limb, and when branches break, blood flows. Cries and wails echo in the sunless, starless air.

Throughout her career, and especially in her latest and most wrenching work—*Sisters, Saints, and Sibyls,* the thirty-nine-minute three-screen lamentation that is a dual memoir of her sister's suicide at eighteen and her own mortifications of the flesh and battles with addiction—the photographer Nan Goldin has been one of the great living suicides of recent art history. Literary critic Charles Baxter has said that novelist Malcolm Lowry captured "the way things radiate just before they turn to ash." At her best, Goldin does this, too.

Sisters begins with images of illuminated manuscripts and Goldin reciting the legend of the third-century Saint Barbara, whose father imprisoned his daughter in a tower for fear that she would be corrupted by a man. After Barbara surreptitiously received a Christian lover and was converted, her father turned her over to the authorities, who tortured her and then allowed the father to behead her himself. He was killed by a bolt of lightning soon thereafter. This is a near perfect allegory for what happened to Goldin's sister, Barbara.

Born in 1946, Barbara was institutionalized at fourteen for the sins of kissing boys at the movies and having a black boyfriend. In 1965, after repeated institutionalizations, Barbara obtained a day pass from the National Institutes of Health, where she was an inpatient. That day she walked several miles, lay down on some train tracks, and was beheaded by a passing train. The first half of *Sisters* tells Barbara's sad story with family photos and filmed sequences of various institutions and homes. We hear Goldin reciting the tragic story, see her visiting the same tracks. In one frightening scene you can see her shadow (with her trusty camera in hand) on a speeding train. It's so close that the engineer blasts his horn.

Goldin then says that Barbara's psychiatrist predicted that Nan, too, would kill herself someday. The three screens go dark and she announces, "I left home at fourteen and found my own family." Yet the images that follow—pictures of Goldin's new family of friends, freaks, and lovers—trace an inexorable downward spiral. "Drugs set me free," she flatly says.

"Later, they became my prison." *Sisters* makes all of Goldin's work much clearer, revitalizing what had been weakened in earlier work. The work's climax, set to Johnny Cash's rendition of the Nine Inch Nails song "Hurt," finds a dazed Goldin in one institution after another, obviously in trouble, on the rocks, her arm bandaged, covered with self-inflicted burns, her eyes glazed over, poised on the precipice of death. Her friends can only look on. Goldin is giving us the moment before she will turn to ash. Yet this only showcases her remarkable gift: regardless of her own condition, she has the uncanny ability to rouse herself, to capture the life and death going on around her. This gift has allowed her to make an astonishingly vulnerable work of art. It might even save her life.

(2006)

The Whole Ball of Wax

According to its two excellent curators, Laura Hoptman and Peter Eleey, *Strange Powers*, their group show about spirituality, magic spells, aura photography, and the like, is an attempt to "explore the transportive power of art." They go an audacious step further and assert that art has the ability to change the world. Are they right?

Most art world denizens would instinctively say yes. But if by "change" you mean, can art on its own change global warming, stop Iran's president from denying the Holocaust, or halt the spread of AIDS, the answer, I'm afraid, is no.

In concert with other things, however, art *can* change the world—incrementally and by osmosis. This is because art is part of a universal force. It has no less purpose or meaning than science, religion, philosophy, politics, or any other discipline, and is as much a form of intelligence or knowing as a first kiss, a last goodbye, or an algebraic equation. Art is an energy source that helps make change possible; it sees things in clusters and constellations rather than rigid systems. It is both a bridge to a new vision and the vision itself, a medium or matrix through which one sees the world. It grants that pleasure is an important form of knowledge. Art is not optional; it is necessary. It is part of the whole ball of wax.

These thoughts, partly inspired by the moral philosopher Mary Midgley, are an attempt to get around all those dogmatists, ideologues, academics, and theorists who demonize and belittle art as a gratuitous, semi-mystical, merely beautiful, purely formal amusement. These aesthetician-scientists regularly reduce art to simplistic, supposedly objective dualisms like mind-body, abstract-representational, reason-imagination, political-apolitical, thinking-feeling, and so on. But all thinking is fed by feeling, and all genuine feeling involves reasoning. As Midgley observes, "It's like saying that shape and size are competing opposites when they're complementary aspects of a larger whole."

The thought police of the art world claim to look at art with unbiased, objective eyes. They abjure value judgments. Of course, their entire system is predicated on the value judgments they were taught, which consequently make it impossible for them to grasp other worldviews. Writing about myopic scientists, philosopher James Lovelock noted that "the most successful among them are the ones who hold on to their ideas the longest and who slow the progress in their fields the most." The same is true in the art world, where many embrace Descartes's model of "I think, therefore I am." They wrongly believe that art is about understanding, when, like almost everything else in the everyday world, art is about experience.

These latter-day Cartesians act like coroners, regularly pronouncing dead that which they don't approve of or can't explain. They say the author is dead, painting is dead, history is dead, and so on. As Midgley points out, "Imaginative systems don't suddenly perish and they don't go away until the things they were invented to deal with have been resolved."

In his eloquent essay "Vermeer in Bosnia," Lawrence Weschler reports that Antonio Cassese, a distinguished Italian jurist serving on the Yugoslav war crimes tribunal in the Hague, would sometimes go to the

Mauritshuis museum after hearing continual testimony about Balkan atrocities. There, he looked at two of the most beautiful things ever made, Vermeer's *Girl with a Pearl Earring* and his *View of Delft*. He did this not because Vermeer's work was "merely beautiful," he said, but because these paintings "radiate[d] a centeredness, a peacefulness, a serenity," because they were "a psychic balm." In other words, when we look at art, we're not only looking at it; we're also looking through the materials—paint, pigment, canvas, what have you—to something else. You're not only seeing yourself and the mind of the maker; in some metaphysical but organic way you're seeing the group mind, and even all the minds that have ever lived. You're seeing a static object with thought and experience embedded in it, a changeless thing that changes through time.

Art is a region where protocols are invented or suspended and things one doesn't understand change one's life. That's why a tiny ivory carving of the Crucifixion can vie for greatness with Bernini, why the Vietnam Veterans Memorial channels a nation's remorse even though it is based on the one thing that most Americans purport to loathe: abstraction. Art is often political when it doesn't seem political, and not political when that's all it seems to be. Neither Andy Warhol nor Donald Judd made overtly political art, yet both changed the way the world looks, and the way we look at the world. That's because art creates new thought structures. Imagine all that would never have existed, that would have gone undiscovered, had all of Shakespeare been lost. Art does far more than meet the eye. It is part of the holistic human biome.

The neo-Cartesians of the art world are aholistic. They believe in their one theory and quote the same seventeen texts by the same seventeen authors—most of whom they've read only in translation—to prove the same points repeatedly. It's time for them to turn the page, to concede that all art is a theory about the way art should look, and that every painting ever made comments on and is a theory about all the paintings ever made.

As Darwin observed, it's not the survival of the *strongest* or the most *intelligent*. Those who survive are those most adaptable to change.

(2006)

Where the Girls Aren't

When it comes to being artists, women can be as bad as men. The problem is that even now, decades after the onset of women's liberation, women aren't being allowed to demonstrate this. I doubt that there's a conscious effort to keep women from showing, yet the percentage of women exhibiting in New York galleries and museums is grievously low. According to the exhibition schedules for 125 well-known New York galleries—42 percent of which are owned or co-owned by women!—amid nearly three hundred one-person shows by living artists taking place this fall, just 23 percent are solos by women.

Some may argue that 23 percent isn't that bad. True, it's not as bad as last fall's 19 percent. And it's certainly not as sorry as the situation at some of our museums. On the fourth and fifth floors of the Museum of Modern Art, in the galleries devoted to the permanent collection of art from 1879 to 1969, there are currently 399 objects. Only 19 of those objects—that's 5 percent—are by women. This is up from last fall's 3 percent, but that's partly thanks to the display of a silver teapot, a brass fruit bowl, and an ashtray by the excellent Marianne Brandt, who technically isn't even in the painting and sculpture (P&S) collection. Yesterday's institutions can't be judged by today's standards. MoMA's shortcomings are built-in: Of all the artists in its P&S collection with work completed before 1970, fewer than 1 percent are women. Even so, MoMA's narrative wouldn't be disrupted by having work on view by Alice Neel, Florine Stettheimer, Sonia Delaunay, Louise Nevelson, Emma Kunz, Hilma af Klint, Adrian Piper, Marisol, Maya Deren, Dorothea Rockburne, Niki de Saint Phalle, Jo Baer, Jay DeFeo, Joan Brown, Grace Hartigan, Leonora Carrington, Leonor Fini, Natalia Goncharova, Gego, Dorothea Tanning, Romaine Brooks, Ree Morton, Howardena Pindell, Lee Lozano, Hanna Höch, and Claude Cahun. If MoMA doesn't own work by all these artists, it needs to rectify this.

Meanwhile, since 2000, only 14 percent of the Guggenheim's solo shows of living artists have been devoted to women. After cringing at that, consider *Full House*, the Whitney's recent installation of its permanent collection. The show was challenging, but familiar in one troubling area: Only 19 percent of its participants were women. Figures, however, aren't always cut-and-dried. Only 23 percent of all the artists in the Whitney's collection are women, so *Full House* reflected its collection. There were forty-eight artists in *Uncertain States of America*, Bard's summer show organized by three European male curators: Only ten were women. Several of these were only in the rotating video program. The prime real estate is still a men's club.

The programmatic exclusion of women is at least partly due to the fact that the art world is a self-replicating organism: Seeing that the art that is shown and sold is made mainly by men, it responds by presenting more art by men. This is how what Adorno called a "negative system" is perpetuated. . . . When the available exhibition space goes mainly to men, it means that more than half the story goes untold. When women tell the story, it will be told in ways it has never been before. If we don't remove the taboo against women, that story could eventually die.

Art historian Griselda Pollock has written about "women's struggle for meaning." However it's described, the situation must be recognized as a failure of the imagination that amounts to apartheid. We must see it as a moral emergency.

(2006)

Charnel Knowledge: Carroll Dunham

By now I no longer know if I like Carroll Dunham's paintings because we're friends or if we're friends because I like his paintings. So anything I say about his work is biased—although over the years I have relentlessly ribbed Dunham about how limiting and wrong it might be that he seems to paint the same male character over and over again. For his part, in published interviews Dunham has denied that this thing is a character at all, identifying it instead as a "shape" or a set of "formal concerns" and "painterly events" in "graphic fields." Whatever it is, it's a no-eyed, fedora-wearing cipher, a gangster, a rogue detective or man in a gray flannel suit, with a dick for a nose and a scrotum on his upper lip or testicles sprouting from the back of his neck. He often sports an L-shaped gun or sometimes a bullwhip. His activities include running amok in some exploding star-filled universe, madly defending homesteads, fighting to keep his head above water, wandering across landscapes, or just posing for an endless array of surrealistic portraits against Art Deco, Cubistic, and Constructivist backgrounds.

By my figuring, this character appeared in Dunham's work as early as 1990, albeit as a multicolored biomorphic blob with multiple sexual organs and a cilia-covered membrane that floated in a psychedelic amniotic sea. Eventually, Dunham gave birth to a brood of similar-looking geometrized monsters, clowns, goons, freaks of nature, snake-oil salesmen, dapper Dans, mercenary businessmen, roving caballeros, and demented goblins.

In the main room of his current exhibition, five of these figures are pictured against canary-yellow backgrounds. If this show contained only these paintings, I wouldn't be breaking my own rule against writing about friends. But something shocking—sensationalistic and, to my mind, sensational— has happened in Dunham's work. In two other rooms, Dunham seems to be painting from a place that not even he knew he had, a place formed by experience, observation, id, current events, mythic history, black magic, and the imagination. Two of these paintings, *Giant* and *Square Mule*, are so intense I felt as if they'd knocked me down, gathered me up, and tossed me about the room again. Three other irregularly shaped diptych-portraits look like fragmentary ruins from some ancient Mayan or Roman fresco cycle. Dunham's character is in all of these paintings, but something has happened to him, or to us, or to the worlds we inhabit. In these two imposing pictures he's bare-assed and bent over, with his anus in the viewer's face like some mad humanoid baboon in a state of sexual presenting. On his left thigh he sports a decorative tribal tattoo; on his right there's an ovular mole or mark of Cain. Things turn really savage, voluptuous, and fractured, however, as the figure also displays his *vagina*, which is painted to resemble a squishy éclair in one canvas, and in the other a bagpipe with flutes and pubic hair. It's as if Dunham is working to capture the power of the vagina even as his characters act out Oedipus's woeful words, "I come to offer you a gift, my tortured body."

In *Square Mule*, this latrine-based incubus sticks a gun into his own ass in order to blow his own brains out and to send him, and presumably us, to kingdom come. The image recalls the words of Dostoevsky—"He who is ready to kill himself becomes a God"—or Nietzsche's imprecation, "One must have chaos in oneself." What's remarkable about *Square Mule* is not only the abjection of the subject matter, but also the way it compels you to see through it to deeper content. This is an image of the end of empire. It is someone getting medieval on his own ass, embodying Homeland Security, turning himself into a war machine. The "Mule" of the title is the hybrid animal that can't reproduce itself—a perfect metaphor for the endgame America may currently be engaged in. This is a portrait of America as a failed state: a picture of humiliation, bloodletting, armament, defiance, kowtowing, idolatry, annihilation, and pleasure. The character becomes a God of death and sex: a suicide bomber, a lone gunman, and a wounded beast. He is us—a collective body in psychic civil war.

(2007)

Deal or No Deal: Takashi Murakami

Takashi Murakami's new show is the latest twist from an artist who in the nineties excelled at ultrathin surfaces and magically vapid images of sex and consumerism. Drawing from the realms of manga—Japanese comics with their often radically distorted creatures—and anime, Murakami painted Mickey Mouse–like characters, sunny mushrooms, and abstract splashes that were part Pop Surrealism, part Hokusai's *Great Wave*, and part porn. Murakami is a craft-master whiz of cuteness, flash, and adolescent male fantasy; he once made a life-size sculpture of a big-eyed girl with shaved pudenda who squeezed her phallic nipples and jump-roped over a money shot of milk spurting from her gigantic breasts. He also curated several lively exhibitions that elucidated the Japanese penchant for mirroring the West back to itself, and shed light on how Japan is insular and xenophobic yet simultaneously open and adaptable. If Japan is like the android that finds life (a common anime theme), Murakami is one who breathed life into contemporary Japanese art.

Unfortunately, since around 2001 Murakami has been so set on merging fine art with commercial product that by now all he's doing is moving merch. The best that can be said about Murakami's new work is that he's making pretty money. Or pretty empty money. The main attractions of this exhibition are fifty little happy-faced flower paintings and six large portraits of a haggard-looking Zen patriarch. The flowers are insipid. So are the portraits, although at least with them Murakami is up to his old extreme stylization. But the real content of Murakami's art is money and marketability. Hence, each of the fifty silly flowers reportedly goes for $90,000; the portraits, about $1.5 mil per unit. Four better, larger flower paintings run about $450,000 apiece; two boring pictures of severed hands, about $400,000. Needless to say, according to the gallery, everything is sold. Not bad for paintings that have the visual oomph of screensavers—that are merely placeholders for gullible collectors, who buy them hoping today's feeding frenzy lasts long enough to fob them off on subsequent happy patsies.

(2007)

Buona Serra

M ission accomplished. The Museum of Modern Art's wide-open, tall-ceilinged, super-reinforced second floor was for all intents and purposes built so that it could accommodate monumental installations and gigantic sculptures if the need should arise. It has arisen.

The artist MoMA was thinking of was Richard Serra, the rajah of weight and steel. The late, great chief curator, Kirk Varnedoe, said that the new building was designed with him in mind; at Serra's opening dinner, the president of MoMA's board of trustees, Marie-Josée Kravis, mused to a crowd of more than five hundred, "Richard, we built this for you." It's as if they were all saying, "Never mind all the rest of you artistic dwarfs." MoMA wanted a mighty Richard Serra show, and it's only fair to say that a mighty Richard Serra show is what they got. *Richard Serra Sculpture: Forty Years* is a gutsy, perception-altering show. When I left the museum, I could feel the vibrations from the exhibition temporarily transforming the world into oscillating wave patterns and semisolid biologic forms and entities.

What is the art world celebrating when it celebrates Serra so unconditionally? Serra is hailed as a God of Sculpture, a kind of mythic king of art. Critics and academics regularly trumpet his preeminence and universality. Few complain that Serra's work is a conservative throwback, inexorably rooted in a time when abstraction was Almighty and any form of narrative was dismissed as somehow sissy. Perhaps the adulation reflects a nostalgia for the days when everyone knew what the issues were, grandeur was good, and men were men. Serra's master-of-the-universe grandiosity and space-eating megalomania can also be off-putting. His sculpture is the apotheosis of public art, in that its existence depends on lots of space, money, power, and large audiences. These are not attributes usually associated with the private transaction between one artist and one viewer, to say nothing of inner lives and intense looking.

Herein lies a paradox. It turns out that *Forty Years* shows that Serra's art is more inner, intense, intimate, and accessible than one might think. More than any artist, Serra makes abstract art that people who hate abstraction can like. His sculptures speak to lay audiences and the art world alike. *Forty Years* is a no-nonsense primer on an artist who emerged in the mid-sixties, looking to explore the ways in which sculpture might involve more than simply a specific object. Like so many of his generation, Serra wanted to make sculpture entail time, movement, and process—to exist in what was then called "the extended field."

Forty Years shows just how extended that field has become. It consists of twenty-seven works spread out over two floors and the sculpture garden. To view the show chronologically is to sense the art historical pendulum swinging away from the object toward something else. My favorite work here, *Delineator*, initially appears to be simply a massive ten-by-twenty-six-foot plate of steel on the floor—until your attention is drawn upward, where another steel plate, the same size, is attached to the ceiling overhead, turned crosswise to the floor plate. The electromagnetic field of the gallery goes berserk, and you realize that Serra has turned the whole room and even the museum itself into a pedestal for this sculpture—or maybe the sculpture is a pedestal for the museum. Either way, it's diabolical. Up and down flip-flop as you perceive that you're inside *Delineator's* volume. The sculpture is attached to the museum the way an organism attaches itself to a host; it looms over you like a giant abstract mutant spider.

The show crescendos on the second floor with three supercolossal new steel pieces, the best of which is *Sequence*. Each curvaceous piece is as big as a barge; together all three weigh more than one million pounds, whatever that means. Allegedly about the twisting ellipses and soaring forms of the Baroque, on the contrary these works feel mouthwateringly lyrical and rococo. Walking around these undulating sidewinders is like being around a herd of otherworldly elephants, or seeing steel skirts blowing in the breeze. Here you understand that Serra's foes are right: His work is not about looking. You don't see a Serra with your eyes; you see it with your whole body. Sheer excess disarms sight. You walk around and through a

Serra, brushing very close to it—closer than to any art I can think of—taking in it its weight, texture, temperature, mass, and volume with parts of you that you didn't know you had. Flow, fullness, and rhythm become ways of knowing. It's like being very close to another person; surprise, tranciness, and enchantment mingle, until you become a walking nerve ending.

One famous female curator I know has disparaged Serra's sculptures as "big-dick art." Serra's work is certainly butch, but in the flesh his ruddy, overlapping plicae and pleats of swelling steel collapse gender. His shapes and configurations and surfaces are silky and puckered; outside and inside merge; folds envelop folds, until the sculptures become almost embarrassingly erotic. These sculptures are so open they're in an almost architectonic state of sexual presentation. And yet, even as they reveal themselves to you, they preserve their wholeness and mystery. They're like Manet's Olympia, posing without shame while also concealing her sex.

After all this, before you head out into the sculpture garden to see the two yonic behemoths, pause before Rodin's great phallic sculpture *Balzac* and think about how the processes, materiality, and sexual vibe you've experienced in the Serra show began here. Seeing the final two huge Serras installed in the sculpture garden, just inches from Matisse's four great back sculptures, is revelatory. Matisse was trying to merge skin and material, surface and figure, support and illusion; he wanted to blur your perception with abundance. Serra wants all this, too. Like the work of Matisse, his is savage, decorative, and enticing. Like Malevich's, it's unrelenting. Eva Hesse said she was trying to make "nothings." Serra is trying to make all-or-nothing somethings. At times this might seem obnoxious or boring. Yet much of the time his work offers the chance to delight in sculptures that call to mind flowers and fortresses, cave walls, and the thrill of the circus coming to town.

(2007)

Bohemian Rhapsody: Elizabeth Murray

lizabeth Murray, who died on August 12, 2007, was among her generation's leading painterly lights. Nearly every artist who emerged in
the 1970s experimented with shaped paintings, but it was Murray's lop-
sided, buckling, asymmetrical, multipaneled canvases that demonstrated
most convincingly that painting needn't only be flat rectangles and squares
but could be irregular, bumpy, and filled with holes. By the time she died,
at sixty-six, Murray was widely recognized. She had exhibited regularly at
the Paula Cooper Gallery since the early seventies, then joined Pace-
Wildenstein in 1995; she had a retrospective at the Whitney in 1988, received
a MacArthur "genius" grant in 1999, and in 2005 had a forty-year-career
survey at the Museum of Modern Art. Her work is even a part of the fabric
of the city itself, in the form of a shimmering Byzantine glass mosaic she
created for the Fifty-Ninth Street stop on the Lexington Avenue subway.

Even so, Murray was underappreciated, maybe because her radical
ideas went beyond the shapes that paintings could take. Her ideas of
beauty were brazen and Dionysian, her colors sunburned and muddy. Her
notion of painterly skill was raw and physical: Surfaces are glutted with
opaque paint, but marked by sketchy patches where pencil marks show
through. Yet her work, as daring and original as it is, came to be seen by
some as excessive, expressionistic, even ugly. And it may have been dismissed as too "female": Although her MoMA exhibition did travel to
Spain, it's significant that Murray was never big in Europe, where, until
very recently, painting was an almost all-male domain. Her bulbous, curl-
ing stretchers are obvious references to painting's otherwise full-frontal,
flat format; Murray wanted to reveal those hidden structures. She wanted
you to see under painting's skirt. This unreservedness rattled people.

Murray mixed things that others kept separate, melding the abstract and the geometric, the private and the public, the formal and the organic. Her subjects, often vaguely recognizable, include canoodling shoes, wiggling beds, fetuses, coffee cups, and broken hearts—all shapes that seem to probe or penetrate one another. In 2005, I asked Murray about the implications of sex and love in these shapes. I knew her, but not that well. Nevertheless, she looked me right in the eye and, out of nowhere, kissed me on the mouth. I was dazed. The act somehow encapsulated her work for me: an imposing combination of formal exuberance, intellectual rigor, lusciousness, troublemaking, and humor, with undertows of darkness and psychology.

Once, when asked by an interviewer where she fit into art history, Murray responded, "That way of seeing historically belongs to the guys. The greatest part about being a woman in the world of painting is that I'm not really part of it. I can do whatever I want."

That's exactly what she did. Like her work, she was a bohemian rhapsody.

(2007)

The American Picasso: Robert Rauschenberg

Robert Rauschenberg was not a giant of American art; he was *the* giant. No American created so many aesthetic openings for so many artists. Jasper Johns, his sometime lover, said that "Rauschenberg was the man who in this century invented the most since Picasso." His output always bordered on the mad and ecstatic; his art could be theatrical, wan, redundant, or just cruddy-looking. In fact, everything he made, good or bad—and many think his late work is junk—has an edge of wit, optical nerve, and invention.

Sometimes those qualities could be almost invisible, as in his 1953

Erased de Kooning Drawing, which is exactly what the title says. On this page of faint smudges, Rauschenberg stumbled onto kryptonite. He'd rocked the boat of Abstract Expressionism and set out toward the more populist shores of art. (It's touching and telling that de Kooning gave the drawing to Rauschenberg freely, knowing what the young artist intended.) This ritualistic killing, however aggressive or loving, gives you a sense of how desperate Rauschenberg and his generation were. They wanted to move on from high-minded heroism to something more vernacular. Rauschenberg seemed to make it all possible.

A year later, saying he "had literally run out of things to paint on," Rauschenberg invented a new form: the combine. Not quite painting, not quite sculpture, this hybrid approach—using everything from bedding to doors to parachutes—was the equivalent of discovering fire. One combine, *Monogram*, features a stuffed goat encircled by a tire atop a horizontal painting. Whether we see Rauschenberg as a mischievous satyr grazing on art history or the goat as a gargoyle protecting the art, the title suggests that Rauschenberg was leaving his mark.

That mark has lasted. Large swaths of the current Whitney Biennial owe him a huge debt. Yet as young artists are still expanding on the idea of the combine, by the late fifties Rauschenberg had tired of it, and he went on to another new technique: using a solvent to transfer images from one surface to another. He used this low-tech, ethereal process to make his set of luminous illustrations for Dante's *Divine Comedy*. Here, Dante and Virgil are athletes out of *Sports Illustrated*; Olympic weightlifters stand in for giants in the eighth circle of hell; astronauts are the sinners. It is one of the most visually literate works ever made, by one of the most articulate artists who ever lived.

I love Rauschenberg. I love that he created a turning point in visual history, that he redefined the idea of beauty, that he combined painting, sculpture, photography, and everyday life with such gall, and that he was interested in, as he put it, "the ability to conceive failure as progress." Most of all, I love him for his fecundity and fearlessness.

(2008)

Frieze After the Freeze

wo weeks ago, the Death Star that has hovered over the art world for the
last two years finally fired its lasers. It was October 15, the day the stock
market fell more than seven hundred points—again—and a month after
Lehman Brothers and Merrill Lynch collapsed and Damien Hirst pawned
off $200 million worth of crapola on clueless rubes at Sotheby's. Against this
backdrop, at eleven a.m., the gates of London's Frieze art fair opened, and in
streamed the international traveling circus of bigwigs, collectors, curators,
advisers, museum directors, trustees, models, movie stars, and critics like *moi*.

Talk of financial doom filled the air. Karl Schweizer, UBS's head of art
banking, told one reporter, "We are in a liquidity crisis." Money manager Randy Slifka added, "There is blood on the streets on Wall Street."
Collectors talked about "sewing up our pockets." Yet much of the art world
was playing on as if nothing had happened. A German dealer told
Artforum.com, "This economic mess will all be over by January." Amy
Cappellazzo of Christie's spun her house's recent sales: "If you bought
something, you bought something real." In truth, most of the speculators
are buying something real bad or badly overpriced.

In fact, though, things *were* different. Those of us who have frequented
Frieze could see that something was off. Dealers and assistants, always
busy with clients in recent years, now stood or sat quietly. Sales were happening, but slowly, one at a time. The claim of "It's sold" was replaced by
"I have it on several holds." Although the megagalleries like Gagosian and
White Cube teemed with moneyed men and very tall women in very high
heels, many younger dealers looked perplexed. A gallerist who entered the
field in the go-go aughts and who had sold only two pieces by five p.m. that
first day asked, "What's going on?"

As I made my way through the 152 booths, I thought about the moment in *Titanic* when the designer of the doomed luxury liner warns Kate
Winslet to find a lifeboat, because soon "all this will be at the bottom of

the Atlantic." When I tried this idea out on attendees, several called me "a buzzkill." I asked, "Isn't the buzz already beginning to disappear?"

If the art economy is as bad as it looks—if worse comes to worst—forty to fifty New York galleries will close. Around the same number of European galleries will, too. At least one art magazine will cease publishing. Museums will cancel shows because they can't raise funds. Art advisers will be out of work. Alternative spaces will become more important for shaping the discourse, although they'll have a hard time making ends meet. As for artists, too many have been getting away with murder, making questionable or derivative work and selling it for inflated prices. They will either lower their prices or stop selling. Many younger artists who made a killing will be forgotten quickly. Others will be seen mainly as relics of a time when marketability equaled likability.

Much good art got made while money ruled; I like a lot of it, and hardship and poverty aren't virtues. The good news is that, since almost no one will be selling art, artists—especially emerging ones—won't have to think about turning out a consistent style or creating a brand. They'll be able to experiment as much as they want.

My schadenfreude side wishes a pox on the auction houses, those shrines to the disconnect between the inner life of art and the outer life of commerce. If they don't go belly-up, or return to dealing mainly with dead artists, they need to stop pretending that they have any interest in art beyond the financial. Additionally, I hope many of the speculators who never really cared about art will go away. Either way, money will no longer be a measure of success. Money has made more art possible, but it has not made art better.

Recessions are hard on people, but not on art. The forties, seventies, and nineties, when money was scarce, were great periods; the art world retracted but it was also reborn. New generations took the stage; new communities spawned energy; things opened up; deadwood washed away. With luck, New Museum curator Laura Hoptman's wish will come true: "Art will flower and triumph not as a hobby, an investment, or a career, but as what it is and was—a life."

(2008)

The art world is
a place that says
it wants people
to be free. . . .
So how did we
come to live in
an insular tribal
sphere where
unwritten
rules and rigid
moralities
are strictly
enforced?

"WHEN DID THE
ART WORLD GET
SO CONSERVATIVE?"
(2014)

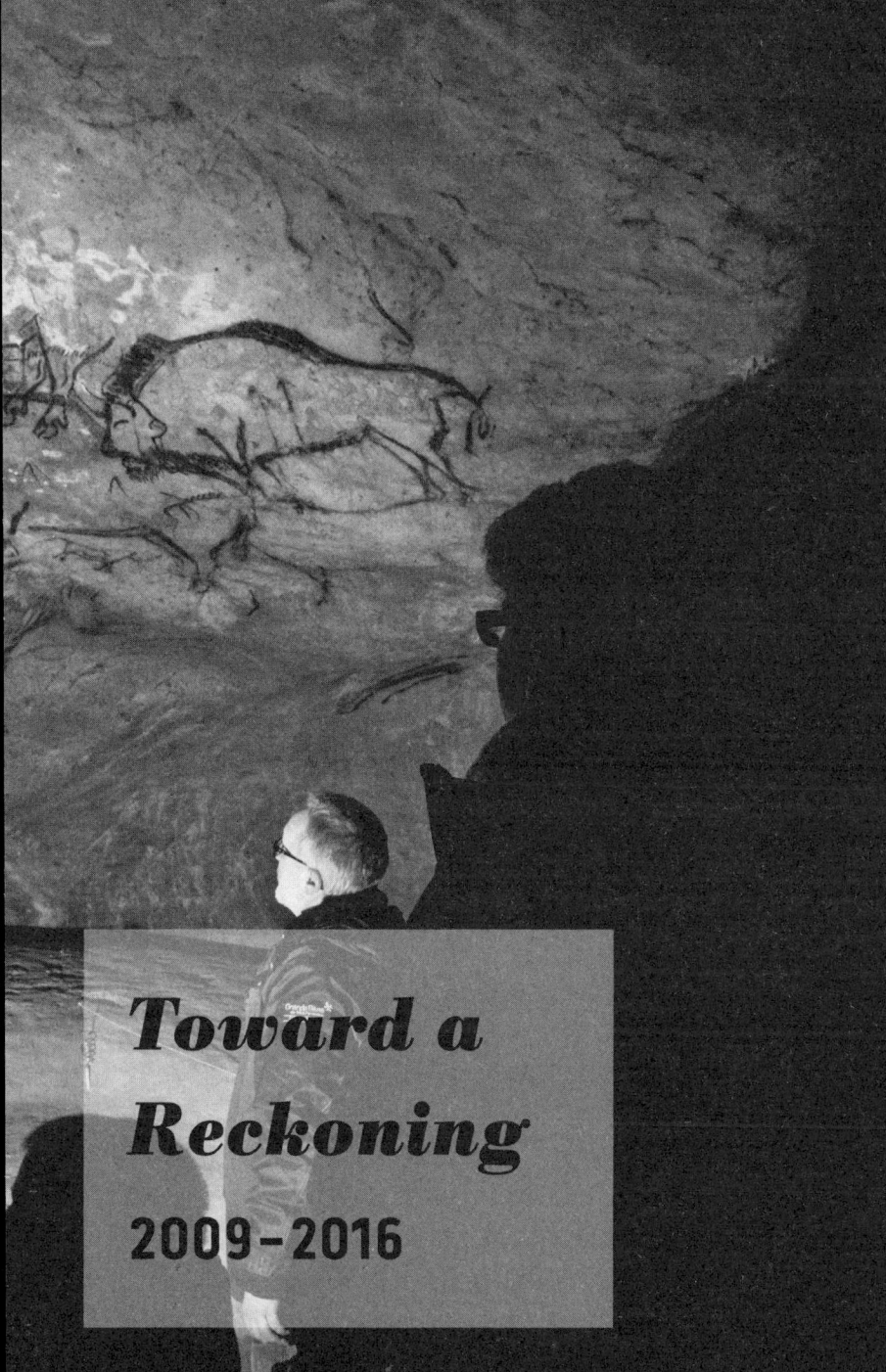

Toward a
Reckoning
2009–2016

Leaving Eden: Pipilotti Rist,
Cheryl Donegan, Kim Rosenfield

I n the closing days of *Pour Your Body Out (7354 Meters)*, Pipilotti Rist's
ravishing wraparound video atrium installation at MoMA, the place
has been packed. Mothers have been making playdates in the atrium, letting kids run around while they gather on the large round couch. Visitors
bring computers and work here, or listen to iPods, or chat or doze or read.

Last Monday I got an intriguing mass email from the artist Cheryl
Donegan and the poet Kim Rosenfield, announcing an unsponsored im-
promptu event called "MoMA Yoga," led by Alexandra Auder. (Auder, a
yogi, is the daughter of Andy Warhol's superstar Viva and the underground-
video phenom Michel Auder.) I couldn't resist. On Friday night, I arrived
to find the darkened atrium teeming with hundreds of people; Rist's wonderful droning, chanting soundtrack filled the air with drowsy delirium,
and her images of gigantic naked floating bodies, lush undergrowth, and
water filled the walls. A few minutes before the appointed starting time, a
dozen or so people, almost all women, shed their coats to reveal workout
clothes. At seven p.m., the tall, fit, and charismatic Auder, outfitted in a

gold lamé leotard and striped leggings, announced that she was leading a free yoga class. She chanted three long loud *om*s and began.

The place went silent. Before I knew it, two Uruguayan girls sitting next to me leaped up and joined in, as did three Japanese women behind me. Soon a group of around twenty-five was following Auder from downward dog to little cobra to pigeon pose. Then Auder called for people to lie on their backs and try not to move a muscle. It became hard to tell the yoga class from the rest of the gallerygoers (except for one kid who was watching a music video on his iPhone). It took audience participation to a new level: doing nothing, absolutely together. At exactly seven thirty, Auder thanked the participants, and that was that. By then the room seemed to have mellowed out in ways I'd never seen before.

I asked Donegan why she staged the event. She said it came from "feeling dissatisfied with the level of audience interaction with both the Rist installation and 'theanyspacewhatever' show at the Guggenheim." She noted that both installations "combined video and carpets and pillows but seemed to ask nothing more of people than to recline and watch. It seemed way too passive." Good point. Just then a guard came over, and I asked him if he had been inclined to stop the performance. He said no, adding that he thought it had been a rehearsal for an organized event taking place on Sunday.

After the yoga group dispersed, I kept watching Rist's artwork, stunned at what she had been able to do to this institution. I wished that her piece could be left here permanently. It would change life in this museum for the better. But all things must pass. Just before eight p.m., we heard an announcement that it would soon shut down for the night. At eight on the dot, the sounds and images disappeared, and the atrium went back to being an enormous blank white cube. The viewers let out a moan I'd never heard in a modern-art museum before. I realized it also sounded like *om*. It was beautiful.

Coda:

Always in search of a perfect moment, I returned to MoMA a half hour before closing time on Monday, February 2, 2009, the last day the Rist was up. I wanted to be there the last time the museum went blank. The atrium was emptier than I'd seen it in weeks. Maybe because it was a Monday; maybe because it was the very end of the day. But the Rist was still working its sensuous magic. I saw a lesbian couple making out inside the donut-shaped couch; outside it, a young woman sat in a young man's lap, kissing him on the mouth. At 5:25 an announcement came over the loudspeakers that the piece was going to be turned off in five minutes. Just then I spied Klaus Biesenbach, the curator of the Rist installation, ushering in a museum honcho from Europe. The crowd began leaving. Soon there were only five or ten of us. I met a few of Rist's assistants as they emerged from the control room. On a whim, I asked if I could be the one to turn off the Rist for the last time. To my surprise the tech guy said, "Sure." He led me to a little closet around the corner from the atrium. Inside, instead of the giant bank of colorful screens I had expected, I found only a small laptop computer on a shelf. He positioned the pointer on the proper place and said, "Go ahead." I listened to the droning sounds coming from around the corner one more time, pictured the luscious flowers, yummy fruit being squished and chewed, the water, waves, and sky, closed my eyes, and clicked. Everything went silent. I walked around the corner and the Rist was gone. It was like leaving Eden.

(2009)

After the Orgy: Lisa Yuskavage

We're on a historical cusp. No one knows what will come next. But in the art world, an aesthetic sorting-out is already beginning. I'm not talking about the purging or comeuppance some critics have gleefully cackled about or howled for. I love art galleries, and worry that a wave of them will close this June when, looking ahead to the traditionally dead months of summer, dealers will be forced to throw in the towel. As for the art: I admire much of the work that came to prominence in the last fifteen years. Recently, though, much of it has been looking dated, not so relevant. At this year's Armory Show, it was stunning to see almost no work by the stars of last season—Murakami, Hirst, Koons, Prince, Reyle, Struth, Gursky. Partly this is a natural process; it doesn't necessarily mean these artists' powers are in decline. But the hypermarket that justly extended the careers of many artists also delayed the winnowing process of many others. Now all this winnowing is occurring at once. Artistic qualities that once seemed undeniable don't seem so now. Sometimes these fluctuations are merely products of the fickleness of taste, momentary glitches in an artist's work, or an artist getting ahead of the audience. (It took me ten years, for instance, to catch up to Albert Oehlen.) At times, however, these problems can indicate a problem with the art. One sign that this is happening is when the same things that were said about an artist a decade ago are still being said today.

The same bogus arguments come up every time Lisa Yuskavage has a show. Is her work feminist? Is she, oy, "critiquing the male gaze"? At the opening of Yuskavage's current solo outing, I was standing between two paintings: *Figure in Interior*, a picture of an anorexic nude on her knees with her legs akimbo, shaved vulva exposed, white cream/semen dripping from her face onto her breasts; and *Reclining Nude*, a picture of a recumbent girl in a glowing green glen, her breasts pointing in two directions, legs splayed to expose pink genitalia protruding from blond pubic hair. A well-known museum curator sidled up and swooned, "Lisa's paintings are as rich as Vermeer's and Boucher's. They're as sumptuous as the background of the *Mona Lisa*." I blinked silently until she mentioned Courbet. Then I bitchily snipped, "If you think these paintings have that kind of mojo, you've either never looked at those paintings or you know nothing about painting." We smiled at each other and parted. I love the art world.

Those who say Yuskavage's figurative skill makes her paintings good don't grasp that, if rendering figures realistically equals skill, then the makers of nineteenth-century Victorian nudes and painters like Bou-guereau would be the greatest artists of all time. Yuskavage's beanpoles, voluptuaries, and ugly ducklings make clear that her work is less connected to classical art than to calendar illustration, cheesecake, dirty playing cards, Vargas, and Thomas Kinkade. This isn't meant as an insult: her influences also include the Hudson River School, Maxfield Parrish, seven-ties *Penthouse* photographers, Impressionists, third-string Italian masters, and the kind of naturalist kitsch the Nazis liked. This mix is kinkier and more interesting than any discourse about technique and critique.

To her credit, Yuskavage has lately been making necessary changes to her formula of putting naked ladies in neon-colored fantasist settings. Her new backgrounds are weird interiors, strange ruins, and primordial bogs. Odd scale shifts occur; women seem as large as mountains or stand thigh-high in lakes; a vulva resembles a vestigial scrotum. The heightened gyne-cological realism is a good move; it may be what it takes to make paintings that feel not simple or blunt but dangerous. I love Yuskavage's palette; I appreciate that she might be in conversation with spread-eagle Modernist masterpieces by Bellmer and Duchamp. But the coy gamesmanship and knowing irony at the core of this work make it feel stuck in another time.

(2009)

Great Artists Steal: The Pictures Generation

Appropriation is the idea that ate the art world. Go to any Chelsea gal-lery or international biennial and you'll find it. It's there in paintings of photographs, photographs of advertising, sculpture with ready-made objects, videos using already-existing film. After its hothouse incubation in the seventies, appropriation breathed important new life into art. This life flowered spectacularly over the decades—even if it's now close to aesthetic kudzu.

The Metropolitan Museum of Art's *The Pictures Generation, 1974–1984* is less a critical survey of a highly influential aesthetic than a feel-good class reunion. Rather than opt for scholarship and tough choices, curator Douglas Eklund has cultivated a gang's-all-here coziness. It's a huge show, with hundreds of objects, books, posters, films, and videos, and works by thirty artists. Had a museum outside New York originated a show this baggy, it's doubtful that the Met would have had anything to do with it. (Although it's fantastic that the fuddy-duddy Met is finally thinking about recent art. It needs to do so more often, and do it better.)

But if you do pick your way through this hodgepodge, you'll find a spirited introduction to a lively moment. In the seventies, a group of American artists seized the means not of production but of reproduction. They tore apart visual culture at a time of no money, no market, and no one paying attention except other artists. Vietnam and Watergate had happened; everything in America was being questioned. In this charged atmosphere, artists braided together three recent styles. They made conceptual art more optical and snazzy. They returned narrative and figuration to minimalism, while retaining its rigor. And rather than "liking things," the way Warhol said Pop Art did, they were skeptical, especially regarding pop culture. This mix was laced with New Wave attitude, French theory, social consciousness, and raw material derived from everything from movies to logos. Pictures artists (as they were called) created a kind of anti-encyclopedia, looking at the world of representation and saying, "This is too good to be true." They changed the way we look at images, ourselves, and the world.

Today, it can be hard to perceive two of the most radical things about Pictures art. First of all, most of it came out of photography. Back then, photographs were entirely separate from the elite fine arts, such as painting (which was going through one of its near-death experiences). Even so-called fine art photography was inexpensive; compared with the other visual arts, it could seem nearly disposable. It was certainly seen as a separate art, with its own history and traditions, and critics and theoreticians didn't much bother with it. The Pictures artists realized that photography could therefore be a theory-free zone—an open field where they could create their own approach. Pictures artists staged their own images or copied or cut out others already in existence. The viewer took them in separately, in sometimes paradoxical waves: an original image, then the manipulations of it, then the places where image and idea intersected. This created a crucial perceptual glitch that irony and understanding filled. It's what makes Jack Goldstein's footage of the roaring MGM lion someone's take on what the lion stands for. Richard Prince's Marlboro men went from familiar and bland to dangerous and funny; Cindy Sherman's dressing up like a model became as strange as dressing up like a model really is. As the Pictures movement photographer James Welling observed, "Images compose our perceptions of the possible." If widely reproduced pictures are often lies, artists wanted to "turn the lie back on itself," as Prince put it. These artists did that with a vengeance.

Which brings us to the other, less visible radicalism of Pictures art: the great representation of women. Back then, it was widely understood that the doors of painting and sculpture were all but closed to female artists. In self-defense, women took up the devalued medium of photography, devoting much of their work to breaking down the visual conventions of gender construction. Feminists who didn't want to be stuck in the "feminist art" ghetto, they forged an art that was forceful, insistent, and seductive. Sarah Charlesworth tore up magazines to show us why we desired what we desired; Louise Lawler made herself a spy in the house of art, taking pictures of work by male artists installed in posh collections; Laurie Simmons created sicko domestic interiors; Barbara Kruger performed shock therapy on advertising; Sherrie Levine rephotographed famous photographs, declaring, "Appropriation is not all that different from wanting to appropriate your father's wife or your mother's husband."

The criticism that grew up around Pictures art was authoritarian if almost unreadable, written in tight knots of language. Painting was called regressive, exhausted, mined-out; graffiti artists like Keith Haring and Jean-Michel Basquiat were written off as lightweights. Sometimes the Pictures artists fought with even their supporters. Adrian Piper (an artist on the fringe of the movement, left out of this show) wrote an open letter to critic Donald Kuspit saying that his writing "dehumanize[d] artists." David Salle, whose work looks outstanding here, dismissed critic Craig Owens's ideas about the way Salle "mystified information" as ludicrous.

Pictures art was never the feel-good fun portrayed here; it was influential, but it was also self-policing and insular. (Salle was essentially cast out of the inner circle for the sin of painting and for using photos of naked women.) But it was a crackling time, and *appropriation* is too nice a word for how potent this style still is: Words like *stealing* and *ransacking* come closer to capturing the atmosphere.

(2009)

Duke Riley's Insane Triumph

There were tossed tomatoes aplenty, although the one that smashed me in the shoulder within minutes of the event's commencement I never saw coming. As I wiped off the runny residue, togas and robes fluttered, dancers dressed as Roman vixens writhed on floating platforms, Black Sabbath's "War Pigs" blasted over loudspeakers, passenger jets roared overhead, and spectators jeered and cheered as leaky boats made of what looked like reeds and junk foundered in shallow water, ramming one another and firing watermelon cannonballs in every direction.

The spectacle was Duke Riley's *Those About to Die Salute You*, billed as a "Naumachia"; the place, a flooded pool on the World's Fair grounds in Flushing Meadows Corona Park; the scene, a gigantic blowout/fraternity food fight by way of a Roman toga party, *Apocalypse Now*, the Crusades, and a Happening. By nine p.m., half an hour after the mayhem began, all that remained were sinking ships, floating spears, hundreds of revelers in the basin, and a burning boat firing off skyrockets.

What I had witnessed was something special—and an example of one way that artists from everywhere are taking matters into their own hands to right the ship that is the New York art world. After months of preparation, and with scores of participants and unending support from that underdog institution the Queens Museum (which either got every type of permit in the book or violated every city code imaginable), artist Duke Riley pulled off one of the finest performance events in recent memory: his own demented simulacra of a naumachia. What's a naumachia? In ancient Greek it literally means "naval combat"—but leave it to the Roman emperors to get really gory with it. The Romans' mock naval battles were held in flooded basins, with real prisoners who'd been condemned to death. Participants saluted the emperor with the famous *Morituri te salutant* ("Those who are about to die salute you"). Then the doomed died.

That night in Queens, none of the combatants died; they just got messy and wet. They were broken into teams, decked out in colored robes, representing various boroughs and their museums: Red was the Queens Museum; yellow, the Bronx Museum; blue, the Brooklyn Museum; and green, El Museo del Barrio. From the start, my money was on the fierce-looking Queens team. After a reedy-voiced announcer revved up the crowd and the boats all entered the faux lake, the battle began. Immediately, the folks from the Bronx made a noble effort to capsize the Queens fighters. But then Brooklyn snuck up on their flank and did them in. At that point, the mighty Queens ship initiated a daring mid-lake maneuver, jumping aboard the Brooklyn boat, hauling toga-clad soldiers off the decks. Next, the Queens mariners jumped into the water and overturned the vessel. Out of nowhere, after the appearance of sundry pirate dinghies and one zebra-striped kayaker, a large replica of the Staten Island Ferry oared in and somehow fell apart. Soon, a giant galleon, part Disney and part amusement-park ride, entered the moat, representing El Museo del Barrio. I don't know what happened then, but somehow Queens got the best of everyone. A weird battleship entered, then was set on fire; the vessel exploded as thousands of attendees danced, cheered, and rocked to Queen's "We Are the Champions."

Riley's squirrelly genius, obsession with all things nautical, and personal acts of public piracy are exactly what the art world needs right now. Last night was a perfect example of an artist taking the rope an institution gave him—more than enough to hang himself—and turning it into a triumph. Riley has been building up to this for a while. In 2005, the art world solemnly gathered at a West Side pier to witness a reenactment of Robert Smithson's famous *Floating Island*. All of a sudden, "after months of planning, days of reconnaissance, and hours of alcohol consumption," Riley and a cohort clambered aboard the island, scampering off almost immediately with the U.S. Coast Guard hot on their trail. (Riley attracted the Coast Guard's attention again not long after, when his homemade submarine, straight out of Jules Verne, got too close to the *Queen Mary 2* in Brooklyn Harbor.)

As I walked with the crowds, under the gigantic utopian globe that dominates Flushing Meadows, I knew that the more wild cards like Riley that get into the mix, the less homogenized the art world will be. And we all know nature hates sameness.

(2009)

Georgia O'Keeffe: Out of the Erotic Ghetto

Poor Georgia O'Keeffe. Even her death failed to soften the art world's opinion of her paintings. Twenty-three years later, many continue to dismiss her as a prissy painter of pretty pictures—or, I should say, pretty genitalia. Even when hailed for being "the most famous and highly paid woman artist in America," she gets saddled with a qualifier.

No other figure in American art history has gone from heights to has-been so quickly. See if these comments, some of them by women, don't raise the hairs on the back of your neck: Critics wrote of the "great painful and ecstatic climaxes" in the art of "this girl," of how she felt "through the womb," and gave us a "sense of woman's flesh in martyrdom." Her paintings were described as a "revelation of the very essence of woman as Life Giver," expressing "dense, quivering, endless life," and "the world as it is known to woman." They wrote of her "outpouring of sexual juices," "loamy hungers of the flesh," saw her work described as "one long, loud blast of sex, sex in youth, sex in adolescence, sex in maturity . . . sex bulging, sex tumescent, sex deflated." And those were the admirers! Clement Greenberg, not a fan, was appalled when the Museum of Modern Art honored O'Keeffe with a retrospective in 1946, one of its first solo shows for a woman; he dismissed her work as "little more than tinted photography." In 1949, when O'Keeffe was elected to the National Institute of Arts and Letters, threatened male artists Edward Hopper and John Sloan were so angry (sex was their territory!) that they tried to have the decision reversed.

Given that reception, it's amazing that O'Keeffe continued making art until close to her death, at ninety-eight. Less surprising is that she did it in relative isolation, spending her last thirty-seven years in New Mexico—which only added to her mythology and popularity outside the art world.

The Whitney Museum's revelatory survey of the work that earned O'Keeffe such derision, the evocative, essentially abstract art she made starting in 1915—phenomenally early for an American artist—should reopen eyes to an undeniable fact: O'Keeffe produced some of the most original and ambitious art of the twentieth century. Her ideas about surface, scale, and color are not only daring; they presaged the work of artists as varied as Barnett Newman, Milton Avery, Mark Rothko, Morris Louis, and Mary Heilmann, as well as movements including Color Field painting, Lyrical Abstraction, and contemporary postmodern abstraction. At her best, she is a formally inventive poetic powerhouse who makes the nonobjective feel mystical, familiar, objective, and subjective all at once.

Born poor on a farm in Wisconsin in 1887, O'Keeffe worked and taught and studied art in Texas, South Carolina, Illinois, and Virginia. Just when it appeared that she'd be a teacher for the rest of her life, fate stepped in. On New Year's Day, 1916, without obtaining her permission, a girlfriend showed O'Keeffe's abstract charcoal drawings to the legendary photographer-proprietor of New York's great 291 gallery, Alfred Stieglitz. With his intrepid eye, he instantly recognized her promise; he'd "never seen a woman express herself so fully on paper . . . I wouldn't mind showing them."

In May, Stieglitz hung ten of her charcoals in a group show. Soon thereafter, she confessed to a friend that she had fallen for the "hot, dark, destructive" (and married) Stieglitz. In 1918, O'Keeffe, then thirty years old, moved to New York; within weeks she became the fifty-four-year-old Stieglitz's lover. As revolutionary as living out of wedlock was in 1918 (the couple married in 1924), a 1921 survey of Stieglitz's photographs, including forty-five pictures of O'Keeffe, many of them nudes, transformed the two of them into an art world Angelina Jolie and Brad Pitt. Stieglitz said, "When I make a photograph I make love." O'Keeffe, who later recalled the "heat and excitement" of the photo sessions, opined that "nothing like them had come into our world before."

Yet the same nude photos that made Stieglitz famous triggered a backlash against O'Keeffe. Forever after, her work was seen in purely sexual terms. "When people read erotic symbols into my paintings they're really talking about their own affairs," O'Keeffe said. Still, the sexualized misconceptions of her work devastated her. "I almost wept," she wrote of one review in 1921.

The Whitney's focused show, carefully organized by curator Barbara Haskell, includes over 125 works and more than a dozen Stieglitz portraits. What strikes you about O'Keeffe's paintings is their restraint and reticence. And the astounding imagination. The sexuality barely registers—which makes the show feel strangely defensive, as if it's scared to let O'Keeffe be as weird, mystical, and suggestive as she really was. I would have appreciated more of her terrified, tentative retreats from and flirtations with abstraction and nature in the twenties, thirties, and forties; her quasi-realist/quasi-figurative hedged bets of the fifties; the oddball flat sixties abstractions; the almost-dissipated work she did during the seventies.

There are naughty bits. But compare her work with that of her closest stylistic contemporary and influence, Arthur Dove, and it's Dove, not O'Keeffe, who comes off as being "about sex." Dove plays the brooding, physical Walt Whitman of *Leaves of Grass* to O'Keeffe's intricate Emily Dickinson. Dove's touch has sensual weight, animalistic body, and shadowy intensity. O'Keeffe's art is Spartan, Apollonian, and cerebral, each painting as structured, layered, and faceted as an abstract sonnet.

In the first two knockout rooms of the Whitney's show, Haskell gives us O'Keeffe's early works on paper and her uncanny ability to conjure indivisible abstract wholes in which all parts are of equal interest and never decorative—something Donald Judd made good on decades later. Aside from one darkened gallery of Stieglitz's superseductive pictures of her, from the third gallery on, you're lowered into O'Keeffe's lapidarian vision, glowing prismatic color, and luscious thin surfaces. She never overworks anything; the relationship of her interior forms to external edges feels found yet pure as Pythagorean geometry.

"The men," as she witheringly referred to male contemporaries, tended to paint dark color with gritty surfaces and romantic symbolism. At the Whitney, you can see O'Keeffe coaxing brilliant hues onto smooth grounds via colossally magnified, closely cropped, disembodied shapes. At the same time, she's assimilated Stieglitz's (and Paul Strand's) ideas of photography into painting. All these things made her, in her own words, "an outsider." O'Keeffe's purer color and form, her surreal scale shifts, were as radical for her time as Warhol's Day-Glo color and pop culture references would be for his. Like Warhol, she was willing to forsake high-minded ideas about what constituted "serious art," and risk being branded with the worst insults the art world could muster: *girly, swishy, pretty.* O'Keeffe disliked such labels, but she wasn't cowed by them. And as the Whitney show demonstrates, her fearless prettiness is also profound and lyrical—an eerie, ineffable joy.

(2010)

Thanks for the Ride, Gavin!

On Wednesday, two young artists took the movement known as Relational Aesthetics for a joyride. The artist Rirkrit Tiravanija has long explored the rich terrain of giving things away for free, of making interactions with art and other people possible, and of sharing. In his current show, he has upped the ante. Setting up a soup kitchen that provides soup for a dollar a bowl, he's removed all the walls and windows of Gavin Brown's gallery. In doing so, he's achieved something Relational Aestheticians have been touting for decades: He's rendered indoors and outdoors the same thing—in this case, leaving the gallery open to anyone who wants to do anything, anytime.

That's where artists Patricia Silva and Eric Clinton Anderson come in. As they were perusing the soup kitchen, they spied Brown's own 2009 Volvo parked inside the gallery—with the keys in the ignition. "We didn't know much about the show beyond the usual 'do as you please' side," Anderson explains. Silva adds, "The absence of authority made it feel so fresh." How fresh? They spontaneously decided to take Brown's car for a spin. "We were really impressed at the boldness of the artist and gallery for having such an anarchic level of interactivity. So we jumped in, pulled out, and took the Volvo up the West Side Highway. Hell yeah!"

Shortly thereafter, Gavin Brown walked into a meeting upstairs in the building and announced, "My car was just stolen." (In classic artist concern-for-the-work-first fashion, the artist Rob Pruitt asked, "This is not going to interfere with our meeting, is it?" Brown looked around, said, "I guess not," and sat down.) Meanwhile, Silva and Anderson were driving up the West Side Highway; Silva was "blasting tweets to the world, announcing our glorious participation in the Tiravanija." She even posted a picture on *my* Facebook page. She found herself rummaging around the car as if it were part of an exhibit. "It seemed so real," she said. "I mean, the parking tickets stuffed in the dash. Wow!"

After driving for around twenty minutes, Anderson and Silva came back to the gallery but found another car blocking the entry. So they took off again, heading down to Varick Street for coffee. Eventually they returned, parked the Volvo across the street, and went in to announce to anyone "who wanted to use the car next that it was back." That's when they ran into a bearded man with a look that said *What the fuck are you doing with my car?* "He seemed really taken aback," says Silva. "Not mad." Only then did they realize that the car's owner was Brown himself. "Isn't it part of the show?" Silva asked. "I suppose it is," Brown replied.

The next day, I asked Brown about the event. "I suppose in some sense I set up the situation. So I've nothing to complain about," he said. "But," he added, "if someone really wanted to do something like this, they should have taken the car for a week, or driven it off the pier." Or "drive their own car into the gallery and leave it here. *I'll* steal *their* cars!"

(2011)

In Praise of Art Gallery Attendants

Dear Jerry,

You've written about the "bad dealer behavior" you experience as a recognizable critic. As an ordinary engaged observer, however, I often experience something very different at galleries: smugness. I'll ask for a piece of information and am dismissed with some uninformative answer. It's not a big deal, since I'm there to look at the art, but it does leave a bad taste. Would you please ask those galleries to be a bit more welcoming?

—Plebeian

Dear Plebeian,

I feel your pain. Walking into galleries can be intimidating. Being cold-shouldered is a drag. Still, allow me to say a few words on behalf of the unsung people who work at art galleries. The people who work at those front desks are usually paid very little. Many have no insurance or benefits. Like you, they're poor, living in dumps with other people, unable to do their laundry, paying off student loans, living on the edge, and working forty hours a week. They're in it more for love or desire than for money. They may be on the "inside," but there's a spiritual cost to that: Dealers are ultra-demanding control types who expect impeccable work out of them.

Moreover, they're on public view and subject to all manner of abuse. They're sneered at and stared at, asked for restaurant recommendations, street directions, bathroom keys, suggestions of what else to see—not to mention fielding less innocent queries, like *Who bought this? How much did it cost? What does this artist think they're doing?* and *Why would the gallery show such crap?* The bigger the gallery, the worse it is. Clueless artists show up unannounced, demanding that the dealer look at their work, then threatening the person behind the desk when they're told that the dealer doesn't consider such submissions. And when the person behind the desk is a woman, it gets really bad: Female attendants are flirted with, hit on, sometimes followed out the door. This goes on all day, even as the attendants are trying to do all the things their dealers have tasked them to do. The pressure is intense. Dealers can hold these people responsible for not recognizing a collector who has come in or for misdirecting a tiny piece of seemingly insignificant information.

In other words, the people behind the desk are more like you than you think. They're probably as concerned about how they're perceived as you are.

Many of the best gallerists today were once those poor people behind desks—among them Gavin Brown, Michelle Maccarone, Lisa Cooley, Rachel Uffner, Kathy Grayson, Risa Needleman, Carol Greene, Friedrich Petzel, Anton Kern, and countless others. #Respect.

(2011, 2015)

The Heroic Louise Bourgeois

Robert Mapplethorpe's iconic 1982 portrait of Louise Bourgeois, who died recently at ninety-eight, speaks volumes about Bourgeois's free-spiritedness, grace, tenacity, and the kinky perversity of her work. In the photograph, the seventy-one-year-old sculptor looks like a shaman seductress, one of Munch's vampiric castration queens, a maker of voodoo dolls, and a diva grandmother rolled into one. Under her arm she casually cradles her twenty-three-inch-long, seven-inch circumference latex-over-plaster sculpture of a phallus, *Fillette* (1968). In French, *fillette* means "helpless little girl." Bourgeois was no little girl, but there's something radically vulnerable about how she's holding the work—she seems almost to pull back the sculpture's foreskin and give the thing a little tickle. Bourgeois said that this gnarly abstract penis, with ovular testicles and a hook at the top, was "the shape of my husband, the shape of the children" (she had three sons). "I wanted to represent something I loved," she said. "I obviously loved representing a little penis." Little? Anyway, as Bourgeois later said, "It's very complicated." Indeed it was. As she said, "I have nothing against the penis. It's the wearer."

For more than seven decades, but in especially mordant, tough, and compelling ways over the last thirty years of her career, Bourgeois—perhaps the last twisted sphinx of surrealistic psychology, and the final vehicle of Abstract Expressionistic seriousness—turned the stuff of childhood trauma, oedipal desire, raging fury, and human sexuality into moving sculptures.

She often recalled her adulterous, psychologically abusive father. (He had an affair with her English governess, which her mother was unable to even acknowledge.) She told of how he regaled dinner guests with stories of how unattractive she was, and ridiculed her large breasts. It's perhaps not surprising, then, to find abstract images of birth, death, fear, and sex in Bourgeois's work: vivisectioned vaginas made of marble, drawings of women with houses for heads, latex dresses made of breasts. One of her installations includes an embroidered handkerchief with the words "I have been to hell and back. And let me tell you, it was wonderful." Another work, *The Destruction of the Father*, features fleshlike mounds and what looks like the jaw of a dinosaur. In the Guggenheim's catalogue for her retrospective there, Bourgeois describes an imaginary situation in which she and her family threw her father "onto the table and pulled his arms and legs apart—dismembered him . . . ate him up . . . It is a fantasy, but sometimes the fantasy is *lived*." For the "lived" part of those fantasies, immerse yourself in her miniature stuffed figurines, many of them housed in glass vitrines, which seem to kill, attack, or make love to one another. She reveled in infernal scenes of headless bodies, big spiders that dominated city plazas like avenging angels, and otherworldly mothers.

After overlooking her work, even dismissing it as latter-day surrealism, I finally became a Bourgeois fan in the eighties. Her images, materiality, scale, and surfaces seemed to get braver and more commanding. The theatricality, surrealism, and Abstract Expressionist angst became more mysterious and disarming. Although I never loved her celebrated spiders, and her pink wooden figures still strike me as derivative, her narratives came totally alive with an almost Kafkaesque darkness and urgency. Her works became horror comedies of sex, memory, and life within the confines of a body. She metamorphosed figures in ways that made them seem to be in the service of forces greater than those of humanity; they became puppets of the gods, expressing a sort of cosmic will. Bourgeois's feminism mutated into a simultaneously heroic and personal state. Where many artists who incorporate their biographies become slaves to them, and flog them in cloying ways, Bourgeois was always removed and skeptical, as filled with anger as she was with wit and incredulity.

(2010)

The Ugly American: Jennifer Allora and Guillermo Calzadilla

This makes me embarrassed to be an American," the megacurator of a well-known art museum groaned to me.

We were standing in front of what was truly a spectacle of American proportions. Directly in front of the U.S. Pavilion in the beautiful Giardini, the main site of the Venice Biennale, the artists Jennifer Allora and Guillermo Calzadilla have placed a sixty-ton army tank. It's a real one, shipped from England at who knows what expense, turned upside-fucking-down, turret and gun barrel on the ground, steel treads to the sky. Atop this warlord wedding cake, they've installed a treadmill where a world-class runner works out for fifteen minutes of every hour. It's the health club from hell, Afghanistan in Venice, and it makes a humongous racket that can be heard all around the Giardini. I looked back at the curator and said, "I think being embarrassed to be an American is partly what this is about."

It was Tanks R Us: We Americans are making this incredible noise, flexing our might, playing police force to the world, entertaining ourselves and anyone who'll watch, being grandiose and goony and needy, all the while trying to stay fit. Yet this monumental, Babel-like totem pole in this place at this time—while ostentatious and appalling in its implications— is, like a lot of art, also an amazing strange fact.

Allora and Calzadilla have found a way to summon, possibly exorcise, and certainly give form to the freaked-out way the world sees the United States. Their work captures what people are thinking before they set foot in the U.S. Pavilion (just as audiences come into the pavilions of Germany, France, Korea, and other countries with entirely different preconceived notions). It's ever-present but always invisible content, accumulated over centuries or decades. As I walked away from this infernal piece, I said to the curator, "Now, that's America."

(2011)

De Kooning: Definitive

D*e Kooning: A Retrospective*, at the Museum of Modern Art, is the most piercing, inexhaustible, and relentlessly intense full-on career survey I have seen in a long time. It could be better only by being bigger. Packing the museum's entire sixth floor with nearly two hundred paintings, prints, sculptures, and drawings (these last the equals of those by Ingres, Seurat, and Picasso), this retrospective should permanently set the art historical record straight on this artist.

Willem de Kooning is generally credited for coming out of the painterly gates strong in the 1940s, revolutionizing art and abstraction and reaching incredible heights by the early fifties, and then tailing off. His work of the late fifties and sixties is commonly maligned as facile or turgid, his sixties sculpture dismissed as kitsch, his abstract-figurative hallucinations of the seventies essentially ignored, his profound paintings of the eighties viewed as suspect. This show, organized by MoMA's chief curator emeritus of painting and sculpture, John Elderfield, proves that de Kooning started great and only got better.

Only two paintings into the show, elements of almost every work in de Kooning's career are already in evidence: figures, fiends, demons, eunuchs, and gargoyles; arcing curves, bowing limbs, windows and doorways in the background to let you in or out; metamorphosing form, uncanny furniture, oscillating geometry, unexpected color combinations, and inchoate spatial constellations that continuously set the graphic fields into visual motion, creating unfixed coordinates that alter before your eyes into subtle structures not quite stable or seen before. From this point on, nothing is either purely abstract or strictly figurative. . . . Start with *Woman I*, long a key piece of MoMA's permanent collection. See it splinter and torque, its voluptuous, tortured half beast turning into an avenging angel. The figure and ground merge and transform into a garish clownishness you've never seen before, a space that is strange, familiar, and credible. Glean how all this is subtly held together by drawing. The figure and the painting become a state of mind, windows onto other kinds of consciousness.

Just as you've reconciled yourself to this paradoxical state of ugly beauty and beautiful ugliness, and this new kind of human being or monster of the id, in *Woman II* de Kooning simultaneously lays waste to and consolidates this new ugliness into something sketchier, less familiar, and more lit up. Then, in *Woman III*, the color reduction, structured abstraction, and multiplying interstitial space of the forties are integrated into the new figurative pictorial field. There's even that same image of a window, echoed from those first two paintings. By the time he gets to *Woman VI*, from 1953, his ball of wax has exploded, and we're in an entirely new world.

De Kooning's both-not-one-or-another position allowed him to engage visionary visual tools to imagine and decipher the universe. Yet at the time this cost him dearly. Clement Greenberg derided his decision to keep the figure in his art, calling it a major mistake, and claimed that de Kooning was in decline. Robert Hughes lambasted his art as "self-parody." Jackson Pollock, whom de Kooning always spoke of admiringly, railed, "Bill, you betrayed it. You're doing the figure. You're still doing the same goddamned thing." In this same historical moment, the gifted young Robert

Rauschenberg showed up at his studio door, asked for and received one of de Kooning's drawings, and erased it.

That was in the mid-fifties, as de Kooning was nearly written off, treated as regressive by an art world that was pronouncing painting dead. At MoMA, we see him continuing at the same accelerated growth rate as before, circling back, striking out, destroying work, starting over, always pushing himself. After the *Women*, there's work here from the late fifties, paintings that I, too, had always written off as murky. Now I see that de Kooning was continuing with his women series—just leaving the women out. In paintings like *Easter Monday, Merritt Parkway, Bolton Landing,* and *Rosy-Fingered Dawn at Louse Point,* made between 1955 and 1963, he takes his vision into the sunlight, enlarging his scale and brushstrokes, going with less drawing, letting more light into spaces he'd always depicted. I was stunned here. As I was with his luscious so-called abstractions from the seventies, paintings I have loved unabashedly, despite their bad rap, for decades. Even in those oceanic fields, which resonate with Turner-like amorphousness and luminous energy, the eye can spot boneless body parts, hints of reclining figures, the windows and doorways of the earlier work, and a wet-on-wet sensuousness. You look at these teeming paintings and know they're made of the same thing we are. As de Kooning put it, "Flesh is the reason oil paint was invented."

In the final gallery comes the wintry incandescence of the last works, and they take the breath away. Exquisitely lyrical looping locutions, lone lines of coral-reef color, umbilical curves: They curl and cut back in viscous fields of mysterious expanding space. The windows and chairs of the first paintings are here, as is his feeling of space, so hard-won. In this gallery is his last rite of visual passage, the perfectly titled *The Cat's Meow*: an image of centrifugal harmonies in pastel that let you see the order and ecstasy in chaos, and the chaos in order and ecstasy. (Some of the paintings from this period are tainted by whispers: that de Kooning was being heavily aided by his assistants, that his developing dementia was robbing him of intellect. I see an artist fully in control.)

Everything on hand makes it impossible to think that, as early as 1959, de Kooning was being accused of repeating himself, betraying causes, making cotton-candy abstractions, turning out second-rate sculpture, or running on painterly fumes. It should also make all those curators who consider painting moribund and regressive, rarely including it in their shows, see the error of their ways. I challenge any of them to name one thing wrong with any work on view here. What we see, from beginning to end, is a cosmos unto itself, visual wisdom for the ages.

(2011)

A Wind That Lashes Everything at Once:
Helen Frankenthaler

For a long time—probably too long—too little thought has been devoted to the far-reaching accomplishments of Helen Frankenthaler, foremost inventor in the 1950s of what is variously called American Color Field painting and post-painterly abstraction. Whatever you call this short-lived movement, Frankenthaler used it to throw up an artistic bridge allowing artists to cross over from the blood-and-thunder-encumbered cosmos of Abstract Expressionism into a new world of Minimalism. The painter Morris Louis called her "a bridge between Jackson Pollock and what was possible." The Minimalist painter Kenneth Noland wrote, "We were interested in Pollock but could gain no lead from him. He was too personal. Frankenthaler showed us a way . . . to think about, and use color."

She did something else, too, although it's even less obvious now. Frankenthaler may have been the first artist not regularly demeaned and defanged by the label "woman artist." Before her, Frida Kahlo, Alice Neel, and Louise Nevelson were routinely relegated to the ghetto.

The sailing wasn't easy. Frankenthaler was often belittled, her work called merely decorative. Critics charged her with making pretty wallpaper. Her marriage to the A-list artist Robert Motherwell was often sniggered about, as was her five-year relationship with the critic Clement Greenberg. Charges of being a privileged rich girl were common, as were the laughably literal readings of her work, which said she was "about menstruation and the liquid world of the feminine." Frankenthaler had to read dismissals of her work, often contrasting it with Pollock's, like this: "Her work excites without quite satisfying . . . she can make a paint-mass spurt like a dike and yet control it till it laps the canvas like a spent wave." Others fretted over the differences between ejaculation and menstruation. (Oy.) Yet Frankenthaler's formal accomplishments somehow broke free of all of this.

She blurred the borders between geometry, order, chaos, the body, atmosphere, and ground. She shunned the overemotional hysteria of Abstract Expressionism, pouring thinned, watered-down, and turpentine-laden mixes of color directly onto raw canvas. Her structures and shapes were open, controlled by natural forces while also describing them. Her paint and canvas became one surface. Back in the day, this was a big deal. Edges evaporated; accident was visible, as were her means and intentions. In her hands, pooling paint created varying viscosities of thickness and thinness, then dried into imagistic riverbeds, isolated islands, clouds, continental masses that all evoked landscape without depicting it or engaging any abstract sublime. There was no paint-flinging, no implied dance around the canvas. There was picture-making, pure and simple. And beauty. Lots of it. Which of course made people run back to labels like "feminine."

It's easy to forget how radical it was for an artist to let go of structure, forsake known geometries, stop using the sides of the painting to define the image, move away from enclosed forms, and meld background and image—all while enthralling the eye, enticing the mind, and allowing others to use the work as a passage to a not-quite known imaginary place. I think of artists as varied as Pipilotti Rist, Lynda Benglis, Albert Oehlen, Sigmar Polke, and Laura Owens catching glimpses of possibility in all this. When I think about Frankenthaler's work—possibly not as often as I should—these things come rushing back into me.

(2011)

Utterly Possessing: Dorothea Tanning

Dorothea Tanning died on January 31, 2012, at the age of one hundred and one, and pieces of history died with her. An artist, a poet, the wife of Max Ernst from 1946 until he died in 1976, and a member of a group of great women Surrealists that also included Frida Kahlo, Leonora Carrington, Kay Sage, Lee Miller, Maya Deren, Remedios Varo, and Leonor Fini, she was at the center of a movement that was also a vicious mill for women, often relegating them to the sidelines of neglected or beset mistresses, muses, and madwomen.

Tanning's memoir describes how she and Ernst fell in love while playing chess, how the two of them lived in Arizona before moving to France, eventually marrying in a double wedding with Man Ray and Juliet Browner; she had longtime friendships with Picasso, André Breton, René Magritte (whom she called "sweet"), Marcel Duchamp, Yves Tanguy, Truman Capote ("a neat little package of dynamite"), Orson Welles (a "scowler"), and Joseph Cornell ("the courtly love of the thirteenth-century troubadours"), and she designed sets and costumes for the great George Balanchine.

Ernst never referred to Tanning as his "wife," a fact that pleased her. "He was very sorry about that wife thing. I'm very much against the arrangement of procreation, at least for humans. If I could have designed it, it would be a tossup who gets pregnant, the man or woman. Boy, that would end rape for one thing. And 'woman artist'? Disgusting."

She writes about being alone on a bus in Chicago and deciding, with no plans or place to live, to go on to New York. There she "ate curry pow-der sandwiches, took Hindu dancing, read the Bhagavad Gita and Emily Dickinson, impartially." In 1936 she saw the MoMA show *Fantastic Art, Dada and Surrealism* and recalled that "here, here in the museum . . . are signposts so imperious, so laden, so seductive and yes, so perverse that . . . they would possess me utterly."

Those signposts startle still in her work. Sexual tension slithers; emo-tional ambiguities multiply. In my mind's eye I see her 1942 *Birthday*, tinted in violet, green, and gray; a woman staring at us, outfitted only in a lacy skirt made of moss or roots, barefoot, bare-breasted but natural, not an object of the gaze, lost in some hall of doors while a winged demon perches by her feet—warning of her presence wherever she might tread. It's Tanning herself, who later said, "My breasts didn't amount to much. Quite unremarkable. Besides, when you are feeling very solemn and painting very intensively, you think only of what you are trying to com-municate."

I see the masterpiece *Eine Kleine Nachtmusik*, a 1943 image of little girls on a landing, becoming undone, one's hair flying to heaven, another's unraveling to the floor, both near a giant sunflower waiting for something, anything to happen, while a force removes them from our world. Without this painting, there is no work by an artist like Neo Rauch. I see Tanning's *Endgame* (1944), its satin pump crushing a bishop's miter atop a chessboard, perhaps thoughts about making her way in an almost all-male art world, perhaps a coy comment on her friend Duchamp. I see her bulbous sculp-ture of a wool-covered couch disgorging or giving birth to itself. In all of these, I see ways paved for artists like Yayoi Kusama, Louise Bourgeois, Lee Bontecou, Francesca Woodman, and many more. Dorothea Tanning is a reminder that all of us should try to live big lives.

(2012)

Cindy Sherman: Becoming

C ecil Beaton once said that "making oneself a work of art" was "that most difficult of all causes." Cindy Sherman not only does that, she's given herself up entirely to the mission. For nearly four decades, she has been braiding together fashion, photography, and the strange internal magic of herself—dressing up, putting on makeup, doing her hair, donning wigs, and posing alone in her studio for the camera. She shows us fashion as costume, compulsion, camp, ritual, and necessity. We see the ways fabric and cosmetics touch our bodies in public and how these performances of self make us visible, invisible, awful, sublime. Fashion helps Cindy hide in plain sight; in turn, she plays havoc with fashion. She is our greatest female impersonator.

A lot of people still think caring about clothes is a dubious, unserious, frivolous, girly thing. Waves of academic critics have insisted, and still insist, that Sherman's work is all about "the male gaze," "the objectification of women," and other such doctrinaire tropes. Sherman is most definitely an artist who thinks about gender roles, but she claims total ignorance of those rigid categorizations. "I was totally unaware of that," she says. "I was trying to come to terms with my own ambivalence about liking to put makeup on . . . dressing up. . . . [It] was a guilty pleasure [that] allowed me to play around with makeup and the sexier, old-fashioned styles." She has talked about being "inspired by how things are made, by fashion as art form." She's shot for *Vogue*, *Harper's Bazaar*, and *New York* magazine's fashion issue. She's been commissioned by Comme des Garçons and Balenciaga.

Yet fashion alone doesn't explain this most complexly uncanny American artist. Sherman delights in the mortification of the self, reveling in it like an epicurean at dinner; I see her as a spawn of de Sade and Rabelais, Daumier and Hogarth. Her survivalist instinct and relentless inventiveness make her a modern-day Scheherazade. Sherman's art is that of someone saving her own life in a mostly male art world, working from deep instinct, ferocious imagination, assertion, self-defense, all while fashioning an elaborate tapestry of grand viziers, demon clowns, Beau Brummells, and Valkyries; frazzled club girls, crinolined courtesans, dandies, macaronis, hippie chicks in Hiawatha fringe, Hollywood housewives, and other women fighting for their places in the world. Sherman is a warrior artist—one who has won her battles so decisively that I can't imagine any future artist embarking on a lifetime of self-portraiture without coming up against her.

I came late to a full appreciation of Sherman's work. After being beguiled by her *Untitled Film Stills* in 1980—the photos that made her famous, in which she imagined herself as a series of anonymous mid-century actresses in mysterious frozen moments—I was baffled when Sherman became the princess of Post-Modernism, the artist who launched a thousand theories. For a decade I was cold on her art. "The Centerfolds," from 1981 and 1982—horizontal pictures of Sherman under sheets or waiting by the phone—and the lurid scenes that followed struck me as pictorially dull. It was obvious noir, New Wave negativity, overconstructed self-consciousness, I thought; it oozed sleepwalking eighties hipness.

Even then, though, I always liked one thing: She consistently asserted that her pictures weren't self-portraits. "I really don't think they're about me," she said. For a moment in 1985, in a series referred to as "fairy tales," I glimpsed the dazing power of this distinction. In these pictures, Sherman's solitude mutated into riskier, more unnerving images of otherness and self-inflicted psychic wounds. We saw Sherman posed as a survivor crawling on a fake beach, a hobgoblin in a field, a banshee wearing a turban and artificial breasts ("I collect breasts," she says), gaping at us from the undergrowth, posed with her prosthetic ass facing the camera. Her work was in seizure. So was my judgment of it. But then she reverted to her melancholy doom, photographing postapocalyptic debris fields, vomit, and other abstract spin-offs. I gave up again.

That changed one evening in January 1990, at the opening of her "history portraits" at her longtime gallery, Metro Pictures, when I saw Sherman explode her own formula. She not only aped the aura, ambience, and look of Old Master paintings, lauding and marauding at the same time; she turned the gaze of male painters and art history into an onslaught of undoing. Wearing brocade gowns, silken cravats, and frills of old, she was in front of and behind the camera, as director, model, artist, inquisitor, subject, costume designer, and disenfranchised human doll. A new female-male Old Master, she posed as a bearded scholar, a dandy, a hag with pendulous fake breasts, a blonde squirting milk from a prosthetic nipple. Backgrounds, clothing, makeup, and props got richer; picture sizes, lighting, textures, pattern, and palette intensified. It was riveting.

Two years later, I went the full Sherman, when she made darkness visible in her horrific-beautiful "sex pictures"—images I've always called, after Goya's paintings of war, "The Disasters of Sex." Fashioned from dismembered and recombined mannequins, some adorned with pubic hair, one posed with tampon in vagina, another with sausages being excreted from vulva, this was anti-porn porn—the unsexiest sex pictures ever made, visions of feigning, fighting, perversion. A studio note to herself from this time reads "should be more toward terror." I'll say.

Today, I think of Cindy Sherman as an artist who only gets better. Right up to the most recent works at MoMA—giant implacable murals featuring Sherman as unknowable beings, sometimes more than one of her, wearing nude full bodysuits or early-twentieth-century frocks, carrying a shield, or bearing flowers. These neorealist pictures are as strange and strong as anything she has ever made. Since around 2005, she's become a great colorist and manipulator of internal scale. Her colors aren't just red or yellow but bloody and ashen, dramatic, vivid, flowering. Faces fill frames; the photographs feel ready to burst or collapse from internal pressure. No part of Sherman's graphic field is now left unconsidered.

Still, for any newcomers (are there Sherman newcomers?) getting bogged down in "Where's Cindy?" games or being turned off by the formal strictness of the basic structures of her art, I offer four pointers from a onetime fellow skeptic:

1. You can never say exactly who the people are in her pictures or what they're doing. Sherman is the master of the "esque"—of creating beings in the manner, likeness, and style of a thing. Frustrated viewers often want her to supply explanations, story lines, even titles (which she hasn't used since the film stills). Sherman, however, adamantly says she strives for "ambiguity" and that viewers are the ones who should "come up with the narrative." Do this. But don't think in traditional terms of plot, continuity, character development, and so on. Her people are actors and inventions, each a tabula rasa and an open program for unformed phantasmagorias.

2. Sherman has talked about her own father unflatteringly: "He was a horrible self-centered person . . . really racist . . . a bigot." Coming into the art world of the seventies, she found more bad fathers: In MoMA's excellent catalogue she speaks to John Waters about being "disgusted . . . with the art world . . . the boy artists, the boy painters." She talks about "female solidarity" and says her pictures are about "provoking men into reassessing their assumptions when they look at pictures of women . . . in a way that would make a male viewer feel uncomfortable." It worked on me. She and her female contemporaries (Louise Lawler, Sherrie Levine, Barbara Kruger, Laurie Simmons, and a few others) "weren't accepted in the guys' world, so we found this whole other way to create." Some of them took up the camera partly because no one cared about photography at the time—it had no market—and they reinvented the medium forever.

3. Her characters have wrongly been compared to those of Diane Arbus, whose subjects look out at us from similarly stark interiors and invite us into a world they're comfortable in. Sherman's characters, on the other hand, are conjured and parodic, removed, un-

comfortable. They never want us to step in. They exude fictive will, detachment. They are effigies.

4. Sherman's pictures are like riddles. Rather than being about understanding, they're about coming to grips with the state of mind that produces them. She has a luminous way of breathing life into things that cannot be described. Giving herself over to her own processes, Sherman opens up thought and makes pictures that subtly withdraw from definition, dislodging meaning, undermining ideology—becoming what I'd call radically passive. She sings the song of her selves.

(2012)

RIP Thomas Kinkade

I view art as an inspirational tool. People who put my paintings on their walls are putting their values on their walls." Those aren't the words of Gerhard Richter or Joseph Beuys, or of Picasso, Mondrian, Malevich, or any other messianic Modernist. They come from Thomas Kinkade, the self-described "painter of light," who died on April 6, 2012, at fifty-four.

Kinkade made dreamy scenes of suburbia, classic cottages, pretty gardens, lighthouses alone on stormy shores, saccharine pictures of small villages, and Christian images celebrating Jesus. As he said himself, "I work to create images that project a serene simplicity that can be appreciated and enjoyed by everyone." His output poses an interesting thought problem involving kitsch, conservative or sentimental artwork, and so-called real art.

As early as the 1930s, Clement Greenberg worried about the power of kitsch and the gap between popular and avant-garde taste, fretting that "real art would not stand a chance next to . . . Norman Rockwell." I've always thought this is fine; people should like whatever they want to like. And they do like Kinkade: He sells around $100 million worth of art *every year*. (By contrast, when Damien Hirst sold just one dopey diamond-encrusted skull trinket for that amount, the art world went nuts.) Kinkade estimated that his work hung in one of every twenty homes in America. Kinkade's admirers love the fact of his massive success; they take it as proof of his worth. But Kinkade's marketing operation also makes a hard pitch for his *values*. As his website says, "Thomas Kinkade devoted his life and career to share an inspirational message of home, faith, family, and inner peace." The paintings are good, in other words, because the values portrayed in them are good. I'm not sure what this makes the many pre-historic statues of giant-breasted women, or the tens of thousands of images of sexual intercourse from Japanese and Indian cultures.

The reason the art world doesn't love Kinkade isn't that it hates life, goodness, or God. We may be silly or soulless, but we don't automatically hate things that involve faith or love. We're not sociopaths. (Well, most of us.) The problem is that none—not one—of his ideas about subject matter, composition, form, or content is remotely original. They're overripe cli-chés, all twice-told tales. This is why his pictures strike artists and critics as ersatz, cynical, or worse. Joan Didion wrote that Kinkade's pictures "typically feature a cottage or a house of such insistent coziness as to seem actually sinister, suggestive of a trap designed to attract Hansel and Gretel. Every window lit, to lurid effect, as if the interior of the structure might be on fire." Work done in such a perfectly balanced, people-pleasing way produces these confected conglomerations: images of things that people want to think they want to think about, democratic paintings whose obvious meanings are meant not to disturb or provoke, not to produce doubt or newness, but to celebrate convention and complacency.

The "serene simplicity" hailed on Kinkade's website wasn't limited to his ideas about imagery. It also involved what Andy Warhol called "business art." Kinkade was willing to go the full Warhol: The secret to his success was that he mass-produced his pictures, creating prints and paintings generated in factories filled with assistants. A recent ad promised "a

Master Highlighter Event . . . an 8-hour personal stage appearance by a certified Thomas Kinkade Master Highlighter. At the event, a highlighter enhances images of the gallery's choice." Needless to say, this is the very thing others have railed about when it's done by Jeff Koons, Takashi Murakami, or Damien Hirst. In fact, Kinkade makes Koons & Co. look like a boutique. After all, Jeff Koons never built his own gated communities in California, with houses and grounds in the likeness of his paintings, with prices starting at $425,000.

Kinkade's paintings are worthless schmaltz; still, someday I'd love to see a museum mount a small show of Kinkade's work. I would like the art world and the wider world to argue about his work in public, to puzzle through what the work—and our divided reactions—really mean. Kinkade once said his goal was to "make people happy." I'm not sure if there's anything to be learned from simple happy reactions at a public exhibition, but I'm more than happy—to borrow an idea—to test our values on their walls.

(2012)

George W. Bush's Painterly Promise Unfulfilled

When I look at the paintings of George W. Bush, it's like seeing an incubus on America, as freakish and off-putting as his presidency was. Yet the art critic in me has to grant that, if I stumbled on three or four of Bush's paintings in a flea market, with no name attached, I'd snap them up. The first batch of his paintings we saw, in 2012, were of landscapes, churches, Bush himself in the bathtub, and other scenes; I liked them for their sheer weird obliviousness, their zonked-out earnest attempts at figuration, the odd feel for form and space, light, color, and softly contoured edges. If I didn't know better, I'd imagine they were made by a diligent high school senior, maybe a beauty queen perfecting her talent, maybe a mischievous frat boy spying on his father, possibly an onanist. They were amateurish, but I liked them for their perverted pictorial twists and psycho subject matter.

When a hacker first made them public in 2012, Bush's paintings were the first things about the man that didn't give me the heebie-jeebies. I fancied this misguided ex-president picturing himself in small spaces, alone, ruminating, naked, without guilt or dark nights of the soul, happily embracing his fragility and know-nothingness. I wondered if they were the beginning of Bush leaving a painterly trail to his inner thinking. I'd buy the paintings of the man in the bathtub and the one of him in the shower, looking back at us plaintively in a shaving mirror. I was stunned by this work at the time. I still am. In 2012, I even urged him to keep painting, to get good enough to let us see more of what he sees and saw.

Now, at his presidential library, Bush is having his first-ever solo exhibition: thirty new oil paintings, most of them portraits of world leaders. Once again, the paintings are weird. The bizarrely skewed portrait of Vladimir Putin makes no pictorial sense whatsoever but somehow coheres as a painting, and I'd buy the one of Tony Blair that looks like one face painted over another, with reedy pinkish lips that might start speaking, as in the old Clutch Cargo cartoons. But, as always, the truth will out. Bush has reverted to aping the idea of what a painter does. Now, as during his presidency, he lacks his own ideas, so he substitutes a notion of how past leaders have acted. The result is like an indirect pseudoportrait of how he learned to behave like a leader—as in the funny way he held his arms when he walked around the White House, or stalked over to the press gaggle on a golf course to threaten the terrorists before saying to reporters, "Now watch this drive." The new paintings include a self-portrait. Tellingly, it is the least finished, least focused, and most vague of all his pictures. There's a labored portrait of his father—the largest head he's ever painted, as if this is the face and figure that really fills his world. In Putin, the man who had Bush at hello, we see W still trying to fathom how he got so played. We see the Dalai Lama (one can only imagine what he made of Bush), King Abdullah (the painting that looks the most like a Luc Tuymans), and—in another painting I might buy, as it has some of the collapsed strangeness and fleshy light of the Blair portrait—Japanese prime minister Junichiro Koizumi.

As with all things Bush, the content suggested by the pictures is not a man exploring his own vision or his deeper feelings. What speaks volumes is what he's *not* painting. His own cronies are missing: Karl Rove, Dick Cheney, Donald Rumsfeld, Colin Powell, Condoleezza Rice, and the Fox News personalities and right-wing talkers who cheered Bush on to war. Imagine Bush painting his view of the 2000 election, or his landing on that aircraft carrier; or the torture at Abu Ghraib; or a self-portrait of him flying over New Orleans after Katrina. Imagine a self-portrait in the Oval Office, working to stop gay marriage or watching Colin Powell talking about yellowcake uranium at the UN. As Stalin edited people out of photographs to erase them from history, Bush occludes the parts of his presidency that don't fit his own story line. He avoids real life and looks away. When I look at Bush's latest paintings I know I'm looking at the true degenerate art.

(2014)

Magic amid the Money

A rt is changing. Again. Here. Now. Opportunities to witness this are rare, so attend and observe.

For nearly ten years, starting in the late nineties, art and money had sex in public. Lots of it. And really publicly. Art became news. Prices were equated with artistic value. The highest sellers were seen as the best artists. Galleries got bigger, then became multinational, opening branches here and then in Europe and Asia.

Wherever money went, art followed. (It should be the other way around.) Larry Gagosian now has eleven outposts; I await Gagosian Kuwait.

Like oil wells, once these operations are turned on, they have to keep pumping product. Lots of it, and most of it crude. For ten years, large, shiny, highly produced, entertaining, ever-more-expensive objects were produced by the system, then snapped up by speculator collectors who rushed in where the rest of us feared to tread. It doesn't matter that most of them don't know what art really is, have never grasped its hallucinatory powers. A lot of people struck it rich and laughed all the way to the bank.

This worldwide rising tide had the benefit of floating many boats. More artists than at any time in history managed to subsist, at least, within this system. And a lot of very good art got made. So it went . . . until it didn't. In 2008, the bubble burst. Or seemed to. Everyone, including me, assumed the art world would shrink. But that didn't happen. Instead, growth surged. It was as if John Travolta's *Pulp Fiction* character had stabbed the art world in the heart with a giant adrenaline needle. More sales and speculators; higher prices; new galleries. And it's still happening. Even as the world is in recession, the art world has remained on a bender.

But something has been happening of late. Large numbers of disconnected and discontented artists, gallerists, and others have taken matters into their own hands, changing the directions of art, its structures, and maybe its internal values. The last decade saw megatons of art produced in factories, turned out by armies of assistants, sometimes never touched by its makers. All you could think about was how much it cost. Collectors and museum curators, eager to be included in the all-out global party, shelled out enormous amounts of money for this sort of art. Often they bought it sight unseen. Everything was impersonal. Meanwhile, things small, unfinished, or chaotic were *ars non grata*.

But now, all of a sudden, more art is coming from private places, looking almost outsider-like, untaught, odd in ways that feel pressing, impatient, and important. In from the wilderness. A lot of it is smaller, made of less expensive or found materials, and more provisional, or at least bad in ways that aren't so annoying.

After too much art that made too much sense, artists are operating blind again. They're more interested in the possible than the probable, the private that speaks publicly rather than the public with no private side at all. Damien Hirst may be able to fill eleven galleries with spot paintings done by other people for other people. But this work has none of the inner power channeled by Joanna Malinowska staging a concert of Beethoven's *Moonlight Sonata* played on toy pianos, then inviting more than a hundred viewers to howl like wolves for five minutes, mourning the fate of Native American prisoner Leonard Peltier.

Much of this art evades categorization; it also tends to defy collectors. It exists in the in-between genres where performance, sculpture, video, sound, photography, and sometimes painting overlap. When it's not in an overlap, it jolts the old categories. I see artists bored by light-without-heat, irked at the gigantic galleries, leaving behind the overdetermined for the undetermined, guided by interior voices. They are bringing us out of a long tunnel to new blueness. Even as our blood still boils at the art-luxury freak show, these insurgent energies have resolved to make it new and make it over. Or die trying.

And the pheromones in the streets have been wild. There have been evenings of more than twenty openings in little spaces on the Lower East Side and in Bushwick, enormous numbers of people filling the streets, looking at one another as if to say, *Yeah. There's a way around the grossness and shell shock.* Most important, it's not about neighborhoods or size. Energy and art go where they will. Peter Freeman just opened a huge, unrenovated ground-floor space on Grand Street that looks and even smells so much like an old SoHo loft gallery that it gave me old-school goose bumps.

Hundreds came, dozens of works were hung, and dancing in the streets ensued a few weeks ago at the opening of the artist Jayson Musson's (known as Hennessy Youngman) everybody-is-welcome-and-everything-gets-hung open-call show at Maurizio Cattelan and Massimiliano Gioni's new pint-size Chelsea non-gallery, Family Business. Cattelan recently hung his career's output from the ceiling at the Guggenheim for a retrospective, and the New Museum's Gioni is the curator of the next Venice Biennale; that two bigwig insiders are running this peewee nonprofit space in the middle of Chelsea shows that people are still trying at all costs not to go along to get along, and to play with the system instead.

Three weeks earlier, I'd seen Marie Lorenz's extraordinary show at Jack Hanley, which includes videos of the artist rowing a small homemade boat around the rivers, waterways, and bays of New York City, exploring unknown reaches of the city, landing on unpeopled beaches. The work is personal; there's nothing corporate about it. It's not a commodity; it's hardly a *thing* at all. Quietly insubordinate and seditious, Lorenz is a one-woman nomad, reimagining the city, letting us see New York anew through a larger, more mysterious lens.

Not long after, I watched Sarah Michelson journey into time and whirling-dervish-dom at the Whitney, choreographing her dancers to twirl in unison, mirroring one another's movements in widening gyres. A dozen people walked out. Yet I saw many happily breathe in. A similar thing happened at Derek Eller Gallery, as Liz Magic Laser had two actors mime the body languages of Barack Obama and George H. W. Bush giving speeches. In this small gallery, no one left; instead a room full of people gaped.

At the peak of these personal mountains is the late Mike Kelley's tremendous three-and-a-half-hour unfinished Whitney Biennial film. We see a mobile-home replica of Kelley's Detroit childhood house being driven up and down a long stretch of Detroit's Michigan Avenue. Along the way, Kelley's interviews with everyday people are spliced in—folks trying to get along, living their lives in unique, amazingly creative ways. Watching it, I saw documentary film sprouting new tentacles. Kelley had the instinctive understanding that reality isn't just something that can be made into art. If seen in the right way, everything already is art. His loss is huge.

Some see this fissuring as a split between market and anti-market forces. Yet we all claim to be on the same side. Nobody is willing to admit to being Establishment anymore, since at this point even the Establishment acknowledges that all the energy is on the romantic fringes. Even Jeff Koons, whose work is utterly salable, is about art first, even as he's trying to create a $25 million hanging-locomotive sculpture to hover above the High Line. Hirst, maker of the $100 million skull bauble, says, "Art is more powerful than money." And those of us who claim to shun or be shunned by the market exist in a larger system that rewards us with money, time, space, grants, residencies, recognition, or respites from full-time-job hell. Not to sound like a holistic hippie, but there are no insiders and outsiders anymore; everyone is both at once.

(2012)

Zombies on the Walls: Why Does So Much New Abstraction Look the Same?

F or the past 150 years, pretty consistently, art movements have moved in thrilling but unmysterious ways. They'd build on the inventions of several extraordinary artists or constellations of artists, gain followings, until they became recognizable as a movement or a school, influencing everything around them; then, almost inevitably, they would become diluted as they were taken up by more and more derivative talents. Soon younger artists would rebel against them, and the movement would fade out. This happened with Impressionism, Post-Impressionism, and Fauvism, and again with Abstract Expressionism after the 1950s. In every case, always, the most original work led the way.

Now something's gone terribly awry with that artistic morphology. An inversion has occurred. In today's greatly expanded art world—and art market—it's the artists making diluted art who have the upper hand. A large swath of the art being made today is driven by the market, and specifically by not very sophisticated speculator-collectors who prey on their wealthy friends and their friends' wealthy friends, getting them to buy the same look-alike art.

The artists themselves are only part of the problem. Many of them are acting in good faith, making what they want to make and then selling it. But at least some of them are complicit, catering to a new breed of hungry, high-

yield risk-averse buyers, eager to be part of a rapidly widening niche industry. Their ersatz art looks, fundamentally, like other art. It's colloquially
been called Modest Abstraction, Neo-Modernism, MFA Abstraction,
and Crapstraction. Rhonda Lieberman gets to the point with "Art of the
One Percent" and "aestheticized loot." I like Dropcloth Abstraction, and
especially the term coined by the artist-critic Walter Robinson: Zombie
Formalism.

Galleries everywhere are awash in these brand-name reductivist canvases, all more or less handsome, harmless, supposedly metacritical, and
just "new"- or "dangerous"-looking enough not to violate anyone's sense of
what "new" or "dangerous" really is. All of it is impersonal, mimicking a set
of preapproved influences. (It's also a global presence: I saw scads of it in
Berlin a few weeks back, and the art fairs are inundated.) These artists are
acting like industrious junior Post-Modernist worker bees, trying to crawl
into the body of and imitate the good old days of abstraction, deploying
visual signals of Suprematism, Color Field Painting, Minimalism, Post-
Minimalism, Italian Arte Povera, Japanese Mono-ha, Process Art, Modi-
fied Action Painting, all gesturing toward guys like Polke, Richter, Warhol,
Christopher Wool, Richard Prince, Martin Kippenberger, Albert Oehlen,
Wade Guyton, Rudolf Stingel, Sergej Jensen, and Michael Krebber.

This work is decorator-friendly, especially in a contemporary apartment
or house. It feels "cerebral" and looks hip in ways that flatter collectors, even
as it offers no insight into anything at all. It's all done in haggard shades of
pale, deployed in uninventive arrangements that ape digital media, or something homespun or dilapidated. Replete with self-conscious comments on
art, recycling, sustainability, appropriation, processes of abstraction, or nature, this array of painting styles shares a common vocabulary of smudges,
stains, spray paint, flecks, spills, splotches, almost-monochromatic fields, silk-
screening, or stenciling. Edge-to-edge, geometric, or biomorphic composition
is de rigueur, as are irregular grids, lattice and moiré patterns, ovular shapes,
and stripes, with maybe some collage. Stretcher bars often play a part. This
is supposed to tell us, "See, I know I'm a painting—and I'm not glitzy, like
something from Takashi Murakami or Jeff Koons." But much of it is just

painters playing scales, doing finger exercises, without the wit or the rapport that makes music. Instead, it's visual Muzak, blending in.

Most Zombie Formalism arrives in a vertical format, tailor-made for instant digital distribution and viewing on portable devices. It looks pretty much the same in person as it does on an iPhone or an iPad, on Twitter, Tumblr, Pinterest, and Instagram. Collectors needn't see shows of this work, since it offers so little visual or material resistance. It has little internal scale; its graphic field is taken in at once. You see and get it fast, and then it doesn't change. There are no complex structural presences to assimilate, few surprises, and no unique visual iconographies or incongruities to come to terms with. It's frictionless, made for trade. Art as Bitcoin.

Almost everyone who paints like this has come through art school. Thus the work harks back to the period these artists were taught to lionize: the supposedly purer days of the sixties and seventies, when their teachers' views were being formed. Teachers and students alike tend to zero in on this period; within that, on a single type of art from the period; and then, within that, on only certain artists representing that type. It's art historical clear-cutting, aesthetic monoculture with no biodiversity. This is semantic painterbation—what an unctuous auction catalogue, in reference to one artist's work, recently called "established postmodern praxis."

Apologists offer convoluted defenses for this tendency, insisting that certain practitioners differ from all the others. Lucien Smith uses fire extinguishers to make his little drips; Dan Colen uses M&M's for his; Adam McEwen deploys chewing gum; Parker Ito paints fields of hazy colored dots. Many artists make art that looks printed but is handmade; others make art that looks handmade when it's printed. We're told that a painting is made by cutting up other paintings, or that it was left outdoors or in a polluted lake or sent through the mail, or that it came from Tahrir Square. We hear that the artist is "commenting on" commodity culture, climate change, social oppression, art history. One well-known curator tried recently to justify the splattered Julian Schnabel–Joe Bradley–Jean-Michel Basquiat manqué of Oscar Murillo—the hottest of all these artists—by connecting his tarp- or tentlike surfaces to the people living under makeshift canvas shelters in Murillo's native Colombia. Never mind that he was educated in England and grew up largely there. At twenty-eight, obviously talented, Murillo's still making his student work; he could turn out to be great. But so many buyers and sellers are already so invested in him that everyone's trying to cover his or her position. In one day at Frieze last month, three major art dealers pulled me aside to admit they agree that we're awash in Crapstraction—but that their artist was "the real deal." I told each dealer what the other had said to me, and that each had named a different hot artist.

I'll admit something, too: I don't hate all of this work. Frankly, I like some of it. The saddest part of this trend is that even better artists who paint this way are getting lost in the onslaught of copycat mediocrity and mechanical art. Going to galleries is becoming less like venturing into individual arks, and more like going to chain stores where everything looks distantly familiar. My guess is that if and when money disappears from the art market again, the bottom will fall out of this genericism. Everyone will instantly stop making the sort of painting that was an answer to a question that no one remembers asking—and it will never be talked about again.

(2014)

Garry Winogrand Captured America As It Split Wide Open

The photographer Garry Winogrand had night vision. With it he saw not only the dark side of his own time in America, but also the first flickering of our hopelessly polarized and fracturing future—its paranoia, rage, and blind righteousness. Winogrand, who was born in 1928, took his first picture when he was twenty years old and never really put down the camera again. He moved like a meteor from city to city, neighborhood to neighborhood, returning to the same sites, always finding people devoured by desire, resignation, and nonbeing. Winogrand peered through the mist of changing America and saw brittle invalids, rich guys with rheumy eyes, figures acting prescribed parts, people frozen in hatred like the plaster figures in Pompeii. His pictures startle with their rawness. Almost always, he draws close—aggressively close—to his subjects. By the end of his life, he was shooting so incessantly he wouldn't even take the time to develop his negatives, much less make prints from them. "I sometimes think I'm a mechanic," he said. "I just take pictures." In those years, he nearly stopped editing, or even looking at, his work. Other people did his printing and put his books and shows together. He died, too, with the same headlong drive. Diagnosed with cancer in January 1984, he went immediately to Tijuana to seek an alternative cure. Two months later, at fifty-six, he was dead.

Winogrand's indelible vision is the subject of a powerful retrospective at the Metropolitan Museum of Art. Densely installed and spilling out of four galleries, it consists of more than 175 of the artist's images—more pictures of his than I've ever seen at once, and they left me wanting more. This sweeping, soup-to-nuts show begins with a 1950 photograph: a lone sailor carrying a suitcase down a dark New York street. It's a perfect metaphor for America right after World War II, embarking on what turned out to be a one-decade "American Century," while already experiencing existential stirrings, a mysterious chafing against cultural values. Subsequent images let us see approaching catharsis, rebellion, reactionary attitudes setting in psychic stone. Stylish women openly smoke on New York avenues, as was once taboo; they're eyed disapprovingly and wantonly by men. Cigar-chomping campaigners for Richard Nixon's failed 1960 campaign form a psychological palimpsest of a mounting resistance to change. Liberations of all kinds come into focus: pictures of women, blacks and Hispanic people, uncloseted gay culture, and a free-for-all of conservative businessmen, construction workers, and military personnel turning cold cheeks to a shifting society.

The dam breaks in the next gallery. From around 1960 to 1970, Winogrand devoured the country as it came unmoored, grew confused, slipped into chaos, convulsing its way to greater freedom. Winogrand is an oracle of unease, seeing tourists in Dealey Plaza yearning for proof of truths and conspiracies; a kid wearing Mouseketeer ears with his camera-toting parents in L.A.'s Forest Lawn cemetery. Women in miniskirts, in tight sweaters, finding sisterhood in public, wearing what they want to wear, acting any way they wish. Winogrand's pictures of women often arouse nettled responses. I adore them, but there's no doubt that this is an artist seeing female bodies not only as agents of change but as objects of his delectation. "I'm still compulsively interested in women," he said.

Winogrand gets one aspect of the sixties better than any other photographer: the visible divide of the contempt of one half of America for the other half. Construction workers bellow at long-haired protesters; everyone peers with hatred at youth. A telling picture from 1969 captures what looks like a family of out-of-towners dumbstruck at the hippies in Central Park. The world opens in the divide between them—a divide that turns cosmic in Winogrand's seventies pictures, as everyone turns into his or her own cathedral, cloistered or fun-loving.

The show also incorporates fifty-six prints made after Winogrand's death—images taken from thousands of proof sheets and rolls of film he never developed, and printed in a larger format and clearly labeled to distinguish them from his own prints. Many fastidious observers consider the creation of these posthumous prints a betrayal, but I'm happier to see them. Many also claim that these late pictures show a falling-off. Again, I disagree. To my eye, they follow the trajectory of America in these years: the way places went from being concentrated to being bland, streets full of burnouts, packed airplanes full of lost souls. These late pictures complete Winogrand's atlas of America, his cosmology of the inner life of a country turning inside out, twisting into half beast, turning back, creating nests of new beings.

Today, the whole world is filled with incredible images—especially on Instagram and other social networks—that owe something to Winogrand's drive for documenting life. Yet the art world and museums are not. Instead they tend to show oversize, very still pictures or images that investigate formal properties and ideas of display and presentation. I love many of those pictures, but what's happening online deserves far more serious scrutiny than it's getting. If the art world doesn't admit more of this sort of deceptively casual-seeming work, the outside world will reject more so-called art photography than it already does. That's a divide we should be trying to close, not to broaden.

(2014)

The Great, Inscrutable Robert Gober

Compared with good art, "great art is much harder to talk about," the sculptor Charles Ray has said, speaking of the phantasmagoric work of Robert Gober, the subject of a forty-year retrospective survey at MoMA called *The Heart Is Not a Metaphor*. "If you were to ask me what his artwork talks about I would not be able to tell you. But this doesn't mean it is not speaking," Ray continued. "What I do understand . . . is that I want to see it again. It asks me to be near. To come closer and look longer or to come back tomorrow and look again. The work whispers 'Be with me.'"

The melancholy narratives of Gober's work have gripped and bewildered me for thirty years. Imagine Proust just presenting a sculpture of a half-eaten madeleine or drawings of only the three windows through which he watched illicit homosexual encounters. In a forthcoming essay about Gober, the novelist and critic Jim Lewis, a longtime close reader of the artist, admits, "I don't understand Robert Gober's work." He notes that most of this artist's commentators have recorded the same reaction, as well. I'm one of them. And that's how I know how good the work is.

The first pieces we encounter inside Gober's stunning new MoMA survey will likely whisk viewers to this never-understand land. There's a recessed closet with no door, a tiny intaglio print of an anonymous cat-sitter ad, and on the floor jutting from the wall—as if crushed by Doro-thy's house crashing down into some eerie Oz—a man's severed leg, complete with pants cuff, hairy shin, and old shoe.

The whole show conjures a house possessed, stripped down, roughed up—Gober's inner home, ours, America's. The second gallery zeroes in on a mad family of contorted sculptures of sinks. All evoke inanimate beings, anomalous anatomies, secret selves, hybrid bodies in pain, absence, emo-tional masks donned and removed. Made in 1984, these are the works that put Gober on the map—albeit off to one side. Famous but never as white-hot as Jeff Koons, Gober has always been viewed by the art world as a sort of "good object," while Koons is seen as the "bad object." This even though the two are pretty comparable: roughly the same age, both from working-class northeastern families, obsessed with sex, religion, and history, blessed with freakish levels of craft, hygiene, and cleanliness. (Gober has his sinks, Koons his vacuum cleaners.) Gober's low-slung sinks, fashioned from plas-ter, wood, wire lath, and coated in layers of bland semigloss enamel, are exoskeletal ghost sculptures, dysfunctional with no running plumbing. All holes and bowls, some look like mouths; they feel like urinals or creatures with needs—clunky, funny, wanting, bizarre. "What do you do when you stand in front of a sink? You clean yourself," Gober has said. His sinks are "about the inability to [do that]."

As you proceed deeper into this apparitional house, the repeated pale-ness of Gober's palette, the hermetic, almost empty rooms, and the aura of surrealism sometimes make his art appear wan, monotonous, joyless. In the next gallery, two crooked playpens might mangle a child's internal compass, but the work is optically inert, emotionally obvious. Gober is better—way better—at ambiguity. Which brings us to something of a skel-eton key to Gober's work. A plain piece of plywood, made in 1987, leans against a wall. That's it. Look closely at the surfaces, edges, and materials. Crafted carefully from laminated fir and particleboard, this is a work cloaked, camouflaged, passing as a piece of plywood passing as sculpture passing as art, blending in, acting one way while *being* another. It is a sculpture in drag.

A work from 1979–1980, a large dollhouse made when Gober was twenty-five, is a nearly perfect hand-rendered re-creation of a typical working-class American home. It is the kind of house you might pass on a shortcut on your way to school, musing idly on how normal life inside it must be. In this exhibition, the work is shown with its sides closed, and therefore hidden, but in other shows they've been thrown open, exposing to all what's within. Inside, the house looks abandoned; the walls are covered with painted scenes of roads, landscapes, shapes of the states. Alarm bells sound: These are images of longing, loneliness, dreaming of other places, getting out, getting away. The empty closet, severed leg, and disembodied sinks all transform into Whitman's "phantoms curiously floating." This is someone's life, prolapsing.

Nearby is another empty doorway—and a work one of Gober's best critics, curator Richard Flood, has called "a curious bag of groceries": a hermaphroditic torso with one male and one female breast, complete with human hair tweezed into the skin. Lumped on the floor and leaning against the wall like a sack of gravel, this is a body in conflict, psychic boundaries bulging, contested, cursed, alive with possibilities. By this point in the show, you've seen all sorts of hyperrealistic attenuated body parts jutting from walls, in corners, on the floor: one pair of man's legs with drains, another that sprouts candles, another that has sheet music imprinted on his naked posterior. A large concrete crucifix spouts a stream of water from Christ's nipples into a jackhammered hole in the museum floor. Tears, nourishment, violence, and sex mingle in this image of sacrifice and violent death. There is an empty wedding dress in a room wallpapered with repeating images of a sleeping white man and a hanged black man. It sends chills. As does as a truncated naked female torso giving birth to a grown man's leg with shoe and pants, foot-first. When this untitled 1993 work was first shown, I remember many viewers being outraged at what they perceived as its misogyny. Gober's own mother said, "Bobby, why would you want to make something like this?" Maybe it just captures something about the physical body—that we're all born this way. Whatever the case, many of Gober's works still make the hair on the back of my neck stand up. The important thing is not what the work says, or what it's about, but what it does *to* you—what it brings up *in* you.

But where does it come from, this strange grotesque netherworld that is both horrifying and unshakably personal, intimate, familiar? Gober's art comes from many places; it can't be reduced to identity politics, sex, religion, race, or psychology. Yet it helps to look at a context that contributed to this art. In 1981, *The New York Times* published a one-column article titled "Rare Cancer Seen in 41 Homosexuals. Outbreak Occurs Among Men in New York and California." AIDS had come into the land. Rather than being protected and cared for by family, religion, and government, gay men were shunned, left to fend for themselves and die with public knowledge but little public support. By the time President Ronald Reagan finally said the word "AIDS" in late 1985, more than 21,000 American citizens had succumbed to the disease. It's hard to convey what New York looked like then, what a ride on the subway was like: Emaciated, marked, scared men everywhere. People afraid, contemptuous of one another. Hate crimes were being directed against gay men and women; sodomy was declared a punishable offense. Gober's home—our home—had turned into a house of death. As Gober has said, "I was a gay man living in the epicenter of twentieth century America's worst health epidemic." He later wrote that "it is primarily gay men . . . who have organized themselves to care for their own when their families and their government recoiled in bewilderment and fear." As he noted, "Should gay men succeed in moving through the discrimination . . . their achievement will be remarkable."

One of the last pieces in the show offers sweet sustenance and hope: a simple potato print of the words of the 1959 Rodgers and Hammerstein song "Climb Ev'ry Mountain." I found myself humming this song as I absorbed all the sorrow, all the lost souls, evoked here. It's pure schmaltz, maybe. But that's a part of what we're made of: gushing, inexplicable feelings. And even when these feelings are evoked by a simple show tune, they can add up to sublimities. Gober's work exhorts, annoys, lulls, sometimes lets boredom slip in. Yet it almost always radiates a disquieting radical strangeness, and that, in its weird way, can bring about healing. He is one of the best American artists of the last thirty years.

(2014)

Chris Ofili's Thumping Art-History Lesson

I t was a shitstorm that ended in a witch hunt. "If this painting is censored, I'm canceling the show," English megacollector Charles Saatchi snapped to me privately in the early hours of September 18, 1999, amid an installation at the Brooklyn Museum. Days before, the New York *Daily News* had run the headline "B'KLYN GALLERY OF HORROR. GRUESOME MUSEUM SHOW STIRS CONTROVERSY." The "gallery" was the Brooklyn Museum. The "horror" was *Sensation*, a show of about forty young British artists from Saatchi's collection who'd emerged in the early 1990s—most of whom were already fading, making the show seem, to those in the art world, something of a nonevent.

That is, until the *Daily News* headline. The "controversy" was one painting: Chris Ofili's beautifully bioluminescent 1996 depiction of a black woman cloaked in cerulean blue. A wavy visage composed of what look like light-emitting microorganisms, she's surrounded by radiating dots of enamel paint and constellations of small, cutout photographic body parts. Her right breast is fashioned of elephant dung secured to the canvas and decorated with black map-tacks. The painting rests on two dung balls, one festooned with pins that say "Virgin," the other, "Mary." Whether it was because of the visage, with its large "negro lips" (Ofili himself is black, a Nigerian-born Catholic and a former altar boy), the sight of the black body parts in the photos, the use of real dung (a material many cultures deem sacred), or the title of the work, *The Holy Virgin Mary*, everything went to hell. Sight unseen,

Rudy Giuliani, then the mayor, opined that the dung had been "flung," called the painting "sick," and vowed to defund the museum of millions of dollars. The Catholic League objected to the Madonna being "black" and railed over "anuses." The Jewish Orthodox Union insidiously suggested that the next defacing might "be a Jewish ritual item." Rather than defending Ofili, many in the art world denounced the museum for colluding with Saatchi to show a private collection in a public institution.

That criticism was, of course, only an alibi. Those in the art world attacking *Sensation* were motivated by cowardice—and I say that as one of the people who did feel genuinely nervous, so much so that, on that same morning when Saatchi made his comment to me, I counseled him toward compromise, suggesting that he place the painting behind ropes. On December 16, seventy-two-year-old retired teacher Dennis Heiner smeared the painting with white paint. His wife later explained that the white "indicates cleanliness." As D. H. Lawrence wrote, "The doom is in America . . . our white abstract end . . . Doom of our white day . . . The last phallic being of the white man."

How distant the New York of the *Sensation* era, and that scrappier art world, feels now. This is a nostalgic city; old-timers love to lament the romantic New York of their youth—the downtown eighties of Madonna and Basquiat, the disco seventies of Warhol and Blondie, long fifties nights at the Cedar Tavern. It's easy to assume the city has lost its potential for new excitement, for a culture where things feel truly up for grabs. But the *Sensation* sensation was only fifteen years and one mayor ago. The city was still roiled by white ethnic-identity politics, and the marriage between contemporary art and global wealth not yet consummated. The result was that fully half of New York could still become enraged by the audaciousness of contemporary art simply for *daring to be contemporary art*.

But hurrah! An exorcism of the bad magic of 1999 has now finally arrived, in the form of the New Museum's breathtaking, building-filling Chris Ofili survey. *Night and Day*, as the show is called, is an endlessly sensuous dive into the most carnivalesque pleasures of painting. This exhibition makes three things clear. First, Ofili is one of the best painters to have come out of England in the last sixty years. For me, he puts painting through far more enticing paces than Lucian Freud or Francis Bacon. Next, this survey gives the lie to the then-prevalent, always-returning canard that "painting is dead." As much as anyone working today, Ofili shows how endlessly expandable painting is, how asinine it is to act like a coroner talking about the death of a medium—or to say that painting can't be "political," when Ofili is as political a painter as any so-called activist artist. Finally, *Night and Day* reminds us how unlikely this sort of cultural-political cross fire is, in our time of art and money flagrantly sleeping together. It's very hard for art to be that threatening when it's embraced by the powerful.

Although at forty-six Ofili is considered a YBA (young British artist), he actually emerged a step after, and a painterly sensibility away from, the ironic neoconceptualism of many of his contemporaries. He didn't even have his first show in a bigger London gallery until 1996—*after* his fabulous 1995 New York debut, after Hirst and the others were showing worldwide. Everything in Ofili's early work is keyed up, on optimum optical overload. (This frontal graphic attack is one quality he does share with other British artists.)

Ofili's early paintings are bedazzling; they come at you with the flamboyant lateral waggle of a swaggering pimp. Canvases here are so layered and dense with dotting, vibrating waves of paint, wild color, washes, and surface inflection that they're thumping visual equivalents to Sun Ra's incredible sonic arks. Note the funkadelic-blaxploitation-like titles: *Afronirvana*; *Monkey Magic—Sex, Money, and Drugs*; and *The Adoration of Captain Shit and the Legend of the Black Stars*. *The Holy Virgin Mary* exudes seductive voluptuousness, mad pizzazz. Racy, raucous, shimmery, *Pimpin' Ain't Easy* depicts an erect brown penis with a smiling face and googly eyes bouncing around a tricked-out iridescent field. Enormous portraits of black goddesses make you aware that there aren't many figures that look like this in Western museums. And all these paintings rest on dung. As does *No Woman, No Cry*, a picture of a woman, Doreen Lawrence, crying for her son Stephen, who'd been stabbed to death in South London. All this is the work of a supremely confident, incredibly skilled artist able to activate and control every millimeter of surface so that it throbs with crazed Blakean energy.

A series of eight paintings made since 2006 bring Ofili from the gaudy neon city night of the early work to thickets of deep indigo, ultramarine, silver, and black. Here the hues and color values are so close that the eye has trouble making anything out; Ofili allows the imagination to see as much as the eye. Interestingly, the best way to see this work is from oblique angles and with sidelong glances. *Iscariot Blues* is a black body hanging from a gallows with a banjo player nearby. Spanish moss dangling at the painting's edges lets Billie Holiday's "Strange Fruit" coil around Judas's suicide. These paintings are so different from what came before that we have to ask why Ofili, when riding so high, would change paths. "At some point I was going to reach a dead end," he said about his early work. "I had to get off the horse . . . and walk. . . . That's what I decided to do." Many artists facing this sort of daunting change just keep making what they always make. That Ofili could cast painting into such a powerful somnambulant fugue state, after doing what he'd done so vibrantly for ten years, is a testament to his talent and control.

But just wait. It turns out that, during those years, not only did Ofili change one modality of his painting—going from psychedelic to somber—he changed another at the same time, as is seen in the huge treat awaiting viewers on the fourth floor: an incredible walk-in installation involving nine paintings all done after 2005, when Ofili left England behind and relocated with his family to Port of Spain, Trinidad. In a serene floor-to-ceiling-painted room of violet, pink, and purple flowers, ferns, and trees—it's like a surround-sound Monet—we see Ofili unleashing all his painterly powers, tapping into art historical sources as varied as Art Nouveau, Romare Bearden, Jacob Lawrence, Bob Thompson, German Expressionism, Gauguin, and Matisse. The lights are back on in this work, but switched from the electricity of the early work to something alien and natural at the same time. This is Ofili fashioning his own history of art, one that shows that the warfare model of Modernism—with each movement successively killing its predecessor in order to live—is less effective than letting all and any art live within one's work. That is the big change from the discourse of 1999: If they want to be, and they have the nerve, artists are no longer obliged to live within the constraints of cant.

Let's end at the beginning, where all ends actually begin. November 20, 1995, the night before the opening of Ofili's first solo show in the United States, at Gavin Brown's gallery. That evening, around eight o'clock, I drove past Brown's little Broome Street storefront. I saw something so startling, it made me pull over, stop, stare, and take pictures. Outside the gallery, with his back to me, Ofili was working on a large vertical painting leaning against the gallery facade. Placing little dots across the surface, he diligently worked with different brushes in his hand, water buckets and other things on the sidewalk all around him. A light might have been propped up as well. I sat transfixed, watching something wonderful come into being. It is simply not possible not to count him among the greatest artists alive.

(2014)

Is There Great Art on Instagram?

For me, Instagram is a land of the midnight sun, a wide-open place that's always lit up, bristling with visions, pictures, strangers, shooting stars, screwballs, and well-known artists posting images from everywhere, together creating an immense, abstract collective missive, an amazing rebus that seems to speak just to me, the curious curator of my own lit-up Instagramland. Strangest in this strange land is the fact that hundreds of thousands of people now follow *me*. Or, at least, their *idea* of me: *New York* magazine's art critic, acting out in pictures online.

On Instagram, I'm searching. But for what? Pictures. My first, best, last, maybe only real language. I love to look. At anything. Anytime. Especially in this still moderately unplumbed space—in terms of openness and weirdness, far beyond the tightening conservatism of Facebook and the whip-fast witticisms of Twitter. To be sure, Instagram is a sort of prescreened "community," where standards of taste and obscenity are strictly enforced, or self-enforced by users intuiting and seeing the unseen, omnipresent censor-world. It only barely echoes the Wild West of the very early days of social media. But patrolled and not, there is more wildness there than elsewhere on the web—or off it. I'm writing this now because I've just come across an artist whose work justifies this interest, gives just a tantalizing taste of all that promise and all the other unknowns who must be out there. But more about that later. First, back to Instagram itself.

Why else do I obsess over Instagram? Passive voyeurism, of course. All these pictures are authored, but I know only a tiny handful of the authors, so there's that mystery and titillation. So these pictures seem to come from nowhere—or, that is, from *other* places, allowing glimpses into other people's lives. I do have some specific tastes: I don't like kids, but pictures of them are okay. I'm not much for dogs or cats. (Although artist Andrew Kuo's cat and dog pics are all hysterically funny and hysterically cute.)

What I do love are the many adults who have an unexplained need to dance naked—not *in public*, the way all artists do, but on social media. How their almost and totally naked pictures don't get censored by Instagram, when I've had pictures of a cow sniffing a man's ass get deleted and a seventeenth-century French painting axed thanks to one dark wisp of pubic hair, is beyond me. Maybe they have some magic body-power that makes them pictorially invulnerable to censors and the censorious.

But what I think I'm really looking for is what I'm always looking for, what I went looking for once upon a time on Facebook and on Twitter: unknown art. Artists who are on social media or Instagram but who haven't shown in so-called real galleries in New York, Los Angeles, Berlin, or London. Artists who don't have reputations, aren't in biennials, aren't collected or celebrated in any way, and yet are really good. Maybe great. Why? I love galleries, but often it seems as if the system that's in place precludes flukes, unexpected twists of artistic fate, things that might not otherwise make it past the waves of gatekeepers. *The New York Times* has reported that the Irish artist Genieve Figgis and Bp Laval, a Canadian artist, were discovered by Richard Prince on Instagram. Figgis has since shown at Half Gallery in New York and had a book of her work published. Raymond Pettibon supposedly found the work of Andrew Pope on Instagram.

I love the idea of finding something that I might not have found otherwise. So I follow one unknown name to another who has liked something on another unknown person's account, who has then liked something on another person's feed, and so on. Linking. Looking. And looking some more. And I have found plenty. I've looked for the many who are much better photographers than they think they might be, and have already come across great "outsider photographers" who are less predictable than many professionals, generating newish ideas about color, composition, subject matter, and cropping. I hope pictures like this might gain greater entrance into popular publications and art galleries. Soon.

But it's not photography I'm looking for, or only pictures of strange things, odd places, visual puns, or formal photographic sensibilities. I want to find something else, before this platform becomes dated and fades into disuse. In this odd golden moment of in-between life, I am looking for art by someone who identifies as an artist and calls what they make "art." Not a hobby or a sideline activity. There's already so much clever visual neo-conceptualism wherever you look, from galleries and museums to print and television ads; that's not what I'm after, either. What I'm really looking for is painting or sculpture—work that might simply work in a gallery as is, without explanation, backstory, or tale. I've been doing this, daily, for almost as long as I've been on Instagram, which is only a couple of years. (I'm nothing if not a *late adapter.*) Hoping to discover a new artist—not necessarily a "great artist," but art I can get excited about, someone who seems to have come up through Instagram, for whom it was a medium as much as a platform.

Four months ago, I stumbled on something. An artist whose name I still don't know, but whose work has a real lusciousness to it, a vision, a fecund sense of color and line, internal scale, odd order, and saucy subject matter. The artist's Instagram name is Alphachanneling. Thinking the artist was a woman, I wrote to her. It turns out he's a man, living near San Francisco. (I should have known just from the New Age side of his work that it was generated in the Bay Area.) At one point the artist told me his name but I lost it in a chain of emails, which seems fine. This fits the profile of what I was looking for: Just as I like to go into galleries *not knowing* about the art, not depending on some carefully packaged explanation, I like that I have only my eye to rely on with Alphachanneling. (Before anyone sniffs about an art critic liking something he's never actually set eyes on, I can only say that I *love* a lot of art I've never seen in the flesh— everything from the Ghent Altarpiece to the Lascaux cave in southwestern France, as well as almost everything I've never seen but that rocks my world from India and Korea. Moreover, in some ways, this art exists *only* on Instagram for me; this *is* its primary format.)

After lurking on his feed, I messaged Alphachanneling to ask him for a very short statement about his work. What I got back fits the work to a tee: "Alphachanneling is a Swiss-born American artist based out of Oakland, California." (I love how he refers to himself in the third person!) "My artwork is a devotional prayer to the feminine principal." (I knew it! The worship of female power, the female body, and pleasure. Not a perv, but someone obsessed with the *idea of something*. Someone inexplicably driven to make a visual philosophy.) "Central to my process is . . . channeling, an ongoing cultivation through a deep relationship I have with several master-teachers." (Makes me wish more in the art world talked about "channeling master-teachers" instead of nattering on about their goddamn "practice" like they're doctors.) "The images I produce are simple thought-waves. . . . I look toward Taoism and tantra, pornography and folk art, BDSM and the divine, the mystical and the occult, indigenous and outsider art alike. . . . Alphachanneling lives in a boundless world called the Utopian Erotic, a world of magical pussy, radiant women, bedroom jungles and temples of light."

Now I'll go art critic on Alphachanneling's ass. All of Alphachanneling's art is erotic without coming off as blatantly gratuitous bad-boy, cartoony, big-tits/big-dick sexism, although he can get close to this occasionally. (A few slap-happy images are just happy buxom voluptuaries.) One image, titled *The Source*, a depiction of a man sniffing or eating a large, lotus-like red flower, apes the vibrant pinks, yellows, and greens of tantric art. In *Surrender*, three different figures are shown in decorative patterned fields. One personage is surrounded by birds and with what looks like a mystic crystal mushrooming from its breasts; another, with a rainbow-colored flower growing from its groin. This work echoes Chris Ofili's later-period black palette and patterning. There's an outsiderish Henri Rousseau quality to some of his careful rendering and large, leafy jungle settings, as if these figures inhabited some netherworld Garden of Earthly Delights. And contemporary artists like Ella Kruglyanskaya, Amy Bessone, and Nadine Faraj come to mind. In one beauty, a male's head seems to beam rays into a vibrating vulva. Or it's a kind of vulva mind-meld on the man's head. A companion drawing finds a woman doing the same thing, or having the same thing done by an erect penis, which she clasps happily with both hands. Either way, these drawings have a delightful Sigmar Polke easiness of line and simplicity of funny form and dicey subject matter. Alphachanneling echoes a couple of my favorite artists, including Ernst Ludwig Kirchner and some of his fellow German Expressionists. In a number of lovely embroiderylike fields and concentric lines depicting coitus, cunnilingus, and coupling in all forms, with any number of people, and mixed races, with flowers standing in for genitals, I am reminded of excellent outsiders like Minnie Evans and Friedrich Schröder-Sonnenstern. In *Love Science, Harmonic Awakening of the Living Temple*, and other wonders, we get great X-ray visions of penetration in rainbow colors.

Someday I'd like to see Alphachanneling's art in the flesh, to size up its scale, touch, and presence. Maybe some art dealer will give this work a shot. Maybe not. Maybe seeing it on Instagram is enough.

(2014)

Iconoclasm Now: *Charlie Hebdo* and the Lethal Power of Art

The world looked on in revulsion as terrorists yelling, "We have avenged the Prophet Muhammad! Allahu akbar!" killed people for making and publishing drawings of the prophet of Islam. Not to oversimplify ideological fanaticism—and not even addressing how smug, snotty, and obnoxious the cartoons actually are (had a magazine regularly published racist or anti-Semitic artwork in America, all sorts of hell would have been raised; guns, of course, eliminate all nuance)—but it's worth underscoring that this non-random, planned act of violence was carried out *because of a drawing.*

Killing over an image is as primitively rooted and as complex as the impulse to kill any who believe in one real or fictional god and not another. All four great monotheistic religions—Judaism, Christianity, Islam, and Zoroastrianism—are based on the Old Testament. About the making of images, the Second Commandment states, "Thou shalt not make unto thee any graven image . . . for I the Lord thy God am a jealous God." This is saying two things. First, that God permits abstraction and unhewn stone (Neolithic circles and the like) but prohibits the creation of *realistic images.* "Cursed be the man that maketh any graven or molten image." Second, that this God *knows there are other gods* out there—be it in Greece, Rome, Egypt, around the Tigris and Euphrates, over the steppe, in northern and sub-Saharan Africa, around the Mediterranean, in the Indian subcontinent and the Far East. The Koran contains this imperious prohibition against images, as well.

Several parts of the Bible reinforce this injunction against realism. Deuteronomy states that "the work of the hands of the craftsman is an abomination unto the Lord." In a hadith, the Prophet Muhammad says, "The angels will not enter a home where there is an image." A companion of the

Prophet, Abdullah ibn Mas'ood, says, "I heard the Prophet (peace and blessings of Allah be upon him) say: 'The people who will be most severely punished on the Day of Resurrection will be the image-makers.'" Interestingly, ninth-century Islamic commentator Al-Azraqi says that on returning to Mecca, the Prophet found the Kaaba covered with paintings. He had all the paintings destroyed, except for one depicting Mary and Jesus.

Over the millennia, the Second Commandment has led to incredible carnage. The Bible says, "Ye shall destroy their altars, break their images." These "image breakers," known as "iconoclasts," killed people and destroyed countless works of art and architecture. Iconoclasts believe that images are not *abstract representations of things* but *the thing itself*, and that, as made not by God, they contain demonic spirits. The horrific paradox then is that these killers believe in the power and divinity of images, art, and architecture *more* than those who make the objects and who see their work as abstract *representations* of ideas and things. A double paradox arises when the iconoclast kills because of an image he or she is eliminating, and— negating the judgment and vengeance of God—taking matters into his or her hands. And the matter becomes even more complicated for nonbelievers like me, who believe that the gods that iconoclasts are killing for are actually superb works of fiction, written so beautifully and compellingly that the protagonists of the stories have come to be worshipped as gods.

The destruction of objects has taken many forms—including razing entire libraries, temples, churches, and mosques—but often includes scratching out eyes or drawing a line across a figure's neck to behead it. Sculptures have their faces or heads smashed, their eyes gouged out. The faces of paintings are removed and burned. Far more art has been destroyed in the name of these four religions than has survived. Looked at through this lens, it's a wonder that any religious art survives at all.

The killers in Paris believed that the drawing was not a drawing but an incarnation of God, an invisible essence made flesh, an object wherein there was no distance between image and God. Whatever they believed, they took this belief to the extent of psychopathy.

(2014)

The Most Powerful Artwork I Have Ever Seen

I have places inside me where there are works of art: internal abysms that feel full, physical, like forces that fuse past and present. In the early 2000s, I spent four straight days in the Prado; all of it's still within me, like some huge, Proustian madeleine. Almost every Bosch, Cézanne, Matisse, Alice Neel, Bill Traylor, Martín Ramírez, and Marsden Hartley that I've ever seen can flash across my mind's eye like lightning. I spent a day enraptured by Matthias Grünewald's Isenheim Altarpiece in Colmar. (I still wonder if I became invisible that day; the guards silently allowed me to remain in the museum even when it closed for its two-hour lunch.) I have a psychic zero point for all the Seurat drawings I've ever seen. And at the center of this point is the small Giovanni di Paolo in Chicago that I saw when I was ten years old, which set me on the course of my life.

These and my other inner alpha points are in me always, churning. What I gleaned from them recalibrated almost everything I knew about art. Even though this internal lightning is always with me, it went bioluminescent a few months ago, when it was announced that paintings found on the island of Sulawesi in Indonesia were estimated to have been made 40,000 years ago. That's 10,000 years older than the Chauvet cave paintings, the oldest cave paintings in Europe. Not long before that came reports of decorative beads and mixed pigments dating back more than 75,000 years. Not to mention the deliberate, delicate symmetries in newly discovered stone axes made 100,000 years ago by an entirely different and extinct species: Neanderthals. (There's evidence that Neanderthals also built and sailed watercraft; there are Neanderthal stone cleavers that date back 170,000 years.)

How could I not use these revelations to revisit my own come-to-cave-art moment?

In 2008, Roberta and I spent a week driving through the stunning

Spanish Pyrenees looking at small Romanesque churches, often alone, with no tourists around. I knew there were Paleolithic caves nearby in France, so before we left New York, I booked a time slot for a group tour inside the Niaux cave. We crossed the Pyrenees, and after being horrified by the hordes of European shoppers who come daily to Andorra for tax-free goods, we passed into a chasm that became a deep mountain gorge. The Niaux cave is located at the southern mouth of this valley. Even 13,000 years ago, this would have been a natural gathering place: a valley with a constant source of fresh water, an abundance of raw materials, fish, game, a perch from which to observe herds and watch for invaders, and a view to die for.

We parked in a large lot. Soon, about fifteen of us met in a predesignated spot near the entrance to the cave. We were greeted by our guide, a twentysomething art historian from Paris. She handed each of us a small flashlight and explained that these would be the only source of light on our trip inside the cave, and that we were to stick together, walking single file, until we got to "the gallery."

Ducking low through a small opening in the stone, we passed into darkness. The cave's original, much-larger entrance had been elsewhere, but it had collapsed millennia ago, sometime after the last ice age. Presumably, these caves were originally not entirely dark, as light was able to flood in through even the small gap that allowed us entry, which is thought to have opened sometime around 1600. As Roberta and I stuck close to the guide, I felt something was happening to me. I loved being in this subterranean world, feeling the atmospheric pressures change, noting the sounds of the world fading, new humidities, air currents and sounds appearing, seeing walls undulate. I felt grateful to be here, and to be very close to my wife and to our guide. I wasn't afraid to be in this alien world, but I was aware that something alien inside me was awakening; my senses were sharpening in strange ways.

After walking for a while, feeling my interior world intensify, we stopped. "Please gather around me," the guide instructed us. "We are about to enter the gallery. Stick together. Do not touch anything or leave the path. Please hand me all of your flashlights. I will have the only light in the gallery." Like children, my wife and I huddled on either side of the guide, walking another two hundred feet in total silence, until we came to a large, irregularly shaped cavern. I can still feel the cool currents on my face. We were in what's known as the "salon noir." Everything remained silent; our guide pointed her light to the ground so our eyes could adjust to the darkness. After a moment, she wordlessly shone the beam upward. A never-ending clap of thunder sounded inside me; one reality was replaced by another. I will try to recount what I saw next and what it made me think.

We were in an amphitheater with images all around us. Of individual animals and groups of animals. Bison, horses, reindeer, boars, ibex, and other mammals I can't identify. Stunned, ecstatic, I felt like I was on the verge of blacking out. Some of the animals were walking; others ran or galloped. Every gait was distinct. Some of these animals seemed to hunt, others were hunted. I think I saw a salmon with a perfectly defined dorsal fin; nearby, something that may have been a pig, drawn vertically because the wall formation suggested it. I perceived a grouping of animals gathering to drink, rest, eat, play. Every image felt palpable, somatic, sensually rendered, real.

Art history teaches us that the principle of perspective was invented in Florence in 1414. Here, that notion collapsed in an instant. On the walls at Niaux, larger mammals are pictured in front of smaller ones who trail behind; animals at the back of packs are smaller than those in front. But there are also examples of what's called *reverse perspective*, the sort of system used in China, where closer things are rendered smaller than farther things. One drawing depicts an ibex, as seen from behind and over the shoulder—an incredibly sophisticated perspective. Another subject, a horse, is seen from a highly accomplished three-quarters view. The artists seemed able to adjust their work to account for curvatures and protrusions in the walls, in the same ways that the painters of Renaissance frescoes adjusted for distortion, distance, and odd viewing angles. I saw a bison with one horn curving up, the other curving down—an accident of birth or battle, but whatever its cause, the artist had *seen* the anomaly and rendered it intentionally. A reindeer evinced shaggy pelage on antlers. Males appeared to sniff females for signs of estrus; others tilted horns, stomped the ground, charged forward, or assumed postures of sexual submission. In one gripping image, I thought I saw a wolf jumping up and bringing down a horse by the neck—the horse's tail is raised in the exact way horses hold their tails when alarmed. Nearby, a bison has three spears in its side. Regardless of whether this and other images depicted hunts, or were instructions for how to approach and bring down bison, these painters loved depicting action, movement, gestures, things happening at very particular times. Nothing seemed only imagined; everything felt observed, studied, thought about, recorded. The psycho-visual acuity of these artists, their understanding of the empirical science of animal behavior—the mind boggled.

Equally notable was their desire for color, which they derived from roots, berries, bark, minerals, clay, red and yellow ocher, and minerals like hematite and manganese oxide, mixing them with water, sap, soot, blood, and viscera. Moreover, these substances had to be gathered and transported; every color evinces the artists' desire to render something more than just graphic outlines. Yet their lines are long, confident, fluid, and drawn from the sort of charcoal sticks you'd find in any fire. The shading I saw on the rear hoof and fetlock of a bison, the first thing that I set eyes on when our guide shone her light in the gallery, never leaves me. It is the punctum—the flash point—of the cave for me. As are long, wavy red strokes that looked familiar. After I got home, during a studio visit, I suddenly remembered where I'd seen those cave lines before: on studio walls, made by artists dragging their paint-covered brushes, fingers, or sticks along the surface to empty their brushes of pigment, test colors, or just make marks.

For me, all this gave the lie to our long-held, egocentric idea that cave paintings were the mystic machinations of master shamans portraying some primitive spirit or dream world. Instead, I saw an astonishing artistic naturalism, a stylized realism that accounted for every individual body part, action, dorsal line, and body language, down to what season or even time of day these images were made (bison chewing their cuds at midday, for instance). When it comes to the best of these paintings, I'd venture that mammals have never been rendered better in the history of our species. These are paintings by a people who watched these animals for more than 30,000 years—far longer than *all* of recorded history combined. I was seeing visual wisdom, the hard work of looking and taking the time and trouble to make exact renditions of what they had seen. Looking at these images, I felt as though I were somehow remembering things that none of us knows anymore but that, as a species, we still know in our bones. I felt the narcotic power of this naturalism, of what Norman Bryson has called "the metaphysics of presence." I gleaned the carnal pleasures of painting textures, surfaces, and fur in variable viscosities; the vision of a world unfolding yet held in exactly these moments, and not framed by drawn lines but within geology. I felt a nobility of subject matter and process.

These astounding levels of visual intelligence tell me that, had these people wanted to make only symbolic images of their mysticism and magic, they could have done just that. One author of a typically romantic book on cave paintings plaintively writes, "We do not know what the images meant to those who made and viewed them." The clap of thunder that sounded for me in the caves was that the world outside and around these people was the same as the world that was inside them. Among the chief subjects of these paintings is the inscribing body of the painters, and the pleasures taken in making these paintings. To turn this gigantic worldview into an either/or proposition—into demeaning all this as merely hunting magic and dream worlds, on the one hand, or going just as far in the other direction, lauding everything here as the masterpieces of a mysterious people, feels false, limiting—another instance of romanticizing the world in one easy way or another.

It's estimated that about 99.9995 percent of *all* Paleolithic art is lost to time. My sparse research suggests that we've discovered about four hundred painted cave sites, and almost that many open-air sites with art. There's evidence our ancestors didn't just *paint rocks*, that they drew in vertical riverbanks, in soft mud, sand, slurries of calcite that coat limestone surfaces; that they engaged in woodworking, body decoration, bark painting, the making of clothing, skin sewing, stone carving, firing clay, carving bone, and the like.

I conjecture that art in caves was, by far, the exception rather than the rule. The very fact that caves were commonly inhabited by enormous cave bears, now extinct, would have made cave-dwelling incredibly risky, if not suicidal. The preservation of cave paintings occurs only under incredibly narrow and lucky circumstances: There must be a very small temperature range (a steady 53.6 degrees Fahrenheit) with no freezing or thawing in 30,000 years, no wind bombardment, plant growth, water inundation, erosion, earthquakes, solar rays, or any such natural disruption. Or human disruption, for that matter: The first person who stumbled on the Niaux cave, in 1600, instantly inscribed his name and the date next to an ibex.

The examples of animal portraiture I saw at Niaux are masterpieces, among the greatest paintings I've ever viewed. However, I also saw images that were crude, clownish, the scrawls of kids, and maybe even doodles. Good and bad alike, they all evinced things we can instantly relate to as zoological, psychological, frightening, funny, or just fun. I didn't notice any of the famous handprints some cave artists made by spitting colored pulp around one's hand. Recent computer studies of these handprints, however, suggest that about half of them are women's. (Bye-bye, male-artist myth.) I saw some of the dotting and dashes that many conjecture are celestial observations or calendar notations, but none of the many vulvas and phalluses found at other sites—the kinds of things kids were drawing then, as kids have always drawn when left alone. Either way, this is by and large the art of a young people, as life expectancy is thought to have been thirty-five years for men and thirty for women.

Still, my romantic self ached for what's not here. There are no images of war. Perhaps it didn't exist yet, or nomadic groups of fifty to one hundred people had no need for war. Given how much these artists loved depicting action, I think they'd have rendered war if it had existed. There are no dogs, because dogs didn't exist yet. But why no pictures of the sun or moon, mountains, trees, or fire? Or tools? Why no fruit, insects, lakes, or rivers? No snow or rain? Other cave sites (though not Niaux) include depictions of sex, but, alas, no human portraiture. *These* are the proclaiming shadows cast by cave art for me.

In Niaux, art grew much bigger for me. The work I saw there became a flying buttress for all the art that would follow, maybe for much that is human. I don't want to sound like an insane art-critic Werner Herzog rhapsodizing about "albino crocodiles" outside the Chauvet cave. All I know is that something seismic hit me at Niaux, some capacious cognizance, cryptic, wakeful. Whatever it was, a new type of human existence entered my consciousness—one that I now recognize as both collective and my own.

(2014)

I Got Kicked off Facebook
for Posting Images of Medieval Art

On Tuesday morning, I tried to log into Facebook via my iPhone. It didn't work. I didn't think anything of it, as I often don't remember my passwords. When I tried again on my laptop, however, I wasn't able to log in either. Instead I got a note saying that, after complaints regarding particular posts, Facebook had decided that I'd violated their "community standards" and was banned from the platform. I don't know how to do screengrabs, so I clicked "I agree." With that, the notice disappeared; now I was able to see my Facebook page again, but I was no longer able to use it. That was that.

My first thought: *Here we go again.* Last December, Instagram had shut down my account after I posted a picture of Charles Ray's great sculptural masterpiece of four nude figures holding hands, *American Romance.*

Instagram reinstated me within three hours, claiming that an errant algorithm had made a mistake. This time, I hadn't run afoul of the Facebook algorithms that evidently scan for nude photographs, pornography, hate speech, civil rights violations, and so on. Instead, it was my "friends" who'd driven me out of town. Apparently, over a period of months, I'd run afoul of a bunch of art world objectors, whose names I recognize from social media—people checking my posts—who objected not to any nude photos, but to my many posts of ancient Roman and Greek art and medieval illuminated manuscripts. Most of these posts sprang from my recent interest in art historical material that has come to light online as a result of the increased availability of high-definition digital photography—much of it art from what we roughly consider the Dark Ages and the medieval era. I loved the idea of communicating through these pictures; though I often attached idiotic jokes to these lost images, I genuinely wanted people to see them. To me they reflect a kind of internal shared consciousness that feels relevant again in this time of ending American empire, and they've sort of taken over my life on social media—though in a way I hadn't exactly planned.

These pictures are powerful. Many were made in the tumultuous period in the West between the collapse of the Roman Empire and the hegemony of Christianity. They can be hard to take. They depict body parts, defecation, plague, death, boils, brutality, emaciation, torture, severe tooth decay, horrific attempts at surgical remedies. Most of all, these pictures portray demons—thousands of them, besetting humanity at every turn, in every color, plumage, and guise, from snakes, birds, pigs, and frogs to flowers and roots to dragons and devils. I love everything about them: the color, scale, subject matter, mythos, even the pain they capture. These were people trying to live by Christ's "Love thy neighbor as thyself." The images, from these stormy centuries more than a thousand years before Freud, remind us that self-hatred is a core part of the human condition.

I first got on Facebook in 2008 when a student created a page for me. I had no idea how it worked or what I'd do with it. After a few months of posting about the weather and what I was wearing, I wrote a few lines explaining why I didn't like the paintings of Marlene Dumas. It was like a bomb went off. Out of nowhere, scores then hundreds of people flooded onto my page to tell me in no uncertain terms why I was wrong. Other than a little bit of *ouch*, in an instant I had a digital epiphany: Facebook might make it possible to invert a model of art criticism. Rather than speaking from on high, from the top of the pyramid to the many, Facebook might make it possible for us all to speak to one another, coherently. I tried. It worked. Like wildfire. And I kept doing it. Trying everything I could think of, following my fancy.

To me, social media seemed to imply a great leap in art criticism, a way to get through a period when print is waning and we're finding our new ways forward. And there's no money to it, so there's nothing to lose and everything to gain. It felt borderless, like the Wild West. I thought I was experimenting with art criticism, although in truth I was never really in control of the experiment; it was in control of me. And it had only very little to do with art or criticism, and much more to do with communication and self-expression.

Online, the boundaries between high and low seemed finally to slip away. Doing criticism in public, live in real time, was thrilling; it satisfied my need to try new things, to reach a much, much wider audience, to be a ham, to alleviate the long terrible hours of aloneness that all writers and artists know well—all the while exercising my own demons and dancing naked in public. First Facebook, then Twitter, then Instagram all changed the way I see criticism and the art world. Social media makes our world much bigger, more participatory, and even possibly more horizontal. It makes me think hierarchies can be flattened, that there are many ways to form communities, even for those of us who don't only want to speak art world to art world, who write for glossy general-interest magazines, who have no degrees, who leave our house only to do our jobs. It offered a voice to the housebound. And it was fun. Being online offers the constant opportunity to take micro-breaks between writing paragraphs to mix it up about art with real artists in real time. I loved that criticism could be practiced in public and not mainly in specialist journals or in classrooms. I'd like to think that on these platforms a sort of accidental criticism happened. And is happening still. And will again.

But what happened this past week made those possibilities seem foreclosed (even if I was relieved, for a bit, to be relieved of my account). Letters to Facebook objected to the centuries-old images I posted as "sexist," "misogynist," and "abusive to women." I was accused of being all these things, too. Soon I was being called "a confirmed sexist." This from people who sought out and read my Facebook page voluntarily, many of them regularly, but then used their energy to criticize how I'm trying to use mine. This seems perverse to me. Especially when we remember that we're all just a few clicks away from pages devoted to white-supremacy groups, guns for children, sex trafficking, the Westboro Baptist Church, and much more. Facebook complainers objecting to medieval illuminated manuscripts clearly have too much time on their hands—and some misplaced illusions about whatever authority critics are supposed to have.

(2015)

The *New* New Museum: The Whitney and the Impossible Problem of Contemporary Art

I. THE MUSEUM AS FAIRY TALE

I've spent much of my life in and in love with museums. When I was ten years old, there was no mention of art in my home. But then one day my mother drove me from the suburbs to the Art Institute of Chicago. There, she looked at art on her own for hours, leaving me to do the same. At the time, I liked being alone, but I hated museums. To me they seemed old and dead, places where people just stood and stared.

By the time I was in my twenties—with no art in my background, just inchoate need—I had gathered together a general idea of what a museum was supposed to be: a place where old art is stored, preserved, and celebrated, if sometimes only dutifully. I also knew that museums could be problematic, that they made imperious judgments, that they excluded whole vital populations. Of course they did: Museums were invented as royal showrooms, triumphal demonstrations of the power of some very brutal states (Napoleon's France, colonialist Britain) to gather up the cultural patrimony of the wider world. When museums first truly came to the United States, it was as part of an American effort to claim a seat at the table of Western civilization by brandishing collections of antiquities and masterpieces. Later, with MoMA especially, the museum itself would become an arm of aggressive cultural diplomacy, promoting Abstract Expressionism as a campaign of the Cold War. So I knew early on that museums were not fairy-tale places: that the practice of enclosing and curating a history of art within marble walls enclosed prejudice and even bloodlust, too. But I also knew that those buildings enclosed touchstones, benchmarks, cultural skeleton keys, divinations, extraordinary probings of the human imagination, and masterpieces like that Saint John the Baptist cycle by Giovanni di Paolo that had floored me in Chicago. I knew, in fact, that they contained something ecstatic and represented something eternal.

Maybe it's naive and romantic, but, beyond the implications of colonialism, princely privilege, the enforcement of taste, and worse, I do still see the museum's Platonic ideal: a centuries-long group effort to preserve, interpret, and commune with artistic ancestors, archetypes, traditions, genres, and methods. Sumerian kings collected antiquities (one scholar has interpreted a tablet from the second millennium BCE as a "museum label"). The practice of collecting and displaying precious objects surfaced in China 3,500 years ago. In the fifth century BCE, the Greeks created a *pinakotheke* to honor the gods. Museums have been with us as long as memory has been with us—"quiet cars," in the words of the *New York Times* critic Holland Cotter, where the act of looking becomes a way of knowing the world and ourselves. And where the past is always alive, sometimes even more vividly than the contemporary moment, the two coalesce into the out-of-body grace of eternal presentness.

II. BRAVE NEW WORLD

But museums have changed—a lot. Slowly over the past quarter century, then quickly in the past decade. The changes have been complicated, piecemeal, and sometimes contradictory, with different museums embracing them in different ways. But the transformation is visible everywhere. Put simply, it is this: The museum used to be a storehouse for the art of the past, the display of supposed masterpieces, the insightful exploration of the present in the context of the long or compressed histories that preceded it. Today, the modern museum—especially as embodied by the Tate Modern, Guggenheim Bilbao, and our beloved MoMA—is a revved-up showcase of the new, the now, the next, an always-activated market of events and experiences, many of which exist purely to occupy the museum industry—an industry that the critic Matthew Collings has called "bloated and foolish, corporatist, ghastly and death-ridden." Whatever long-view curating and collecting museums do now—and many of them still do it well—the institutions that are sucking up the most energy are the ones that have made themselves platforms for spectacle.

With this new model taking over, the museums of New York can already feel alien. And we're really at the beginning rather than the end of the transformation. All four of Manhattan's big museums—the Met, MoMA, the Whitney, and the Guggenheim—are all involved in massive expansion, renovation, and rebuilding. These are more than just infrastructure updates: We are witnessing a four-way battle for supremacy in the new art-museum universe. What makes this all so startling is that these museums have never been all-out competitors before. Until now, they had distinct missions, collections, and curatorial identities: The Met specialized in breadth, embracing five thousand years of art; the Whitney was devoted to American art; MoMA was Modernism's Francophile Garden of Eden; and the Guggenheim—well, the Guggenheim has always been a bit confused, distinguished mostly by its incredible building. But now, all of a sudden and for the first time, it is not unusual for curators to speak of being unable to mount a show because the artist they have in mind is "already taken."

Each of these museums still preserves, collects, and exhibits the art of the past. But with all the action, and the big money, centered on contemporary art, galleries, auctions, art fairs, and biennials, each is more committed than ever to the cult of the new. Every curator, artist, gallerist, and collector I've discussed this with acknowledges the ongoing shift. "The problem is museums trying to be as up-to-date with contemporary art as galleries are," says the painter and critic Peter Plagens. "The cultural distance between what a museum preserves (Cézanne, Joan Mitchell, etc.) and how it spotlights the present (Björk, interactive art, etc.) is greater than ever." Of course, he acknowledges, "museums will survive. But in what form?"

III. THE WHITNEY REBORN

The new Whitney, opening May 1, 2015, and designed by Renzo Piano, is the first totally new museum to be unveiled in this era. It's an angular, asymmetrical, ship-shaped building at the base of the High Line, deep in tourist country and adjacent to the heart of the art market beast: Chelsea, the bluest-chip gallery district in the world. The move marks the first time one of the four major Manhattan museums has abandoned its flagship for another neighborhood since 1966, when the Whitney moved into the Breuer building from West Fifty-Fourth Street. The move downtown is significant, returning the museum to its roots in a place of bohemian tribal identity, even if the downtown it's returning to has been built by developers for the very rich—and the Whitney's very presence will help make the area even tonier than the Upper East Side.

The audacity of the building leaves no doubt that the Whitney will survive the new era. The better question is whether it has found a way to thrive in it. And, believe it or not, so far I am in love with what this building represents—including its perfectly titled inaugural show, *America Is Hard to See*. The show includes six hundred works by around four hundred artists, drawn entirely from the museum's collection of more than twenty-one thousand works by three thousand artists, and it makes me think this museum might just point to one way through the current morass.

Why? Let's start with the building. From the outside it looks like a hospital or a pharmaceutical company, but I don't care what it looks like; as an art lover, I'm concerned only with the inside of museums. For me, the genericism of the building suggests that what matters to the Whitney isn't the vanity or grandeur of so-called destination architecture—it's what goes on under its auspices.

So what is inside? First, space. By today's bombastic standards, the new Whitney is modest. The place could become overcrowded overnight. Yet there's lots and lots more space than the museum has ever had before, and more of it will be devoted to showcasing the museum's permanent collection, which is crucial. Until now, the Whitney has had only meager galleries for its permanent collection—about 7,725 of the old museum's roughly 32,000 square feet of exhibition space. The Piano building has about 50,000 square feet of indoor exhibition space (plus 13,000 outside), of which 20,500 over two floors is devoted to the permanent collection. The space in the new building is open, simple, Shaker-like; the wide-plank pine floors are perfect. This means the Whitney has devoted $422 million, at least in part, to doing something the other three big Manhattan museums haven't: to make a lot more and a lot better space for older art *and* a lot more, better space for newer art.

Second, a team of curators with the wisdom to resist contemporary mania—to make use of new energy without pandering or prostrating themselves. These days, the museum and its staff are the objects of much affection and admiration in the art world—and while goodwill might seem like an intangible asset to praise in a museum, it does reflect something, namely that artists have faith in these people and this institution. Much of the guarded optimism around the new building has to do with the museum's director, Adam Weinberg, an old-school true believer in art and artists. Weinberg and his team are also operating under unusual terms, thanks to the mission of the museum, which is the third reason the Whitney seems so well suited to the new era. As the museum's chief curator and deputy director, Donna De Salvo, said, "The Whitney is not a building. It's an idea," and that idea is actually a question: "What is American art?" Founded in 1930 to collect, explore, explain, and interrogate American art, the Whitney has always had a fluid sense of its own mission. But its curators have also brilliantly reimagined their mission for our new crazy era—an era defined not just by commerce but also by globalization and encyclopedic knowledge, an art world full of people who can access every iota of art history online but who are guided far less by the narrow old art historical teleology than by their own access to a bottomless, almost ahistorical well of source material.

The Whitney knows how to consider new work alongside old, how to throw together pieces produced in entirely different contexts and watch the sparks fly. Freed from the need to consign works forever to, say, a room dedicated to Ashcan School painting or Pop, curators are free to hang a single painting in multiple shows over decades, alongside different paintings from different decades each time, each time prompting a different reckoning with the work. The first show demonstrates these advantages quite powerfully. More than a quarter of the works on display have not been seen in decades; many have never been shown at all. The effect is to recast ideas about American art history by bringing new work into the fold without surrendering the tradition to people born since 1975. The show treats those artists and their work as part of a running conversation, one designed to provoke constant reevaluation. Over and over, artists whose work I thought I knew looked brand-new and suddenly relevant; second-stringers stepped forcefully to the fore, more prescient and pertinent than they've ever seemed. Revelations like this are one very vital way to lever-age the fresh energy of contemporary art into new insights about the past, without entirely handing over the keys to the museum to the galleries up Tenth Avenue.

Thankfully, the museum is already endowed with a permanent collec-tion perfectly suited to this project, which is the fourth reason I think the Whitney is in such good shape. Skeptics have long pooh-poohed the Whit-ney's holdings, but I think that not only is the collection singular but also we've never really seen it before. It's a marvel to see Allan D'Arcangelo's *Madonna and Child*, an empty-faced image evoking Jackie Kennedy, and Malcolm Bailey's hand-painted 1969 depiction of a slave ship take their places on a wall of Pop masterpieces by Warhol, Johns, and others. En-countering Alma Thomas's brightly colored part-by-part painting *Mars Dust* (1972) in the Whitney (even as one of her works hangs in the Obama White House) only makes you realize how much optical DNA still lies buried in this supposedly lesser collection.

The large, striking 1932 painting of boat parts by I. Rice Pereira gives us almost Guston-like levels of gaga gnarliness. And the salon-style wall depicting America in convulsion in the 1930s will stop you in your tracks. One floor down, along with a 1935 painting by Alice Neel of coal and steel strikes, there's Harry Sternberg's 1935 satanic lithograph *Southern Holiday*. Sternberg's work portrays the hell on earth suffered by twenty-three-year-old Claude Neal, who was accused of raping a white woman in Florida. Neal's lynching was advertised in newspapers; vigilantes kidnapped him from jail, tied him to a post, cut off his fingers and toes, castrated him, and forced him to eat his penis. His broken body was then dragged behind a car and delivered to the home of the alleged victim. America *is* hard to see.

(2015)

Does the New Whitney Show That Modernism Never Really Happened in America?

I n 2015, David Wallace-Wells, my longtime editor at New York *magazine—the best editor I ever had, now known as the author of the* New York Times *bestseller* The Uninhabitable Earth—*interviewed me about the new Whitney and the artists in its collection. David has recently moved on to write for* The New York Times; *I miss him every day.*

David Wallace-Wells: I wanted to ask you about a couple of artists from [the mid-twentieth century] who aren't being rediscovered now, who've been with us in very big ways all along: Edward Hopper and Georgia O'Keeffe. Hopper especially is the sort of spiritual center of the Whitney, and always has been. O'Keeffe is less central to their collection, but is probably the most recognizable (and surely the most posterized) painter of those decades. How do they fit into this story?

Jerry Saltz: Many outside America still pooh-pooh them as either just-fine but not modern, or as merely illustrators. In fact, both were more modern than people know, and as original in their ways as any Suprematist, Surrealist, or mad Dada anarchist. Hopper is the Leonard Cohen, Roy Orbison, and Bruce Springsteen of painting, an only-the-lonely artist of ordinary life. His modernity is in the radical ways he redefined the conventions of good painting, Modernist and traditional alike. He brought ideas of illustration to art, roughing up traditional painting while smoothing out Modernism's stuttering touch, turning his blocky composition into his own narrative versions of Mondrian and Malevich. At the Whitney, his image of an empty storefront at seven a.m. at the end of a town street on the edge of the woods rides that thin American line between lives perused, lives lived, and lives lost along the way.

DWW: He's also been sort of casually derided, for decades, at least, as a sentimentalist. Which does make me think that's another way that these American painters were different, in addition to their relative lack of interest in avant-garde-ishly trying out new forms and new styles. I'm simplifying in the extreme, obviously, but this work is also so much more powered by sentiment than the European stuff of the era. Why is that? I mean, theirs was the civilization that was completely falling apart!

JS: Yes. Now we know what those Europeans knew—that end of empire. Hopper knew something different: the solitude of American freedom, living in this country that was on the verge of an "American century," but with the original sin of slavery ever-present, feeling that cathedral of longing inside of us, proud to be Americans but knowing that glory and specificity are fleeting, filled with fear, a well of alienation. Hopper painted that. It may come off as sentimentality to some. At the Whitney, look closer: You see something darker, more searching, colder nights.

(2015)

Chris Burden's Work Was Like an Atomic Bomb

How great was Chris Burden? On November 19, 1971, out of nowhere, as if from some punk Plato's cave of aesthetic contamination and perfection, Burden created a work of art so pure, perfect, self-evident, riveting, and revealing that it became an instant masterpiece of modern sculpture—even though no one ever saw it. At 7:45 p.m., in an alternative space in Santa Ana, California, he had himself shot in the left arm by a friend with a .22 long rifle from fifteen feet away. His vision: the artist as a body that acts, is acted upon, and absorbs and changes material, becoming a meaning machine. A living sculpture come to dangerous life in the blink of an eye, sacrificing for his work while enacting a complex sadomasochism of love, hate, desire, and aggression. *Shoot*, as the work is known, is America's Duchamp's urinal: a cipher and a defining zero point of art. Lawrence Weiner once said that art isn't just something that messes up the viewer's day, it should "fuck up their whole life." That's what Burden did to art from that day forward, until he died yesterday, at sixty-nine.

Burden's first piece, created while he was still a graduate student at the University of California, Irvine, was pure Kafka's "Hunger Artist." From April 26 until April 30, 1971, for his graduate thesis, Burden had himself locked in a two-foot-high, two-foot-wide, three-foot-deep locker. He stayed there without leaving for five days. The locker above him contained five gallons of water; the locker below him contained an empty five-gallon container. At the age of twenty-five, Burden had distilled sculpture into a perfect system whereby the artist acted in public and private at the same time, functioning as a medium and passing point between states of being, transforming liquid within his body and excreting it in his own form. Another work of art so powerfully compact and dense in its implications, ideas, and intensity that it need not be seen. Only imagined.

In the 1970s, when Burden first took the stage, the art world was having one of its periodic nervous breakdowns. Painting was said to be dead; sculpture was starting over. Artists were dematerializing the art object, breaking it down, using their bodies as tools. Marina Abramović worked as a prostitute during her show; Vito Acconci masturbated under a gallery floor; Joseph Beuys lived in a gallery with a live coyote; Jack Goldstein buried himself alive. Burden was part of this revolutionary aesthetic palace coup.

I loved Burden's work. Twice, very early on, I was lucky enough to come into contact with it. On May 7, 1974, he performed *Velvet Water* in Chicago. For five minutes, a small group of us sat on metal folding chairs, watching on a video monitor as, in an adjacent room, Burden relentlessly dunked his head in a filled-up sink, trying to inhale the oxygen-rich water. We sat stupefied, paralyzed, until he seemed to pass out and the monitor went dark, and that was it. He'd tried to return to his amniotic amphibian state in real time. In that moment, I knew art was a place where I wanted to be.

Back then, I was working as a guard at Chicago's Museum of Contemporary Art. There, on April 11, 1975, Burden performed a piece called *Doomed*. He walked into the museum's main gallery and lay down beneath a sheet of tilted glass. There was a clock nearby. Then he did nothing. He didn't move, eat, drink, speak. The audience seated on the floor in front of him sat there. And did nothing. It was one of those 1970s moments where your ideas of time, boredom, creativity, credulity, faith, and passion were tested. I left when my shift was over; he was still there. The next afternoon, I heard, he was still there. The day after that, I heard that he still hadn't moved. This thing had gone from art to psycho. I knew that something important was happening, not only to him but to me and to art. I rushed back to the museum. A handful of people were sitting there, transfixed, freaked out. *Sun-Times* film critic Roger Ebert later reported that a museum employee said, "It's a really strange scene here right now." Finally, forty-five hours into this excruciating thing, fearing uremic poisoning or dehydration, my friend and fellow guard Dennis O'Shea placed a pitcher of water next to Burden. Just like that, Burden got up, got a hammer from another room, and broke the clock. The performance was over. So were lots of ideas about art. Burden told Ebert, "I thought, My God . . . are they going to leave me here to die?"

I could recount twenty more Burden pieces of similar protean density and abstract essence. In the eighties, Burden turned to making objects with the same immensity of emotion and mysterious cathartic power. A few years ago, in a great retrospective of his work at the New Museum, viewers could behold the ugly *Big Wheel* (1979). An eight-foot, six-thousand-pound cast-iron flywheel is mounted on a wooden pyramid-like structure. A real motorcycle is placed so that its rear wheel can make contact with the big iron one. A couple of times a day, a rider mounts the bike, shifts it so that the rear wheel makes contact with the flywheel, and revs the bike up to its top speed. Then the bike is turned off and pushed away. The iron wheel ominously spins for up to two hours. You are seeing oil chemically and mechanically converted into movement, flirting with perpetual motion, and on the edge of destruction—and nothing actually goes anywhere. Burden describes the piece as a "Neanderthal atomic bomb."

It's almost impossible to grasp the reach of Burden's work, even if he always functioned as an outlaw, coming into the art world in bursts from out in the wilds. His importance to late-twentieth-century art cannot be overstated. Thank you, Chris, for fucking up my whole life.

(2015)

Why Have There Been No Great Women Bad-Boy Artists? There Have Been, of Course

D ana Schutz and Katherine Bernhardt are among the liveliest American painters to emerge in this country in fifteen years, and both opened big new shows over two nights a few weeks ago. Before we get to the exhibitions, a little history to help explain why the reputations of these two painters have careened so much over that time: They've been celebrated, passed over for big shows, and become dark horses, all while helping to shape our current moment for charismatic painting.

Schutz and Bernhardt were born a year apart, in 1976 and 1975 respectively. Both hail from the Midwest: Schutz from Livonia, Michigan, and Bernhardt from St. Louis. Both got their MFA in New York—Schutz at Columbia, then approaching the height of hip; and Bernhardt at the School of Visual Arts, always an underdog school. Schutz had her much-noticed New York debut in 2002; Bernhardt had hers in 2000, although to almost no fanfare. In different ways, each has been instrumental in a transition that painting has made since then, a shift away from the more traditionally skillful, twisted figuration practiced in this country, especially by John Currin, Lisa Yuskavage, and Elizabeth Peyton, among others.

Perhaps more interesting, they have also sidestepped many of the other micro-movements that have unfolded in painting since. Neither Schutz nor Bernhardt employs photographic tools, digital approaches, or outright appropriation in her work, in the manners of Peter Doig, Wilhelm Sasnal, or Luc Tuymans. There's no sign of the glitzy digital flatness of Takashi Murakami, or the never-ending European river of imitative post-Richter painters. Neither deals with issues of mechanical reproduction in the vein of Wade Guyton or Kelly Walker. Nor has either of these artists gone down the superpopular, yawn-inducing "critique of painting" rabbit hole—the perennial, syllogistic business of painting about painting about painting, until it's paintings all the way down. Ours is a time when art history has been simplified in order to be gentrified, so that it's palatable to the widest market share—so that anyone can look at a painting and link it to one of the magic names: Warhol, Richter, Kippenberger, Krebber, Koons, Guyton, or another from a small, preapproved list of artists or isms. Not only could most of this work have been made anywhere, at any time since 1945, but much of it looks like it came from one small painting mill, churning out collectibles. It's as if artists, academics, curators, and critics are comfortable in a tractor beam of nostalgia that draws them forever back to some imagined wound in painting, a scab to peel back, a place where the same problems can forever be solved in similar ways.

Contrary to these sentimental journeys, Schutz and Bernhardt have been endlessly idiosyncratic, continually creating new variances of material, scale, surface, touch, tools, technique, color, and figuration. Schutz conjures unsteady cornucopia compositions that build out of her paint, shifting spatial planes that flip-flop, flickering in confetti color; until recently she worked with an especially creamy paint, which flowered into bucolic clusterfucks. Hers is an everything-but-the-kitchen-sink approach to space. Bernhardt is much looser, her color more electric and intense, bordering on tropical fish that pool in psychedelic lagoons, thinning out, then building up in gluts that turn into brambly palimpsests and clammy reservoirs of iridescence. Her mode of composition is more organized than Schutz's, taxonomical in nature, with everyday images, like toilet paper, fashion models, and shoes, spray-painted, laid out as if found in a pop-culture specimen bed. When it comes to Bernhardt's work, you can forget narrative; a spitfire magpie, she follows Warhol's credo of "liking things," and paints what she likes the way she likes to paint it. At their worst, her latticeworks can look like wallpaper and place mats; at their best, they become rich visual tidal pools.

Schutz and Bernhardt are both wildly admired among their fellow artists, but neither has ever been in a Whitney Biennial, a Documenta, an Istanbul Biennial, or any of those big international cattle calls. (Schutz was included in the vast 2003 Venice Biennale, along with more than three hundred other artists.) Nor was either included in MoMA's recent foray into contemporary painting, though theirs are the two names most often cited as artists whose work should have been included.

Why these omissions? The short answer, I'm afraid, amounts to something like a crime—the crime of being a woman. Long careers of female bad-boy painters have always been rare; there have been so few of them over the past fifty years that I can count them on one hand. The art world has never really known what to do with them, mostly responding from fear. For five thousand years, art has been treated almost exclusively as the domain of men. As Linda Nochlin famously pointed out in 1971, for centuries women were excluded from even attending the academies; they were never invited to learn the tools and skills of painting, and were considered persona non grata among those who defined the status quo and controlled the flow of ideas and capital. Men were the geniuses and ordained shamans of art; women were the flesh that made muses move. Or they were cast as regressive or crafty, or corralled into erotic ghettos. Or they were just witches. In this nightmarish way, almost all Western notions of beauty, form, technique, color, composition, subject matter, skill, surface, scale, and narrative have been shaped and controlled.

Thankfully, over the last few decades women in the art world have rebelled, redefining painting again and again—which means that, today, there are probably plenty of women whose names might spring to mind as examples of true pathbreakers. But there's still a significant restriction in place, one that's almost never mentioned: Very few of the female painters who've forged long-term careers have painted in expressionistic or more unleashed ways, deploying high-keyed color or ropy surfaces, or painting in ways that strike people as irrational, out of control, or noncerebral. For a woman to paint in any way excessively, loudly, using thick paint or brash color, is a near taboo. When it comes to women painters, the art world is chromaphobic, gesture-phobic, and effluvia-phobic. Unless—and this is key—the woman, say, Charline von Heyl or Jacqueline Humphries, both of whom deftly deploy gesture, color, and expression, is said to be doing so self-consciously, "using painting's languages" cerebrally, with conceptual underpinnings and art historical structure. (As if all art doesn't have varying degrees of these things.) Even now, Thames & Hudson's *Abstract Expressionism*, recently published in a new edition, includes only two paintings by women among its 172 pictures—both by Lee Krasner. These prohibitions and strictures filter into and infect the present.

Whatever else she did, Dana Schutz—along with Nicole Eisenman—was among the first women to cross these invisible lines in recent years. Indeed, when I wrote about Schutz's great 2002 debut, her work was so wild, so out there and unexpected, that I mused that she might have some unknown form of mind that made her imagine things this way. But that daring has made many people wary of Schutz's work, especially in the context of the contemporary market, whose fluctuations can transform the careers of even the most exciting and independent-minded artists.

In this respect, you could call Schutz the Artist Zero of the aughts art boom. She shot to overnight fame in 2002. Her first solo show in a small new gallery—LFL, now Zach Feuer—included an array of canvases of different sizes, all of them in high-keyed, unfixed color, depicting collapsing scenes of noses exploding, faces fracturing, figures in combat, and lanky men with droopy dicks. The show sold out; the work was written about widely. It felt like a blast of air blowing open a door in the House of Painting. First her fellow artists took notice; collectors followed—which is where the complications set in. Almost immediately, there was word of speculators buying and selling her work for huge figures. Soon Schutz's paintings were being sold at auction for almost half a million dollars. At the same time, almost anyone who'd met Schutz claimed to have "discovered" her—teachers, dealers, art advisers, everyone. It got to be a creepy joke, but a telling one. Something in the art world was splintering, and people sensed it.

What happened to Schutz happened fast. She is among the most open, honest artists anywhere—on a personal level, everyone adores her—and yet her fate over the next decade was, to my way of thinking, sad. The art world has a place for sensations, of course, but it offers a much more comfortable home if those sensations are men. (See Nate Lowman, Urs Fischer, Joe Bradley, Mark Grotjahn, Dan Colen, Paul Chan, and many others.) Schutz, by contrast, was the canary in the market coal mine. While the optical power in her work, her wild imagery and color, helped free even artists who were her elders—able painters like von Heyl, Humphries, Amy Sillman—Schutz was soon being dismissed as a "market artist," somehow not part of the art community. As other artists got deservedly included in important group shows and biennials, the same curators almost entirely bypassed Schutz.

That's not the sad part, though. What's sad is the way this market backlash and prohibitions against wildness in women painters now seem to shadow what she's actually doing. I love Schutz's work. Yet in her current exhibition—her first since 2013, at Petzel gallery—she seems overly self-conscious, tighter, caught between urges, alternately cartoonish and figurative but also more abstract and all-over. Few artists her age are as fearless when it comes to color; here she's working in a profusion of citrus colors, Creamsicle orange, Lik-m-aid yellows, violet, pear shades of green. Her shattered, multicolored, disjunctive compositional fields are rivaled only by elders like Peter Saul, Elizabeth Murray, David Salle, Jörg Immendorff, and James Rosenquist. She can seemingly master any space and scale. In the mural-size *Shaking Out the Bed*, figures—seen perhaps from the side, maybe lying down, reaching to the painting's right side to adjust perspectival vantage point—appear from above, slipping into different pictorial spaces, or try to get outside the frame. It's a kind of history painting unmoored from history.

In two of the best works here—*Fight in an Elevator*, which looks part

Harlem Renaissance and part *Who Framed Roger Rabbit*, and the square-looking but not-square *Slow Motion Shower*—Schutz forces two of painting's major formal subplots to the fore. The first is the way that everything in any painting is always pressured, held in, defined, or in dialogue with the edges of frame. The fracturing Cubo-Futurist construction and structure of these works, the ways Schutz is crossing the glittery temporal and planar shifts of Boccioni with Peter Saul's insane, all-over narratives in blazing acrid color, strikes me as the work of an artist undertaking a remarkable painterly feat. There is a lot going on in every one of these works. And yet: except for a couple of canvases, I'm not sure that there's *any one thing* going on. This is a problem. Schutz's skill at mustering frontal energy and her painterly verve are immense, but in viewing the work I felt I was mainly looking at parts, never a whole. Too often the work tightened into something like a *New Yorker* cover illustration. I think back to a great work of hers from 2004, another allegory of painting: a huge horizontal figure being dissected by doctor types amid a large number of onlooking heads. The picture was busy, but so iconic that it tattooed itself permanently on my mind. The work here, by contrast, is cartoony, crazy, exuding fabulously unfixed visual pheromones.

But taste has changed around Schutz; painting has gotten more abstract, even as Schutz's work has gotten more figurative, controlled, illustrative, and defined, and not necessarily in a good way. I miss the mushy subterranean rhythms and uncanny abstractness of her earlier work; her current paintings feel somehow more isolated than before.

Which brings us to Katherine Bernhardt. One of the most exuberant, almost feral, slashing painters around, Bernhardt—whose new large canvases pulsate like hallucinogenic magnetic fields and have the retinal bite-force of crocodiles—is, with a couple of dozen solo shows since 2000, something of a veteran around town. Yet many people haven't heard of her. Why? Her new paintings—groupings of hammerhead sharks, fronds, cell phones, toucans, plantains—bring something of Basquiat's mind-boggling border-to-border busyness, combined with Bernhardt's own spray-painted, psychedelic phosphorescent fields, which transform before the eye into fossil beds of modern life. Whatever is going on in these paintings, they exude obsession, endlessness, and germinating optical power.

As much as her career parallels Schutz's, however, and as beloved among artists and shunned by curators as she is, Bernhardt's market story is very different. On the upside, this has shielded her from the kind of backlash that was unfairly aimed at Schutz in the early 2000s. On the downside, as recently as 2007, Bernhardt said she was still creating her art on "one side of my bedroom, about four square feet." It was only that year that she finally got a proper studio. (Like Schutz, she now has a son. She and her husband, Youssef Jdia, who is Moroccan, buy and sell incredible Berber rugs, sometimes bringing them to her gallery, Canada, piling them on the floor, hanging out, as people come and go, just having tea or playing, with all the kids hanging around. Whatever it is, it's pretty old-school. And wonderful.)

As with Schutz, Bernhardt's work is more untamed and eccentric than much of the current crop of monochromatic, process-based abstractions that fill art fairs, galleries, art schools, auction catalogues, and more than a few museums. Bernhardt's paintings are information stored in amber-glowing paint; Schutz's are deployments of the "one million colors" and imaging programs available to the human mind, the only thing as complicated as the universe itself. But none of this seems to matter to those who like their painting only if it has air quotes around it, or if it somehow "makes sense"—that is, fits into the canonical interpretation of history.

Almost all of Bernhardt's two dozen solo shows, some of which saw her covering walls with advertisements from Spanish bodegas or collaborating with Jdia, often—as in her current exhibition—activating the space by covering the floors (in this case, with burlap coffee sacks), have been downtown, in small group shows, and around the globe. Until now, she's never shown uptown at a great posh gallery like Venus Over Manhattan. Nor has she sold to that strata of collectors. I'm glad to hear that, with her work available in the area, and with Bernhardt not leaving her own Lower East Side gallery (more artists should take a page from this book, not just going to megagalleries for the payday), the bigger-fish collectors have finally caught on. When I asked if any of our local museums had gotten on board as well, however, the person behind the desk just blinked knowingly and shook her head as if to say, *Of course not; they like their newer painters more predictable. More cerebral. Not so wild.*

Lately, though, the faithful among us are starting to see signs that painting is escaping this genericism. Batons are being passed. Let's hope that a little of what animates the work of Schutz and Bernhardt is part of the new mix. And that we're finally wise enough, and open enough, to celebrate it for what it is.

(2015)

The Whitney Rejected
This Masterpiece Sculpture

For all its promise, the new Whitney Museum of American Art is and will be marked by an invisible original sin that can't be lifted. It's an aesthetic sin, one that perfectly mirrors America's hysteria and mania around race, what D. H. Lawrence called the fear of our "old, hoary, monstrous," "unspeakably terrible," "snow-white," "abstract end."

After boldly commissioning the eminent American artist Charles Ray to design a sculpture to be permanently installed on the public plaza outside the new museum, the Whitney blinked and declined Ray's proposal. According to Calvin Tomkins, the museum feared that the work would "offend non-museumgoing visitors." And just like that, a gigantic chance was lost. The proposed work—which Ray has since created, exhibiting it at Chicago's Art Institute—is not only a twenty-first-century sculptural masterpiece, it embodies so much of America's past and current struggles that it might have become a beacon, a second Statue of Liberty, in New

York City. And there are layers of paradox to this tragedy: The work is a classically traditional Western figurative sculpture—a nod to the kind of ancient Greek and Roman art that helped establish Western standards of beauty. It's a work of High Realism, rendered with incredible skill and a fealty to canonical form and academic history. Beyond all that, the subject matter is totally familiar, even banal or boring: two large, naked figures, both male—nothing not already seen in probably a hundred other American museums. Yet Ray's public sculpture crackles and fractures with historical counterforce, presenting a fact so shattering that the Whitney decided the work could not be exhibited in public. Let's look at why.

The figures are big, looming over us at about one and a half times natural size. As realistic as they are, and as much space and attention as they command, they also feel abstracted, once removed. At no point do the two figures actually touch, yet they're locked in cosmic orbit with each other, almost inseparable. A standing man towers over us at about nine feet. He's probably about forty years old, fit, but not a colossus. Still, he's something of an augur, perhaps owning to how he peers into a distance over our heads as if we're not here. As if he's been swallowed up in something we can't see. He extends his right hand over the bending figure of the boy, who is looking into his own open hand, or down to the ground. He's lost, absorbed in something. Ray says that the figure "reaches down into the river and pulls up a frog." Either way, nothing untoward, freakish, or even flashy is happening. The standing man's hand over the boy might be seen as a gesture of blessing. For me, the small of the boy's back seems like a vulnerable point, a place where injury could be inflicted with very little force—especially given the distracted, rapt way the boy is stooping, oblivious to the world around him. The standing man's consciousness, meanwhile, is split, conflicted, weighed on, filled with pathos. He is far more aware of the boy than the boy is of him. Still, however academic the realism, neither figure feels Greek or godlike; the body language and type are familiar, the hair is contemporary, expressions are commonplace. The figures are cast in stainless steel, but their surfaces feel digital, pixelated, as if they were fashioned by 3D printing. Also, unlike classical sculptures on pedestals, these figures stand on the ground, in our world. Maybe due to their size and the stark white of their surface, however, they still exude an enigmatic otherness. The sculpture is neither sensual and translucent, like marble, nor reflective and cold, like steel. These figures are in limbo.

This is where the hysteria sets in. I can't recall a contemporary artist better electrifying a work of art with its title: The sculpture is called *Huck and Jim*.

Of course. We are looking at a representation of Mark Twain's famous characters in *The Adventures of Huckleberry Finn*. The man is Jim Watson, escaping Missouri for the free territory of Illinois and Ohio. Huck is the novel's namesake, a small-town Missouri boy running from his drunkard father, who wants to kill him for a treasure found in a previous book. In the middle of the night, on Jackson's Island in the Mississippi River, Huck finds Jim hiding from slave-catchers who will either kill him or chain him to claim the reward for his return. As told by Twain, Huck is escaping but also looking for adventure and fun. He's no angel. Throughout the book, we read of how he wrestles with his conscience, dogged by the question of whether the right thing to do is to return this piece of "property" to its rightful owner. By the story's end, Huck deigns to let Jim go because, as he puts it, "I knowed he was white inside." Huck becomes the hero of the book, Jim the cause of his heroism and redemption. We know that Huck will eventually have access to the money he found. We don't know what will happen to Jim: if he'll be able to return to Missouri for his wife and two children, if he's killed making his way back from Arkansas, where Huck steered him in order to seek adventure.

The hysteria comes from Ray flipping the script. This is no longer Huck's story. It is Jim's. Or whatever version of Jim's story could be truly authored by a white sculptor. Huck is depicted in the privileged precincts of the imagination, stooping to study something, lost in speculation, surrendering mindfulness to wonder and the luxury of marveling. Ray brilliantly reflects his callowness by obscuring his identity. It's impossible to see his face without lying down on the floor. Or stooping over and peering up at it—which puts you in the exact same position as the figure you're lost looking at, lost in aesthetic wonder. (When you do get under Huck, you also notice that he has no pubic hair, another sign of youthfulness or innocence.)

Jim is the lodestar of this sculpture, the locus of psychological and physical magnitude. This isn't his *Adventures of Huckleberry Finn*. It's his "Penal Colony," his *Inferno*—in modern parlance, a state of terrorism. Jim is running for his life, for the fate of his family. Indeed, Huck's lust for abstract adventure has the effect of leading Jim deeper into slave country, rather than crossing the river into a free state. Even when they reach the point where the Ohio River branches north from the Mississippi, Huck misses the turn in the fog—and continues south. As a result, Jim is captured twice. Both times, he barely escapes. In Ray's sculpture, Jim is a man thinking about something serious; in the words of artist Kara Walker, "His inner plantation . . . this grand place where to some extent, we knew our place; a place where one is whole . . . and knows what to fight against, or what not to fight against, or who to obey, or how to hold on to oneself in the face of oppression." This is Jim's Gethsemane—an in-between moment of wanting this cup to be taken from him, even as he knows that America offers him no such hope. All this felt ambiguity, confusion, innocence, violence, betrayal, and grand defiance radiates from *Huck and Jim*. Here Huck may be well-meaning and innocent, but he is still the racist who needs the black man more than he is needed. And we're back to that "hoary, monstrous" fear that the old codes will go away. As James Baldwin writes, "It is the innocence which constitutes the crime."

And then there is a second kind of in-betweenness at work. The standing man is black; the stooping boy is white; the man's genitals are large and uncircumcised; the boy's penis is small and without pubic hair; Ray is white.

Sexual racial tension is old in America, and deep. In 1851, Herman Melville pictured Ishmael sleeping in the sheltering arms of dark-skinned Queequeg and having torn feelings—later saying, "I must turn idolater." Twain has Jim call Huck "honey," and Huck talks about how "we was always naked, day and night." American shadows become visible. In his famous 1948 essay "Come Back to the Raft Ag'in, Huck Honey!," Leslie Fiedler writes of the relationship between the boy runaway and the slave runaway as an archetypal case of American literature's fetish, so to speak, of "chaste male love as the ultimate emotional experience." It's a love not quite so chaste of mind as we are typically taught, he writes, even putting aside what he calls the "shackling cliché" of "the white man's sexual envy of the Negro male" and the underlying fear, "the white American's nightmare that someday . . . he will be rejected." As Fiedler notes, "In each generation we *play out* the impossible mythos, and we live to see our children play it, the white boy and the black we can discover wrestling affectionately on any American sidewalk, along which they will walk in adulthood, eyes averted from each other, unwilling to touch even by accident. The dream recedes; the immaculate passion and the astonishing reconciliation become a memory, and less, a regret, at last the unrecognized motifs of a child's book. 'It's too good to be true, Honey,' Jim says to Huck. 'It's too good to be true.'" This is the minefield too far that Ray's *Huck and Jim* occupies.

And yet no outcry erupted when the sculpture was installed at the Art Institute of Chicago, part of a tremendous exhibition of Ray's later work. Perhaps because it was inside a public institution called a *museum*, within the confines of rooms known as *galleries*, where people know to allow ambiguity, nakedness, sexual tension, and unstable subject matter, even around race.

In his sculpture, Ray hits us with visual fact, the belief that form carries meaning, dispensing with all the familiar, distancing tropes that keep stories safe and pathology at bay. Other than its mildly operatic scale, there's no romanticizing of subject, no nostalgia, sentimentalizing, myth, or fantasy. No palliative parable or moral. Just the bare facts. Twain's novel was set in the 1830s or 1840s; Ray's story, set in an eternal present, is nonfiction. Here, in Wallace Stevens's words, it's a "constant cry against an old order."

(2015)

How Philip Guston Reinvented the Sublime

As late as he came to the style, by 1957 Philip Guston was a highly admired first-generation Abstract Expressionist—a phrase he hated. How late to the party was Guston? In the 1940s, peers like Arshile Gorky, Franz Kline, Jackson Pollock, and Mark Rothko were already finding their ways into all-out abstraction. Yet throughout that time Guston was still experimenting with figures, grounds, solid spaces, and objects. Pollock, who attended high school with Guston in Los Angeles (the two were expelled for designing satirical leaflets) and who urged Guston to move to New York in 1935, had been making abstract paintings since 1939. Gorky had done so since 1932; Rothko and Willem de Kooning reached these farther shores by the early 1940s. Guston didn't go fully abstract until about 1950. History is lucky; had he waited a minute longer, the Ab Ex train would have left without him and we might never have heard of him.

Guston was always hesitant, and when he finally did get to real abstraction he stayed ambivalent about it. "Every real painter wants to be, and his greatest desire is to be, a realist," he said. The abstract works that deservedly won him fame are beautiful shimmering lyrical fields of broken brushstrokes, flickering grounds of pearly blue and pink, serene combinations of Monet and Turner with inflections of Mondrian's early piers-reflected-in-water. But Guston started to feel that he was only taking small bites in his work. By the 1950s, he felt he "had nowhere to go." Saying "I hope sometime to get to the point where I'll have the courage to paint my face . . . to paint a single form in the middle of the canvas," he started doing exactly that. And he had the courage to do it at the apex of his career.

By 1970, he'd finished "clearing the decks." From then until his death, in 1980, at the age of sixty-six, Guston left abstraction behind and made some of the most memorable and influential paintings of the late twentieth century, big and small: huge, gloppy, opaque-colored images of what appear to be Ku Klux Klansmen driving around in convertibles, smoking cigars; cyclops heads, in bed, staring at bare lightbulbs; piles of legs and shoes; figures hiding under blankets, clutching paintbrushes in bed. Many of these are so narratively accessible they can seem almost like panels from comic strips. But they are also cryptic. In this body of work I see spiders, newts, malignant clouds, boatmen, snake charmers, lanterns lighting up existential nights. The list of artists influenced by this incredible work includes Nicole Eisenman, Amy Sillman, Albert Oehlen, Carroll Dunham, Elizabeth Murray, and Georg Baselitz, who saw as early as 1959 that Guston was involved with "a distortion of the abstract [that was] full of concrete forms." Jasper Johns saw that, too.

But the stakes of abandoning abstraction were high. Recognition had come late to Guston's generation. The Abstract Expressionists had labored alone in America, dirt poor, with no audience, no art world apparatus to support them—only one another. As Barnett Newman famously put it, "We were making it out of ourselves." And those selves were obsessed with going beyond Picasso and into nonobjective painting. They had bet their entire lives on the gamble, and as a result any sign of apostasy or disaffection was seen as a threat to all. Even after America took notice of the group, in the early 1950s, they were the constant butt of jokes about "my three-year-old" being able to paint like that. Worse yet, no sooner had they arrived than a new group of artists—led by Jasper Johns and Robert Rauschenberg—arrived on the stage doing totally antithetical work. The world turned on a dime. In 1962, the Sidney Janis Gallery organized a show including Andy Warhol, Roy Lichtenstein, Wayne Thiebaud, and Claes Oldenburg. This was seen as a betrayal by Guston, Rothko, Robert Motherwell, and Adolph Gottlieb, who all quit the gallery in protest. It was at this show that de Kooning reportedly told Warhol that he was "a killer of art, a killer of beauty." But Guston wasn't really in line with his colleagues; amid all this he harbored a secret yearning to change.

By 1957, he'd done everything he could do to avoid doing what he had to do, and his work began to solidify into something new. The lesson of his career is that, in order to really be themselves, *all* artists must find their

inner Guston: an artist who forgoes easy answers, who looks for and channels doubt and not-knowing. An artist like this understands that he or she
isn't really *controlling* their art—that on some cosmic level the art controls
the artist. All great artists must be able to create a machine that can make
things that they cannot predict. Even when they make what might be
nightmarish or ugly to them.

Which is why *Philip Guston: Painter, 1957–1967*, at Hauser & Wirth, a
showcase of Guston at the turning point of his career, is an incantatory lesson for all artists. Perfectly curated by the gallery's Paul Schimmel, the
exhibition sounds a secret chord for artists in search of one of art's many
strange grails: how to make art that is original and entirely one's own. This
is especially pressing now that there are promising signs of new artists everywhere who are trying to break through the fog of professionalism and ca-
reerism that have crept into the art world. These new artists are rejecting
the corporate cautiousness that's made too many painters rely on minor
moves in known directions, toeing preapproved formal lines, and making
the system feel clogged up, static, sterile. Guston, who was desperate to
change his work, knew this. "I got sick and tired of all that purity," he said,
"the extreme codification of beliefs and the institutionalism of everything."
If that sounds painfully familiar, make it your business to see this show.

On view in the airplane-hangar-scaled museum-level gallery show are
thirty-five paintings and forty-eight drawings from this lesser-known decade of Guston's career, 1957 to 1967. This grouping of work has not been
exhibited in one place since the 1960s, so that spectacle itself will be new
information for many in the art world. What we see is a lead-up to what is
perhaps the greatest final act in twentieth-century American art history:
Guston's all-hell-broken-loose, id-under-pressure late figurative paintings.

The change comes slowly at first; Guston is always fighting it. As Jasper
Johns said about being an artist, "If you avoid *everything* you can avoid, then
you *do* what you can't avoid doing, and you *do* what is *helpless*, and unavoidable." Guston did that. The opening gallery shows his first steps—so small
you might not see them, thinking, *Oh, he's getting choppier, is all. I guess that
triangle could be a hood or something.* In 1957, Guston's colors turn more opaque;

warm tones turn frosty and muddy; odd, armlike shapes appear, torsos or trunks, hillocks, shadowy head configurations. But nothing definite. Being figurative was so strictly verboten that at one point Guston said he painted a can with paintbrushes in it, then lost his nerve and scraped it off. It was just too much. In the next gallery, Guston's backgrounds turn blocky. The shimmery thing is gone. So are the little snaky strokes. Things are thickening. A huge maroon handlike thing emerges from the top of one canvas. Compositions get optically bolder. In *Garden of M*, named after his wife and daughter (both named Musa), we spot something like a patchy garden grid, or maybe two lumpy figures clutching each other in bed. Sooty grays, yellows, and crimsons abound. But things stay abstract. What's happening is that Guston is looking for every way possible *not to make* a figurative painting. He couldn't just paint that single thing inside a canvas, a head, or even a can, without retreating back into abstraction. These works are almost ugly; creating them must have been hellish.

Then, in 1963, he just blows through the fear. A big, black-hat-wearing, egg-shaped head appears with a shaky arm, holding what might be a paintbrush and maybe a small canvas. This wasn't Ab Ex, it wasn't Pop, it wasn't like anything. The title *Painter III* tells us what's going on; it's a self-portrait, and a collective portrait of every artist's inner temperament when venturing into realms unknown. But it's too much for Guston and he pulls back. Again. *Looking* is just a smooshed figure that might be gazing at a black rectangle. It's almost self-as-grub. This one-step-forward, one-step-back crab dance continues as Guston looks for biomorphic, architectural, or geometric solutions rather than what's staring him in the face: the horror of going both figurative *and* expressionistic. In the last work in the show, Guston hits the wall of all the implied image-making. An all-gray field that is so confusing to Guston he doesn't even go to the edges, leaving swaths of canvas unpainted. In the middle of this is what looks like a black sun hovering—as if everything that Guston *can* empty out has been emptied out, except the truth. The implication of figure, ground, narrative, image. He'd reached Johns's "helpless" place.

Guston must have known that the return to figuration could no longer be denied. And still he refused. He was in a battle of wills with his art—so much so that, after the last canvas in this show, he stopped painting altogether for three years. He didn't exhibit his work again until 1970. Critics had slammed that work as "displeasingly raw"; the canvases were said to have "unpleasant texture." His colleagues were shocked, suspicious; they thought he was trying to hop on the Pop bandwagon. One painter friend asked why he had "to go and ruin everything." Lee Krasner was said to find the work "embarrassing." The *New York Times* critic Hilton Kramer lambasted Guston as "a mandarin pretending to be a stumblebum," dismissing the work as "cartoon anecdotage . . . funky, clumsy and demotic," and concluding, "We are asked to take seriously his new persona as an urban primitive[,] and this is asking too much." But the die was cast. While Pollock was the first to truly break through to pure nonobjective painting, it was Guston who was the first to break back out. And yet nobody seemed to understand. He'd risked everything and lost.

But Guston had crossed the Rubicon; even as he was being rejected by all around him, he was becoming the great painter of the American night. Not the night that follows day—the night of self. He wasn't painting "pictures," as he saw it, but rendering "one's experiences and one's enlargement of self." Guston moved the sublime—the bigness of it all—away from abstraction, where the Abstract Expressionists located it; away from nature, where the nineteenth century placed it; off the ceilings of churches, where it went in the Renaissance. He was shifting it back, finally, to where it probably has always been, since it left the fires in the caves: The sublime is in *us*! To see that, captured in art, is to bring Emerson's "alienated majesty" back to us.

Philip Guston helped push aside all the preoccupations of his moment: all the classicizing, romanticizing, philosophizing, the ambition to be a theologian of the sublime. This is epic. And it's present in all of Guston's late work. Of his contemporaries, only the always generous Willem de Kooning recognized the depth, the real content, of this final period of Guston's career. The subject of this art, he said, is "freedom."

(2016)

Taryn Simon Brings You
Face-to-Face with Death

The mysterious transit of the soul to the afterlife, soothing wounds, collective bereavement, inscriptions in sound and song of thought that words cannot express: These subjects and more are beautifully brought forth in a somber, stirring, sepulchral forty-minute interactive performance, *An Occupation of Loss*, organized by artist Taryn Simon in the vast darkened Drill Hall at the Park Avenue Armory.

After being admitted through a second-story side entrance, fifty or so viewers descend a long staircase to see eleven concrete silos or circular towers almost fifty feet high, open at the top and arranged in a semicircle. It's like a giant pipe organ. Long ramps lead to a slightly elevated oblong opening at the foot of each tower. Viewers may duck inside. There, in intimate quarters, usually seated on a bench, are professional mourners from eleven different countries, including Albania, Azerbaijan, Ecuador, and Ghana. There are people in robes, gowns, full body wraps, giant masks, or covered entirely in black. Forget about Simon's highly staged theatricality, all the operatic imperiousness and astronomical budget it took to build this set and bring this global group together. Instead, allow Simon's vision to usher you into the presence of the archaic.

In the beginning I watched from outside, afraid to go into any of the towers. When finally I ducked into one, I was shaken. Inside was a woman seated on a bench; as I stood there she cried, rocking back and forth, thumping her thigh, moaning, singing, and speaking words I couldn't understand. It was a universal language of loss and inconsolability. The woman was grasping an American-flag handkerchief, and in her mournful cries I heard what sounded like the words *bibi* and, perhaps, *niente*—words I took to mean "baby" and "nothing." I looked down, felt embarrassed at my own presence: a spectator looking on at her world of unrelieved pain. (Later, I learned she was a dirge singer from Ghana.) Time stopped. I had similar experiences inside every silo.

When I tried to enter another silo, this one sheltering two veiled women in black, I was told by an attendant that "these women mourn only in the presence of women." Many of the mourners were women: Just as we're brought into the world to the screams of women in labor, Simon's art reminds us how often we are ushered out to the sounds of women in grief. Rituals like these are meant to shepherd the soul to its next incarnation, to ward off demons, to comfort the dead and console the living, to level karmic forces, and to usher a body back "home" to its cosmic collective family. Being a professional mourner is a higher calling, but it also comes with a stigma: The Cambodian musicians here, playing ceremonial songs reserved for the moment the soul leaves the body, were forbidden to practice at all during the Khmer Rouge's reign of terror. Mourners here from Russia, Albania, Romania, and other countries were forbidden to practice as well. This oppression of proper burial is as old as our earliest stories: In the *Iliad*, Priam steals into Achilles's tent begging for the body of his dead son Hector, whom Achilles has dragged in the dirt for days. Without proper burial and mourning there is no eternity. No peace.

Somehow, at the Armory, this intense listening in the dark releases sorrow, absolves, soothes wounds. In its very stylized, yet direct, respectful, and guttural way, Simon's world of warbling choristers and companion-priests opens doors for us future travelers, letting us feel the pulse of things bigger than we are, yet things we are composed of.

(2016)

The Mysteries of *Dying Gaul*

D*ying Gaul* is a world masterpiece. A once-in-a-lifetime loan from the National Archaeological Museum in Naples, the two-thousand-year-old sculpture is part of the Met's luminescent exhibition of more than 250 incredible objects of Hellenistic art, *Pergamon and the Hellenistic Kingdoms of the Ancient World*. It is a slightly larger than life-size marble sculpture of a partially naked man on the ground—apparently felled here, supporting himself with one arm, the other resting weakly on an outstretched leg. The hand on the ground is atop a broken sword; his head is bent downward to the point where we can't really see his face at all. He is bleeding from a large chest wound, dying.

You knew this sculpture before you saw it. The pose is almost as well-known in the mind as that of another sculpture from the ancient world—also on hand, no less—of a boy removing a thorn from his foot. But there's a piercing difference. We engage with the boy with sweetness, this softness, youth, incipient-innocence-on-the-verge experience. *Dying Gaul* speaks to us in a tenor of tremulous enmeshed cosmic pathos.

Dying Gaul was part of a large sculptural grouping in an epic monument to commemorate decisive Hellenistic victories over the invading Gauls from nearby Galatia, in what is modern-day Turkey. Made between 100 and 200 BCE, it is a Roman copy of a lost bronze Greek original made about a century before by the great Hellenistic sculptor Epigonos. The bronze original—lost, probably melted down—was unceremoniously taken from Turkey by the emperor Nero to Rome, where it was used to decorate his gigantic gold, jewel-encrusted Golden House. Copy or not, time and distance collapse when you stand before it; a mysterious abyss opens between the viewer and the sculpture, and recognition rushes in. We are seeing layers of beauty, strength, inwardness, isolation, vulnerability, and the sensuous antecedents of Michelangelo's beautiful *David*—all the way to the even older wisdom of Homer.

No one grasped death the way Homer did—the way a human being turns into a corpse, a mere thing that is "dearer to the vultures" than to loved ones, as Homer wrote, "dropping to the world of night." Homer gives us death replacing life, both in an instant and millimeter by millimeter; in his poetry we glean spears piercing armor, rending fabric, entering flesh, penetrating viscera, severing veins, piercing bone, marrow giving way, swords going all the way through bodies into the earth below. Homer does this with no romanticizing distance, redemption, thunderbolts, whooshes of resurrection, or even florid poetry. Nothing, just unalterable descriptive direct detailed death.

Which brings us back to *Dying Gaul*. Almost every art historian and scholar has seen in this sculpture the last heroic act of a noble soldier gallantly rising to try to fight again, defying fate, staving off death, elevated by this last heroic effort. I don't see this at all. This is what I'd call the *Roman interpretation* of this sculpture. Roman aesthetics revel in melodrama, theatrics, power, exaggerated form, outward emotion, even Mannerism. Bodies are often deformed, poses are flashy, faces sometimes wildly expressive, narratives pronounced. Which makes sense for an empire like the Roman one, with more than two million soldiers, a Roman population estimated at more than a million, half its inhabitants slaves. While its forms might have emulated Greek art, the power projected was meant to be Egyptian—all-powerful, unassailable, imperial. The Romans had beaten back everyone: Egyptians, Asians, North Africans, Iberians, the French, the British. Even after Alexander the Great took over the known world, three centuries before, the Romans defeated them. That's absolute power.

But while *Dying Gaul* is a Roman copy, its real meaning is buried deeper, and it is deeply Greek. Unlike the work we know from Rome, Greek art was marked by gravitas; it took a grander, philosophical form, imbued with restrained sensuousness. To the Greeks, theatrics were for the theater. In *Dying Gaul*, I see a soul submitting to the physical and profound mysteries at hand—someone in the act of becoming a thing, a person who is suddenly "not there" but still in the act of recognizing this; a person who is lost, enveloped by death. The moment of death takes away hope, leaving only the eternal. This is not the grand drama of a man rising mightily to inner crescendos against death; it's a vision of pathos, pain, sadness without sunlight, of a person cut off from all of life. Nothing heroic is happening here, no last burst of vengeance or Roman self-sacrifice; nothing amasses here against death. Instead, in encountering the sculpture, we are wrapped in death. Absence telescopes into something withdrawn, not available to us. Epigonos has his figure look down, obscuring his features from us, making him less a person, more abstract. With no drama, no clues, it exists almost in the same *other* world as its subject. That's miraculous, like a thunderbolt. And it's what connects to Greece again.

The first time I think I more fully gathered what dying means—and why the Greeks had it right—was when I first saw Sam Peckinpah's 1973 film *Pat Garrett and Billy the Kid*, with music by Bob Dylan. In the movie, a remorseless gun-for-hire (James Coburn), a local sheriff, and his deputized wife come looking for Billy the Kid. The setting is nowhere—a little shack. A skirmish erupts; guns are fired. It's a minor scene. But in the middle of this exchange the sheriff, played by Slim Pickens, starts, falls back a little, looks down, and sees he's been shot in the stomach. As the action goes on around him he's already entering another world—Homer's world. He holds his wound and walks away and drops to his knees near a riverbank. His wife then looks up, sees he's not there, looks around and is horrified by the sight of her husband on his knees looking into the distance. She runs to him, drops to her knees about twenty feet from him, and just weeps, rocking back and forth, knowing what this is. He looks over at her. She looks at him in agony. Then he looks away and inward again. Like the *Dying Gaul*. I was twenty-two when I saw that in the movie, and right there, in that moment, I lost my religion. But I gained something else, something bigger, that is still in me today: surrender, supplication, freedom from fabricated ideas, and access to a something more intense, a bigger inwardness, our collective inner *Dying Gaul*.

(2016)

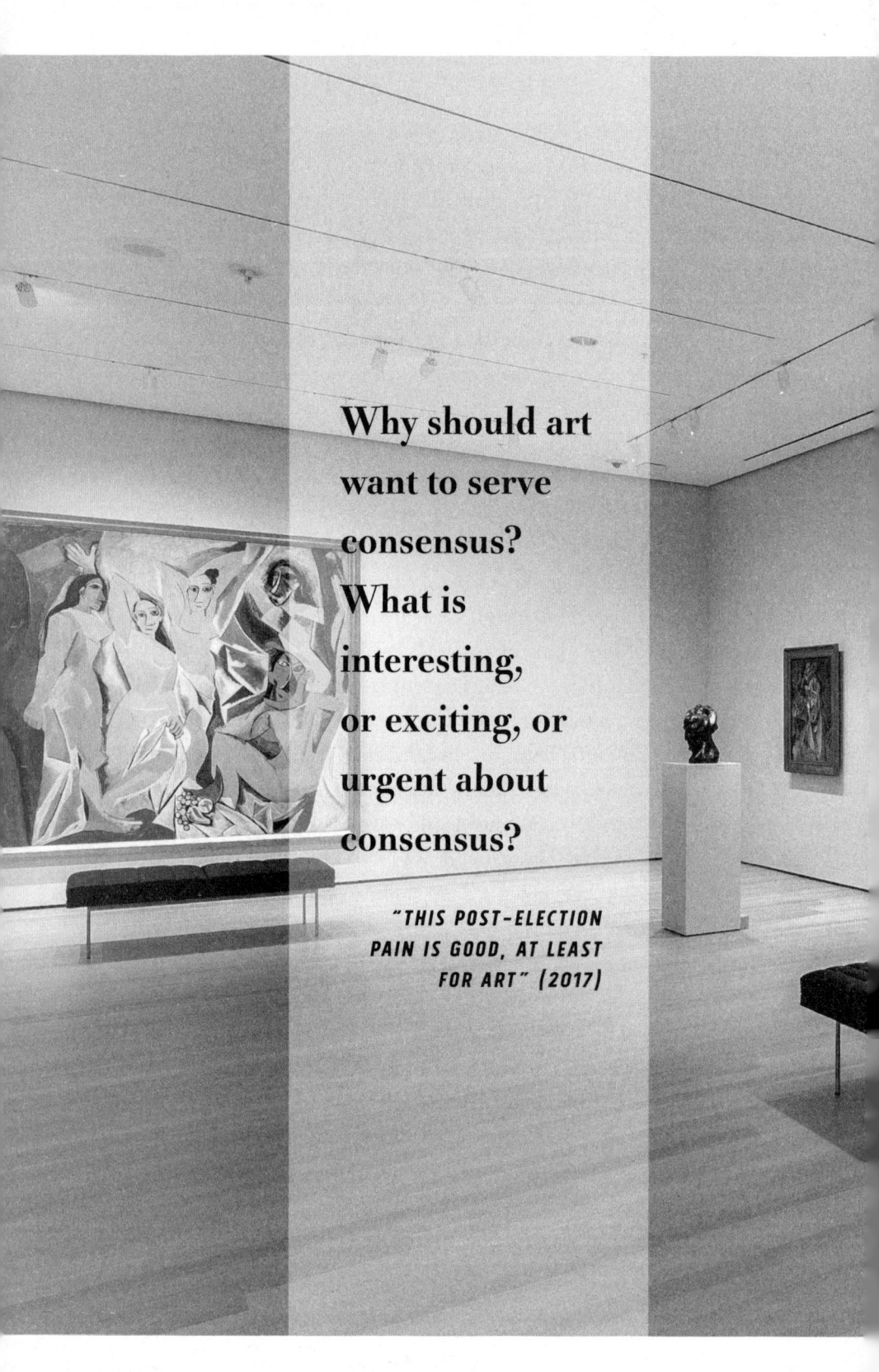

Why should art
want to serve
consensus?
What is
interesting,
or exciting, or
urgent about
consensus?

*"THIS POST-ELECTION
PAIN IS GOOD, AT LEAST
FOR ART" (2017)*

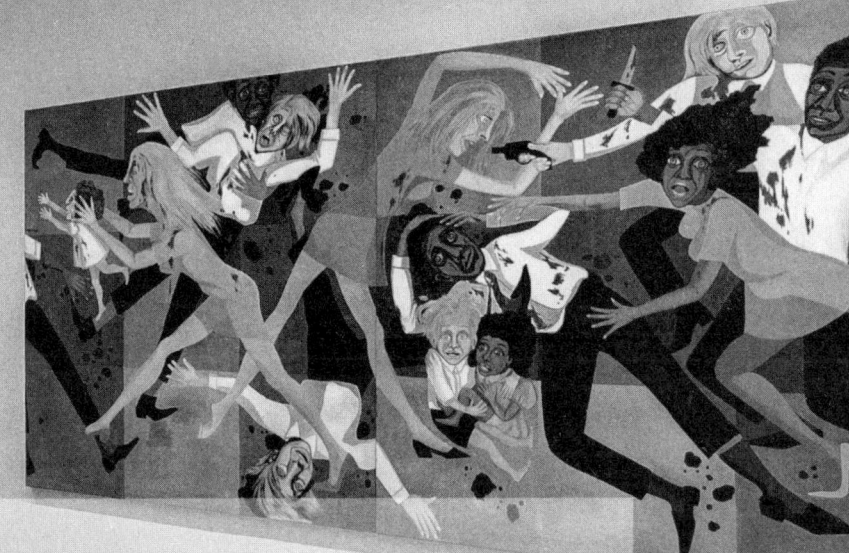

The Long American Night

2016–2021

The Painting I Can't Stop Thinking About:
Kerry James Marshall

Kerry James Marshall's tiny egg-tempera icon *A Portrait of the Artist as a Shadow of His Former Self* fires like a time bomb in the mind. The painting haunts *Mastry*, Marshall's newly opened, magnificent retrospective at the Met Breuer, like an avenging angel of art history. Small, spectral, cartoonish, smoky, frightening, an uncomfortably racial self-caricature, it reverberates with a power reminiscent of Ralph Ellison's horrific line: "I am invisible, understand, simply because people refuse to see me." Made in 1980, when the artist was only twenty-five—the astounding first figurative image he made after years of abstraction—the self-portrait is one of the most potent of the twentieth century.

(2016)

The Tyranny of Art History in Contemporary Art

Even the greatest art, whatever its power, cannot stop famine in sub-Saharan Africa. It cannot eradicate a virus. But I've written that art *does* change the world, if only by osmosis: typically by first changing how we see, and thereby how we remember. Raymond Chandler invented early-twentieth-century L.A. Francis Ford Coppola forged our vision of the Vietnam War. Andy Warhol combined clashing colors that had never been coupled before into a palette that is now ubiquitous. God creating Adam looks, for most of us, the way Michelangelo painted it. As Oscar Wilde noted, "the mysterious loveliness" of fog didn't exist before poets and painters. That's big stuff.

Yet art, as we now know it, has narrowed. These days, much of what we define as art is work that's mainly informed by other art and by art history. Especially in the last two centuries—and tenaciously of late—art has been obsessed with examining its own essences, ordinances, techniques, tools, materials, presentational modes, and forms. To be thought of as an artist, an artist must *self-identify as an artist*, must make work that they consider to be art.

This center cannot hold. Why? It is far too tight to let real art breathe.

Right now, the New Museum is hosting a show that casts a much wider net, that gives weirder and more idiosyncratic work much more air to breathe—and that makes everything we're used to seeing in museums (and even galleries) seem constrained by comparison. Organized by a superb team overseen by Massimiliano Gioni, *The Keeper* is a museum full of museums, possible encyclopedias, indexes of other orders, and miniature models of pain. Most of the work takes the form of collection: virtual coral-reef phantasmagorias collected and collated from things as strange as dead languages, detritus, cat's cradles, agate, and snowflakes, things that aren't included in any accepted category of art. Often, we call the people who make collections like these outsider artists—when we call them artists at all. Many of the thirty-some makers and collectors in *The Keeper* didn't self-identify as artists, or call what they made art. Their work isn't grounded in art history; probably they didn't care about this history. They were busy plumbing other depths. A small portion of such work can be found in art museums. But most is relegated to specialty collections, foundations, barred, or forgotten.

This is because our art history is not chronological; it's not neutral, not a matter of tracking simultaneous cross styles, outliers, or other activities that may have been going on at any given moment. Our art history is organized teleologically—it's an arrow. Things are always said to be going forward; progress is measured mainly in formal ways, by changes in ideas of space, color, composition, subject matter, and the like. Artists and isms follow one another in a biblical begetting, based on the impression of progress toward a goal or a higher stage. Cubism was "a race toward flatness." Suprematism was "the zero point of painting." Rodchenko declared that he'd made "the last painting." Ad Reinhardt one-upped him, saying he was "making the last painting which anyone can make." In this system, synthetic shifts and tics combine into things we call movements: Art Nouveau, Futurism, Cubism, Constructivism, Color Field, and so on. The problem is, anyone who doesn't fall into this timeline is out of luck. This paradigm has been in place for two hundred years.

I love the art in our museums and galleries. I don't want museums to stop staging exhibitions of it. I don't want them to look like science fairs, flea markets, exploratoriums, laboratories, *Wunderkabinette*, or thrift stores. But our idea of art history is dead; it just doesn't know it. Its terms are so specialized and vague they're useful only to those in the know. To categorize an artwork as Post-Minimalism tells you only that it came after something called Minimalism. Only aficionados know why both Barnett Newman's monochrome paintings and Willem de Kooning's wild style are considered Abstract Expressionist; why the über-controlled David Salle is a Neo-Expressionist. Unfortunately, so many academics, curators, collectors, and artists are so invested in this system that the result is an art world full of nonstop formalist twists, micro-moves in monochrome painting, photography about photography, readymades galore, formulaic institutional critique, and ironies only comprehensible to those who read the long, jargon-filled labels attached to the work. This is Zombie Art History.

But there are different paradigms, different methodologies—countless numbers of them, many of them on display in *The Keeper*. The artists here short-circuit art history. Not only do most of them not identify as artists, they don't see the world in any linear way. For these artists, every object contains the whole world, is part of a family of forms. Their inspiration is drawn not from art history but from within themselves. For them, the whole shapes the parts; taxonomical units cohere into clouds; microcosms mushroom into macrocosms; webs of interrelationship form. These artists are in search of what might be called ur-forms, conceptual templates, archetypal systems, inner rhythms, flows—things that have been here for millions of centuries, that are embedded in materials and in the fabric of time.

What's in *The Keeper*? The author of *Lolita*, Vladimir Nabokov, dissected butterfly penises—in his words, "sculptured sex"—and arranged them in cabinets to identify individual species. At the New Museum, his beautifully notated Frankensteinian collages of butterfly-wing patterns show an aesthetic intelligence equal to that of Kurt Schwitters, Wallace Berman, and Rauschenberg. Also here is Korbinian Aigner, a priest, painter, and pomologist (scholar of fruit), who, from around 1912 through his time in Dachau to his death in 1966, painted dusky still lifes of apples on glowing monochrome backgrounds. His obsessional focus, power of observation, fleshy texture, and subtleness of color are as mesmerizing as Giorgio Morandi, as strange as Cézanne, as formally distinct as El Lissitzky. André Malraux, author of *Museum Without Walls*, said, "We can feel only by comparison." Neither Aigner nor Nabokov is represented in our traditional art museums. Neither is Hilma af Klint, whose sixteen glorious paintings from 1914 to 1915 cover three walls here. Her highly hued work, filled with spirals, squares, circles, and corkscrewing seashell shapes, shows that she's not just a great painter but one of the inventors of abstraction itself. Her plain, blocky fields of color are revolutionary; we don't see them again in painting until the backgrounds of Francis Bacon. Af Klint still isn't allotted her deserved place in art history. Maybe because she called her work *Paintings for the Temple*, said she was inspired by "high masters," and designated her work to not be seen until twenty years after her death. Somehow this cast her as some sort of zodiacal spiritualist.

Suffering a similar fate is Olga Fröbe-Kapteyn, who called her geometric paintings "meditation drawings" and founded a school of spiritual research in 1930. Her twelve paintings from the twenties and thirties in the New Museum show have such a snappy graphic quality that you might mistake them for Pop or psychedelic posters of the sixties. Nearby are eighty-one wild black-and-white abstract-geometric photographs by Wilson Bentley, who fashioned his own camera to make photomicrographs of individual snow crystals. Bentley is in a few museums, but even though his work is abstract photography—decades before it became an ism in art—his work is considered primarily scientific. At the New Museum 300,000 of the 500,000 pencil drawings of contemporary artist Vanda Vieira-Schmidt suggest an original voice that is also a kind of synthesis of Paul Klee and Louise Bourgeois. She believes that her drawings are "countering the forces of evil in this world"—the same claim made by Byzantine and Early Renaissance artists about their work. Her pieces can otherwise only be seen in a Dresden military museum.

The funny thing is, however unusual the collections look within the context of a museum—however powerfully *The Keeper* shows us that there is more in the category of art than our present system has dreamt of—in truth I think that all great artists understand this cosmic complexity already. Every maker has an individual idea of what needs to exist; great imagination is always a force from within. Whether one knows art history or not, art begins pre-intellectually, beyond language. It is a search for new paths of encounter and poetic structures, images and things that go beyond themselves. Af Klint and Fröbe-Kapteyn might have believed their work was inspired by cosmic forces. Kandinsky described his art as a "penetration of collected forces." Franz Marc called his a "pantheistic penetration." Marsden Hartley called his "cosmic Cubism." Marcel Duchamp suspended twelve hundred coal bags from a ceiling. That piece would have been right at home in *The Keeper,* along with the cat's cradle–like string-figure configurations collected by filmmaker and ethnomusicologist Harry Smith.

It's beyond time for a new generation of art historians to change all this: not just to open up the system and let art be the garden that it is, a home to exotic blooms of known and unknown phenomena, but to *work against* this system. We can't declare "Painting is dead" just as women and artists of color have started to enter the bigger story of art history. Our art history has stiffened into an ideology that clear-cuts a medium, pronounces it dead, and moves on like a conquistador to the next stage. The idea that art has an overall goal of advancing or perfecting its terms and techniques is imagined. It's idiotic. And it's worthless—except to those who devote all their energies to exploiting this intellectual fundamentalism. Someday, people will look back at this phase of art history the way we look back at manifest destiny and colonialism.

(2016)

Eric Fischl's Great New Work of American Art

At 10:17 p.m. on December 13, 2016—one month and one week after the presidential election—the well-known artist Eric Fischl did something he'd never done before. On Facebook, he posted an image with the words "New painting fresh off the easel." It was of a large canvas, begun days after the election, depicting what seems to be the group mind going blind and growing paranoid, possessed, self-annulled, vulnerable, perverse, rotten. In it, Fischl returns to ideas found in his earliest work: family, child-hood, parent-child relationships, sexual taboos, swimming pools, and sub-urbia. But there was something new, too. Looking at Fischl's new work, I felt I'd fallen through a trapdoor into a landscape of festering wounds formed by the election—a place artists will surely be exploring for a very, very long time.

The scene is a stylish backyard dominated by an in-ground pool; an array of four upholstered designer chaise longues, with matching tables; and a large green-poled deck umbrella. The surroundings are immacu-late, minimalistic, barren, a cliché out of any lifestyle magazine. Simply but lushly painted in blazing blue, white, green, and flesh tones, it's a suburban-American idyll—the territory behind bushes, hedges, walls, or within gated communities, isolated and invisible from the outside. Eden run on a skeleton crew. In the center of the painting, however, is a psychic avalanche: A hulking male figure, seeming half human and half creature of animal instinct, lies on his side on a towel on the concrete at the edge of the pool, contorted in some fetal seizure. His scrotum pokes between his legs. He's clown, clod, monster, victim. You don't know if this is a pose of fear, self-loathing, shame, insanity, radical exposure, masturbation, or ri-gor mortis.

One hallmark of Fischl's work is an absence of sequential narrative, which often leads to a kind of pictorial syntactic slippage—you don't know what you're looking at, exactly, nor how to look at it. Like a Zen koan, Fischl's work often manages to slow things down, to create both doubt and a new philosophical framework. Those elements are strong here. To the right of the man stands a boy, maybe ten years old. He carries a stuffed animal, wears white swim trunks, and is draped in an American-flag towel. He looks down at the man with his mouth slightly open. There's no other reaction; he's accepting, bored, as if at any time he might ask his dad for the remote control. In the background lurk a pair of male gardeners—dark shapes and guardian figures, props and prisoners. Other than con-firming that the painting was begun after the election, Fischl says only that he "wanted to see if the man was sick, wounded, unconscious, depressed, a figment of the imagination. I kept putting people in and taking them out as I tried to figure it out. The boy was the final addition, and though he doesn't answer any of the questions directly, he feels he must be there also."

I read the painting a dozen different ways, watched dozens of different American narratives unfold. Full of male figures, it's a story of the wreck of masculinity, something bankrupt, buckling, sick, unconscious of everything around it. In the naked man, who is totally somaticized, I see an empire ending in an infantile whimper, a country identified by the heroism and pain it is forgetting, turning inward, being consumed by itself. The man in Fischl's portrait is pampered, deluded, duped, marooned; he seems desperate for someone else, some other, to show the self-confidence he lacks, to make those he fears go away. So that he can be great again. Or at least forget that he hasn't lived up to his own expectations. The boy wrapped in the flag is cathecting on a stuffed animal in place of real love; he sees his potential future as a man blown to emotional smithereens before him, in a shapeless shambles. The most present-tense emotion in the painting comes from the workers in the background, who stifle their contempt as they're left to clean up the mess.

A great dysfunctional family unravels in Fischl's picture. This cowering, traumatized, naked man being seen this way by a child or his son evokes perversity, incest, and irresponsibility. And, to be honest, I have to admit that in this man I can also see myself, in my foul inconsolability, having witnessed the complete failure of almost every source of news and every institution in this country; losing faith, but trying to be reborn in stronger skin to pick up the fight. I also see my fellow privileged liberals, their technocratic universe no longer ascendant, horrified by the aberrant figure who is now president. The son becomes an orphan, or perhaps a new nativist, in this dawning American landscape. Apathetic, scornful, idle, he replaces the annihilated father on the spot. If we view this as a sequential narrative, read from left to right, the monstrosity of the father seems to beget the blasé nationalistic scion, indifferent to his father's chaotic collapse. Standing in the painting's dark light, I remembered Faulkner's line from *Absalom, Absalom!* "Now the period began which ended in the catastrophe."

The painting is titled, perfectly, *Late America*. To me, the *late* imparts the current darkness. I don't know what the *America* means anymore.

(2016)

Andreas Gursky Predicted the Future—and the Present

Artists often channel the future, seeing patterns before they form and putting them in their work, so that later, in hindsight, the work explodes like a time bomb.

In the months before September 11, 2001, in the long stupor following George W. Bush's selection as president by the Supreme Court, German über-photographer Andreas Gursky—known for his totalizing pictures of atriums, raves, hotel lobbies, and trading floors—made a spectacular color photograph of a Los Angeles big-box store. *99 Cent II Diptychon* presents us with mesmerizing rows of shelves, stocked with a prismatic array of inexpensive goods arranged for shoppers' delight. This picture seems to channel the comfortable cherry-cola numbness soon shattered by the attacks, which followed repeated ignored warnings of international foreboding.

Now, Gursky has done it again with *Amazon*—a boat-size picture made months before the 2016 U.S. election, in which he foreshadows something in our information systems, which exist in a state of such high complexity, such near unmaintainability, that they live only on the verge of our understanding.

Amazon is a portrait of the unknowable patterns of contemporary mass consumption and the hyperdistribution of goods. Behold its amorphous Sargasso Sea. More than thirteen feet long and almost eight feet tall, the picture is simple, recognizable, even banal—the vast interior of an Amazon warehouse in Phoenix. It's empty of everything but endless rows of shelves with goods. Once a year Amazon conducts inventory, clearing all workers. It was on this no-ghosts-in-the-machine day that Gursky took his picture of the near future.

Amazon is a single image—not hundreds tiled together, as is often the case in digital photography. Everything is equally in focus, giving the picture an uncanny vividness—as if we're seeing the world the way an insect might see it. It's like a modernized Monet, with a shimmering, undifferentiated, optically equal field of flecked color. There are three pillars in the background, each sporting an almost Stalinist bromide: *Work Hard, Have Fun, Make History.* The bins in the distance become skyboxes or maybe a mountain range.

Even though they picture similar things, there's a huge difference between *99 Cent* and *Amazon*. In the 2001 picture, viewers reveled in endless order, looking within a contained space we've all navigated. *Amazon* is another superspecies altogether. We are not really looking at a space at all, let alone one we're familiar with. Instead we are seeing an algorithm made physical, a Borgesian or Kafkaesque labyrinth of causes, effects, rhythms, and ratios. The art critic in me sees an indoor earthwork, a consumer-based Robert Smithson *Spiral Jetty*. Or a hyperversion of Ed Ruscha's *Every Building on the Sunset Strip*, from 1966—a landmark fold-out photographic record of exactly that. From *Amazon*, I glean what Malevich called "the supremacy of pure sensation," where "every real form is a world." The strangest part is, this nonspace is where we all live.

A narcotic power radiates from this kaleidoscopic picture. Nothing is arranged alphabetically. Or by product type, size, shape, weight, material, origin of manufacture. A different principle is at work. You could call it *space-time*: Goods stocked to be retrieved as quickly and efficiently as possible, so that what we're seeing are cross-referenced patterns and configurations of consumption—the rhythms of the way we live (and consume), but mapped in ways that are unintelligible to us. Here, packages of Spanx sit near thermometers next to posters next to Play-Doh near *Jeter Unfiltered*, all of it cheek by jowl with dolls, Japanese calendars, books on hypnotism, construction manuals, toner cartridges, aerobic instructions. A police exam lives next to a yoga mat, near a fire extinguisher, near knapsacks and a book of Jackson Pollock's recipes.

I knew when I saw it that this work was really thumping with something. And then, the week after the election, I saw the picture for the second time—and saw something that made the hair on my neck stand up. In the lower part of the picture, a *Donald Trump for President* cup. I wondered who else bought items near this one. I saw cups, Christmas cards, Ian W. Toll's World War II book *The Conquering Tide*, a *Star Wars* game, books on biology and mathematics, toys, a stuffed monkey, boxing gloves, candy bars, a plastic fossil of a beetle, envelopes, a tie rack, a hairbrush, Trojan prophylactics. All the cryptologists and Egyptologists in the world wouldn't be able to discern the political patterns of these physical hieroglyphics. But they are still there: patterns that go beyond buying habits, capturing deeper codes: of class, age, gender, geography, race, religion, economics, educational level, sexuality, even voting. I yearned to see a preelection twelve-month time-lapse film of *Amazon:* individual items and groupings going in and out of stock—appearing, ebbing, flowing, changing placement, reconfiguring, appearing elsewhere—to see whether they corresponded to other constellations of goods. I imagined the colors of the shelves changing like an octopus skin altering to adapt to new environments. It might show us the group mind and multiple patterns of hundreds of millions of people.

But those patterns can't be seen, not all at once, not properly. Only the algorithm knows them—and the algorithm is buggy in ways even it doesn't recognize, and is predicting things that then turn out to be false. Like us, it fails to see patterns that were there the whole time.

I thought back a week to the night before the election, to the last Hillary Clinton rally, in Philadelphia, where Bon Jovi and Bruce Springsteen both sang sets before the Clintons and Obamas spoke for the last time before the election. In song and words, both musicians seemed to be imploring their core demographic—undereducated white males—*not* to vote for Trump. Remembering the event now, their melancholic sets reminded me of *Amazon*. The script had been flipped and no one knew it yet, although the patterns were there. Not with an apocalyptic bang or a Romantic cataclysm, but with a quiet electronic whirr, a paradigm shift was already in action.

(2016)

Considering the Ankara Assassination Photos as History Painting

I've never seen anything like the photographs by Burhan Özbilici of the assassination of the Russian ambassador at an art gallery in Ankara, Turkey. The event itself was a pathological act of terrorism, a nationalist bloodletting, a state of political siege. But in the pristine, stark-white setting of a contemporary art gallery, with patrons, assassin, and victim all dressed in elegant black, the photographs themselves look strikingly surreal—uncanny, even—and, in some very painful ways, beautiful.

What makes these pictures so different from all the other pictures of death that we see? The poses are almost classical in appearance; the figures they depict are frozen, as if captured during some theater or ballet rehearsal, some painting or mannequin display. The photographer, working the art opening for the Associated Press, deserves the enormous credit he's received for responding as fluidly as a war photographer to the sudden outbreak of violence. But if I told you that the images were fake, or staged, you might believe me. As Kurt Andersen put it on Twitter, "The great photojournalism of 2016 is continuing to resemble stills from a scary, not-entirely-realistic movie"—and that strange familiarity we feel in look-ing at the images is one reason they are so uncomfortable to contemplate. Everything in the images is emotion articulated, caught, performed, and real. All of this triggers an unreal internal visual dance. It's a new surreal-ism of modern life, made all the more harrowing because it could not be more truly real.

The most instantly iconic picture is the assassin standing, brandishing a gun, gesturing, pointing a finger overhead, admonishing onlookers with the corpse sprawled and dramatically foreshortened behind him. The scene could be a modern-day martyrdom by the most theatrical painter of them all, Caravaggio; the prelude to Jacques-Louis David's *Oath of the Horatii*; or one of Robert Longo's large black-and-white drawings of figures in dramatic arrested motion—human beings seemingly cut out from the world, thrust onto this pictorial stage.

In this image, frozen perpetual motion: An entire scene of action and worldview is caught in an instant. Notice the picture is in perfect focus. This is not the shaky, out-of-focus, ill-framed onlooker shot of assassinations and revolutions past. Özbilici is obviously a pro, and the setting, both quo-tidian and stagey, is surely an element of the image's strangeness. The gal-lery lighting balances and color-corrects everything, theatricalizes it all the more, making the action that much more striking. Look close and notice the key factor: This picture is taken from eye level. The photographer isn't running away, hiding, in another room or in a crouch. Whether cravenly or by instinct, the photographer immediately reacted, moved into the action from almost straight on, framing the picture perfectly. His eye instinctively invested the images with frontality, clarity, structure, density, form. This is far from an accidental image; it is radically self-determined, powerfully formal; whatever the photographer's intent, its effect is polemical.

The picture of the group of onlookers huddled in a corner is taken from close up. Although it, too, was captured from a standing position, it ap-pears as though the photographer stooped over these people to take the picture. None of them takes notice of him. The photographer is absolutely present, yet simultaneously *not there*. (Even the assassin didn't look at him.)

In an effect familiar from great paintings of dramatic crowd scenes, this neatly cropped group photo is an encyclopedia of individual reactions. The weeping woman on the left is held by a man; she looks into herself, at the agony within, more than at the room. The man is on one knee, ready to move, but with one eye on the still-unfolding action in front of him. He gives the picture its eternal *now*, helped by the rolled-up magazine he holds. Next to him is a crouching man, a figure that could have been drawn during any academic figure-drawing class. His profile is strong, his pose stable, his body clad in black. (As with the central figures, his head obscures the identity of the two women behind him.) Next is what looks to be a couple: She's on the floor with her knees up, her purse poised on her skirt, her eyes attentive but still turned inward. Finally, what passes as a figure of wisdom in this picture: He's older, with a bush of curly, thinning hair, looking on forlornly, knowingly, as if he's aware that this is history, happening beyond his control.

The only person violating the frame, getting out of the scene, is in color: a woman, dressed in blue, entering another existence. Looking at her, we realize that we are stuck with her in this configuration—looking for, but unable to find, a way out.

(2017)

Look Outward, Artist: What Photography Can Learn from Danny Lyon

Were there any artists who documented the rise of Trump? His rallies, his voters, his America? If the election was a sudden return to history—one liberals were too self-confident to see coming—where was the history painting of the era? Where are all the close-up pictures of fomenting populist rage, the burgeoning racism, nativism, bigotry? As far as I know, no artist captured this, unless in some abstract, still indiscernible way. *All* of our visual images of Trumpism have come from two sources, neither very reliable: First, Trump supporters themselves. (I follow as many as I can: Students for Trump, Women for Trump, and so on. But their pictures are all the same: unironic small groups of happy, waving white people in red MAGA hats.) Second, from the news, whose focus in the end was *only* on Trump's behavior and words. And as much as he loved the gaze of the camera banks at his rallies, Trump was right to say, panderingly, that the cameras should have been turned away from him, should have been focused on the crowd. Only C-SPAN showed these crowds in extended unedited pre- and post-speech detail shots. (The media were much more fond of tracking the crowds of Bernie Sanders.)

So why didn't any artists rush in to fill the void? First of all, because Trump's candidacy happened fast. Few saw his rise as a void to fill until it was too late. More to the point, by 2015, even the most topical art had trained its sights on large, deeply rooted structures such as systemic racism, homophobia, sexism, capitalism, or colonialism—except when artists were working out *their own* issues, usually involving aspects of identity and personal history. This often prioritized subject matter and autobiography over visual originality. But artists don't have to choose, and their work does not have to advocate to be political, or even to take politics as its subject. Instead, it can choose injustice, or outrage, despair, community, vengeance, doom—that is, the world and all the ways it is perpetually and violently disrupted.

But something else happened, by and large during Obama's presidency. By the end of his eight years, many had come to treat their politics as an outward projection of their position and activism. This narrowed the political discourse and subtly discouraged critical dissent. If a given artwork was presented as confronting misogyny, any criticism of the work could result in charges of sexism—even if the work was simplistic, derivative, or just bad. Exclusion of such work from exhibitions or collections could bring accusations of bias. In this way, the art world politically insulated itself while placing itself above its larger audience, often preaching in elaborate formal languages that only the choir knew.

Still, the era did give us great art. One artist whose work was recently on view at Gavin Brown's enterprise demands attention in this context—especially when it comes to photography. Even after his godsend of a Whitney retrospective last summer, it's probable that most people have still never heard of one of the most powerful and political photographers in history: Danny Lyon. This is partly because his work couldn't be more different from what is often celebrated as good photography today; more on that later. But it may have more to do with the fact that Lyon had disappeared almost completely from the art world radar. So much so that, three years ago, despite being a lifelong fan, I embarrassed myself by asking Lyon's excellent artist son, Noah, "Is your dad still alive?" Yes, he was, and working nonstop as he always has, now in Bernalillo, New Mexico, where he lives with his wife and dogs. Yet I hadn't seen a gallery show of Lyon's work in decades.

That just changed with the fantastic look back at his pictures from the early sixties at Gavin Brown last month. Born in 1942 and raised in Queens—a self-described "white boy from Forest Hills"—in 1962 he took a camera and hitchhiked to Cairo, Illinois, to be part of the civil rights movement. "The movement became my life," he told me. "The law was wrong and it was our responsibility to break it." There he encountered and was inspired by John Lewis, then chairman of the Student Nonviolent Coordinating Committee (SNCC) and an organizer of the 1963 March on Washington, now a civil rights hero and congressman, and one of Trump's continual bêtes noires. That fall, the white boy from Forest Hills became SNCC's "official photographer." Lyon saw it all: sit-ins, riots, prison cells, marchers, mobs, Martin Luther King, Jr., Muhammad Ali. Lyon ran from white gangs, hid in cars with guns, escaped police by giving false names (including "Paul Newman") at airports. Yet he was so adroit that part of our collective impression of what this struggle looked like—its bravery, camaraderie, suffering, danger, triumph, and violence—derives from Lyon. The famous *One Man One Vote* poster of a black man in overalls; fifteen young black women held in a Georgia stockade; a black choir singing at the March on Washington; mobs turning on demonstrators—all these are Lyon's pictures. In some ways he sums up the look and feel of the political early sixties as much as Jackson Pollock's drips define the look and feel of the cultural early fifties.

Like many Americans, I saw many of these photographs at the time; they were part of our news wallpaper. But I never knew these were Lyon's pictures until much later. I just thought they were incredible and scary. After this, he recorded the authorized architectural destruction of lower Manhattan as witnessed from his downtown loft. Soon, he was a member of Chicago's notorious Outlaws motorcycle gang. I grew up around Chicago and these guys were genuine "tough hombres." By the end of the sixties, he was photographing Southern chain gangs, which is when I first saw *Conversations with the Dead*. His book on the subject changed my life.

Like practically everyone of my generation, I was pretty politically active when I was young. In 1968, when I was in high school, I took the subway from my comfy suburb to Grant Park, where Chicago police didn't wait long before starting to beat us protesters. (It was on that very night, when the police were shown beating white kids rather than people of color, that my right-wing stepmother and all her friends turned against the war. When white kids are beaten, change happens.) But Lyon's close-up black-and-white photos, his personal interviews of prisoners, his involvement in the minutiae of their lives, showed me that great art and activism could commingle and still retain art's mysterious ability to invite our gaze a thousand times and have it affect us differently every time. (I still study Lyon's pictures.) Lyon went on to do this with immigrants at the southern border, and more recently in China. He was one of an array of fellow geniuses who also took to the streets to make their work, including Diane Arbus, Garry Winogrand (my fave), Robert Frank, and the visionary Weegee, as well as photographers like Robert Adams, Lewis Baltz, and Stephen Shore (collectively known as the New Topographics—a group that recorded suburbia's encroachment on the landscape, implicitly showing the rape of the land, the socioeconomics, and the white flight that were shaping America). The work of these artists was as visually and politically radical as any history painting, as stylistically risky as the Impressionists. They were models of what I thought photographers should be.

But this future was not to be. In the seventies, America turned inward. So-called political activism and street photography were back-burnered. The art market as we know it today was still nascent; universities were mainly where art was coming from. For the first time in history, almost all artists had come through art school. This changed the art world in many ways. First, the teachers—mostly older white men who believed that art had been better in the sixties, their heyday—tended to shunt aside women, and they also promulgated their own internal biases against painting. This made the very act of painting itself seem radical. (I remember how shocked I was when I started smelling oil paint again in galleries in around 1980!) For women to paint, in that moment, seemed especially revolutionary. Schools also professionalized the art world, foregrounding a focus on careers, galleries, networking, and the art market.

By the eighties, these artists—many of them women who had found the doors of painting closed to them—took up the camera as a tool and a weapon. In doing so, they created a new and powerful activist art. Using images and found objects, the artists of the Pictures Generation—like Barbara Kruger, Louise Lawler, Laurie Simmons, and Cindy Sherman, as well as Richard Prince and many others—were warriors who used cameras without partaking of traditional street or landscape photography or overt journalism. They weren't recording the news; they were making it, using the photograph not just to record found reality but to transform what it captured into a new reality. This work was thrilling to me—as thrilling, probably, as the work I had seen by Lyon and others in the sixties. The artist's identity was always present in the overt manipulation of these images; the artist was never a passive bystander. It's impossible to look at a Kruger image-text piece and not think, "What side am I on?" They still put me on inner notice.

After Pictures art came a group of artists—almost none of them American, almost all of them men—who scaled up the ideas of New

Topographics into a new universe of huge, glitzy pictures, then color-
ized, spectacularized, theatricalized, and theorized them. Artists like Andreas Gursky, Thomas Struth, and Thomas Ruff (so ubiquitous in the
nineties that I collectively called them Struffsky, prompting a nasty note
from one of them), as well as Canadians like Jeff Wall and Rodney Graham, pulled photography in a bigger, more narrative direction, influenced
by the storytelling and production values of movies and billboards as well
as traditional history painting. Wall's gigantic-setup aesthetic, with its numerous allusions to other art, makes him, for me, the best art history student ever. (Never mind that only art world denizens might catch his
allusions.) The politics here involved seduction, toward the end of addressing great systems: industrial farming, world trade, museums, architecture,
and the like. Instead of the politics of the body, their work focused on the
buzzy hum of modern life, and on what Rem Koolhaas famously called
Junkspace.

After September 11, 2001, the movement's preoccupation with the spec-
tacles of the 1990s—think the Berlin Wall—were suddenly passé. The medium turned inward, until it had become essentially a matter of photography
about photography. We were flooded with photographs of cameras, of photographs, of ads; with scenes shot against TV green screens; with commercial photography color cards, light fixtures, film boxes, film, digital
patterns, even pictures of the chemicals used in old-style photography. This
was Zombie Photography. And in the Bush era, believe it or not, I totally
understood and embraced some of it. We all got that administration's message loud and clear: "We don't give a shit what you think. We make up our
own reality." In an era when war and economic collapse were foisted on
America, it's not surprising that artists should turn their backs, gather
around their own artistic campfires to commiserate, hone their ideas into
finer and finer bytes. It was, in its way, an act of defiance, even if that defiance was comprehensible only to those in the know.

But Donald Trump is different from George W. Bush. The history
we're living today is of a type we haven't experienced since the eras of civil
rights, the Vietnam War, and the AIDS crisis. Everyone feels the urgency:

We are being invaded, and the impact is fracturing us. This is what a test of time feels like. And the government isn't going to save us.

My favorite scene in *Apocalypse Now* is when the Martin Sheen character asks a soldier in a firefight, "Do you know who's in charge here?" The terrified soldier pleads, "I thought you were!" Next he asks another soldier the same question and he calmly replies, "Yes." Meaning, *We are in charge.* Our current moment gives all of us agency: It falls to us to take matters into our own hands. No one is a spectator. We're in it. Individuality and the group mind are mingling in new ways. This is why we mustn't become art police, demanding that art must "be political." *All art is political,* because within every contemporary artist is the *deep content* of our time. All of that is in their work—even if it's just stripes or squiggles, done unoriginally, in a fever, with insight. Art, in other words, is going through the same changes you are, that we all are. Last week, for instance, I saw a great protest sign: a stark blue, geometric abstract painting by Cary Smith, an image that seemed to say, "Focus on this, motherfuckers."

The challenge of our moment is already changing our consciousness, replacing hopelessness and passive alienation. This isn't to call on artists to make "political art." God save us from the reams of explicit, insipid political art that may well wash over us. This isn't a call for the end of formalist or conceptual photography, either. Nevertheless, it does seem that something is stirring in younger artists that stirred in Danny Lyon long ago. Some photographers may hitchhike to the heartland to take pictures of Trump supporters; others may focus on the new faces of those of us who feel like we're part of a countermovement. Either way, for this stain to be erased from America, two things need to happen: First, right-wing overreach and failure must lead to sustained protest; second, the energy of the streets can recruit us all as change agents. At a moment when America hangs in the balance again, we need to see how the world looks without the filters of the news and its rogues' gallery of zealots. We need to see America singing.

(2017)

Basquiat Painting Becomes Priciest Work
Ever Sold by a U.S. Artist

ulu Garcia-Navarro, NPR: It's been splashed on screens large and small
this past week . . . the exhilarating painting of a big disembodied
skull clenching its teeth, outlined with violent slashes of black and red
paint against a sky-blue background. The late Jean-Michel Basquiat is the
artist, and it just sold for an unprecedented $110.5 million at Sotheby's.
We're joined by Jerry Saltz to talk about the significance of the work and
its price tag.

So tell me about this painting. Maybe take us back to 1982, when he was
painting it at twenty-one years old, a few years before he died of a heroin
overdose at twenty-seven.

Jerry Saltz: It's 1981, 1982. You have this twenty-one-year-old artist
having their debut in New York, and it goes off like an atomic bomb. Basquiat, of course, is probably the only artist of color involved in any part
of the art world at that time, and he was a spectacle to behold. I saw him
on the streets of New York, and he truly was what he was called—a radiant child.

LGN: He's of Haitian and Puerto Rican descent. He's been called
America's van Gogh. Talk about his importance to the art world.

JS: Basquiat is an extraordinary example of taking his own identity,
growing up as a black man in New York, and combining it with art history
via a lot of expressionistic wild-style painting, where every single inch of the
surface is activated and coming at you with optical power aggressively so,
really hard. He has a kind of graffiti energy, where he's writing words,
making references to Muhammad Ali, famous bluesmen, writing numbers.
There's a kind of almost overload, overspeeding, hyperbolic activities. And

this style is singular, and it also sings of an American spirit, of this amazing hodgepodge but also the long American night.

LGN: In your view, what is the correlation between the price of a work and its value? Does the enormous sum paid at auction for this particular work make this Basquiat his most important piece?

JS: Absolutely not. In fact, the art world has been so distracted by ridiculously obscenely high prices that mainly the only art that people are even aware of is art that costs a lot of money. But no artist of color has ever entered this kind of pantheon—you know, Picasso, van Gogh, those whose work does sometimes sell for over $100 million. So you know what? I have to make a strange exception to my rule. In this case, I kind of love that Jean-Michel Basquiat has broken that barrier. More power to women, more power to artists of color. These lives do matter, and they're going to continue to matter.

(2017)

The Obamas' Official Portraits Rise to the Occasion

On Abraham Lincoln's 209th birthday, four American firsts have brought dignity, respect, and art together to remind us that this country can embody love, hope, and things bigger than the misrule and chaos that seem to define who we are today and will be for at least the near future. Today at the National Portrait Gallery in Washington, D.C., four shots of love: the first official portrait of an African American president, painted by an African American artist, and the first portrait of an African American first lady, painted by an African American woman artist.

The president's portrait is by Kehinde Wiley, a forty-year-old art world megastar. Wiley is known as a maker of highly precise, plastic-looking photorealistic images of black men and women placed in fabulous surroundings, pictured in the guises of mythic figures, ancient gods, and historical hotshots like Napoleon. Known for his sartorial snazz, the chief of a major studio where assistants work on canvases, Wiley is an artist in demand, his work commanding astronomical prices. Explaining his choice of Wiley, the former president said, "What I was always struck by when I saw his portraits was the degree to which they challenged our ideas of power and privilege."

Happily, Wiley rises to the occasion. His Barack Obama is a troubled human Rock of Gibraltar, seated on a hard wooden seat that hints at the bare-bones look of African tribal chairs. The president is seated in and among—not out in front of—a verdigris overgrowth of flowers. He's almost fighting for the stage that is already growing over him. But he remains. Real, insistent, evidently pure of heart, a reminder or compass. Steering clear of his usual bravado and grandiosity, which tends to so elevate his subjects that the paintings approach kitsch, Wiley's treatment of Obama allows the person to bloom more fully. Positioning the president this way, enmeshed in an overabundant, colorful natural setting, gives him a much more mysteriously human presence—not merely *knowing*, separate, but somehow both brooding and kindled with innate curiosity, seated at the border of the ordinary and the extraordinary. It's exactly the metaphysical place Obama embodied as president of all America. Many may dislike Obama being presented this way—may feel he's been made too normal, too small, denied the grandeur of an imperial god. I think the picture is true to the way Obama carries himself. He's clearly the central subject but not entirely; he's open to his surroundings, part of them but not the only thing present. He's still fighting for space. Wiley even gets some of Obama's melancholy, his tranquilizing thoughtfulness, the whispering sense that he will not be smote.

Then there's the portrait of Michelle Obama by Amy Sherald,

forty-four, who lives in Baltimore. Sherald had a heart transplant in her thirties; her work has come to light only recently, under the aegis of a portrait exhibition overseen by National Portrait Gallery curator Dorothy Moss. At the unveiling, the president noted that Sherald's portrait of the first lady captures "the grace and beauty and intelligence and charm and hotness of the woman that I love." Indeed, Sherald portrays this woman, whose great-great-grandfather and great-great-great-grandmother were slaves, in ways that challenge every convention. Seated, wearing a chic black-and-white Michelle Smith–designed gown, her hair down and wavy, her bare arms blazing, chin resting on her hand, she is an everyday queen of heaven: grand, elegant, gorgeous, but her jackrabbit-quick wit is right there. Set against a monochrome flat powder blue, the first lady is a compass star to another kind of glamour, a serious spirit whose face suggests a sly sense of humor, warmth, and protectiveness. And a different idea of female power and beauty: As the first lady said at the unveiling, Sherald's work will have impact on "girls and girls of color . . . They will see an image of someone who looks like them hanging on the wall of this great American institution. I know the kind of impact that will have on their lives because I was one of those girls."

Looking at the paintings, President Obama talked about art that can picture the "beauty and the grace and the dignity of people who are so often invisible in our lives, and put them on a grand stage." Of those people, he said, "Kehinde lifted them up and gave them a platform and said they belonged at the center of American life." Amen. Then he casually mused that, as far as he could tell, he and Michelle were the only people in their family trees ever to have their portraits made. These four firsts, and the larger truths they represent, transcend any minor quibbles about these pictures and offer new reason to believe America might yet be delivered from its current moral, spiritual, and political disarray.

(2018)

The Drawing I Can't Stop Thinking About: Bear's Heart at Frieze

A great work of art from 1875, never before seen in any museum, almost never seen by anyone—indeed, all but lost to history—recently sat radioactive on the wall of a small gallery at the Frieze New York art fair. A simple depiction in prismatic hues—pencil and lustrous color—it somehow seemed to express a thousand anxieties, lost freedoms, secreted emotions, omens of anger, empty worlds, tears, and the life of a captive. In the image, we see a canary-yellow locomotive pulling a decorated red coal car and an invisible payload moving against a landscape of fields of corn, front yards, wooden fences, towns, buildings, and tracks, all running through the back of America's memory. This is the end of the journey of seventy-two Cheyenne, Arapaho, and Kiowa prisoners of war who were found guilty without trial, then removed from their native lands of eastern Colorado, western Kansas, northern New Mexico, Oklahoma, and the Texas panhandle—the site of their traditional Plains way of life, a region that once teemed with herds of wild horses and bison. They were piled on horse carts, ships, and train cars, and carried to a prison camp at Fort Marion in St. Augustine, Florida.

The artist is Bear's Heart, one of the seventy-two prisoners on that forgotten train. Once the captives reached Fort Marion, they were subjected to forced labor. However, to please visiting tourists the prisoners were also encouraged to draw. Thus, like prisoners everywhere, these artists found coded ways to depict their captivity. The resulting image gives us an instantaneous spatial and emotional estuary of integrated opposites. The vantage point of the drawing flips from frontal and straight on—the left being the bottom of the image with the tracks turning right—to an overhead depiction of a planted field, with fences curving in every direction. It seems to capture the last lost moment of life outside camp walls, with color, a sense of life in the world, a world that is enjoyed, not endured. The thought that the person who made this paid with years of his life for the "honor" of creating it drills into my heart.

In other drawings, the twenty-four-year-old Bear's Heart depicted Cheyenne cosmology, dragonflies, and butterflies. For millennia it was imagined that art could heal wounds, serve as a balm to defeat, death, loss, and the injustices of history. In our museums we feel this. But we cannot know this with Bear's Heart's gleaming hellish drawing, because almost none of the many great ledger drawings made in this period have ever been integrated into any museum's permanent collection. I think this artist's work could go up against anything made anywhere in 1875. And should—soon. As for Bear's Heart, in 1881 he settled at the Cheyenne-Arapaho Agency in Oklahoma, where he died of tuberculosis in the year of his thirtieth birthday.

(2017)

Kara Walker's Triumphant New Show Is the Best Art Made About America in This Century

James Baldwin once said that "No true account really of black life can be held, can be contained, in the American vocabulary." Kara Walker's devastating new exhibition suggests that such an account might be given visually. Or at least that Walker is coming close.

Walker's Boschian American Babylon—a tableau of race and rage, dominance and submission, barbarity, hatred, irredeemable evil, self-cretinizing white people, modern Black Power figures, shuffling black cleaning ladies, Civil War soldiers, beneficent whites, plantation owners drawn and quartered by rebellious slaves, pickaninnies and Sambos sexually servicing white masters or being castrated—is as terrifyingly beautiful as Bosch, as haunted and mysterious as Conrad's *Heart of Darkness*.

It is not, and should not be, a surprise that Walker has achieved something this monstrously magnificent. I've written on Walker since 1994, the year I was thunderstruck when I saw her student work at RISD—a drawing, rendered in chocolate, of a "white" child trying to wash the color off a "black" child. Here was a coming avenging angel. Beginning with the cut-paper silhouette mural she exhibited at the Drawing Center that same year, which also focused on historical brutality and ugliness, Walker has been exactly that. And yet she has also been attacked by established artists of color who said—and still say!—she's gone too far, making work they consider a disservice to their political cause. Since then, she's only gotten better, braver, stronger, more skilled, more fearless.

The name of her show is written in barker banter. (Walker is tremendous with language.) It reads, in part: "Collectors of Fine Art will Flock to see the latest Kara Walker offerings, and what is she offering but the Finest Selection of *artworks* by an African-American Living Woman Artist this side of the Mississippi." It continues: "Students of Color will eye her work suspiciously and exercise their free right to Culturally Annihilate her on social media. Parents will cover the eyes of innocent children. . . . The Final President of the United States will visibly wince. Empires will fall . . ." An accompanying artist's statement, meanwhile, reads as a manifesto for artists of color: "I am tired, tired of standing up, being counted, tired of 'having a voice' or worse 'being a role model.' Tired, true, of being a featured member of my racial group and/or my gender niche. It's too much. . . . My capacity to live in this Godforsaken country as a (proudly) raced and (urgently) gendered person is under threat by random groups of white (male) supremacist goons who flaunt a kind of patched together notion of race purity with flags and torches and impressive displays of perpetrator-as-victim sociopathy." It concludes by marveling at "how many ways will the racists among our countrymen act out their *Turner Diaries* race war fantasy combination Nazi Germany and Antebellum South—states which, incidentally, *lost the wars they started*, and always will, precisely because there is no way those white racisms can survive the earth." We're optical geographers in Walker's grotesque phantasmagorical landscape of American racial dreams: a United Failed States of America. Walker is reclaiming her name, declaring, essentially, *I am an artist*—not a *black artist*—*who is sick and tired of the long American night of racism, and I will now use my work to attack it head-on.*

In addition to a number of smaller paintings, the show contains two large and venomous masterpieces, *The Pool Party of Sardanapalus (after Delacroix, Kienholz)* and *U.S.A. Idioms.* These are done in a process that is new to Walker, but so perfect that it's extraordinary she didn't hit on it sooner, if only as a way to solve the kinds of problems that can arise when compositions get large and can't be changed: She deploys cutout images drawn in sumi ink onto giant white sheets of paper by blowing up her drawings, which allows her to move them around within her giant compositions (rather than never being able to change a single part without affecting the whole). This offers new possibilities of scale, surface, and spatial organization, raising drawing to the level of history painting as Walker achieves with collage and drawing what she has already pioneered with silhouette. Included in these two audacious works are images of slave children seeking rescue from a tree topped by a Confederate banner, slaves burying dead soldiers, and an urban gangster knifing a shirtless black man as a white man tries to restrain him. Finally, a black woman—Walker herself?—sticks a knife or pen into the bloated belly of a fat, hands-up, naked Donald Trump. It's extraordinary to see an artist responding so sharply to the incredible political storm blowing all around us. I am told that these giants have been done in the last few months.

Another of her new works, however, rises above even these two standouts. Along with Walker's gigantic 2014 sugarcoated, sphinxlike Aunt Jemima, it is perhaps the greatest work about America made in the twenty-first century. The painting, titled *Christ's Entry into Journalism*, should be installed permanently next to the Met's *Washington Crossing the Delaware* as a post–Civil War/contemporary counterbalance. It is as big as a barge, an inchoate Sadean vision of nearly one hundred figures drawn in Walker's signature style, a vision that evokes Brueghel, Daumier, Goya, and Ensor.

Most directly, the work echoes James Ensor's gigantic 1888 masterpiece *Christ's Entry into Brussels in 1889*. Walker's painting depicts an uncentered mystic mountain of murder, pillage, carpetbaggers, lumpen golems, and historical figures, including Trayvon Martin's hoodie-clad head presented on a platter borne by a white lady—perhaps an allegorical figure of Justice—surrounded by a Batman figure fleeing with a mummy-wrapped Uncle Ben–like man while a black church lady begs for the boy's body.

Elsewhere in the composition, a black man is clubbed by a white policeman in riot gear who videos it on his iPhone. Walker is out for blood. An explorer applies calipers to the naked ass of Sarah Baartman, a real-life figure who was taken into captivity in Africa, brought to Europe, and humiliated before throngs as the "Hottentot Venus." A process-haired James Brown belts into a microphone; marchers with protest signs march; a naked man with an enormous penis performs cunnilingus on a screaming naked black woman as a white church lady strikes him with her umbrella. At the bottom right is Martin Luther King, Jr. Lest you think you are projecting identities onto these figures, near the top are two birdman figures or Klansmen. One has a thought balloon that reads OBVIOUSLY WE'RE CONTEMPORARY REFERENCES.

This brings us to the crescendo of this empire-destroying machine. At the bottom, a Black Panther–like figure stands beside a Frederick Douglass look-alike, giving the Black Power salute as he holds the severed head of Donald Trump aloft by its hair, a swastika penciled on its forehead. Finally, at the top of this pile, a corpulent, double-hooded Klansman stands between the two birdmen. From beneath the legs of this KKK member, an impish personage lifts his robes and sticks his tongue out at us while excreting. And there he is again: Donald Trump. Nearby, two swinging black girls perform a trapeze act from a branch that also holds a lynched body. The scene encapsulates Walker's lethal ability to mix the historical grotesque with carnivalesque madness in ways that horrify and accuse, sparing no one—and that keep us forever afire in a vent of psychic perdition. If this work doesn't end up on permanent display in a prominent New York museum, it will be a crime.

(2017)

Christie's Is Selling This Painting for $100 Million. They Say It's by Leonardo. I Have Doubts. Big Doubts

S andwiched between onlookers who'd waited in line outside in the cold to be ushered into the dimmed Christie's gallery, to gaze and gawk at what the auction house trumpets as "the greatest and most unexpected artistic rediscovery of the twenty-first century"—that is, a brand-new Leonardo da Vinci lost in the 1600s, scheduled to be auctioned off this week—a well-known expert in the field leaned over and asked me a question. "Why is a Leonardo in a Modern and Contemporary auction?" Before I could say *Yeah! Why?* he answered, "Because ninety percent of it was painted in the last fifty years."

He's right. Not only does this supposed lost masterpiece look like someone's dreamed-up version of a missing Leonardo, an array of X-ray techniques have revealed scratches and gouges in the work, paint missing, a warping board, a beard here and gone, and other parts of the painting that appear to have been brushed up and corrected to make this probable copy look more like an original.

The painting, titled *Salvator Mundi* (*Savior of the World*), is a portrait of a smoky floating man in a blue robe looking at us, raising his right hand in blessing, holding a crystal orb in his left hand, pictured against a black background. It's said to have been painted around 1500, when the real Leonardo would have been forty-eight years old and already the most famous artist alive. On Wednesday night, this small picture is being auctioned off by Christie's with massive jubilation. The opening bid is set at $100 million. (Which might seem cheap when you remember that Damien Hirst's 2007 *For the Love of God*, a diamond-and-platinum-encrusted human skull, carried the same price.) This explains why one Christie's official rapturously primed the collector pump by wondering aloud if someone might bid $2 billion. In a world this out of whack, that could happen. Promoting the sale is a glossy 162-page book with quotes from Dostoyevsky, Freud, and Leonardo, and several platitudinal Christie's videos of enraptured gazers gawking in wonder at "the new masterpiece." Don't miss the extended clip of three male company bigwigs pitching the painting to Hong Kong clients as "the holy grail of our business, a male Mona Lisa, the last da Vinci, our baby, something with blockbuster appeal, akin to the discovery of a new planet, and more valuable than a petrochemical plant."

I'm no art historian, or any kind of expert in Old Masters. But I've looked at art for almost fifty years, and one look at this painting tells me it's no Leonardo. The painting is absolutely dead. Its surface is both lurid and inert, scrubbed over, varnished, and repainted so many times that it looks simultaneously new and old. This explains why Christie's pitches it with vague terms like "mysterious," filled with "aura," and something that "could go viral." Go viral? As a poster, maybe. A two-dimensional ersatz dashboard Jesus.

Why else do I think this is a sham? Experts estimate that there are only fifteen to twenty Leonardo paintings in existence. Not a single one of them pictures a person straight on, as this painting does. Nor is there a single painting picturing an individual Jesus. All of Leonardo's work, including his single portraits, depicts figures in far more complex poses. Even the figure that comes remotely close to this painting, *Saint John the Baptist*, also from 1500, gives us a young, turning, randy-looking man with hair utterly different from that of the figure shown here, much more developed than the few curls Christie's is raving about in their picture. Leonardo was an inventor of—and in love with—the practice of posing people in dynamic positions; his figures are shown weaving, curving, corkscrewing, their positions predicting the compositions of Raphael, then in his twenties, and already being highly influenced by his contemporary Leonardo. Renaissance masters were all about letting figures interact with the surface and the structure of the painting, bending space, involving the viewer far more than an old-fashioned direct headshot could. Leonardo never let a subject come at you all at once in the style of this painting, with its flat, forward-facing Byzantine symmetry. No other Renaissance master dabbled in Byzantine portraiture like this either. By then, they were all pushing way beyond such old conventions.

Christie's marketing has played the "golden ratio" card heavily here. The golden section, or golden ratio—widely employed in ancient Greek art, and which had a huge influence in the Renaissance—is a mathematical system of measuring space whereby rectangles and proportions within the painting can in turn be divided into an almost endless, fractal series of repeating smaller rectangles, squares, ovals, and the like. The Christie's painting *is* riddled with this proportion. However, I'd imagine that no great artist worth their name would stoop to being this obvious, especially this far into their career, when they had total freedom to do as they wished—and had spent a lifetime doing so in increasingly original ways. All those enthralled by the idea that *Salvator Mundi* is based on a perfect golden section need to get a grip, to remember that the golden section can be imposed, to one extent or another, on almost any image. Leonardo, an inventor with each new work, would have been laughed out of Italy if he expected to gain anything with such an old trick.

If we're to believe that this painting was made in around the year 1500, that means Leonardo himself had already surpassed such primitive portraiture ideas many times over—in his many Madonnas, his beautiful *Portrait of a Musician* from 1485, and the two versions of the great *Virgin of the Rocks*, painted between 1483 and 1499—not to mention his consciousness-expanding *Last Supper*, completed in 1498. By 1500, Michelangelo had already finished his tremendous *Pietà* in Rome and was in Florence working on the *David*. Botticelli was there, too. It's hard to imagine that, upon arriving in Florence, within range of the young Michelangelo—who was being hailed as "the new Leonardo"—the master would produce such a conservative, backward-looking picture. These artists were as competitive as any artists today: When Leonardo sat on the committee to decide where the still-unfinished *David* was to be situated in Florence, he voted *against* giving it the pride of place it eventually won, next to the Palazzo Vecchio. The Christie's narrative suggests that Leonardo came to Florence only to become a hack painter of post-Byzantine portraits—when in fact we know that Leonardo did just the opposite, because in 1502 he painted the *Mona Lisa*. This *Salvator Mundi* doesn't fit the story, no matter how you try to make it so.

If we want to give Christie's the benefit of the doubt, we can be generous and accept the argument that this work *does* date from that time; we might even grant that Leonardo could have painted a ringlet of hair, perhaps a hand. Even if that holds, however, the rest of the painting—including the intricate patterning and clear glass, which would have been a specialty of numerous studio assistants at the time—is still sensuously and physically inert. The painting is spooky and olden-looking, following a period convention of images of Jesus blessing saints—another argument against this being made by an artist of Leonardo's epic skill.

This kind of salesmanship is an old game: an irresponsible knowing flimflam that defrauds a mass audience into thinking it is "appreciating" an Old Master, when all that's really on offer is smoky spectacle and mirrors. One of the first things you'll hear from a Christie's official is that "the only way to know what this painting is worth is to bring it to auction." This is patently untrue, a reminder of how out of touch Christie's has become. But it's also a sign of a new system of authority, of the power the auction houses have acquired: that one of them is pushing a "new" Old Master—a work that may have been accepted by some experts but which many others view with high skepticism—and yet no furor has been raised. Those experts are probably thinking, *Well, scholarship changes every twenty years; this will be corrected later*, unwilling to rock the already splintering institutional boat. As in the wider world where people sit by for fear of losing position, it's no wonder that many Old Master experts are keeping quiet on the subject.

(2017)

LaToya Ruby Frazier Is a Goya for Black America

In the searingly honest, empathetic documentary images of LaToya Ruby Frazier—who describes herself as an "artist, curator, educator, and photographer"—I see the rotten social malignancy of racial discrimination as it is deeply inscribed into our legal, financial, and health-care systems. I also see obdurate white tribalism, the 55 percent of all white people and 75 percent of all Republicans who concede that racial discrimination persists, but only against white people.

I look at Frazier's beautiful activist art—depictions of people with the courage and strength to live life amid Trumpian statecraft and everything that made it possible—and behold an aesthetic passionate enough that it just might jar the art world from its ten-year fixation on insular formalist photography-about-photography. The films, texts, and photographs of this recent MacArthur "genius" grant awardee mark her as one of the strongest artists to emerge in this country this century—a thirty-six-year-old oracle calling for a new engaged "movement in photography" that bears witness to our legacy of state-sanctioned economic racism and environmental atrocity.

What do Frazier's photographs actually document? Everything. The entire postwar American Dream, as it has been stacked against black Americans. It begins with the dream of owning a home, and the denial of that right to black citizens who could not get loans from banks or government agencies because they already lived in poor neighborhoods, or who were redlined in similar ways so that they paid more for less where they already lived, while getting fewer services, bad schools, lesser health care, than white residents. In her first-ever New York gallery solo show, at Gavin Brown's Enterprise, Frazier explores this disenfranchisement in three trenchant bodies of work. Frazier's mode of operation involves getting very close to her subjects, without ever being predatory or voyeuristic. She shares intimate moments, allows her collaborators to set up photos, record their voices and poetry, and document their own family histories. Her images are a shadowy, stark black-and-white that conjures the tonal grounds and preternatural observational powers of Rembrandt and Goya.

Frazier's is a world on the edge, pushed to the brink of extinction. But this is not just ruin porn, or just another photographer visiting and recording nodes of poverty from a privileged position. While Frazier has been diligent about providing health statistics, legal proceedings, corporate records to bolster her portrait of American life, the most powerful content is often the subject's words as they accompany her imagery. Frazier has talked about imagining what might have happened had Dorothea Lange allowed Florence Thompson—the nameless "migrant mother" in her iconic 1936 image of poverty in America—to photograph herself, her family, tell her own story. That's a radical leap. And it's what Frazier has undertaken, drawing in her subjects as collaborators. Frazier starts to see the world through the eyes of others—channeling their dreams, melancholies, hells, joys—and accesses their inner visions.

Frazier's series *Flint Is Family*, made between 2016 and 2017, explores the effects of the water crisis in Flint, Michigan, a majority-black city. We are given micro and macro views of Flint's environmental catastrophe, scenes of factories, decrepit streets. She zeroes in especially on three generations of women from the Cobb family: grandmother Ms. Reneé, mother Shea, and Shea's daughter, Zion. Here we see the firsthand effects of how state-supported ecological disaster leads to businesses and jobs leaving, the breakdown of social structures, and a lack of health care that means anyone unable to escape must fend for themselves in a situation that is none of their making.

Frazier uses her camera as a weapon that reveals the two-tiered Jim Crow laws of racial environmentalism, in which heavily African American cities like Flint grow ever blacker and ever poorer. It is impossible to imagine a systemic thirty-year environmental disaster unfolding this unchecked and unaided in Manhattan—or, say, Arlington, Virginia. She records how Flint residents still pay some of the highest water bills in the country, even as their local Nestlé factory is allowed to pump four hundred gallons per minute of pure Lake Michigan water for free. In an eleven-minute video, Shea Cobb calls this what it is, murder by the state—a process whereby the environment leads to self-destruction, hollowed-out bodies, and Flint as a modern plantation where workers whose very lives are under assault are derided as "bottom-feeders."

Next is *The Notion of Family*, begun when Frazier, then just sixteen, started documenting herself, her family, and her surroundings. (A teacher seeing her first photo told the teenager that she had a destiny to work with the camera.) *Notion* is already a landmark of American photography—a new American *Disasters of War*. We see her hometown, Braddock, Pennsylvania, nine miles from Pittsburgh on the banks of the great Monongahela River, home of Andrew Carnegie's first steel mill, the famous Edgar Thomson Works, in operation since 1875. The pictures are raw, beautiful, intense, subtle, prophetic. She focuses on three generations of Frazier women: herself; her mother, Cynthia; and her late grandmother Ruby. In *Notion*, ideas of genre collapse. It is family portrait, autobiography, case study, manifesto, indictment, and howl. It is a picture of thirty years of official negligence and deindustrialization, which have brought about the near-annihilation of the black working class.

It's no coincidence that Braddock, too, is a majority-black city. Companies have been cited for chemical emissions of benzene, mercury, chloroform, lead, and tetrachloroethylene—a colorless liquid now found in Braddock's water that brings risks of cancer and immune-related diseases.

Here is the human cost of systemic negligence, redlining, and other malevolent policy.

In another group of pictures, we witness the death of Frazier's grandmother from pancreatic cancer. Next we see her mother's terrible backlength scar from spinal surgery. Frazier calls her "a prisoner in her own home." Cynthia, a nurse's aide, lives two blocks from Braddock's former hospital, now torn down. Yet even after she collapsed from a series of maladies last year, it took over three hours for her to be rescued and brought to intensive care. After she was examined, she was told to go home because she had no chance of survival.

That's when Frazier contacted Dr. Esa Davis, a doctor of color from Pittsburgh who knew of Frazier's work. Davis soon arrived and, working with Frazier, prescribed treatment that expressly required her mother to stay in the hospital. This was done against the wishes of the white doctor. With permission, Frazier stood vigil over her mother to make sure she wasn't sent home to die or be neglected again. That's health care in much of America. So is this: A white physician then falsely accused Frazier of "laying hands on him," and security and police arrived and ushered her out of the hospital. Fortunately, Davis—"Dr. Esa," as she's known— stepped in again and saw to it that her mother wasn't sent home. Last week, I saw Cynthia looking great and doing well speaking on a panel at the gallery about her life and her daughter's work.

Frazier pictures the not-so-secret but almost entirely unacknowledged war against the black working class in America. Over an image of her grandmother's stepfather in his coffin, Frazier reports that he "worked hard labor in high temperatures tearing down and rebuilding furnaces, cleaning up spilt metal and slag . . . his labor-consumed body discarded and thrown away." After this, we see the topless self-portrait of the artist seated on a bed, *Self-Portrait (Lupus Attack)*. Frazier eyes us directly in this picture of a person paying the price of her mind, body, and energy in this undeclared war.

Today, around the country, the war is being ramped up. Under Ben

Carson, Trump's head of public housing, the agency has already delayed measures to strengthen civil rights–era requirements for local governments to take active steps to undo racial segregation. Instead, it is rolling back measures imposed during the Obama administration that were designed to undo systemic racism. Carson has said that the creators of these laws "meant well . . . and had no intention of entrapping people"—only to dismiss the programs under the nativist label of "social engineering." Julián Castro, his predecessor as HUD secretary, has lamented that "benign neglect is the best way to describe" conditions in public housing today. And housing, of course, is just the start.

Frazier somehow captures even these unraveling catastrophes in images of local citizens standing up for their rights, demanding clean water, access to health care, the right to live dignified lives. What gives these pictures resonance is that they're from 2016—*before* the election. We see groups peacefully holding signs outside factories, hospitals, and at a local Flint high school awaiting the arrival of then-president Obama—who drank Flint water in solidarity.

These pictures speak volumes to our current situation. As horrible, complex, and frustrating as these situations are, we see that protests like these, back then, at least made America look at the problem, notice it. Or so we hoped. Back in 2016, it almost felt as though, under pressure from the Black Lives Matter movement, black lives might *actually* start to matter to all Americans—that bodies like these, in Flint, Braddock, and ten thousand other American towns and cities would not continue to be "discarded and thrown away." But then whites in every demographic category voted Trump their president, and the Republican Party—a de facto white people's party—only intensified its take-back-our-nation last stand.

(2018)

Cy Twombly and the Transforming
Power of Art

The first time I saw Cy Twombly's aphrodisiacal paintings, I felt the way Patti Smith felt upon first hearing the Rolling Stones: "I was doing all my thinking between my legs." Something unrecognizable and distorted within me quivered. Twombly's fevered glowing blooms of runny jellyfish chrysanthemums, with their elongated, pulpy, tentacular sacs; his iridescent storms of inchoate cryptographic scribbles, floral scrawls, jittery jutting lines; his pustules rising and falling like raw nerve endings, flying vagina dentata, plaited anuses, priapic phalluses spouting involuntarily or drooping defenseless; what his closest reader, the late Kirk Varnedoe of MoMA, called "anteater tongues"—all of it metamorphosed into my own inner *Kama Sutra* of urge. Sensory networks lit up; a new barometer fluctuated. It was abstract yet explicitly erotic. I was in voluptuous rut. But something like gravitas and immensity was moving within me, too.

Somehow, by deploying only the barest rudiments of art—jots, dots, lines, doodles, dashes, loops, scribbles, scratches, little glyphs, weird ruins, the skeletons of Gothic structures, ziggurats, wobbly frame shapes, and (perhaps more effectively than any other Western artist) hard-to-read handwritten words and phrases, whole poems, and the names of ancient poets and places—Twombly has been able to make an art that rises to the level of epic poetry and fills you up with the sweep of history and fiction. He's one of the few twentieth-century painters who produces some of the same capacious sensations we get while reading Virgil, Homer, Sappho, Keats, and others. A silent sonorous world opens before you. Twombly brings mythos and antiquity together with the erotic urge, and with an undertow of the elemental interiority and abjection of Francis Bacon.

Right now, there are two spectacular Cy Twombly shows at Gagosian.

(None of the work is said to be for sale, so . . . thank you, Larry.) Uptown are the stately so-called solar-barges of the sun—the ten-part painting cycle from 2000 titled *Coronation of Sesostris*. (It's the second time this work is being shown: The group was installed almost exactly this way on the same walls that year. For whatever reason, Twombly changed the third painting, and I liked it more before he did.) *Sesostris* is ostensibly based on the stories of three twelfth-dynasty Egyptian pharaohs by that name. Even that arcane Egyptian word conjures obscure twinges, the physiological effect we feel when gazing at hieroglyphics. This wraparound room-filling undertaking finds the artist, then seventy-three, developing and deploying the multi-colored fireballs, ship prows and oarsmen, waterfall smears, and giant float-ing clots that had been appearing in his work since 1987. In this tour de force, Twombly, who died in 2011, was reborn once again and began put-ting all this together, commencing the colossal final years of his work.

The fifty-year concatenation that led to all this is on view in the equally unmissable show at Gagosian's Twenty-First Street space. In almost one hundred works dating from 1951 to 2008, it gives an account of Twom-bly's ever-changing drawing methods. His hand is a Geiger counter of in-definite interior synesthetic sensations that break the surface of painting and telepathically distend into us. This huge show begins with a table laid out with a series of small notebook pages from 1951. Here, at twenty-three, Twombly sketches cage, grill, grid, window, and fence-like configura-tions with sprigs and sticks, nodes and nodules affixed to rickety, stiff lines. Already he's using marks and structure to get around Abstract Expression-ist gesture and Gorky's biomorphic composition, and even looking past not-yet-extant Minimalism to something stranger and more personal. That was the year after Twombly had met his then-lover, Robert Rauschen-berg. A fellow Southerner, Rauschenberg brought Twombly to Black Mountain College in North Carolina, where he met Jasper Johns, John Cage, Merce Cunningham, Charles Olson, and many others. Twombly and Rauschenberg soon traveled together to Naples, Palermo, Rome, Florence, Casablanca, Tangier, and Morocco, where they met and trav-eled with Paul Bowles. These first drawings also show Twombly already internalizing the inspiration that Rauschenberg seems to have imparted to all those who came into contact with him in those days. Indeed, careful readings of Twombly's career suggest that almost every time the two had sustained contact—even long after their romantic relationship ended—Rauschenberg's titanic talents caused Twombly's work to explode. The final drawings in the Twenty-First Street show are the ecstatic last blasts and Whitmanesque effusions that flowed into Twombly's paintings and drawings at the end.

Take just two beauties from 1992, both titled *Naumachia*: Note the arc-shaped boats, the idea of the canvas imposing some enclosed sea, ships sailing, maybe magnolias blooming, a feeling of a violent order being dis-ordered at the same time that an essential unity is portrayed. *Naumachia* is an ancient Greek word, but in Rome the word referred to gigantic war games staged as mass entertainments. Julius Caesar once deployed more than two thousand combatants and four thousand rowers, all prisoners of war, to restage one of his recent victories. Twombly suggests that on a for-mal level, at its core, *this* is what all painting is—a willed, staged presenta-tion within artificially imposed borders where imagination, chance, order, intention, experimentation, audacity, and ideas are all put into play and are meant to captivate.

To grasp just how much experimental and staged pictorial and graphic information springs from Twombly's drawings, recall that imme-diately after the nineteen-year-old Jean-Michel Basquiat saw Twombly's Whitney Museum retrospective in 1979—a show that included several of these exact drawings, notably *Apollo and the Artist,* in which the words *Apollo* and *artist* appear on a surface surrounded with free-floating notations—Basquiat aesthetically detonated and began making his own assembled works with words, graffiti, crowns, arrows, and names. In this moment of genesis, he took Twombly's speed of history and amped it up to the speed of life. In that same Whitney show Basquiat saw the beautiful *Ode to Psyche,* with its great arch at the bottom of the page, counting numbers enumer-ated, and references to the text of Keats's "Ode to Psyche." Feel the lumi-nous atmospheric streamers and charged particles that must have ignited in Basquiat's mind in the same ways that Twombly must have experienced Rauschenberg. I fancy the prospect of young artists coming to this show and extending that arc.

I'm not going to delve into the encyclopedic trove of aesthetic possibilities implied in all these drawings. I only urge viewers to suspend any notion that Twombly is some charlatan wisenheimer trying to put one over on you. Don't place yourself in this cynical cul-de-sac—it'll prevent your mind and eye from grasping Twombly's gigantic indexical range. Allow his shapes to congeal into narratives, temples on fire, tidal waves washing over inscriptions, chariots on the plain, Leonardesque deluges, bedsheets after lovemaking, burial mounds with flowers stuck in them, panoramic battle scenes with armies of marks surging or being wiped out in erasure. Let Twombly's eroticism, formalism, and visceral brio reach you. Accept the gall and glee of titles like *Leda and the Swan, School of Athens, In Beauty it is finished, Delian Ode,* or *Hero and Leander.* Let Twombly's way of redefining skill redefine your ideas about skill, too.

Back uptown, *Coronation of Sesostris* moves from left to right in large canvases of varying shapes and sizes, arrayed around three walls. (A careful study of Twombly's drawings reveals that he first drew this "solar barge of Sesostris" motif as far back as 1985.) Consider the whole as a retinal-emotional musing on the soul's journey to the afterlife—on loss, glory, love, homesickness, painting, even a kind of passing Proustian dream. We see barges in the shape of closed eyelids, with what look like oars sunk in water like eyelashes; we see wobbly suns rising high and setting low. The last canvas in the show has a blocky top-hat shape that might be derived from a figure Degas painted of his brother, Achille, in 1873's *The Cotton Exchange in New Orleans.* (Even if it isn't based on the Degas, the possible connection to the name of a Greek hero is irresistible.) The overall palette is white-primed canvas, with tones of saffron mustard, lemon yellows, purples, violets, ruby and rose-madder reds, and Turneresque washes of glowing color. Words drift in and out of focus; none are easy to read; all make you nearly chant them aloud.

You can view the work in this show in any order. The sixth canvas, which looks like a page from a book, features two dozen blood-red glops around the stabbing words—all jumbled and hard to read, in Twombly's scrawled hand—of American poet Patricia Waters: "When they leave do you think they hesitate, turn and make a farewell sign, some gesture of regret?" Soon you make out the words "the sun high . . . you dizzy with wine, befuddled with being, sink into your body, as though it were real, as if yours to keep." There's a real sense of trying to hold on to life, love, or memory. The penultimate canvas is a black-outlined lone boat and the phrase "Leaving Paphos ringed with waves." Paphos is located on Cyprus, also known as the "Island of Love," the supposed birthplace of Aphrodite. The cycle transmutes into some sort of final farewell. The second canvas finds the words "Solar barge of Sesostris" hovering over an image of a double sun. In the last Degas-inspired panel, all the color has drained as we read Sappho's aching refrain: "Eros weaver of myth, Eros sweet and bitter, Eros bringer of pain." Thus Twombly has given us rising and setting suns, the passage of a day or a life or an era, ships ablaze on flowered grounds, and this final call to psychic and physical shore. The cycle is complete. All that remains is every nerve in your body straining with this overload of irrational beauty, desire, pretension and need, esoteric information, cryptic incantation, and what look like the footprints of birds, running through milky paint to some farther Mediterranean shore.

(2018)

The Future Belonged to Hilma af Klint

The Guggenheim is making a full-barrel bid to canonize Hilma af Klint, the early-twentieth-century Swedish mystical abstract painter. It's only a hundred years late. But then the show is titled *Paintings for the Future*, so perhaps the future she envisioned has arrived at last. The exhibition makes a conclusive case for af Klint as the first Modernist artist to paint entirely abstract.

On display: more than 160 of the most beguilingly uncanny and imaginative works of the last century. They amount to cosmic sonograms, the unseen forces in af Klint's very large, iridescent canvases, with their biomorphic shapes, auras, algae blooms of color, arabesque jellyfish tentacles coiling, geometric configurations, all of them intended to "awaken humanity" to unseen astral-transcendental energies. Each of her works imparts an elemental force, intense shifts between micro and macro scales—you might think you're looking at a molecular world, then an instant later into celestial infinity—and seems to point to some Gaia-like grand plan. Af Klint created her own optical language with visual, chromatic, structural, and narrative syntax. Her artistic ship sails some of the deepest waters around.

Af Klint was wellborn, in Stockholm in 1862, and attended Sweden's Royal Academy of Fine Arts, where she was such a standout that she was awarded a free studio in the same building where Edvard Munch exhibited. She was in the middle of everything going on in that art world. She also spent decades conducting studies of biblical, mythological, Rosicrucian, Buddhist, scientific, and theosophical sources, while holding regular séances as part of a circle of female intellectuals called "the Five." Her paintings illustrate the group's complex spiritual concepts. The Five were obsessed with the idea that you could make contact with "higher spirits," and in 1906, when af Klint was forty-three, two of those spirits instructed her to create a cycle of works to be titled *The Paintings for the Temple*—and to design the temple herself.

The current consensus holds that the "inventors" of modern abstraction are Kandinsky, Kupka, Mondrian, Goncharova, O'Keeffe, Popova, and Malevich, among others. Af Klint has never been counted among them. In fact, af Klint made her totally abstract paintings before any of these others. By 1908, she'd completed more than one hundred paintings in her celestial commission. (That's roughly as many paintings as Mondrian or Barnett Newman made in their lifetimes.) She was on fire; history was changing in her hands.

That's when af Klint had what the artist Amy Sillman aptly calls "the worst studio visit of all time." Excited to share her efforts, af Klint invited the famous theosophist Rudolf Steiner to examine her work. On seeing the epic project, he disparaged her ideas of relinquishing agency to the forces of the universe, of "translating" ideas imparted to her by divine others. Never mind that no artists can really tell you where their work springs from, that all feel commanded in some way to do their work and helpless to do otherwise. Steiner's dismissive comment threw af Klint off; she stopped painting for four years. Luckily for us, she started again and never stopped. Af Klint died in 1944 at eighty-one, her "letter to the world" complete.

She'd also had a vision for that temple for her paintings: "a round building," she foresaw, "where visitors would progress upward along a spiraling path." Rather like the Guggenheim itself.

(2018)

How Does the Art World Live with Itself?

The lush new art world documentary *The Price of Everything* shows us a system so waist-deep in hypermarketing and excess that it's hard to look at art without being overcome by money, prices, auctions, art fairs, celebrities, well-known artists, and megacollectors who fancy themselves conquistadors. In this, it's a lot like most recent accounts of the art world—which are, all told, pretty accurate. I hate this toxic rot, this junkie-like behavior. Yet I love art and the art world. I hate the portrait of that world contained in this movie, but I also recognize in it what I love.

That may sound like a paradox, but it feels to me like something else. I used to believe the art world was at war with itself, that money was fighting art and vice versa. But I've been living in this ambivalence for a decade now, or more, and I'm starting to think that this is not a war but a new state of equilibrium, defined by that ambivalence. In other words, it's not just me. Everyone complains about money in the art world, but few would ever leave. Everyone hates the system—struggling artists and billionaire gallerists and everyone in between. But none of us can live outside it, nor would we want to. Why would we? How could we?

The Price of Everything is a portrait of this damaged system. It's a place where big-ticket art made by only a handful of people—maybe seventy-five artists, mostly male—appears in high-end galleries, auction houses, and art fairs before being sold off at astronomically inflated prices. Art and money have always slept together; they're just doing it more profligately now than ever. The patter of the high-enders, as shown in *Price*, is so imperious and spiteful that it's no wonder the public—and even many insiders—have grown cynical about it all. I left the premiere feeling sick to my stomach, full of shame.

(Oh, and also: I appear in this documentary. More on that later.)

Price opens with a balletic dance of white-gloved workers hastening about the immaculate showrooms of Sotheby's auction house, moving works of art around their tony galleries. The paintings are by the usual market suspects: Damien Hirst, Jeff Koons, Andy Warhol, Roy Lichtenstein, Rudolf Stingel, Richard Prince, Jasper Johns, Gerhard Richter, Takashi Murakami, Banksy, Christopher Wool, and many others. *Price*'s director is Nathaniel Kahn, maker of the 2003 Academy Award–nominated *My Architect*—a beautiful look at the architecture and life of his late, great father, Louis Kahn. Throughout the ninety-eight minutes of *The Price of Everything*, alpha dogs talk money, plot prices, and act snarky about those who aren't as upper echelon as themselves. It's one insane earmark of this film that each potentate who appears in it believes his behavior to be better than that of all his peers. *No one else is a connoisseur anymore*, grouse a series of collectors whose cookie-cutter collections reveal their market-driven taste.

Soon we see the works themselves, paraded onstage before an almost all-white, well-dressed crowd. Paddles are raised, catalogues marked, necks craned to see who's buying what. The potential bidders sneer, marvel, make knowing gestures to one another. It's a modern danse macabre, the superrich buying their art in public: a performance of power, clout, social status, sublimated sexuality, and price manipulation. The auctioneer is the pole dancer/dominatrix of the proceedings, moving in his mannered fashion, pointing to bidders, cooing at them, calling some by their first names, being cheeky, coaxing, cudgeling, always closing, reciting the prices as they climb. You hear him calling out a chant of numbers: "I'm going to start the bidding at three hundred thousand. Three hundred and fifty thousand, four hundred thousand." Then a move to his right. "Oh, six hundred thousand, six hundred and fifty thousand," he says, "there's seven hundred thousand in the back of the room." Soon, "I have one million dollars on my right." The magic number: a murmur goes over the crowd. Then he looks up—at a skybox? a chandelier?—and crows, "I have one million, two hundred thousand dollars." He gives "fair warning," hesitates, counts to three, cracks the hammer down, and shouts, "Sold!" The crowd erupts in applause; your skin crawls. Mine did, at least.

Cut to Simon de Pury, the so-called Mick Jagger of auctioneers. (He was once suspended by cables over a roomful of rich bidders, calling out bids from the air.) "It's important that good art be expensive," he purrs—a perfect and ridiculous echo of Tobias Meyer, Sotheby's former worldwide head of contemporary art, who once chirped, "The best art is the most expensive because the market is so smart."

The thing is, some of the work on these trading floors is great. Most of it, however, is middling, iffy, or bad. The collectors themselves even seem to recognize this, obliquely. "We're lemmings," one of them concedes. Another acknowledges that she "always wants more," and a third admits that her friends now own the same sculpture she proudly displays in her home. (Her friends' versions are "different colors," she clarifies.) The craziest thing about this documentary is that, while the artists in it all acknowledge the powerful presence of the market, those who are in the market barely seem to notice the artists themselves.

And yet those artists continue to work—some of them magnificently—and their appearances give the film some of its wonderful high points. *Price* brings us into artists' studios, where we're allowed to watch them work in silence, often alone. This is amazing access. To me, an artist working is still one of the more mysterious sights a human being can witness, and one we see so rarely. I love these scenes.

We're not dealing with unknowns here, however. Each of the artists Kahn shows us is or has been famous, now or in the past. As they work, he queries them about money. All of them acknowledge the market's shadow; they admit that life is easier when money comes, and that it's good not to suffer. Each of the artists, however, also informs Kahn that with or without money, they still can't not do what they do. "I don't care if people buy [my paintings]," says Marilyn Minter, "I just need to make them." MacArthur recipient Njideka Akunyili Crosby talks about "urgency." All the artists explain that art and the market are very separate things—a message lost on Kahn, who seems to want to reduce the work to its value and the art world to its business.

The artists Kahn interviews talk about art as being the only "defense" they have "against fate." These artists gave me faith. Except, maybe, for Jeff Koons.

The Price of Everything gives us Koons in his sprawling studio, overseeing scores of assistants quietly making his paintings, matching colors down to the tiniest scintillas of pigment. As Koons speaks in his Ronald Reagan voice about wanting to "make people happy and give them permission," Kahn peppers him with questions about costs, prices, power, and being "the most expensive artist alive." This stops even the squirrelly Koons, who looks hurt, winces, and says he's "humbled." Then he adds, plaintively: "All I have are my interests." For this one second, even an artist as annoying as Koons is deeply human, vulnerable, desperate.

Success can be disorienting—for individuals, and to whole communities. Just forty years ago, the art world was small; artists did their work with no market, no money, and little outside audience. People with no money started galleries on the fly; some, like Larry Gagosian or Paula Cooper, became powerful industry forces. People who had never bought art before started buying some of this art, at then-low prices. A few who had no training whatsoever called themselves (ahem, *our*selves) art critics and started writing art criticism. In the ensuing decades, however, art and its market have become central fixtures of mainstream culture: Artists are now celebrities, prices are news, collectors try to enter art history by paying the highest prices for art, and auction houses—once dusky places—are now hubs where contemporary art can go from studio to trading floor without ever being shown at all.

Now, it's thrilling to witness art playing a huge role in culture, and to know that many of these self-made people built this art world with their own obsessions, their own sweat. It makes me proud, even. But we seem to be in a kind of end-game phase that is more than disorienting to many of us.

THE TOP-HEAVY APPROACH of *The Price of Everything* has been a feature of art world documentaries made for the general public since Morley Safer's infamously snippy 1993 takedown on *60 Minutes*. In that thirteen-minute segment, Safer mocked new art, artists, auctions, art fairs, rich collectors, high prices, and all the other low-hanging fruit *Price* features. Some of the same people in the *60 Minutes* episode appear in *Price*, including, of course, Koons. It's as though there's some publicly available software specifically for making such films.

Which brings us to me. Aside from vanity, neediness, and FOMO, one big reason I agreed to appear in *Price* was that I loved Kahn's *My Architect*. A bigger reason, however, was the film's producer, Jennifer Blei Stockman, former president of the board of the Guggenheim Museum. I've known and admired Stockman from afar for more than twenty years. In the 1990s, she called out of the blue to ask if I'd give a talk about art at her Connecticut home. At that point, I was only just starting to write—in fact, I was still driving a truck—and she was offering money. I took it. All I recall is that the group was tickled by the pornographic paintings Jeff Koons made starring himself and his porn-star wife.

In 2015, Stockman emailed me about my being in a film she was co-producing about the art world. Sure, I said, assuming that—as with most of the excited calls I get about "making a film about the art world"—this one would vanish, too. But Stockman followed up. I tried to get out of it, but when she cornered me and my wife at a packed Guggenheim performance, Stockman made a passionate pitch, pleading about how bad the art world had become, and pledging that her filmmaking team was trying to portray the real art world—"the one we love, Jerry." I bought it.

In the foul weeks after the 2016 election, I met Stockman, Kahn, and a small crew in the office of the director of the Whitney Museum. Equipment got set up; lights went on; I sat down. Facing me was Kahn with a clipboard. He started asking questions. He did this for hours; in the finished film, I appear three or four times.

As Kahn posed his questions, I noted a series of consistent themes. First of all, many of his queries concerned what art "means." He seemed to make a mistake that's common among lay audiences, imagining that we're supposed to *understand* art. Beneath this is a strange fear—that maybe, if you don't understand a work of art, the art might be trying to put one over on you, to take your money and give nothing in return. Those who think this way are afraid that an artwork might be laughing at them, that it might mean nothing at all, and if so, that it must be bad, or at least fake. I tried to get him to see that understanding art has very little to do with it. Of course there are things we do understand in this world: movies, TV, sports. We understand the Kardashians. And money. But it's meaningless to talk about "understanding" Mozart, the *Mona Lisa*, or the floating, fuzzy, Buddhist TV-screen paintings of Mark Rothko. We don't "understand" works of art in this way. We dive into them.

Maybe all this made me defensive, or exasperated, or afraid. I kept trying to bring us back to our point of connection: I hate all this stuff, too, I insisted, but galleries are still where new art comes from, and I love going to them. I reminded Kahn that most dealers have no money. Only about 1 percent of 1 percent of all artists make any money. I talked about artists living on the edge, and reminded him that a lot of good art is still getting made and shown. The big-money scene he was asking about was really just a teeny sliver of the art world. At one point, getting a bit carried away, I think I said we'd all stand over the imaginary caskets of all the speculators until we were sure they were dead, then dance on their graves. Thankfully, this was cut.

Still, he persisted. Finally, exhausted, I had what felt like an insight into the deep background of his questions. In the middle of a question, I stopped him. "You're a cynic!" I said. "You hate the art world!" Everything stopped. There was silence in the room. Behind him I saw Stockman staring at me, amazed.

Kahn and I looked at each other for a while, blinking. Finally he seemed to catch his breath. "Yes," he said. "I am cynical."

Then I went a step further. I said, "You hate the art world and these megastructures of power and things like this for destroying your father, ignoring his greatness, and allowing him to die forgotten, in poverty. The art world is a stand-in for what tragically and unjustly happened to him. And to you." Total stillness. His eyes misted. After a moment he admitted he was crying.

As he recovered, Kahn spoke movingly about how awful and brutal the creative sphere can be to artists, how hard and callous it is. I told him I knew this, that maybe it's always been that way. But this is a reason to *love* artists, I said, and not to spurn them or be cynical about what they do or even the market their work enters. The art world may be broken now, I said, but it will change again when the money goes away. I wondered if the film was a way for him to secure revenge for his father. After seeing it, I still believe this.

The film's two heroes—or villains, depending on your point of view—are the nonagenarian über-collector Stefan T. Edlis and my old friend and sparring partner, Amy Cappellazzo, chair of the Fine Art division of Sotheby's. When we first see Edlis, he is sitting at a desk, high above the clouds in his skyscraper Chicago apartment, scrolling on his computer as he reads from an inventory of his vast collection. Throughout the film, Edlis can be heard reciting the prices he's paid for the artwork he owns, making comments about big killings and market drubbings. But it was Cappellazzo's patter—a spot-on reflection of what's going on in this world—that gave me the heebie-jeebies. Pelting us with prices and investment strategies, she talks about hedge funds, about selling short. She holds a picture of Willem de Kooning standing in front of a painting she's about to auction off, calling the photo a "money shot." You think, "This world should explode." For me, the film's nadir comes when Edlis and Cappellazzo offer a series of sales tips: Red is better than brown! (Goodbye, Rembrandt.) No pictures with fish! (Bye-bye, Matisse.) Once an artist is installed in a lobby, he/she is forever reduced to the status of "a lobby artist." (*Hasta la vista*, Alexander Calder.)

FOR ME, THE DEEP CONTENT of *The Price of Everything*—as with so much about the current moment—involves the troubling undercurrents that surfaced in the summer before the 2016 election. That July, I was flown in to speak at the rich persons' self-help summer camp known as the Aspen Ideas Festival. On my last night there, I attended a fancy dinner of about twenty people in the art world. Stefan Edlis was there—it was the first time we'd met—and Jennifer Stockman and Marilyn Minter were, too. Almost everyone else was a collector. The conversation was typical—shows, museums, gossip, the news—until midnight.

At that point, from down the table, I heard Edlis animatedly carrying on about how Trump could be good for America. I was stunned. In my dumb pre-election art world bubble, this had seemed impossible. Across from Edlis was none other than the Reagan-era economist David Stockman, Jennifer's husband, whom I've met and chided over the years. He agreed that the whole system needed to be shaken up and seemed to suggest that he was voting for Trump. I barked, "You're just trying to make up for the damage you did with Reaganomics." This had no effect on him. I challenged him to tell his daughter how he was voting. This seemed to stop him, but only momentarily. Down the table, a woman married to one of the world's largest machine-gun manufacturers babbled on about how she was adamantly against any kind of gun control.

Three artists were present that night, and they joined the two gallerists and me as we argued with this group. At one point, I think the dealer Jeanne Greenberg Rohatyn actually got up on a table and yelled at them.

But they all just gawked at us, as if we dumb clucks should just shut up and stick to art—the same way right-wingers are always telling liberal musicians to "shut up and sing." Two guests—the art dealer Michelle Maccarone and the artist Carol Bove—got up and walked out. I never said anything to Edlis directly, but Minter and I did start bellowing that none of them had any idea what art really was, that they shouldn't be around art at all. They only smiled more, doubtless thinking, *How cute.*

Minter and I left soon after, and as I walked home, I grew cold, newly aware of a fact that many in the art world tacitly know but rarely talk about: Probably more than half of the collectors, advisers, auctioneers, and others in the American art world are Republican. And voted for Trump.

That paradox is part of the reason I said nothing to the ninety-one-year-old Edlis. As I walked home, I thought, "Who am I to judge him?" The film sheds light on this, too. As a boy, Edlis heard Hitler speak in Germany, looked into the Führer's eyes. He and his family barely escaped the Holocaust. In the film we see his old passport, with its large red *J* for *Juden.* In one of the film's most affecting scenes, Edlis shows us a sculpture by Maurizio Cattelan. It's a masterpiece, a super-real, child-size, lederhosen-clad adult figure of Hitler, kneeling, hands clasped in prayer. The work, whose title is *Him*, is not front and center in Edlis's grand room. Instead, it is displayed facing a wall between two large bookcases—lurking, insidious, frightening, uncanny. Pay attention to Edlis in the scenes with this sculpture: He cannot or will not say the name Hitler. He refers to *Him*, to him, only as "him." The work and Edlis himself are melding, redoubling, delivering, and redeeming one another. He never looks directly at *Him*, either, only gesturing with his head or his hand. We feel something that he feels while looking at the sculpture. In this way, *Price* gives us a glimpse into the metaphysical transformations that art creates.

In the movie, Edlis says that he hopes to do something "meaningful" in his life. It's a moving moment. Soon we learn that he and his wife have generously donated more than forty pieces to the Art Institute of Chicago—works by Jasper Johns, Roy Lichtenstein, Andy Warhol, Gerhard Richter,

Jeff Koons (*Rabbit*, valued at $65 million), Cindy Sherman, Cy Twombly, Robert Rauschenberg, John Currin, Brice Marden, and many others.

Welcome to the art world of this moment: a place of cravenness and tropospheric wealth even as it still provides space for artists, gallerists, and collectors to do their work, to take chances, to assert themselves, to step outside themselves, to act, and maybe to do "something meaningful." A place where Jeff Koons can make you crazy and still make good work; where Amy Cappellazzo can act batty but shine with intelligence; where former art-star octogenarian Larry Poons—cast as the film's Tiny Tim battling against the evil Scrooge art world—might appear to be on a kind of famous-male-artist automatic pilot, not really pushing his work enough, yet still following a deep calling.

The Price of Everything is a masterpiece of its genre. It's amazingly well-made. Yet it's also a blinkered picture of a very big, very knotty ball of art world wax. Oh, and it never mentions the source of its title: a phrase from Oscar Wilde, talking about cynics who know "the price of everything and the value of nothing."

(2018)

This Too Is Andy Warhol: The Story of an American Revolutionary in Eight Works

Andy is in the air we breathe. Among the most revolutionary artists who ever lived, Warhol, in his work from the magical years of 1962 to 1964—Coca-Cola bottles, Campbell's soup cans, Brillo boxes, Marilyn, Jackie, Brando, Elvis, electric chairs, paint-by-number paintings, the fabulous dance-step diptych, the Empire State Building film, flower paintings, and superstars—gives us an artist in a state of creative grace feeding on, mirroring, doubling, and actually changing the culture he pictured. Willem de Kooning may have thought him "a killer of beauty," but I think he invented a new beauty. Warhol was a philosophical assassin and vampiric social figure, ever interested in and hyper-observant of the culture around him. True, in interviews he would sometimes speak not a word, even ask the interviewer what he should say; invited to lecture, he sent body doubles to appear in his place. But his performance of fame, as much as it might dominate the memory of him outside the art world, was just one part of what he did. The Whitney's new retrospective looks through all that to his art: its primitive hits of optical power, poisonously alive color that doubles as makeup and war paint, tragic glamour, coolness, heat, voyeurism, secret sexualities, bulletproof sincerity, visual originality, and brave refusal of and resistance to all pictorial norms. Beautifully curated by Donna De Salvo, it allows viewers to take in an artist who was world-famous by the time he died at fifty-eight—endorsing brands, starring as himself on TV—yet still shunned in the art world. He was considered overexposed, over the hill—someone Robert Hughes disdained as "abnormal," "homosexual," and "malevolent," all in one sentence. As Warhol said, "All my reviews are bad."

He also famously said that anyone who wants to know about his work only has to "look at the surface of my paintings." Let's do that.

1. *LIVING ROOM*, 1948

When he was twenty years old and a senior at Carnegie Institute of Technology, majoring in "pictorial design," Andrew Warhola painted a watercolor of the living room of his working-class Pittsburgh home at 3253 Dawson Street. Warhol was raised in the Depression, and he lived here with his two brothers and his mother and father, Julia and Andrej, émigrés from Czechoslovakia. *Living Room* is a startlingly condensed, precociously complicated, and bewitching picture that pulls us into its world. Think of this living room as Warhol's van Gogh's *Bedroom*—a weighing of some sort of ragged truth, one that pictures not the place where we sleep (he made a whole film of that) but where we live, where our private and public lives take place at the same time. It may be a beginner's effort, but, knowing who Warhol became, it's an almost indispensable document of where he came from. The room is small, worn, shabby but still tidy, with a run-down sofa and overstuffed maroon armchair, covered in patterned fabrics and pillows. The space is organized, full, almost modular in its arrangement. The only decorative touch is the cross on the mantelpiece.

According to Warhol's mother, this is also the room where Warhol's father was laid out for three days in 1942 after he died from drinking poisoned water from the coal mine. The young Andy was too afraid to come downstairs to view the body. By then the boy had already contracted Sydenham's chorea (also known as Saint Vitus' dance), which made him shake and gave him skin blotches that lasted many years—and sparked his obsession with the people he called "the beauties," believing perhaps that his beauty would come from being around them. His sickness kept him out of school, where he'd been ridiculed by boys but befriended by girls; at home, he and his mother bonded even more. Warhol spent his weeks at home cutting out paper flowers, making decorations, playing with dolls; he also began a lifelong collection of autographed pictures of movie stars. (Shirley Temple was his first favorite.)

There's no view outdoors in *Living Room*. Everything you need to know is right there, in Warhol's dusky cluttered room.

2. *MALE GENITALS*, 1950s

In June 1949—after working in the display department of a Pittsburgh department store, where he'd show up with fingernails painted different colors and shoes dyed odd colors—Warhol, still twenty and now a Carnegie graduate, boarded a train to New York with his artist friend Philip

Pearlstein. In one of those fabulous New York stories, on his second day in the city he went to see Tina Fredericks, the art director of *Glamour* magazine. Not only did she buy one of his drawings for ten dollars, she told him, "I need some drawings of shoes, Mr. Warhola . . . tomorrow morning at 10 a.m. Can you do them?" Andy loved feet and shoes and fashion—and deadlines. And yes, he could draw anything.

Look closely at the work in this show from this period. These years are often dismissed as Warhol's juvenilia, his commercial years, but almost everything he'd do in the rest of his career surfaced in that decade. There are pictures of people sleeping, advertising images, portraits of the famous and portraits of freaks, drawings of shoes. They are dedicated to Elvis, Mae West, and Christine Jorgensen—a man who became a woman who became a successful cabaret artist. There are images of money, soup cans, men in jeans, car crashes, flowers, newspaper headlines, and endless drawings of the male body in all states of dress, undress, relaxation, and having sex. Scores of drawings of penises, too. As Pearlstein rightly put it, all "totally unacceptable" subjects in the art world of that time. So if you want the political revolutionary, look no further.

There's more though. In the fifties, Warhol found the prototype of his own future factories: the wild Fifty-Eighth Street studio of fashion photographer Otto Fenn, who always had an assortment of strange, beautiful, and famous creatures around him. It was in this underground gay scene where Andy was nurtured, and where he thrived. Not the "straight" art world of the Abstract Expressionists, or even the new scenes around Johns, Rauschenberg, Twombly, Merce Cunningham, and John Cage. His "outness" made Warhol an outsider to all this. Wayne Koestenbaum writes, "How gay was Warhol? As gay as you can get." As he notes, for "Warhol, everything is sexual . . . Movement is sexual. Stillness is sexual. Looking and being looked at are sexual. Time is sexual." Warhol's sexuality—however we may define the term—went deeper than voyeurism; he was simultaneously observer, participant, wallflower, cannibal, agent provocateur, and lover.

Taking a cue from Fenn, Warhol soon began holding "coloring parties," where people would come over to color his work or to help create it.

His mother signed his name to his artworks. It was here that he regularly asked male visitors to disrobe so that he could draw their penises. Andy liked to look. As many have reported, he sometimes became turned on and flustered while making these drawings, retiring to the bathroom for what he called a "private organza." So beautiful. Here, a direct, disarming, sweet, strange, suggestive mode that involved loving, laughter, need, reticence, and immense focus. His art shows us male genitals doubled as cake candle, gift-wrapped, tied in a pretty bow, decorated with hearts and flowers—all done with Matissean flair and simplicity.

By the early 1960s, he had removed the *a* from his last name to remove any Slovak associations, had a nose job, took to wearing a glued-on wig, and mounted shows of his so-called illustration and commercial work. Though he had arrived in New York with only $200, and slept for years with his mother next to him on a mattress on the floor, and lived sometimes with dozens of cats, by 1959 Warhol was so successful that he was able to pay $67,000 for a town house at 1342 Lexington Avenue. He continued to live with Julia for decades.

3. *MARILYN DIPTYCH*, 1962

His 1960s work is what Warhol is most known for. As radical as this work might appear now, Warhol didn't invent Pop; at the time, he was viewed as derivative of artists like James Rosenquist and Claes Oldenburg, a lightweight compared to Jasper Johns, a latecomer for appearing after Roy Lichtenstein. Nevertheless, he was an insurrectionist, though it is true that an often-breathless hagiography surrounds him.

To appreciate just how original he is, here is an essential exercise for looking at Warhol's work: First, identify the subject matter; it might be Liz, Jackie, Liza, Mick, Natalie Wood, Dennis Hopper, Dick Tracy, Superman, a car crash, a suicide, a sunset (he did more than 630 of them), the *Mona Lisa*, flowers, criminals, the telegram announcing JFK's death, hammers and sickles, or Andy's own face. Next, set aside the subject matter—or, rather, look through it, to focus on how Warhol paints. The first thing you'll notice is his color. It's electric, psychedelic, vibrating, merging; it clashes, flips, and flickers. He's also prone to monochrome that doesn't read as serious, doesn't convey gravitas (as in formalist painting), but instead registers as more aggressive, contradictory, "problematized." What are these colors? As with the humble drip—which was there in the caves but never really exploited until Pollock—Warhol's colors have been with us for millennia. It's just that no one in the history of art had ever combined them this way. It's like finding another note on the saxophone. This note has since been used to create whole visual cultures. With color, he is a rival to van Gogh and Matisse.

There's more. Note how Andy uses the silkscreen. What makes his portraits unforgettable isn't his choice of so-called low subjects. It isn't that he painted photographic images. It isn't even his serial, gridded, repeating images. What gives Warhol's work its singularly yelping optical intensity is the way his screens smudge, skid, streak. They get overloaded, wander off-register, out of alignment. This turns the still and repeating images he chooses into quixotic filmic experiences, changing the retinal read; it makes seeing and deciphering them trickier, more mysterious, even after the subject becomes clear. As in Monet or Seurat, what's pictured and how he pictures it fuses; you can't see one without the other. Moreover, you're not just seeing repeating images out of register: Warhol leaves in the grain-iness of the original photographic images. This reminds you that these paintings are removed from the original sources, that they come from somewhere else. The degrading of the silkscreen makes the process even more present, even stranger. Warhol is showing us that the way we usually respond to repeating images—like advertisements, Coke cans, celebrities, the news—is to see them and then *stop* seeing them. They blend together until they begin to go unnoticed. Warhol continually pulls you back to the image, the thing, its source, what it is, how it's been deployed, and the way it's been rendered. This is as big as *La Grande Jatte*.

For real spice, add that the primary "paintbrushes" he used to make this work were the bodies of others: his assistants, always male, often shirtless, muscular, and sweaty. (The screens used to make silkscreen images are *heavy*.) Andy would stand to the side, directing them. This is important. The entire history of Western painting had always rested on the artist's hand—the artist's skill with paint and the brush. But Warhol forwent such institutional and historical approval. He sidestepped traditional uses of paint, tools, materials, surfaces, subject matter, even photography. (As Koestenbaum said, "as gay as you can get.") Just as Warhol often wore makeup and a wig, with pantyhose under his jeans, and posed regularly in drag, he subverted every traditional, approved way to make art.

Marilyn Diptych may be Warhol's *Flag*. The fifty repeating Marilyns are his stars. The picture is from Monroe's first starring role, in *Niagara*; it's the only image of her he ever used. "When Marilyn Monroe happened to die that month [in 1962] I got the idea to make screens of her beautiful face," he coolly said. Here, the Marilyns mirror one another. Half the painting is vibrant contrasting color. The other half—after she's dead—turns ghostly black, gray, and white. The colored half is perfect; the other half is filled with smudges and gluts. Paint sluices over one row, almost blotting out this star. Monroe, Liz, and Jackie are Warhol's beautiful, tragic trinity of heroines. There's Jackie, so young and lovely in the White House, so stunned by grief after the assassination. Liz, drug-addled divorcée, the eventual warrior queen of AIDS. And Marilyn, probable American suicide at thirty-six. In another of the odd prefigurations that mark Warhol's life, in 1964 a self-styled witch and Factory character named Dorothy Podber donned a pair of white gloves, aimed a pistol at a stack of Marilyn paintings, and shot through four of them. When the paintings were exhibited, the holes were painted over with makeup; these portraits were titled *Shot Marilyn*. Warhol used everything.

4. MUSTARD RACE RIOT, 1963

People have complained that Warhol wasn't political. I disagree. I've called Warhol revolutionary for changing the way the world looks and the way we look at the world. But Warhol was political in other ways. And not only as a swish gay man who openly celebrated queer sex and sexuality. Warhol may have voted only once, but he noticed things and then painted what he noticed. He noticed with a vengeance—and never stopped at just noticing. He made charged, confrontational pictures of gay icons, communists, capital punishment, cross-dressers, beefcake, penises, semen paintings made with semen, abstractions made by urinating and having others urinate on canvases, headlines about Harlem stabbings, Lenin, the FBI's thirteen most wanted men (a list officials had removed from a World's Fair pavilion; Warhol and his assistants surreptitiously painted over the mural with silver paint, preserving the image), hammers and sickles (some with vibrators), guns, and Mao Zedong. He also painted among the greatest so-called protest paintings ever made. *Vote McGovern, 1972*, an ugly portrait of Nixon with a yellow mouth, blue jowls, green upper face—a president as a Goya-like gargoyle—raised $40,000 for the George McGovern presidential campaign. After this portrait, Warhol (along with other McGovern-supporting artists, including Rauschenberg, Terry Southern, and Norman Mailer) was audited by the IRS. He was audited thereafter until he died.

Another example of Warhol's knack for painting what he noticed is *Mustard Race Riot*, a powerful almost-gold silkscreen showing police with dogs beating black protesters. The right side—the all-mustard-color part (he's always telling you things you might not notice?)—hits you with flat, blank monochrome undeniability and leaves a sickening political taste in your mouth. Another kind of flag painting.

5. *COW WALLPAPER AND SILVER CLOUDS*, APRIL 1966

In April 1966, Warhol celebrated his "retirement from painting" with an exhibition at Leo Castelli Gallery. This involved covering one room in pink, yellow, and black cow wallpaper, and in another room placing free-floating silver helium-filled pillows (originally created as set design for Merce Cunningham's *Rain Forest*), a work he called *Clouds*. This installation/

happening was his "farewell to art." Warhol also declared Pop Art "dead" and went all-in on what he'd been doing for the last few years anyway: making films. These feature some of his pixilated hangers-on, oddballs, acolytes, and outsiders, figures like Viva, Ultra Violet, Sugar Plum Fairy, Holly Woodlawn, Edie Sedgwick, "Little Joe" Dallesandro, Taylor Mead, Ondine, Ingrid Superstar, John Giorno, and others. Mostly very little happens in Warhol's movies—or so much that it turns into a monumental immersion in otherness. These include *Blow Job*, *Hand Job*, *Sleep*, *Chelsea Girls*, and, perhaps most famous of all, *Empire*. This masterpiece was filmed starting at six p.m. from the forty-fourth floor of the Time-Life Building. Warhol framed the shot. Filmmaker Jonas Mekas and assistant Gerard Malanga changed the film rolls every thirty minutes. The crew stopped filming around one a.m. The first two rolls are overexposed—Andy had set the exposure wrong—but no matter. Warhol called the whole thing "an eight-hour hard-on. It's so beautiful. The lights come on and the stars come out and it sways." As with his other movies, *Empire* is shown at the speed of silent films, so that it lasts longer than it took to make—another typically Warholian way of manipulating time.

6. *BIG ELECTRIC CHAIR*, 1967–1968

This is one of the last works Warhol completed before Monday, June 3, 1968. It is a jarring, chilling, hard-to-read image, almost abstract, masterful, optically complicated, emotionally alienating, a cipher, a constellation unto itself, malevolent, flaglike. Nothing that followed would be the same.

That June day began for Warhol like most other days. He awoke uptown, prayed with his mother in the basement, shopped at Bloomingdale's, and procured more Obetrol—an amphetamine then widely used as a diet aid. At 4:15 p.m., he got out of a cab in front of his studio at 33 Union Square West. (Dallesandro claimed it was his first official day working at the Factory.) Warhol's boyfriend, Jed Johnson, was walking up to the door at the same time. They got into the elevator and were joined by a Warhol hanger-on named Valerie Solanas, who had been lurking around on the street near the Factory looking for Warhol after being told he wasn't there. As the three rode up in the elevator, Warhol noticed Solanas was wearing a heavy coat, despite the hot weather, and tightly clutching a paper bag. Studio manager Fred Hughes was at his desk; also inside were the critic and curator Mario Amaya and the filmmaker Paul Morrissey, who was on the phone with Viva. Morrissey handed her off to Andy, who handed the phone to Hughes and went in the back to the bathroom.

Just then, Solanas pulled a .32 automatic pistol from the paper bag and pointed it at Warhol, who was standing in front of her. "No! No! Valerie! Don't do it!" he screamed. She fired two shots. Andy fell to the floor and tried to crawl under a desk. She walked toward him, pointed the gun, and fired again. The third bullet entered Andy's right side and exited through his back, leaving a huge wound. His lungs had been punctured; he couldn't breathe. He later said he felt a "horrible, horrible pain, as if a firecracker had exploded inside me." Thinking he was dead, Solanas fired at Amaya and missed; he ran away, but a fifth shot hit him in his flank. After Morrissey and Billy Name kept her out of the back room, she returned to the office, stood in front of Hughes, and said, "I have to shoot you." He fell to his knees, pleading with her: "I didn't do anything to you. Just leave." She pointed the gun between his eyes and pulled the trigger, but the gun jammed. Just then, the elevator doors opened. Hughes screamed, "There's the elevator, Valerie. Just take it!" She did.

On the floor, Warhol was dying. He was passing in and out of consciousness. Billy cradled Andy's head in his lap and started to wail. Andy said, "Oh, please don't make me laugh, Billy . . . please, it hurts too much." Name said, "I'm not laughing, Andy . . . I'm crying." At 4:35, fifteen minutes after the incident began, an EMS team arrived and put Warhol on a stretcher, but the stretcher wouldn't fit in the elevator, so they had to carry Warhol, seated, in their arms, down the stairs. His pain was agonizing. He lost consciousness. At 4:45, Warhol was brought into the Columbus Hospital ER, where Dr. Giuseppe Rossi and a team began working on him. Amaya was in the bed next to him. He heard the doctors say that the pulse was faint. Andy's wounds were devastating; the bullet had penetrated his esophagus, liver, spleen, intestines, and—fatefully—his gallbladder. "Forget it," the doctor said, there was "no chance." At 4:51 p.m., Warhol was pronounced clinically dead. Amaya screamed, "Don't you know who this is? It's Andy Warhol. He's famous. And he's rich. He can afford to pay for an operation. For Christ's sake, do something." They resumed work, massaging his heart until he revived.

Police detectives searched the Factory, scoffing in disapproval at all the male porn and death-and-disaster paintings, and brought Hughes and Johnson into custody as suspects. At eight p.m., Solanas walked up to a twenty-two-year-old rookie cop in Times Square and said, "The police are looking for me." Robert Kennedy was shot and killed the next night. The sixties ended many times. These two nights are among them.

"Before I was shot," Warhol said, "I always suspected I was watching TV instead of living life. Right when I was being shot I knew I was watching television. Since I was shot everything is such a dream to me. I don't know whether or not I'm really alive—whether I died. It's sad." It is.

7. LADIES AND GENTLEMEN (MARSHA P. JOHNSON), 1975

When Warhol returned to painting, it was by commencing his endless series of commissioned portraits. No one knows how many he painted; he saw the project as an overall portrait of society. It's said that the going rate for commissioning one was $25,000. The format was almost always the same: Starting with a Polaroid taken by the Big Shot camera, which is only in focus at a distance of forty inches, Warhol took as many as fifty pictures, always using a flash. He then selected a single shot and rephotographed it with a 35mm camera, transferred it to acetate to silkscreen, and then printed it, always at the same forty-by-forty-inch size to preserve the Polaroid framing. Warhol sometimes subjected the images to his own "kind of plastic surgery," bringing features out or collaging elements in. This endless series includes Muhammad Ali, Brigitte Bardot, Sylvester Stallone,

Princess Diana, Aretha Franklin, Gianni Versace, Jimmy Carter, Carly Simon, Martha Graham, unknown businessmen and society women, and O. J. Simpson. The work was panned as "shallow" and "boring" by the *Times*' Hilton Kramer; in the pages of *Time*, Robert Hughes said they "hardly exist within the sphere of aesthetic debate."

One 1975 series stands out: *Ladies and Gentlemen*—a set of drag queens, each of whom was paid fifty dollars to sit for a photo session—and particularly the portrait of Marsha P. Johnson, a black drag queen with pink teeth, blond hair in a twist, a beaded necklace, and a red streak down the right side of her hair. Warhol probably never knew it, but, as the artist Glenn Ligon notes in a brilliant essay on the series in the show's superb catalogue, Johnson was "already a star."

On June 28, 1969, according to legend, it was Johnson who threw "the shot glass that was heard around the world." She was, Ligon writes, "an integral part of the uprising that followed a police raid at the Stonewall Inn," throwing the fateful glass into a mirror "while shouting, 'I got my civil rights!'" "Black Marsha," as she called herself, became a leading activist in the fight for transgender rights; by her own estimation, she was arrested "over 100 times" for sex work. But her life was lived on the margins, on the streets; she had nervous breakdowns, walked naked on Christopher Street. The P of her middle initial, she said, stood for "Pay it no mind." Shortly after the 1992 Gay Pride Parade, her body was found in the Hudson River. Despite a massive wound in the back of her head, her death was ruled a suicide. In 2012, activist Mariah Lopez got the NYPD to reopen the case as a possible homicide. RuPaul calls her "the true Drag Mother."

Now look at all of Warhol's *Ladies and Gentlemen* paintings again.

8. *AIDS, JEEP, BICYCLE*, 1985–1986

Another common charge against Warhol is that he supposedly ignored AIDS. In fact, AIDS struck often and close to Andy; he knew many who died of the disease. In 1984, Warhol's boyfriend of several years—Jon

Gould, whom he photographed more than four hundred times—was diagnosed with AIDS. He was hospitalized twice that year; he lost his sight, his weight plummeted to seventy pounds, and two years later he was dead.

AIDS is everywhere in Warhol's late work—as in his paintings of words, like *666 the Mark of the Beast, Are You Different?, Heaven and Hell Are Just One Breath Away*, and *Repent and Sin No More!* In a painting modeled on *The Last Supper*, he silkscreens the words "The Big C" under Christ; the C stands for cancer, as attested in Warhol's source material. And, in one of his last paintings, he just comes out and says it: Along the bottom left side of the enormous canvas, stenciled and painted in patchy black, is the word "AIDS." Above it, you can make out the sort of scare headlines that the *New York Post* used to run about the disease, which helped to stigmatize the disease and spread hatred of gay men. The words "New York," from the *Post* logo, appear above, along with the date "Friday August 30 1985." All this is offset by a set of random images from consumer ads—a Jeep, a bicycle, a sale price—and other text, as if to suggest how the culture was looking away. Warhol noticed, with a vengeance.

In the same year Warhol made *AIDS, Jeep, Bicycle*, Rock Hudson died of AIDS. Mario Amaya, who had pleaded with doctors not to give up on Andy after Solanas shot them both, died of AIDS the following year. ACT UP was founded the year after that.

On Saturday, February 14, 1987, Warhol complained to his dermatologist of abdominal pain. He spent the weekend in bed, not telling friends what was going on. On Tuesday, he kept an appointment so he could be photographed with Miles Davis. That same day, he told another doctor he'd been feeling ill for four weeks. The doctor diagnosed him with an acutely infected gallbladder and advised that it be removed as soon as possible. Warhol waited two more days to see what would happen. On Thursday, he caught a chill. The gallbladder had become severely inflamed with fluid and had to be removed at once. He went to New York Hospital, where he was scheduled for surgery on Saturday. "Oh, I'm not going to make it," he said, and locked many of his valuables in his safe. After surgery, he was administered Cefoxitin, a drug very similar to penicillin, which he was allergic to. Staff nurses failed to properly measure his fluids; a malfunctioning suction device that allowed a reduction in fluids was not replaced. As biographer Victor Bockris notes, "The chances of dying from complications of routine gallbladder surgery are thousands to one." Andy Warhol died at 6:31 a.m., Sunday, February 22, 1987.

(2018)

Why Did It Take So Long for the World to Recognize the Genius of Joseph Yoakum?

An array of more than sixty exquisite, quasi-abstract colored-pencil landscapes by the Native and African American visionary Joseph Yoakum—drawings that look like they might have been made on Mars—is emitting optical auroras at the gallery Venus Over Manhattan. Though he is still little-known and underappreciated, Yoakum's time may finally have come.

Yoakum was born in Missouri in 1890; his mother was a former slave, his father a Native American—Cherokee, though Yoakum himself liked to boast of Navajo ancestry. One of ten children, he worked from an early age with railroad circuses: Ringling Brothers, Buffalo Bill Cody's Wild West show, and others. He did stints as a horse-handler, billposter, miner, carpenter, shoeshine, janitor, mechanic, foundry worker; in 1918, he served in France in World War I. He married twice, fathered children in both marriages, but traveled the world, including to Asia, Australia, and all over America, and hoboed across Canada. In 1962, while retired in Chicago, the seventy-two-year-old Yoakum was inspired by a dream to try drawing. By the time he died, on Christmas Day ten years later, he had produced around two thousand radiant drawings.

Yoakum's work is dominated by landscapes, images filled with strange shapes that look like segmented islands and elephant skin, geological maps and sedimentary core samples, marked with nerve systems and erosion; visual calypsos of meandering landmass, evening rains in lagoons, shadows falling across mystic bays, protozoa and lava that seems to flow into clouds, claw configurations, and biomorphic jigsaw puzzles, all glimmering with prismatic secondary colors. There are repeating curves and forest patterns, rising and falling hills. Individual elements of each image are depicted from all directions at once: from above and below, left and right. You see the world from a great distance, as if passing on a train, or remembered, or imagined, or as seen through some kind of tunnel vision. This gives Yoakum's work a metaphysical quality; viewing it recalls the effect of studying illuminated manuscripts and amorphous Chinese-landscape ink paintings, which are continually reconfiguring themselves into different spaces.

Although Yoakum did create portraits, he never depicts people in his landscapes. Yet each of these vistas represents a world people have visited, lived on, traveled through, and altered. Yoakum wasn't looking for the end of the world. As a Native American and black man, he always appears to be looking from a distance toward a world he knows well but is never quite within or part of. When he needs to populate a farm or field with livestock, he uses images taken from contemporary sources: picture books and magazines. He uses the same cows, chickens, and horses repeatedly. All of this gives his work its otherworldly wistfulness, makes it feel a little lonely.

Yoakum was no outlier in any of this. His fellow Chicagoan Henry Darger was using found images in much the same way, and space in the work of Martín Ramírez and Adolf Wölfli has a similar nonnarrative all-at-once quality, marked by curving cones and off-world compositions filled with terrestrial phenomena. So-called real artists like Arthur Dove have also employed flat fields of swelling forms and furrowed fields; Charles Burchfield's waving world is marked by a similar cosmic glow. Yoakum's tangled arrangements even recall the ecstatic confusions of William Blake. It seems clear that Yoakum was familiar with the majestic black-and-white photos of the American West by giants like Carleton Watkins and Timothy

O'Sullivan, not to mention the railroad and circus posters he would have known from his youth. And his titles suggest a strange cross between atlas, textbook, magazine caption, and Walt Whitman's encyclopedic assessment of the world.

Yoakum has loomed large in my imagination since 1971, when I was twenty years old. That year, I had a teeny space across from the noisy El train in an annex of the School of the Art Institute of Chicago. There, in the school's Wabash Transit Gallery, just thirty feet from my studio—on the same floor—I was permanently imprinted by one of the first-ever showings of Yoakum's work. I met the man that day, but remember only his weathered face, strong hands, a jasmine scent, and something that seemed to hum around him. I knew I'd encountered a life force, and glimpsed a kind of aesthetic possibleness. These possibilities multiplied when—in life-changing rapid succession—I saw the first exhibitions of two other newly discovered so-called outsiders, Ramírez and Darger, who lived a few miles from Yoakum and just blocks from my apartment. Suddenly, Chicago was artistic Mecca.

In Chicago, such miracles seemed commonplace. The grudging Second City mentality has always led us to develop our own "regional" preferences and tastes. We were always looking in out-of-the-way places: at junk shops, garage sales, and most famously at the huge outdoor Maxwell Street flea markets on Sunday, where it wasn't uncommon to hear blues and gospel musicians as we browsed around looking for inspiration.

In 1967, the year after he took a small storefront studio on Chicago's South Side, Yoakum's work captured the attention of a local teacher named John Hopgood when he saw a handful of beautiful drawings in the artist's window. Beguiled, he entered the studio and purchased a few of the drawings for less than ten dollars. Very soon, Hopgood got him a show in the small foyer at the nearby St. Bartholomew's Church, and began spreading the word. Two years later, Whitney Halstead, who had organized that 1971 SAIC show—and who also happened to be my teacher—discovered Yoakum's work and started showing it to Chicago artists like Jim Nutt, Gladys Nilsson, Roger Brown, Christina Ramberg, Karl Wirsum, and others. All these admirers began promoting Yoakum, buying his work themselves, talking it up, and arranging shows for him. Finally, a year after my revelation and one month before his death, legendary curator Marcia Tucker organized a show at the Whitney Museum of American Art.

But this was the early 1970s. And while Chicago may have seemed like a new Jerusalem to me, the winds of mainstream art were blowing in other directions. Over the previous twenty-five years, New York had exploded with a series of art movements that defined and redefined the art world: Abstract Expressionism, Lyrical Abstraction, Pop Art, Minimalism, conceptual art, video and performance art, and much more. Outsider artists stayed outside. By the time I moved to New York, Post-Minimalism and a hundred other styles had taken root in New York and around the world. And I suppressed my love for all those artists who'd meant so much to me in Chicago. I wanted to get with the program, and the world I'd left behind—Chicago Imagism, funk, and outsider art—wasn't part of that. It hurt me personally to walk away from such vital work, and the art world itself suffered for excluding so many of these artists for so long. It's not outlandish to say that artists like Yoakum, Ramírez, and Darger—and many others who remain unaccounted for today—are among the greatest artists of the twentieth century.

Go see the Yoakum show, and take it from me: Never deny the sources of your pleasure. Always honor your eye. Follow your taste. Love will find a way.

(2019)

What the Hell Was Modernism?

Can a museum devoted to Modernism survive the death of the movement? Can it bring that death about? Ever since the beginnings of the Renaissance in the fourteenth century, most art movements have lasted one generation, sometimes two. Today, after more than 130 years, Modernism is, at least by some measures, insanely and incongruously popular—a world brand. The first thing oligarchs do to signal sophistication, and to cleanse and store money, is collect and build personal museums of modern art, and there's nothing museumgoers love more than a survey of a mid-century giant. In the United States, Modernism represents the triumph of American greatness and wealth; it's considered the height of twentieth-century European culture—which Americans bought and brought across the Atlantic, which is to say poached.

Today, kids sport tattoos of artwork by Gustav Klimt, Henri Matisse, Salvador Dalí, Edvard Munch, Piet Mondrian, and Andy Warhol. (You might not think of Warhol as a Modernist, but we'll get to that.) Our cities are crowded with glass-walled luxury riffs on High Modernist architecture, the apartments inside full of knockoffs of "mid-century modern" furniture. Donald Judd's headquarters/studio outpost in Marfa is now East Hampton in West Texas, a secular pilgrimage site for millionaire collectors, full of expensive restaurants and fancy second homes. (As recently as 1994, my wife and I were offered a house there for $5,000.)

And people pay—not just at the auction houses, but just to see the work, even briefly. Witness the Museum of Modern Art's daily crowds, the daily lines of full-price guests forking over twenty-five dollars. Last year's annual attendance was just over three million. (Do the math.) People take selfies with van Gogh's *Starry Night*; adolescents feel big feelings because the world didn't understand Vincent, though he's been understood clearly for well over a century. His life has inspired movies, as have the lives of Pablo Picasso, Paul Gauguin, Frida Kahlo, Jackson Pollock, Warhol (and the woman who shot him), and Jean-Michel Basquiat—the most recent in the long line of world-straddling geniuses. We all know the stories, from destroying one's own work and committing suicide to womanizing and pissing in fireplaces. (In this way, Modernism is Hollywood Babylon.) And while we take our parents to the Met to appreciate old art, tradition, and "good technique," we go to MoMA because Modernism is still *cool*—a sequence of revolutionary gestures, shocks, and succession stories that we're convinced tell a foundational story about radicalism and experimentation.

That sequence of succession dramas, and the reputation it created, are not an accident. They were forged by MoMA in cooperation with artists who very much wanted to see their own work as the natural end point of all art history. (Who wouldn't?) All this has prevailed since the museum's founding by wealthy New Yorkers in the late twenties. The museum opened nine days after the onset of the Great Depression in 1929, and even today, three-quarters of a century after Modernism's true peak, the movement's grip is like a vise. It is why we are still so captivated by the allure of the avant-garde, long after the avant-garde started sleepwalking. And it may be why we still believe artists are like gods, long after they start sleeping with money and celebrity. People still quote Duchamp saying, "A painting that doesn't shock isn't worth painting." Why are people still set on shocking their nanas? Modernism. Museums still present art history as one long story that breaks, dramatically, with the twentieth century. Why? Modernism! Why do I keep asking myself, Is Modernism over yet? Modernism!

I love Modernism. It's a movement, and a culture, that can be defined in as many ways as there are art historians. I believe, and MoMA has long seemed to assert, that it began with Paul Cézanne's *The Bather*, in around 1885. Your take on its start and end points may vary, but surely we can all agree on the impact of the formally daring work that defined the first half of the twentieth century in Europe and America—work that's been familiar to many of us from our earliest school museum trips and postcards on our dorm-room walls: Picasso and Matisse, O'Keeffe and Pollock. Much of this work can still feel truly shocking. Thousands of the ideas generated by Modernism continue to challenge artists today, and I still love many of the movement's defining artists. All of Picasso, Pollock's giant drip paintings, and Hilma af Klint's first forays into the deepest precincts of abstraction take my breath away.

But much of Modernism and its concerns now feel long ago, forged in a time of rapid industrial change when white European males assumed they ruled the world. The demands of our times call for something else. And before you object that we've been living for fifty years in Post-Modernism, not Modernism, reflect on what it means that the movement following Modernism was defined by, even named after, what preceded it. (Daddy issues, anyone?) The shift that began in the fifties and sixties with Pop Art and the work of Andy Warhol looked like a break from Modernism, but it also extended Modernism's fetishizing of novelty and its canon of iconoclasts. Modernism is part of my life story, all of our life stories; it has shaped the ways we see the world and how the world sees itself. But the past couple of decades have seen seismic shifts, moving the art world for the first time far beyond the dictates of the movement. Modernism is not headed for the dustbin, but in terms of experimental one-upmanship, and the conviction that each new work could break and redefine all of art history, a page is finally turning—slowly, a bit, at least.

Of course, this kind of change—the fading of a movement that once conquered the world—has happened before. Usually, it happens much faster. The heyday of rococo artists like François Boucher, Jean-Honoré Fragonard, and Antoine Watteau lasted just fifteen years before neoclassicism shouldered them aside, deeming their work effeminate and gauche. Instead, artists like Jacques-Louis David emerged with gigantic, "masculine" portrayals of Roman virtue, the glories of Napoleon, the French Revolution, and mythic scenes of death—until David was arrested and thrown in prison. Impressionism lasted all of twenty-five years. Even the High Renaissance came and went in less than fifty. By comparison, by this point Modernism is ancient. Modeling it as something new and cool today would be like the original Modernists modeling themselves after the art and values of 130 years before them: Boucher, Jean-Auguste-Dominique Ingres, and Antonio Canova. That Modernism has been so canonized is especially ironic given that the earliest Modernists were so desperate to break away from the art of the past that they scrapped Renaissance approaches to perspective and space. (Duchamp wrote that he wanted to use a Rembrandt as an ironing board.)

Which raises the question: If Modernism wasn't the end point of art history, the ultimate form of artistic expression, what was it? If we don't let it bully its way to the front of the line and center stage, crowding out everything that came before, during, and whatever comes after, what does it look like? And what will it look like as it recedes farther and farther in the rearview mirror, until it finally appears not as some grand finale for everything that came before, but simply as one period in a never-ending sequence—one set of mannerisms followed by another?

As great as many of Modernism's artists were, much of the art is about itself. For the most part, it's a matter of white people arguing over other white people's art history. Once we've left those arguments behind, it may be that Modernism's most striking legacy is the cult of the male artist and the competitive aesthetic messianism it spawned.

ON OCTOBER 21, the greatest collection of modern art on the planet will reopen at the new Museum of Modern Art. The newness is not due to a big move to another location, or a billion-dollar structure springing up in the old footprint (that last happened in 2004, to so-so reviews), though much of the interior of the iconic—and blandly slick and cramped—building on Fifty-Third Street has been redone, and new galleries are now located at the base of yet another new MoMA skyscraper full of very expensive condominiums. The MoMA is new, this time, because of what will be presented inside, and how.

The museum has traditionally hung its collection chronologically, in order to tell a particular story: He begat him, who begat him, and so on, until finally Modernism hung a sign on its door saying CLOSED (just as a new generation showed up at the door). Of course, the story acknowledged, Modernism had its roots in various kinds of source material (see Picasso); of course, it was marked by rivalries (see Picasso vs. Matisse, for instance). But the story has always been told as if it were a matter of rigid progression—to the point where, on the museum walls, its evolution appeared almost inevitable. In 1941, MoMA's great founding director, Alfred Barr, famously drew a diagram of the museum's ideal permanent collection—in the shape of a torpedo. (This was during World War II, after all.) At the tail were Cézanne, van Gogh, and Seurat. And the point of the weapon? After 1950, Barr predicted, art would come only from America and Mexico. His successor, Bill Rubin, tripled down on his formulation. (Except for Mexico, of course.)

Now, at last, the museum is moving past this timeline. It's getting rid of the very idea of movements. Good! Measuring things that way does a disservice to art and to artists; as Willem de Kooning said, "It is disastrous to name ourselves." MoMA will be hanging works from different eras, and different places, next to one another, opening up what had begun to seem like an airless, self-referential canon into something much more dynamic. The museum is even discarding its eighty-nine-year aversion to showing different mediums together. As a geezer, I relish back-to-back galleries of killer paintings, but it's fitting to stop showing art in only this way, in part because the new strategy allows us to go back and ask new questions of work we thought we understood, and in part because it reflects how artists themselves see art history, today especially: not as a timeline of progress, but as a beautiful trash heap or costume shop in which to play. (In the age of the internet, with the art world globalized and at least some of the old barriers to entry collapsing, this probably isn't too surprising.)

Most exciting of all, MoMA's permanent collection will no longer be a static thing. Every six months, a third of it will be reinstalled. I presume that the twin peaks of Picasso and Matisse will always be on display somewhere, along with other trophy works and big names. But there will be many more names, too, belonging to artists who are less well-known, less hoary with age, less white, less male, and less exclusively American and European. This means that every eighteen months, MoMA will be entirely new. If you're irked by the way the collection looks now, come back in six months; you never know what you'll find. Goodbye, canon! At least the static, teleological Old Testament version we all grew up with.

In 2004, when MoMA reopened in a then-new glass-and-steel campus, only 5 percent of the art on view in the permanent collection was by women. Today, the museum estimates that 28 percent of the works on view are by women, and 21 percent by artists from outside Western Europe, the United States, and Canada. That's gigantic for MoMA, Modernism, and art.

"This past five to ten years is the most change-making, radical re-thinking of art history and, by extension, museum curation in a half-century," Ann Temkin, the museum's chief curator of painting and sculpture, has said. "Things that were assumed over the last forty, twenty, ten, or even five years have exploded." Amen.

So what were those assumptions? Let's look at five big ones.

First, there was Ezra Pound's cri de coeur "Make it new." In Modernism, only newness was given value. Everything old was considered passé, inadequate to address the times—which led Modernism to claim a monopoly not just on newness but also on importance. One Dadaist says "Art is dead"? Case closed. What this overlooked is that *all* art was once new. Cave painters painted over older cave paintings; the ceramic artists of ancient Rome signed their work with boasts like "No one could ever make a grain pot as good as this." It's the same as each generation thinking it has invented sex. Newness is as old as time. The Modernists were just a lot cockier about saying so.

Second, Modernism called itself reality. Which meant, perversely, that it didn't have to bother to address the *actual* reality—instead, it offered itself as the only thing that mattered. Kandinsky wrote, "Realism = Abstraction. Abstraction = Realism." The critic Clement Greenberg said that art was meant to "undeceive the eye." Much of modern art turned away from the world and into itself, erasing subject matter and narrative altogether. Or denying, at least, the *importance* of subject matter, since of course many of the Modernists employed traditional subject matter: nudes, landscapes, still lifes, more nudes, everyday scenes, nature, architecture, and more nudes. What an artist had to render new was *how* these things looked. Viewers were expected to look through the subject matter of a given work. You weren't seeing a landscape; you were seeing the way this artist has reinvented the landscape. As late as the end of the twentieth century, Gerhard Richter said he was "indifferent" to subject matter (although he made paintings of Nazis, terrorists, and 9/11). One implication of this is that Modernism places you in the narrow world of the artist's studio—amid a cloud of optical shoptalk. This is what allowed artists to occupy themselves making squiggles, squares, rectangles, pictures of violins, color arrangements, street scenes, and naked ladies even during the worst days of World War I and World War II. By the time I was trying to enter the art world in the seventies, the only thing painting was supposed to be about was itself, its materials, and "flatness."

Third, Modernism was built on the principle that formal experimentation is the only thing that matters. The doctrine can't be emphasized enough. Every artist had to create his [*sic*] own forms and world. These forms had to follow visual strictures: Art had to be seen all at once, not sequentially or with any formal hierarchy. (That alone eliminated any possibility of narrative.) Think of how you view a Pollock: all at once, even though it has parts and details. Similarly, in viewing a Modernist work, you're not supposed to observe any distinction between process and material; the viewer is meant to take them in just as religious observers of the medieval era were meant to see the mosaics of the time—as image, color, surface, process, and material all coalesced into a single thing. Modernism was philosophically colonialist this way; its adherents loved declaring every idea as its own, even as they insisted they were inventing what they were stealing.

Fourth was the principle that modern art would "kill history"—a manic grasping toward finality. Modernism was born in an era of multiple revolutions, mass industrialization, and colonial empire, coincident with inventions like photography, movies, flight, automobiles, X-rays, and Einstein's theory of relativity. Duchamp said painting should "avoid all contact with traditional" art. In wanting to destroy the whole history of Western art, Modernists were like an aesthetic Taliban. Except for what they approved of, all art was dismissed as bourgeois, bad taste, or kitsch.

When Americans took up the mantle with Abstract Expressionism, they were no less absolutist. They had not seen their culture destroyed by war, as the Europeans had, but they were still Modernists at heart. Barnett

Newman said American artists had to "start from scratch." Ad Reinhardt said, "I am merely making the last painting which anyone can make." History didn't exist unless you were making it. (In Modernism, it's always the end times again.)

Finally, there was Modernism's grand teleology: the wack-rationalist idea that history proceeds in a predetermined order. If you don't know or care about that order, if you don't fit its prescriptions—or if you happen to be an artist of color, a woman, a visionary of any kind—you're out of luck. The only goal was progress, as defined by the movement's white male leaders.

For those who actually lived Modernism, of course, the whole project was way messier and more rivalrous than any set of principles could contain. After all, before MoMA got its hands on Modernism, it wasn't propaganda. It was just a name for a broad array of artists and their work. Which also meant a lot of different, competing strains of propaganda.

In fact, Modernism was less a unified movement than a wrestling match of competing egos vying for top-dog status, each claiming he'd replaced or repudiated his predecessor. Picasso was against abstraction. (What a pill!) Mondrian wrote, "Cubism did not accept the logical consequences of its own discoveries." His goal? "Pure plastics." (I'm still not sure what this means.) Kazimir Malevich, the high priest of Russian Suprematism, demanded "victory over the sun" and "the supremacy of pure feeling." (What?) In 1912, Duchamp declared that "Painting is over." Nine years later, the Constructivist Aleksandr Rodchenko announced, "I have reduced painting to its logical conclusion . . . I affirmed it's all over." (Hello, Dr. Death.)

Marcel Duchamp did take a less bellicose posture, musing, "Can one make works of art that are not 'works' of art?" (I love that!) In response, Clement Greenberg dismissed Duchamp as "sub-art." (What a bully!) The so-called Pope of Surrealism, André Breton, "excommunicated" heretics like Alberto Giacometti. (God complexes and control freaks are a Modernist feature, not a glitch.) Minimalist Donald Judd opined that Duchamp had invented fire with his "readymade" art, but that he failed to do enough with it. Much later, Duchamp himself sniped that contemporary artists "no longer make pictures; they make checks." Before long, Chris Burden and Richard Prince were making art out of checks. Now artists make art out of Prince.

Things have come a long way since the Armory Show of 1913—the first in-depth look Americans got at European Modernism, and arguably the true catalyst for all that might be called modern art in America. In New York, 85,000 people saw the show; in Chicago, attendance was 188,000. It's no exaggeration to say the founding of MoMA stems from those twenty-seven earthshaking days in New York. One New York critic wrote, "American artists did not so much visit the exhibition as live at it." Albert Barnes, Henry Frick, and the Met bought works from the Armory Show. American salon impresario Mabel Dodge wrote to Gertrude Stein that the show's New York appearance was "the most important public event . . . since the signing of the Declaration of Independence" and added that "things will never be the same." She was right.

At the time, the Armory Show's impact was reflected most conclusively by the resistance it encountered. Traditionalists protested that the show was like "visiting a lunatic asylum." Matisse, a prominent feature of the show, was burned in effigy. Teddy Roosevelt called the art "repellent from every standpoint" and asserted that there was "no reason why people should not call themselves Cubists, or Octagonists, or Parallelopipedonists, or Knights of the Isosceles Triangle . . . one term is as fatuous as another." The show's most scandalous work was Duchamp's *Nude Descending a Staircase, No. 2*; newspapers derided it as "Rush Hour in the Subway" and "Explosion in a Shingle Factory."

The spectacle of the masses mocking avant-garde art is so familiar today that it's hard to believe no one had bothered to do it before Modernism (though such ribbing had occurred in the rarefied air of the French and English salons). But why would anyone have bothered before? Until Modernism, no art movement had ever offered as totalizing and threatening a proposition as Modernism did: that art would remake the world.

It did, and it didn't. First, in America at least, Modernism itself would have to be reimagined. By 1948, Barnett Newman was filling large canvases with stripes and monochromatic fields of bright color. Jackson Pollock began to drip in 1947. Peggy Guggenheim opened the Art of This Century gallery in New York, exhibiting both European Modernists and starving, struggling Americans, among them Clyfford Still, William Baziotes, Alexander Calder, Adolph Gottlieb, Joseph Cornell, Robert Motherwell, Willem de Kooning, and Mark Rothko. She gave Pollock his first solo show in 1943. A new game was in the offing: America claiming the European avant-garde as its own imperial patrimony.

The values of Abstract Expressionism included enormous scale: Its defining image was that of the male painter, alone in the arena, painting in pursuit of total abstraction. (Except for de Kooning, who Pollock felt had "betrayed" abstraction.) These artists embraced myth, the sublime, transcendence, existential and spiritual terror, cosmic light and darkness—all that hocus-pocus, and celebrity, too. Pollock was featured in *Life* magazine, caught in the act of painting and smoking. Abstract Expressionism had restarted Modernism wonderfully—until 1953, when twenty-seven-year-old Robert Rauschenberg arrived at de Kooning's studio carrying a bottle of liquor, offering to trade it for a drawing of de Kooning's, which he promised to erase. De Kooning's best biographers, Mark Stevens and Annalyn Swan, call this rendezvous "a ghostly Greek messenger come to warn the king of hubris." De Kooning said, "I know what you're doing," and granted the request.

That same year, Rauschenberg and composer-artist John Cage made *Automobile Tire Print*, a long, narrow strip of paper on which Cage had driven a car, leaving a long track in black ink. All this was a direct attack on the life-or-death gravitas of Abstract Expressionism—and indeed all of Modernism. Art would soon be riven with irony—a factor absent from the art world for some time—and the ironies would multiply all over the world for decades. In 1956, the first Pop Art show took place in London. In Europe, Yves Klein and Piero Manzoni were ascendant. The year 1957 brought the most political international postwar art movement of them all: Situationism, which railed against personality-based individualism, asserting instead that art is determined by real-world conditions and situations. Artists today still work from that premise.

The coup de grâce came on January 1, 1958, when a collage called *Target with Four Faces* garnered the cover of the era's leading art magazine, *ARTnews*. The work was by twenty-seven-year-old unknown Jasper Johns. Three weeks later, things lurched into hyperspeed when Johns's debut solo show opened at Leo Castelli's new fourth-floor gallery on East Seventy-Seventh Street in Manhattan, and American art turned on a dime. MoMA acquired three works from the show and arranged for a fourth, *Flag*, to be purchased as a gift for the museum (for a price of $900). All are now Modernist icons. A new world was released.

While many of the younger artists were still white and male, in this moment one new factor did come to the fore: Many of them were gay. Moreover, all of them held views that were diametrically opposed to the lofty academic values they'd inherited.

These artists painted smaller, and often figuratively. They chose and employed their subject matter deliberately, not spontaneously. They were uninterested in spiritualism or strict formal ideas like "flatness" or the sublime; they had little attraction to cathedrals of the self; they even violated the sacrosanct surfaces of their art by attaching real objects to them. (Ed Ruscha and Robert Indiana made paintings of words.) Like all artists after them, they were formalist and anti-formalist, sincere and ironic, at the same time. (The latter is a condition of life.) These artists didn't turn away from the mass culture around them, but rather embraced it. They brought life back into art. All of this was intentional. Rauschenberg said he and Johns "used to start each day by having to move out from Abstract Expressionism."

These innovations were important, of course. Yet, in attacking their Modernist forebears, the Pop artists were also affirming the reign of their ideology. In 1961, Robert Smithson described himself as "a Modern artist dying of Modernism." He was right. Pop Art and Minimalism were derived from mass taste, sources, and material; they were ironic, but like their immediate predecessors they were also committed to *making it new*, to the idea of the work of art as a closed perfect space, to formal experimentation and innovation above all else, to repudiating previous art history, and to the conception of art as a teleological project. And, of course, their work shocked your nana.

WHAT WILL IT BE LIKE to live without the old Modernist canon? Thrilling and scary, I expect. I don't want Picasso and the rest to go away, and of course they won't; we can't forget these titans, even as we rehang and reconsider their work every year.

But here's how art has already moved on. To artists today, Modernism is now just part of art history, and not even the only or best part. Artists are ranging through history, happy to make things new by returning to older unused, overlooked art. I've seen countless artists deploy Cubism and Post-Impressionism in ways that make the ur-Modernist movements just another segment of the aesthetic double helix. Artists like Jenna Gribbon, Louis Fratino, Carroll Dunham, Sarah Peters, and Jonathan Lyndon Chase actually cross the beams of Modernism with motives on Greek vases. And it's not pastiche or gamesmanship: Kerry James Marshall goes all the way back to neoclassical history painting to tell new stories, picturing black bodies rather than white heroes.

Subject matter and narrative are on the rise in art everywhere. With a hungry, documenting eye as lucid as Walker Evans's or Robert Frank's, LaToya Ruby Frazier photographs working-class American cities and people decimated by toxic environments and jerry-rigged governmental policy. Is her work "didactic"? It is! In the works of numerous artists, collectives, and collaborations, we're seeing brilliant portrayals of institutional cruelty. In other words, the real world—and not just as it's reflected in the artist's studio. You don't need a wall label to feel the gut punch. Ditto the set-up photographs of queer quadriplegic Robert Andy Coombs, which show the artist as explicitly sexual, as a human being with agency and desire. Christine Sun Kim retrofits the charts of strict minimalism and conceptualism to express the rage of her own deaf community.

Modernism began in many places, at different times. Today, artists aren't robbing or trying to kill the past. They're collaborating with it. Subject matter and other forms of imagination have emerged as the electric center of artistic innovation. Narrative, biography, autobiography, history, cultural context, and family trees, all long dismissed as unserious or provincial concerns, have been injected into art. The purities of Modernism don't mean a thing; recent minimalist, monochrome, conceptual art-about-art tends to feel like the work of artists posing as junior Post-Modernists. Art no longer seems locked in a competitive struggle for artistic supremacy. (Except in the market, where it has always been this way.)

But the monolith of Modernism is gone. Artists are no longer content to crawl into the skins of former styles. They're consuming, using, changing, and cannibalizing them. Gone is the bullying certainty of the old order. Instead we find subjectivity, a concern with ethics and responsibility, an engagement with the social contract, an embrace of personal obsession, and a renewed, earnest attempt to communicate with less insider-y audiences. Rather than worrying over where such art fits on the teleological-formalist timeline, consider the monumental power of Romanesque and medieval church facades—masterpieces that tell essential stories in visually sophisticated, visionary ways, making extraordinary use of material, scale, and craft, yet creating an experience that anyone may read, grasp, and become part of. They are open books.

These are the possibilities of art today. Art has landed on another moon.

Where does this leave MoMA? Alas, I'm no radical, so I am glad the museum won't be changing altogether. Flawed as they are, I have no desire to see MoMA or other museums of Modernism destroyed. I still need to return to their spaces regularly, in order to commune with the ancestors. Others will come forward to fix and replace the system. If MoMA is guided by a radical love of art, rather than a love of its underlying systems, it will play a leading role in the generations to come—and it may be that future art historians point to this new rehanging as a turning point, the central institution of Modernism committing to a new set of ideas about what it was, what it represents, and what it offers us today. I say to MoMA, go into storage and bring out your dead—the artists who were deemed "wrong," not part of the old story. Put them all on view. Let us decide. We all love art. But as James Baldwin wrote, "Love is a battle . . . love is growing up." After a century, we are finally beginning to outgrow Modernism.

(2019)

Beauford Delaney, Black and Gay, Very Nearly Disappeared from Art History

He is amazing . . . this Beauford," the novelist Henry Miller wrote of his lifelong friend Beauford Delaney in a 1945 essay that helped make the painter a legendary attraction in Greenwich Village. Delaney was so well-known that people often gathered outside his building on Greene Street, where he lived and worked on the top floor—a walk-up lit only by a woodburning potbelly stove—to catch a glimpse of him. Miller called Beauford Delaney a "black monarch," an artist capable of making "the great white world . . . grow smaller."

Born in Knoxville, Tennessee, in 1901, Delaney migrated north to Boston in 1923 to study art; he moved to New York in November 1929, days after the onset of the Great Depression. On his first day in New York, he slept on a bench in Union Square, where someone stole his shoes. The next morning, he set out to walk uptown to Harlem in a pair of new shoes. When he reached Central Park, he stopped because of his severely blistered feet.

Things had never been tougher for American artists—let alone black ones. Art schools didn't take black artists, and independent-studio classes banned black artists from figure-drawing sessions with white models. Undaunted, Delaney started drawing at a Midtown dance studio. Somehow, his career took off almost overnight. Four months after he arrived in New York, the *New York Telegraph* ran an article about Delaney's portraits of dancers and society figures.

He met and charmed everyone. A list of his friends and acquaintances includes Stuart Davis, his closest painter compatriot; W. E. B. Du Bois, whose portrait he did; Georgia O'Keeffe, who did a portrait of him; Duke Ellington; Louis Armstrong; Jacob Lawrence; Alfred Stieglitz; Edward Steichen; Dorothy Norman; Anaïs Nin, who intimidated him; Jackson Pollock; and Jean Genet. His closest lifelong friend, however, was James Baldwin, who had looked up Delaney in the Village after fleeing his own father at sixteen. Delaney became a kind of surrogate father to the writer; Baldwin later called the artist his "principal witness." Judging by his 1941 painting *Dark Rapture (James Baldwin)*, a steamy nude portrait of the sixteen-year-old writer (one of several Baldwin portraits he made over the decades), Delaney seems to have been in love with the lithe young man, twenty-two years his junior.

In October 1938, more than a decade before Pollock graced the same pages, *Life* magazine featured a photo of Delaney smiling beatifically at the Washington Square Outdoor Art Exhibit. "One of the most talented Negro painters," the caption read. Yet by the time he died in 1979, Delaney was alone, alcoholic, hallucinating, paranoid, and penniless in a Paris psychiatric hospital. What started as a great American story is now a near absence in the history of American art and an American Dream forestalled.

Through the thirties and forties, while most American artists were either struggling along as fifth-rate Cubists, regionalists, or academics, or desperately looking for ways around Picasso via Surrealism, Delaney made his own thoroughly contemporary way. In street and park scenes, still lifes, and portraits, he built upon the work of his good friend Davis, arriving at his own compact, flat fields of creamy, opaque color. His sense of visual, jigsawing geometry and strong, graphic distillation of structure is second only to Davis's. Delaney's work, however, has a much more human aura, atmosphere, and arc, almost to a mystical degree, seen only in Marsden Hartley.

So why has Delaney been disappeared from our collective memory? Partly it's due to the racial bias of art history; even while he was celebrated, it was less as a painterly equal to his contemporaries than as some kind of Negro seer or spiritual black Buddha. But timing also played a role: In 1953, at the age of fifty-one, Delaney left New York at perhaps the worst possible moment. When other American artists, like Jasper Johns, Robert Rauschenberg, Cy Twombly, John Cage, and Merce Cunningham—many of them open in their sexuality—were meeting up and staying out late together, Delaney was in Paris, where Baldwin had told him he could escape the long American night of racism. Baldwin was right, but Delaney struggled with French and became even more isolated. Twombly, Baldwin, and Miller returned often to New York; Delaney never did, so he never got to rejoin the conversation.

By the sixties, Delaney's abstraction was more connected to the French Art Informel—a primarily European response to Abstract Expressionism—and his paintings, influenced as they were by Monet's *Water Lilies* and Turner's glowing use of color, had little of the ironic, direct quality of Pop Art or the systemic rigor of Minimalism. At a distance, Delaney's work seemed passé—an artist painting in a void, outside the canon.

But I love Delaney's work, especially his highly colored, optically intense, dense figurative paintings. He is almost an exact contemporary of—and a New York compatriot of—another great painter-portraitist who captured the power and magic of being stylishly poor, who lived on the margins but eventually came to be recognized as a visionary: Alice Neel. Delaney should be held in the same high regard.

(2020)

No One Looked at New York Like Jason Polan

Jason Polan's powers of observation, and his hand—so simple, quick, supple, fun, and visually intelligent—made him one of the consummate draftsmen of the early twenty-first century. Thinking of him after hearing of his death at thirty-seven, I realize that I never saw him not drawing. He was always on a street somewhere in New York, notebook in hand, sitting off to the side, watching, a slight smile on his lips, a human seeing-machine who saw and drew it all.

In Polan's short life he must have made hundreds of thousands of cartoonish, scrawling drawings, including many that were part of radiantly impossible projects. He drew every object on view in the Museum of Modern Art, then self-published the results as a brilliant book. (Art aficionados will marvel at how authentically he renders every detail: the shape of a Lee Bontecou wall sculpture, the exact angles of Barnett Newman's *Broken Obelisk*.) Like a Borges character, he set out to draw "every person in New York," which became another amazing book—this one with thirty thousand squiggly ink drawings. His line is puckish, wonderful, kooky—akin to Alexander Calder's—and almost impossible not to at least smile at. His craft arcs out of the art world and into the real world in the ways Keith Haring's did. He was a bit of a weirdo, too, like that other watcher, Andy Warhol. (Indeed, Polan thrilled at seeing stars: "Just wandering around I notice celebrities because I'm looking at everybody's face," he told *New York* in 2009. "I think it's exciting to see a celebrity." Note the low-affect, deadpan love. Then he added, "I've never talked to any of them.")

Polan emitted his own kind of beautiful psychic sunshine. There was no irony in his work. His oeuvre is a mirthful illustrated encyclopedia of modern life, body language, styles, and habits. City life is the deep content of Polan's work. (He's a real Jane Jacobs artist.) Just as early itinerant photographers set up studios in storefronts or on city streets to take pictures of passersby, Polan placed an open call on his website offering to make "an hour's worth of drawings for $125," and posted where he'd be at a certain time if anyone wanted him to draw them. He had gallery shows, but he was never big in the art world. Instead, his art was beloved and well known by everyday people. When word came of his death, Instagram was flooded with messages proclaiming love and gratitude for Polan and the amazing grace of his art.

I knew Polan a little. Not long after he arrived in New York from Michigan in the early 2000s, he introduced himself to me on the street. (Where else?) He showed me the sketchbook he was carrying—I never saw him without one—and I was instantly smitten. He drew me, sometimes with Roberta, at least six times. I never spotted him doing it. I love how and where he depicted us: always in galleries or museums, where critics spend most of their lives, as he did, looking, observing. In one image he captures how my wife touches me lightly, calling my attention to something we're looking at. In another, we're depicted from behind, walking arm in arm. (Although in Jason's drawing I appear much balder than I think I am.)

Each of us has no art but our own. Jason found his, shared it with the world, and gave us all his small joys and tender mercies of a life lived in looking.

(2020)

Vida Americana: Harbinger of Immeasurable Abundance

Here is the most relevant show of the twenty-first century: the Whitney Museum's *Vida Americana: Mexican Muralists Remake American Art, 1925–1945*, which gathers together the adamantly political public art of Diego Rivera, Frida Kahlo, David Siqueiros, José Orozco, and others.

Once upon a time these artists were called "the greatest Renaissance in the contemporary world," a group whose art made "the aesthetic experiments of Paris [seem like] trifling matters." I agree: Those years were extraordinary. The muralists' painterly montage compositions reimagined the social order in high-keyed color and in-your-face power. Along with the recent shows *Posing Modernity* at Columbia's Wallach Gallery, which focused on black models in modern art, and *Hilma af Klint* at the Guggenheim, this show makes the course of art history look different. Not least for revealing the influence this still underrecognized movement exerted on the rest of the world before it was, as the catalogue puts it, "written out of American art history."

How did this happen? The erasure began in the early thirties, a time when President Herbert Hoover was railing about "American jobs for real Americans," and some 1.8 million people were deported and "repatriated." Even American artists sent complaint letters when Mexican muralists received commissions—forgetting that the artists in question were not immigrants but, rather, visiting dignitaries. Next, World War II and its Cold War aftermath gave American politicians the pretext to ban these artists' work for its "communist sympathies." (And there were other, more prosaic factors: These artists often painted huge murals, for instance, so much of their art cannot travel to faraway museums.)

Still, American artists of the time, looking for a way around the broad shadow of Picasso, were highly aware of what the Mexicans had to offer. The work of the young Philip Guston, trying to introduce new subject matter into his art, and Jackson Pollock's widely maligned, early pre-drip paintings, which attempted to wrestle the lessons of the Mexican artists into dense configurations of mythic subject matter, are both mind-boggling shows-within-a-show, early steps in those artists' campaigns to reset the trajectory of American painting.

Vida Americana gives us artists who were being modern without Cubism or abstraction—who instead reconstituted these and much else into entirely new aesthetic languages that still offer possibilities today. For me— and, I hope, the artists who study this work—the aesthetic lesson of *Vida*

Americana is that art can be so formally, physically, and visually convincing that it challenges long-held assumptions about whether "good subject matter" is necessary to the creation of good art. Instead, this art insists that "good subject matter" requires original form.

The Whitney show is full of big figurative paintings with daring compositions: raking diagonals, dramatic foreshortenings, full-frontals. They are Hellenistic by way of Aztec culture, with a monumentality that recalls the scale of Mesopotamian and Renaissance-era work. The rigid blockiness of the bodies and flat, shallow space comes from Egypt, Rome, and Giotto: Each figure is posed, purposeful, determined (sometimes over-determined), extremely theatrical. This is intended to create a visual vernacular that's eminently readable, yet bolts beyond the confines of the avant-garde art world. At the Whitney, huge crowds gather to marvel at—and decipher—the work. In contrast to the European Modernists, with their vocabulary of abstract grids, squiggles, and monochromes (and inherited forms like nudes, still lifes, and landscapes), the Mexicans set out to capture their own social and political life, through a gaze informed by 10,000 years of art history. At this show you'll see paintings of peasants, politicians, factory workers, child labor, race riots, economic injustice, the slave trade (the most barbarian phrase in any language), totalitarianism, guerrilla warfare, Pancho Villa, Henry Ford, Zapata, Lenin, Sojourner Truth, martyrs of the revolution, and images recalling the genocide of 90 percent of the pre-Columbian indigenous population, thought to be as many as 100 million people.

The show revolves around "los tres grandes," Rivera, Siqueiros, and Orozco. My hands-down fave is Siqueiros, who joined the Mexican Revolutionary Army at eighteen, then the Communist Party, was jailed in and exiled from Mexico, and mentored Pollock and Guston directly. Siqueiros's mad paintings look like end-time raptures; they are among the most physically original and innovative paintings of the twentieth century. (Talk about undervalued: In today's idiotic art market a small drawing by Siqueiros can still be bought for less than $2,000, while the latest MFA artist can sell for ten times that.) He was showing Pollock how to drip, splatter, smear, attack the canvas, and overlay skeins of paint in the 1930s! (Pollock himself called one Siqueiros work "the greatest painting done in modern times.")

In 1922, Siqueiros published a manifesto addressed to, among others, "Painters and . . . the indigenous races humiliated through centuries; to the soldiers converted into hangmen by their chiefs; to the workers and peasants who are oppressed by the rich; and to the intellectuals who are not servile to the bourgeoisie." For Siqueiros, art was blood sport. He and his cohorts meant to "overthrow [the] old . . . inhuman system within which you . . . produce riches . . . while you starve." Then he went after art: "We repudiate the so-called easel art and all such art which springs from ultra-intellectual circles, for it is essentially aristocratic. . . . Art must no longer be the expression of individual satisfaction, but should aim to become a fighting, educative art for all." This could almost have been written by artists today, looking for ways to address the politics of our current social and economic crisis.

The greatest colorist and most famous of los tres grandes is the preternaturally talented Diego Rivera, who called himself a "guerrilla fighter," and is perhaps better known today as the womanizing Mr. Frida Kahlo. (She called him "evil fat toad.") Born in 1886, Rivera studied in Paris; he was a great Modernist before he broke ranks with the movement. The natural environment captured in his work, full of succulent undergrowths of green, and his socially urgent subject matter, conspired to send a global SOS at as large a scale as possible. At the Whitney, Rivera's work—especially his simple line drawings—bring us eyeball-to-eyeball with larger-than-life pictures of Mesoamerican deities, lynched bodies, men with beaten backs, Zapata planting his foot on the sword of a dead soldier.

In the thirties, American artists flocked to Mexico to see the work of these artists firsthand. Critics wrote that they had "brought painting back to its vital function in society." Soon the Mexican artists were being commissioned to create monumental frescoes all over the United States. In 1932, Rivera accepted a commission from Edsel Ford, son of Henry, to create a gigantic, wraparound mural called *Detroit Industry*, featuring the Ford Motor Company's massive River Rouge automobile plant. Rivera depicted masses of humanity at work, from the smelting of iron to the winding pipes, stamping presses, and car chassis of the production line that created the celebrated Ford V-8—all merged with the image of Coatlicue, the ancient Aztec creating and destroying goddess. (The mural also featured a portrait of Henry Ford.) This is when the art world turned on him: For his dalliance with the capitalist titan, Rivera was denounced as a counterrevolutionary who had abandoned the revolution. Siqueiros blasted him as a demagogue, mental tourist, opportunist, saboteur, a J. P. Morgan of the Mexican art market. (It was Twitter cancel culture almost a century before the fact.) Indeed it lingers: At the show, I met two young women who rebuked Rivera for being "an artist of rich people." A chilling coincidence, then, that *Vida Americana* opened almost eighty-six years to the day in February 1934 when Rivera's huge mural in the lobby of the RCA Building at Rockefeller Center at Fifty-Third Street was destroyed by jackhammers after he refused to paint over a portrait of Vladimir Lenin embedded in the image. Back then, *New York Sun* critic Henry McBride sniffed, "When politics comes to the door, art flies out the window." As with many critics today, he neglected another truth: that, at its best, art is inseparable from politics.

(2020)

The Art World Goes Dark

I t felt like the end of something last Friday, as my wife and I made our way through the last few deserted galleries still open in Chelsea. Each was staffed by one or two people preparing to suspend gallery hours for a nondetermined time into the foreseeable future. It was very sad and very scary. In these last few hours before total shutdown, I saw three shows that would have been in contention for best of 2020—if such lists will even be compiled nine months from now. But it's hard to think that far into the future; "now" seems so brutal, so constantly present.

The first of these three shows was Donald Judd's gigantic plywood wall sculpture, unseen in New York since 1981. This masterpiece extends the entire length of one of Gagosian's grand palaces. Next I made my way to Sikkema Jenkins & Co. to see Kara Walker's large, impassioned portraits of Barack Obama, including one of him as Shakespeare's Othello, holding the severed head of Trump—an image that struck such a bare place within me that I shuddered. Another depicts the former president as a black savage in a loincloth, carrying a spear, sitting on a hog. This is Walker presenting Obama not as a man but as a mythic figure, complicated and provocative. Last was an exhibition at DC Moore Gallery of Romare Bearden's abstract paintings of the sixties—a shock, as I'd never known he made paintings like this! All of these shows sit empty now, along with hundreds of others in galleries and museums around the country. The time has run out to see the jewel of a show dedicated to the little-seen American visionary Karla Knight at Andrew Edlin. Or the beautiful thirties and forties visions of Agnes Pelton at the Whitney. All over the world, galleries and museums have gone dark. And they'll stay that way, probably, for some time.

No one knows what the economic damage will be, or how fully the art world will be remade, in the wake of cataclysm. Theirs is a complex infrastructure, including people at every economic level, all but the highest echelon among them living precarious lives in the best of times—dependent on the patronage of the very wealthy, but not themselves secure at all. Things could return to quasi-normal when galleries open again—much as the art world soared after the market collapse of 2008 and 2009, as inequality accelerated and money sought refuge in the so-called safer vessels of art. (Art—*safe?!*) Prices skyrocketed at the top, megagalleries mushroomed, and so on. But it's also possible that, this time, many smaller galleries won't make it through to the other side of this unknowable storm. Certainly many who work in and around art will lose jobs and health insurance. Whole art sub-scenes could be economically wiped out. If buyers aren't buying art, and museumgoers aren't coming to see art, if teaching jobs are suspended and employment curtailed, what happens to the already fragile financial support systems artists depend on? Art will go on. It always has. But everything will be different; we don't know how, only that it is. The unimaginable is now reality.

And that's the rub: Art's primary metaphysical building block is that which has never been imagined. This is why I can say—and know—that art will go on. Art is an advanced, abstract operating system devised for imagining the unseen, for gleaning the ideas and qualities of the group mind. It's a tool to invent new protocols; to generate rapture from form; to explore consciousness, map reality, create constellations of unspoken communication that echo across millennia. These things never change, but they are different for every person who sees a work of art, and different each time we look at the same work anew. This is because art is the practice of embedding the unimaginable in the material.

Creativity is a survival strategy. It's in every bone in an artist's body.

Darwin knew this; hence his insistence that the survival of a species depended not on the strongest or the most intelligent—it's tragic that he was misread this way—but on those who were "most adaptive to change." Boom! That's what art does, maybe better than anything: It is flexible, adaptive, pervious, hungry for change. Otherwise, all art today would be variations on Egyptian hieroglyphs, Mesopotamian carvings, the Raphael Madonna. (I have sometimes wondered whether art has its own agency— whether it might be using us to reproduce and evolve itself. But then, I would think that.)

Yet even with all this ingenuity, the last few decades have seen a surge in the tendency to demonize art as frivolous, gratuitous, useless, decadent. Art *is* all of these things, and it always has been, because those things are part of us. Pleasure is a form of knowledge. The decorative is a force—a creative force. So are all the rest of those supposedly shallow values. From the first bead bracelets made in caves and the earliest painted Paleolithic stone axes to Hokusai's ornamental *Great Wave* and Matisse's art as a "good armchair," art has always had a decorative thread to its fabric. Even Goya's *Saturn Devouring His Son* was painted to decorate a dining room.

If the question is "Can art change the world?" the answer is no, or at least not enough—not when it comes to those suffering and about to suffer. However, art does change lives, and lives can change the world.

None of this is to say that art will play the deciding role—will be of special use or special importance—in the gruesome future we are all about to enter. It's just part of the whole ball of wax. But it can help. Yesterday, on Instagram, I happened on a short video posted by the Prado, featuring its magnificent El Greco gallery. Watching it, my whole day changed. I feel it still. In the same spirit, galleries and museums around the world are trying to make art available online. I can imagine MoMA hosting a 24/7 live feed of *The Starry Night*; the Met could do a roving tour of its Egyptian collection. Let the New Museum post videos of its wild Peter Saul show. Critics could write about art that exists anywhere, rather than art that is on public view, or new. Maybe I will.

Maybe things will be different in two years, when we reemerge battered and bruised. If I live, I may have written more obituaries than I will want to remember. We did this during AIDS, and it was shattering. Maybe we will travel less, not run around from biennial to art fair to museum show to biennial to more endless art fairs. Forced isolation might favor more intimate artistic practices: work done in small spaces, at kitchen tables, with the kids reading or drawing or wreaking chaos nearby. Maybe all those gigantic artist studios, with scores of assistants, will suddenly seem unnecessary; maybe we'll no longer attend event installations in grand exhibition halls and massive atriums.

Or, maybe, after two years of more social and economic suffering and disruption than has been witnessed in generations, not much will have been learned. This is what happened after September 11. At first, many of us thought that everything would be different, even if we didn't know how. As it turned out, though, the same forces that were ascendant leading up to 9/11—the Bush-Cheney war machine, the culture of willful neglect that poisoned the water in Flint, Michigan—only tightened their grip on our culture. Rather than changing, it is possible that coronavirus will make things more of what they already were before this was visited on the world. Coronavirus feels very different from 9/11: bigger, more mysterious, more terrifying and far-reaching. Whether we change or not, the world around us is being changed by forces beyond our control. All we know is that viruses come—but viruses also go. *Ars longa.*

(2020)

My Appetites

As soon as my wife and I started sheltering in place, I started getting concerned emails and queries on social media: "Jerry, how are you eating and drinking coffee during this?" It's a question I haven't seen asked of anyone else. Many people have asked after me and Roberta, who has been battling cancer since 2014. Today she's doing well on immunotherapy drugs, though she is in several high-risk categories for COVID-19, and our sheltering in place involves a lot of moving parts.

But that's not the only reason people ask us about food and coffee. There's another big reason: Namely, that anyone who has ever heard about how we eat and drink thinks we are insane.

First, coffee. In normal times, every few nights I buy six large black deli coffees: three caffeinated and three decaf. I put them in the fridge. Each morning, I combine one caffeinated and one decaf into a 7-Eleven Double Gulp cup, add ice, Lactaid, and stevia. I drink two a day, which I tell myself equals one big cup of coffee. We bought a dozen of these 7-Eleven cups and tops in 2017, along with four metal straws, and we wash and reuse them constantly. The foodies, and many in the art world, are aghast when I post about our routine. Of course, I grew up in an art world where everyone drank this kind of coffee. But the world has changed, and I get it.

Neither of us really cooks. Roberta can but doesn't; I can't but do, in a manner of speaking. We rarely go out to eat. It takes too much time. We can't plan it with two regular deadlines in the same house—two critics trying to write, daily battling the demons that tell every writer "You're through! Time to quit." We do go out for pizza slices on weekends, after the galleries have closed and the openings are over and other people are off to big dinners and after-parties. I don't think I've been to more than five sit-down art world dinners in ten years. Instead, over slices on paper plates, Roberta and I go over lists of things we've seen, what we missed, gossiping about which dealers wouldn't leave us to look in peace (Hi, Gavin, you know we adore you!), and scraping away at each other's wrong ideas about shows and artists and work.

We don't do takeout either. It just seems like an invitation to overeat, which is something I worry about constantly. I haven't had a pancake, waffle, or piece of French toast in decades—afraid I'd instantly become addicted, the same way I know that if I took one puff of a cigarette I'd start smoking again. I did this once in 1986, a month after Roberta and I met. I wanted to show her how cool I looked with a butt in my mouth. I took a drag, and as the smoke filled my lungs, I still remember thinking, I am going to dedicate the rest of my life to smoking. And so I did, for eighteen months from that day, before going cold turkey. Do I sound like someone with food or possible substance-abuse issues? I do. But I've white-knuckled it this far.

Once a week or so, I stop by a nearby place called Agata & Valentina and buy two large boxes of something called chicken paillard—unbreaded chicken with a teriyaki-ish sauce. The chicken goes into the fridge, in Tupperware containers; we microwave one for lunch, one for dinner. Ditto bags of greens. I boil potatoes and steam Brussels sprouts or broccoli. For breakfast, it's scrambled eggs and toast. These, I cook. Other than snacks, fruit, sugar, carbo binges, and whatever grazing we do while we're out at galleries and museums, that's it. I am a hunter-gatherer-microwaver, providing for my wife, who is my eyes and mind. We got these lives and learned to make them talk. We adapt to our environment, shortcomings and all, and we survive.

At least, that's how I see it. But I know that with food, as with everything else, I have acquired only partial self-knowledge. At different times, I think of myself as a glutton and an ascetic. I can see myself as a person of endless appetites and curiosity, who can imagine going everywhere and seeing everything and eating anything. But I can also straight-facedly say that I have no interest in food or a social life that is anything other than monkish. Barack Obama has talked about narrowing down his clothing—to suits of one or two colors—so he didn't have to think about anything when getting dressed. (Bernie Madoff, actually, got dressed the same way.) I get that: eliminating certain options in your life in order to open up time and space for the things you really love. For me, that thing is looking at art and writing about it. Everything else feels like a wind blowing dead leaves away.

But narrowing and focusing also sound like lame productivity hacks, and I wonder whether Obama was fighting to bottle something up within himself—to continue living in denial and contradiction. Like me. I've made a place for myself in a world, the art world, that is both aesthetic and sensual, abstract and bodiless. I made that place within it by being a puritan who also happens to have an insane appetite for art. I no longer know which of these is the pathology and which is the coping mechanism.

Except for my closest friends, it will shock most to know that I am unimaginably bashful. Going out in public in anything but a crowd costs me emotionally. Sometimes I get antsy for days before a nothing event. I never pick up the phone when it rings. As soon as quarantine began, I started to dread someday having to go back into the world. This exile has been one of heaven for me—a version of life that I've dreamed of many times. To paraphrase the legendary coach Al Davis, ours is a tunnel life; we're not really part of "society," even if others see us this way.

Many find my coffee and food ritual disturbing, even disgusting. Maybe it is. Even Roberta reminds me that "Pleasure is an important form of knowledge." And yet, by nearly anyone else's standards, we live almost at war against pleasure. But we're happy with what we've made together. Could we have more pleasure? Sure. But not more time. For me, beauty is what works—the way an odd baseball swing producing a .300

hitter is beautiful, or how Goya's *Saturn Devouring His Son* is beautiful. Yes, it's probably harder to eat in a pandemic when you can't cook. But we don't feel deprived eating food stored in Tupperware.

So to all of you asking, we're eating just fine, thanks.

SO FAR, I'VE DODGED the big question of why I eat the way I do. It's not all speed, efficiency, and deadlines.

I was raised by animals. Or to eat like one. I grew up in a small apartment on the South Side of Chicago. My life was fine. I spent days gazing at dust motes in sunlight, flipping over on my back to pretend the ceiling was the floor, and feeling whole other worlds in these things—all like some happy domestic cat. When I was seven, my father made a lot of money on a handheld plastic invention called the Dexter Sewing Machine. You squeezed it, and it sewed and reattached buttons, mended seams, and the like. It was advertised in cheapo commercials late at night, along with all the other handy gadgets that used to dot the air: the Veg-O-Matic, the Clapper, the Ginsu knife. For the rest of my years in that house, I remember my father sitting in our basement, at a card table lit by a single bulb, trying to find another invention as successful as his handheld sewing machine. There were self-closing venetian blinds, an envelope licker, and others—many others. None of them panned out.

During the day, he and his four brothers owned a woman's lingerie company in Chicago called American Maid. I loved going to their office, with its curved desks and wet bars, watching the masterful old Jewish fabric-cutters working with big scissors at enormous tables of satin, and glimpsing models. It was an American Dream to me. With the money my father made from the invention, our family of five moved to a Jewish suburb north of Chicago. There were brand-new homes and construction sites everywhere. I played baseball, ran around, played kick the can, rode my bike, and was happy. There was no art in my life whatsoever. I didn't know what art was, other than the smeary twenty-dollar fake French Impressionist paintings that hung in our living room and a faux-Brancusi bird shape on a Formica table in our rec room, which was dominated by two Naugahyde Barcaloungers and a TV embedded in a bar. I remember an art history book where—when my parents weren't home—I'd search for nudes. That was art to me. I once masturbated to Jean-Auguste-Dominique Ingres's *The Turkish Bath*, from 1862. I loved my life.

Then the bottom fell out. When I was ten years old, my mother drove me in her powder-blue Buick Wildcat to the Art Institute of Chicago. I loved looking out the window as we drove. I had never been to a museum before. I wandered around, without direction, until I started looking back and forth at a colorful little diptych. The light in it was intense; the colors were like coral-reef fish. In the left panel, a man in a prison cell chats through the bars with two friends outside his cell. In the next image, his head is on the ground; blood spurts everywhere from his neck, which is still sticking through the window; a swordsman holsters a huge blade with blood on it. (Decades later, I realized these were Giovanni di Paolo's fifteenth-century depictions of the imprisonment and beheading of Saint John the Baptist.) Then it hit me: This painting was telling a story. I looked around and realized: *Everything* here was telling a story. And I realized that I could *hear* all these stories, if I looked close enough. My mind was blown.

A month later, my mother committed suicide.

The next day, my two brothers and I were dropped off at our house after Sunday school. On the way in, I saw lots of cars parked outside our house. That was strange; they weren't there when we left. We walked into our rec room through the built-in garage, where I passed my mother's blue car. My father was waiting just inside the door. He had never done this before. He sat us down in front of him, on our ersatz Modernist couch, and asked us how Sunday school was. Then he said, "Your mother has gone to live with the angels." To me, the "angels" were a Los Angeles baseball team. I asked, "When is she coming back?" He said, "She's not coming back." I asked, "What will we do with her car?" He looked at me like there was something wrong with me.

As I walked upstairs, the sound of my shoes on the steps made me remember something that had happened that morning: when we were heading out, I'd heard my father running down those same stairs, saying something about a "relapse." It terrified me. With that memory still in my mind, I made my way upstairs to my bedroom. Looking down from the third-floor landing, I saw lots of old strangers in my living room. When they looked up at me, they all went silent. As if I was suddenly different somehow. From that day forward, for the rest of my father's life, my mother was never mentioned again in our household. Not once. All my memories of her, except for that trip to the Art Institute—and one of her on that drive, telling me, "We might not see each other again"—vanished. There was no funeral, no memorial service, no nothing. I went to school the next day.

My life had changed in an instant, but I didn't know how, or why, let alone what had happened. In my early twenties, when a friend of the family gravely talked about "the way your mother died," I said, "What do you mean? How did she die?" All I knew at that point was what I'd been told, accidentally, at a birthday party as a kid: As I was drinking something out of a glass, someone mentioned something about "Jerry's mother," and out of nowhere I bit the glass and it broke. There was no injury, but I always wondered what had happened in that moment. The woman was shocked that I'd never been told. She told me that my mother jumped out of a third-story window. That she thought she had "female problems." She might have been in a hospital. That phrase and the word *relapse* have haunted me ever since. That's still all I really know. That and the date: November 11, 1961. I called it "the upside-down year," because 1961 looks the same right side up as it does inverted, and 11/11 is a visual palindrome. The date mattered, not the event. Ever since, my mind has held its thoughts in patterns, systems, and internal, non-optical arrangements, which subsume everything that might go into them.

My life changed, and didn't change at all. *Why don't I feel anything?* I wondered. *I can't cry. Why should I cry? Nothing has happened.* If nothing had happened, why was everyone treating me differently? Parents were fidgety around me. So were teachers. My friends treated me differently, but I couldn't say how; some stopped seeing me. No one asked me to play baseball anymore. The girls in school fell silent around me. Were these "female problems"? I was alone. Over the course of a year, I became the worst student in school, started acting out with teachers. Something else was happening, though: I grew invisible antennae, grew sensitive to nonverbal vibrations and cues around me. I was special, a kind of social-insect empath who didn't care about anyone, didn't communicate, but who sensed what everyone felt and thought. I was delusional. None of this made me sad. I had simply decided that I had no emotions. I developed a protective, grandiose mantra, which I'd chant to myself: *I am death.* It meant that I was separate now, a member of an excluded order. Like many who live through trauma, all this was my normal, all just my story. You've got yours.

Two years later, unannounced, my father remarried and brought home his new wife, my new stepmother, and her two sons. One minute, I was the eldest of three boys; the next, I was a twin with an older brother and two younger ones. Having an older brother was bad; being a twin was worse. I felt a competition and comparison I'd never known before—the root of things I fight inside myself today, always judging whether something is fair. (Roberta always laughs at this; "Who said anything about fair?" she asks, and my resentment melts.) A year or so later, my father pulled me out of school and we went to a courthouse, where my stepmother adopted me (my father never adopted her sons), and we moved to a much bigger house in another suburb.

No longer on my home turf, I was plunged into a civil war.

My stepmother was a working-class Polish Catholic from Chicago's South Side. My new brothers were what used to be called "greasers": tough guys who picked fights, small-time troublemakers. When he was still in high school, my older stepbrother got a girl pregnant and had to marry her. They had a kid and lived a shitty life in an apartment in the city and had to drop out of high school. They later divorced. (All of this was a secret we were never to tell anyone.) On the first night I shared a room with my new twin brother, Paul, he came over to me as soon as things went dark and said, "We're sneaking out." We crawled through our second-story window and lowered ourselves to the ground. I'd never done anything like this before. It was dark, thrilling, and quiet. He had a bunch of tools with him, and we went around our silent suburb in the darkness, dismantling street signs. After a couple of hours, we crawled back up to our window and went to bed. He slipped a sign under his mattress and fell asleep.

The next morning, my father walked past our room and saw the sign sticking out from under Paul's mattress. "Where did that come from?" he asked. My heart pounded. After a silence, Paul said, "I don't know," and stared at my father. I stared at Paul. My father stood still, staring at us both, blinked, then glowered at us with a look I'd never seen before. He turned and left. In that moment, a new paradigm had formed. None of this was in the Jewish-suburban playbook, but from then on, that's the way it was in our house. I was on the other side of the law, living in two different houses under one roof. Enemies: parents versus children; children versus parents; brother versus brother. It was survival of the meanest. I survived.

My life jumped the track. Soon I was riding bikes around with Paul, setting leaf fires, smoking, climbing on people's roofs, committing minor acts of vandalism, having the police called on us, fleeing. I never did another piece of homework in my life. I graduated at the bottom of my very large high school class. There was never any talk of college in my house; I completed the SAT answer sheet by making geometric patterns in the answer slots. I developed impetigo, a chronic skin condition that made me scratch my scalp and forearms till they oozed. I never saw a doctor for it. "What a neurotic," my stepmother said.

Violence happened in that house, a lot. Not all-out physical violence, and it was never sexual, but there were beatings: some as punishment, some in the form of older brothers bullying and beating up younger brothers. About ten years ago, one of my younger brothers told me that Paul and I once hung him up by his hands with a rope from a pipe in our basement . . . and just left him there. Why? He hadn't poured our Pepsi the right way. My heart broke hearing this. I had no memory of it at all. I'd never known that I'd been as cruel in those years as they were. It kills me to write that; my internal script has always said *I'm the good one*, the permanently aggrieved one with a chip on his shoulder. That persecuted fury was the fuel of my inner locomotive.

On the refrigerator door in our home hung a two-foot leather strap. My stepmother had gotten it from steel truckers who worked at the mills in Gary, Indiana, and had it shaped to fit her hand for a better grip. It was used for strapping us. She and my father would tell us how many lashes we were getting, usually between five and ten; we bent over and they'd strap us. My heart grew cold; I turned mean. I scowled so hard at them during these sessions—making certain they never saw me crack or wince with pain and shame—that deep wrinkles mark my forehead to this day. Every time I look in the mirror, I see that ancient affront. It was chaos.

But I had a secret garden that redeemed me, a place I could always go to, one that in many ways pointed to ideal forms, beauty, narratives— eccentricity and imaginings leading out of the pandemonium I was in. Every morning, on the way to high school, I took a series of circuitous shortcuts—crawling through bushes, smelling dirt—until I emerged in the backyards of almost a dozen different Frank Lloyd Wright homes. It was as if some other god had descended to make these grand private palaces in the Chicago neighborhood of Oak Park; to me, they were foyers of some-thing enormous. Oak Park was filled with clusters of these brilliant Wright homes and other Prairie School jewels, including my high school. I re-member gazing at these homes, imagining happier lives, warmer colors, better ways of being—the ways things could look and be. I still take walks every day; now, as then, I talk to myself, telling myself elaborate stories, weaving together constellations of as many facts as I can, getting lost in them, making them into new inner geographies and possible compasses. Once, I kissed a girl in one of these homes, but we were caught by her parents and told to leave, so all of this has an odd erotics for me, too. Meanwhile, I think I hated all men.

There was no learning in my house. Not even talk of it. Anything you knew, you picked up on your own. This included cooking—which meant that I learned nothing about cooking. I never had a meal with my parents. My parents had a separate entrance; a different dining and living room. We were never even permitted to use the front door.

This all suited us fine. We hated them; they hated us.

I have no memory of any hot cooked meals in our home. Cooking wasn't something you did. There was only eating. Our refrigerator was stocked with Oscar Mayer bologna, corned beef, tongue, salami, and roast beef. There was mayonnaise, ketchup, peanut butter, and other things I don't remember. We had a large shiny bread basket filled with Wonder Bread. This was home base for me. The pantry had cereal, cookies, and crackers. A snack, for me, was cutting off all the crusts of an entire loaf of white bread, wadding up the dough into a big ball, sitting in front of the TV, and eating it. I pretended I was a carp, snipping and snapping at the ball till it was gone. Once a week, a Polish maid came in to clean the house and make a large pot of something called "grub"—a gray mealy mix of rice, lentils, peas, hamburger meat, and other stuff. It was placed in the fridge, and we heated it up anytime we wished. There were no dinner hours; we ate alone, with each other, at the table, in our rooms, in the basement, wherever. We never went out to dinner as a family. Paul would come down to the dining room table wearing only his tighty-whities, picking away at some grub with his fingers while sitting on the back of the chair, drinking a beer, talking about getting stoned, and making racist comments.

We all had DO NOT DISTURB signs on our doors. So did my parents.

Soon I stopped eating regular meals; the only thing I drank was Coca-Cola. Going out to eat, for me, meant picking up a few containers of fries at McDonald's and eating them on the way home. Or I'd buy boxes of Wheat Thins and eat them by the baseball diamond near our house. None of this seemed strange to me. (I'm still addicted to Wheat Thins.) Before my father remarried, I'd always been the tallest person in my class, a good athlete and runner. I played football. With girls watching nearby, I won races at our track and field meets. I believe now that my growth was stunted in those years. It's only recently that I've really realized how short I am—I never grew an inch after ninth grade. By the time I was a senior, I weighed more than two hundred pounds. I worked at an ice cream store and ate vats of vanilla ice cream. It never occurred to me that any of this had anything to do with my weight. I never saw myself as fat. When I heard myself called "husky," I told myself it was because the Huskies were our high school football team. On the night I graduated, I went home, handed my parents my diploma, retrieved two packed suitcases from under my bed, and moved into an apartment that my friends and I had secretly set up in the city. After that, I never had any real fights with my parents, no real falling-out with them. We all just pretended everything was great. We acted that way for the rest of their lives.

It struck me as normal that I would go many years without seeing my family. After I left home, I don't think I saw my stepbrothers more than a handful of times. As far as I was concerned, none of that part of my life had happened. A couple of years back, after not thinking about my stepbrothers for decades, I googled their names. From what I could gather, at least one of them is dead. Paul was already a pothead in high school; in the last two years I lived with my parents, he never left his bedroom. He didn't graduate with the rest of the class. I guess I won that battle.

That first summer out of that house was as huge in my life as the day I was told my mother was with the angels. I got a job in a paper-and-drafting-supply factory and worked as a doorman. I lost seventy pounds. I was free of everything that had happened in the past. All of that was forever behind me, dead.

In high school, I had noticed that the people having sex were either in theater or art. When I was nineteen, I chose art. It never helped me with sex, but I felt like a freedom machine. The next ten years were the best years of my life up to that point. I met hundreds of new people, hung out, made art, commenced my huge twenty-five-year project to illustrate the cantos of Dante's *Divine Comedy*. I kept myself fed at a happy mix of diners and coffee shops, where my friends and I would eat and smoke and talk about art. I never shopped for food or cooked it. Looking back, I don't think I knew where the grocery store was.

Then, in my twenties, my long-silenced subterranean demons rose up all at once. I started having panic attacks. The first one was over breakfast, coffee, and cigarettes with friends at the corner diner.

These attacks made me afraid to be with anyone. Or to go out in public, or at least too far from home. I became all but cut off from society. My apartment had no kitchen, only a hot plate, so as I stopped going out to eat with friends, I got all my meals from fast-food and takeout places—any place I could get into and out of quickly. I did this three times a day, and it was a battle every time. I spent the rest of the day trying to calm myself down. I took my pulse obsessively, counting my heartbeats. It was then that I stopped making art.

Still, I needed a job, so I started working as a helper on local art-delivery trucks. I found I could be in a confined space as long as the scenery around me was changing, so at the age of thirty I became a long-distance truck driver. Until then, I had actually never had a driver's license. I'd failed my driver test at the age of sixteen—we had driver education in high school, but I never got a practice drive at home. My parents just said, "Go take the test. You need a license to work." In my house, of course, failing the test didn't mean not driving. I owned cars, drove them everywhere, without a license or insurance. On a European trip with a girlfriend, I bought a 1961 Sunbeam, a little English sports car, for twenty bucks at the Luxembourg airport when I landed there from New York. I drove it as far as Switzerland, where the engine blew up inside an enormous tunnel under the Alps. (I knew only forward and reverse. I drove the whole time in first gear.) My girlfriend and I got out and hitchhiked to Communist Warsaw. A few years later, I was driving through the Midwest with another girlfriend when I blew the engine out of my big beautiful 1959 Chevrolet because I hadn't changed the oil. We left the car on the road in Sault Sainte Marie, Michigan, and hitchhiked through Canada to New York and then back to Chicago. I mention this because driving, for me, was as alien as cooking: No one ever showed me about how to use a stick shift or told me about changing the oil. Since I didn't know how to learn, I didn't know how or what to ask.

Driving a truck was a romantic dream of mine. I would be a nomad, not connected to anyone, riding my own psychological wheels of fire, driving to Florida or Texas once a month for about fourteen days with stories of the open road, truck stops, women, drugs, everything that sounded cool. Only none of that ever happened. I never got a single story like that to tell.

Instead, each day was the same as the last: Get up, order breakfast, grab a thermos of coffee and a jumbo bucket of Colonel Sanders's chicken. Maybe some bags of potato chips or Fritos. I would eat while driving all through the day, stopping only for gas and bathroom breaks, getting to a motel around eight or nine o'clock at night. Zonked, I'd crash on the bed, buzzing. The bucket stayed on my night table, and a bite of cold chicken got me going in the morning. Food was fuel. I tried to eat in truck stops, bars, and restaurants along the way, tried to strike up friendly conversations with people, do what it looked like everyone else was doing. But I couldn't meet anyone. When I tried to strike up friendly conversations with people, I got no reply at all, just looks. I sat in booths reading the only thing I ever read on the road: my road atlas. Maps were another system I loved getting lost in. I can still tell you the distance between almost any two cities on the East Coast.

My dream version of the job was that I would sleep with a different woman in a different place every night. Here's how that went: On my second-ever night on the job, I stayed at a motel off Route 95 outside Jacksonville, Florida. Determined to find a bar and look for women, I put on a cowboy shirt, left my room, and paused for a cigarette on the second-floor balcony. As I stared out at the broken asphalt and weeds in the parking lot, I noticed a young woman standing about twenty feet to my left. After a minute or two, she looked over at me and asked for a cigarette. I walked over, and she said, "You want a date." All the blood left my face—and my penis, probably. I stared at her for a minute and then heard my mouth say, in a much higher voice than normal: "Nooooooo, ma'am!" I ran back into my room, freaked out. "Oh my God! It just happened! And I blew it! Crap!" With my back leaning against that motel-room door, I resolved never to do that again; from now on, I would only say yes. But the lords of trucking knew what I was made of. In my entire career driving trucks, I never met, spoke to, or slept with a woman. Boy, though, could I drive! Six hundred miles or more at a clip. Back then, I couldn't go much over sixty-five miles per hour.

(By the way, I don't want to give the wrong impression about what I was carrying. I wasn't delivering steel, meat, or plywood. I wasn't driving an eighteen-wheeler, either. I'm Jewish; I delivered art and drove a ten-wheeler. My CB handle was "The Jewish Cowboy." I'd get on the CB and say, "Shalom, partner," and try to make conversation. No one ever responded. Not once. Mostly they talked about cops and spewed racist shit. It felt like listening in on my stepmother and -brothers again.)

Did I see America? Not really, unless you count either side of all the interstates in the Lower 48. I was pretty switched off. Manic. I had no curiosity. I simply drove from point A to point B. I never took side roads, had an afternoon off, did any sightseeing, detoured to see anything—not even to take in a scenic overlook. It didn't occur to me. Except once, in Arizona: I drove about an hour north of the highway to the Grand Canyon. I parked the truck and walked to the canyon ledge. *Cool*, I thought. (We didn't carry cameras everywhere back then.) Then I got back in the truck and on the road. Another time, in Miami, I threw out my back lifting crates of Carl Andre steel plates. I got so sunburned so often that, today, I have pre-cancers on the top of my head from years spent under the Texas and Florida sun. If you want romantic stories of the road or tales of what that life was like then, I don't have them.

Worse, I was so mad at the world for not giving me a living that I was abusive with the cargo. I didn't secure the art; often, it got banged up. If someone asked me how something was damaged, I'd learned from Paul to go stone cold and lie. "Who, me? It must have been that way when I picked it up. You got insurance?" Sometimes I'd just throw stuff in the truck and cover it with blankets with no strapping at all. In the end, I was fired. Which was fine. I knew, at that point, that I had to get back into the art world somehow—but I also knew I couldn't return to being an artist. I ruled out being a curator, because I knew I didn't want to do everything artists told me to do. I eliminated being an art adviser because I don't know anything about money. I toyed with being a dealer, until it dawned on me that I had no money and no idea how to open and run a real business. Finally, I decided to become an art critic. Until then, I'd never written a word in my life; I had barely read a word of art criticism. As anyone who's ever written knows, writing is really hard! To me, it still is. But I had to get out of the trucks, and anything on earth would have been better than what I was living.

Now that I was saying I was an art critic (it still feels exotic to say so), I started meeting new people in the New York art world. I tried going to parties, tried being with others in restaurants. I remember how the simple ritual of eating in public made me start to feel part of the world again. I was taking baby social steps. Somehow I understood that nothing I was doing could be a mistake, because at least I was trying to do something. The painter Eric Fischl did me two big favors. First, he asked me to help him with a book of assignments for young art students, including conduct interviews with artists. Second, he got me a job as a driver for a wealthy Texas collector. Once a month, when she came to New York, I'd spend a few days driving her around to galleries in her garaged Mercedes. For this, I was paid $1,000 a month. Whenever she left me with the car, I'd blast the radio, and use her newfangled car phone to call friends. (In the process I accidentally rang up a bill of more than $1,500.) At one point, without her permission, I even took the car to the Hamptons to go to the beach; while it was sitting in the parking lot, someone bashed into it, and I had to have it fixed before she came back. And once, without knowing that my life's whole destiny was in the car, I picked up Roberta—whom I'd never met— and took her and the collector to a Broadway play. Roberta tells me she remembers thinking how "cute" the driver's neck looked.

In between limo stints, I was back in the trucks. Depressed. But that's where I taught myself to be a critic. I bought stacks of *Artforum* magazine, the art world school paper, and read them at night in my motel room, over my chicken bucket. The problem was, I never understood a word of what I read. Everyone seemed to be quoting the same fifteen or twenty theoreticians I hadn't read. All the artists were reviewing one another's shows, writing in one another's catalogues. Not only did I feel like an outsider; I felt like an idiot. I even tried to hang out with some of these people, but even though we were around the same age, I was sort of an odd duck to them. I thought I was a loser—but I knew I wanted to write about art that I was seeing in the present and didn't want to have to read all those books that all those critics were always referring to. I was forty years old! I didn't have twenty years to go read all that theory. My reading skills weren't up to it, anyway. One summer, I tried to read some of the standard texts of the time; I don't think I retained a single thing. To me, it seemed like a bunch of people writing about a toothache without ever mentioning teeth.

Then two beautiful things happened. The first was that I was ushered into what was then one of the great art salons in the world: the huge loft of the curator-seer-gallerist Clarissa Dalrymple, one of the smartest people I've ever met. Her loft had once been home to the 1970s art world legend Gordon Matta-Clark, a fact that cast a kind of magic spell over the place—and the Paula Cooper Gallery was in the same building. I was in the right place at the right time. Several nights a week, Clarissa cooked a huge amount of food, laid the platters out on tables, and invited fifteen, twenty, or thirty people or more into her home. She was insatiable, curious, and brilliant. I met everyone there. There were famous people—Jasper Johns, Joan Jonas, Alex Katz, Brice Marden—but mostly it was a group of unknowns who'd go on to become the art world of the nineties: Damien Hirst, Sir Nicholas Serota, Sadie Coles, John Currin, Chris Ofili, Cecily Brown, Matthew Barney, David Zwirner, Anton Kern, Peter Doig, Maurizio Cattelan, the founders of *Frieze* magazine, the editors of *Artforum*, independent curators from everywhere, Jeff Koons, and many others.

Somehow, I also talked my way into teaching gigs at three schools. I would fly to RISD in Providence, teach two classes, go to the airport, fly to Chicago, wake up the next morning and teach all day in Chicago, go to the airport, fly to New York, get up the next day and teach at SVA. Soon I was making as many as one hundred studio visits a year and had scores of visiting-critic gigs all over the country. In the meantime, I was scrounging just enough of my savings to take myself to places like the Venice Biennale and Documenta. John Cage said, "Always be around," and I was. All that allowed me to finally see the sun.

That, of course, is Roberta. When we met, I hadn't really started writing reviews. I was still sponging up all this new information, going everywhere, doing everything I could—all to get into the world I wanted to be part of, looking for ways to create some sort of a role for myself. Roberta had recently been fired from *The Village Voice*. She wasn't writing anywhere. She was going out with a guy in Japan. I knew of her, but I'd never read her work. I asked her to write the essay for a crapola book I was doing at the time. When we finally met for real, it was like two orphans finding one another. Really, we were never not together again—from that moment to this. (Except when I had to throw a fit about her also wanting to see the Japanese guy.) When we fell in love, she was pretty clear about not wanting to be with another critic. Her attitude was like what Roger Angell said to other baseball writers: "Leave it all to me."

In 1998, I was hired for Roberta's old job at the *Voice*. By this time, she was writing for *The New York Times*. Naturally, she started reading my work. After going through a batch of pieces, she walked into my office and dropped a stack of my reviews on my desk. I was expecting her to compliment me. Instead she said, "If you don't get better, I'm going to kill myself!" That put the fear of God into me fast. I learned on the job—like all people. After Roberta cut through my laziness, I started writing the best I could, in my own idiot voice, the way I talk and think—saying what I actually saw, making judgments and trying to back them up. So I guess I saved Roberta's life—and I know I saved my own. She still bristles when she sees me wanting to write on a show she's interested in. "This is my show," she'll say. "I want to write on it." Here's a secret: I always agree. I love my work madly—even when I hate it. But let's be honest: Who would you rather have write about your work, Roberta Smith or me?

ON MONDAY, OCTOBER 13, 2014, as I emerged from the Seventy-Ninth Street subway station, my phone rang. I was on the way to pick up Roberta from a doctor's visit before a preview of a new show at the Met. It was Roberta. She paused, then said simply, "We need to talk. Meet me on Park and Eighty-First." I seemed to know right then what the next six years might look like. Something inside me collected a storm of impalpable pulses of fiery desire and resolve, and recomposed them to summon the strength to meet whatever was required of me. *I can do this*, I thought.

Roberta had been diagnosed with uterine cancer. Everything changed, and nothing changed. Except what changed. She has had three big operations, two recurrences, and one near-cataclysmic extended emergency hospital stay. Today, thanks to the treatment, she is doing well. We have gone through the entire process without ever googling her disease, or even looking it up in a book. We never ask questions about "the odds," "the prognosis," or the future. I don't think this amounts to denial or incuriosity. Rather, I would say that instead of crawling down a million digital self-help wormholes, or fielding advice about kale diets, we threw everything we had at finding a doctor we trusted, then treated him like a field general sending us to the front, into war. Dr. Sabbatini told us where to go, what to do, how to act. We followed orders. I stopped taking notes after another doctor looked at me and said, "I see. You are trying to maintain control by taking notes." I'm not telling others to follow this example, but I think this was the best decision I ever made. It left all of our energies and focus for the nonstop tasks at hand.

Those tasks multiplied. And we found a way to deal with them together. As Roberta woke up in the middle of a November night from her first major surgery, and I told her that her tumor was malignant, we swore to one another that whatever might come, we would "write our way through this." We knew that art and writing about it had gotten us to this point, and that it could be what got us past it. We spent the rest of that dark night talking about the connection between Matisse's late paper cutouts and how Donald Judd used color in his last works. It saved us that night. It saves us today. If you were a fly on the wall of our house, you wouldn't know we live with cancer 24/7, except on those high-pressure days when we go to doctors, have tests, scans, and the like. We had built a fortress of work so total even cancer couldn't get it, not really.

The day before I brought Roberta home after that first surgery, I went to Kmart and bought something I'd never used in my life: a microwave oven. I put it on my shoulders and walked home. Our diet stayed pretty much the same, but our prep time of fifteen minutes of steaming everything was reduced to about ninety seconds. We loved the microwave; it stream-lined our routine, leaving us even more time for looking and writing. (We have still never used our antique dishwasher or had anyone to our home for a prepared meal.) Even this diet changed, however, after Roberta's second big surgery, which was followed by months of chemo and a harrowing four-teen days in the hospital. Our restricted diet became more restricted. We were told to serve only the mildest, blandest foods; the color white was fa-vored. This suited us fine: potatoes, white bread, simple white-meat chicken, white rice, and the like with a sprinkling of greens. We've since added more greens and other meats. But microwaving it all from our already prepared food has allowed us both to "write our way through this."

Today, we're lucky. We're self-isolating two hours north of New York, in northwest Connecticut, in a home we rent year-round from a close friend. Getting Roberta up to Connecticut has always been like pulling teeth; she likes going places only if there is a lot of looking at art involved and the space can be reached by public transportation.

For weeks before we left our apartment for Connecticut, I began to see the same American unraveling as most saw. I kept nudging Roberta that we'd have to go; she kept telling me to get a grip, reminding me that it was *our job* to stay in New York and pay attention to what art and artists were doing. Two weeks before we left, another patient forwarded me a doctor's email that said, essentially: *The city is berserk with coronavirus. Get her out of the city. Now!* I showed Roberta the email. She wanted to keep going until the last gallery closed. Finally, late one Friday afternoon in March, that hap-pened. The very last galleries, already run by skeleton crews, shuttered their doors—some probably forever. Finally and reluctantly, she called a handful of galleries to make sure we weren't leaving anyone on the battle-field. All of them were closing, too. Late that night, we packed and left.

Which brings us back to eating. The Greek definition of *catastrophe* involves an "overturning," an end to the status quo. The order that has been overturned in this crisis is not in the way Roberta and I eat or shop.

It is how everyone else does these things. Now, all the former restaurant-goers shop for three meals a day, seven days a week, with only takeout to break the monotony. My shopping routine is the exact same as it ever was—except that we've traded the chicken paillards of Manhattan for local whole roasted chickens, frozen hot dogs, hamburger meat, and occasional pieces of baked salmon I pick up here. I get our coffee at the local gas station. I do all the shopping and errands; Roberta hasn't been more than five miles from this home.

But going to the grocery store now is like taking a journey under the volcano. On cold Connecticut days, I see the steam of my breath and others intermingling. I hear the beating of my own heart, thinking of this meshwork of air, our every respiration a risk. I sense solitude of self in every eye. We're all in this together—but alone, our facial expressions disappeared beneath homemade or fancy face masks. The ways we used to communicate across space are gone, at least for now. Uncertainty and disjunction reign. It reminds me of my life after my mother left.

I feel a withering of spirit in public, an absence of the old shared yearning to be among one another. Time turns staccato; little actions feel big; large ones aren't taken lightly; everything comes with a residuum of doubt. This is how socializing has always felt to me, but now I see how it looks in other people, too. Movement is awkward, hesitant. This is our sleepwalking universe, our slow death at the grocery store. It's a psychic sorcery, full of imaginary spells and lingering questions: *Did that person cough? Why isn't she wearing a mask? That older man is walking too close to people. Are you my enemy? Am I yours?* My voice is theirs. We are cobras coiling through aisles, allowing space for the other. Unsure, we stop, eye one another. I turn, that person walks in the other direction. Someone in a line snaps at the person behind them, "I'm not done. Get back." We wonder, *Have I just undone all my consecutive days of seclusion all for one lousy package of green beans?* Every errand is apocalyptic. I never remember everything I need—I neglect stops, forget items, have to double back. Often I decide I just can't make another stop. My internal software hasn't updated, hasn't retrofitted my hardware to handle the demands of the new world.

Yesterday, at the checkout, I was bagging my groceries, trying to see over my mask and through my perpetually fogged glasses, when my gloved hand bumped the gloved hand of the checkout woman. We both froze; startled, sad, a little angry, we said nothing. *Don't tell me that you are my angel of death?*

Amid this overturning, I have lost my defensiveness and embarrassment about the way I eat. I no longer overcompensate with excuses, self-pity, guardedness. In this terrible pause, I can say that—as someone who didn't find writing until he was forty years old, and then always felt frantic, out of time, and at the end of the line—I took my limitations and pared my life down to art, work, and Roberta. I couldn't be happier.

(2020)

This Is the Saddest Picture
I Have Ever Seen: Botticelli

Sandro Botticelli's small, nearly unknown fifteenth-century master-piece gives us a human being stripped of all hope. The painting is a metaphysical crucible, filled with the woes of the external world: invisible emotions, shame, wailing last words, cataclysmic loss, silence, final jour-neys, the closing down of life, demonic intensity, and the retraction of self. Often called, perfectly, *La Derelitta* (or *The Desperate One*), it is the saddest painting I have ever seen, though I've never seen it in the flesh. It's a paint-ing I first saw in my twenties, when I'd talked my way into a job showing slides for art history classes at the School of the Art Institute of Chicago. The afternoon I projected it, it smote me.

There's no visual way into or out of this picture—no space to hide or escape into. It's all wall, a kind of premodern brutalism and rigid mini-malism. Everything is stripped of adornment, rendered in low relief, un-real, dreamlike, diminished but concrete. Botticelli made *The Desperate One* in Florence when he was approaching a life crisis. He was born there in 1446 and died there in 1510. He never lived for long more than a few miles from where he was born—like Bruce Springsteen, who also has imagined encyclopedic universes filled with operatic casts. Springsteen once re-marked, "I made it all up; that's how good I am."

Botticelli saw it all. He was an eyewitness to the birth of a new world and the beginning of its death. Florence was the center of the Italian Re-naissance, indeed of the entire West. Botticelli was at the center of this center. He worked in the service of the Medici, including Lorenzo de' Medici, known as Lorenzo the Magnificent. The Medicis' bank was the biggest in Europe; they were brokers to the pope and to potentates. Lo-renzo was less about business, though, and more about culture. A noted poet, he gathered around him a cadre of philosophers, poets, and sculptors and painters of the future: Botticelli, Michelangelo, Verrocchio, Ghirlan-daio, and Leonardo. Together they delved into recently rediscovered Greek philosophers like Aristotle and Plato, and in doing so helped invent human-ism. They were archaeologists as well, identifying extraordinary lost works of pagan, Greek, early Roman, and early Christian art. During their life-times, a whole new ancient world was revealed for the first time in over a thousand years. It was as if these artists and thinkers had found a new sun.

Almost overnight, hundreds of years of medieval, Byzantine, and Gothic art dissolved. Gone was the stiff, flat, linear, ultra-religious piety of these styles. Then, in the beginning of the fifteenth century, came some-thing as earthshaking as the invention of the camera: the rediscovery of the kinds of perspective seen in ancient Roman wall painting. Soon fol-lowed the reinvention of portraiture and landscape painting, a way to de-pict objects in a new, more "realistic" kind of receding space. It was like seeing movies for the first time: objects painted onto a flat plane suddenly seemed to move toward or away from you! People were flabbergasted.

With the new humanism came the reintroduction of all sorts of lost and found pagan and mythological stories. These included mythical beings, satyrs, and subjects like homosexuality, debauchery, and the sensuous pleasures of the world. (It was a time when calling someone a Florentine meant "homosexual.")

In 1482, when Botticelli was at his full power as a painter, the preacher-prophet Girolamo Savonarola came to Florence. Assigned to one of the city's most important churches (where the beatified Fra Angelico painted), Savonarola arrived breathing fire and brimstone. He railed against aristocrats, the Medicis, wealth, the corrupt Church, and the papacy, and advocated a return to ascetic Christianity. Anything pagan was wickedness. Savonarola soon had his own roving gangs of young supporters, who turned belligerent enforcing his will. On the eve of Lent, the thugs went from home to home in Florence rounding up all things considered "vanities." This could mean mirrors, clothing, furniture, keepsakes, jewelry, books, and much more—including art. Particularly art like Botticelli's, which was deemed unchristian, sacrilegious, sinful, and pagan. These items were taken to Florence's central square, where they were stacked into an enormous pile, then set aflame. This was the infamous "bonfire of the vanities." Legend has it that, under Savonarola's sway, Botticelli burned some of his own work. If so, the loss reverberates still.

Aside from the pope, Savonarola was now perhaps the most powerful man in Italy. He held so many under his influence that the pope himself finally reached his limit. In 1497, he excommunicated Savonarola and soon threatened the rulers of Florence with an interdict should the city continue to harbor the demagogue. The following May, Savonarola was hanged and burned as a heretic in the same square as the former bonfire.

The Desperate One, seemingly painted in prophetic anticipation of all of this, offers glimpses of the internal ruin Botticelli experienced. This is a scorched, depleted world. The grieving figure in the painting is bent over. No face is visible, only flowing hair. He is barefoot, like the dancing Dionysian figures and nymphs Botticelli had painted and now despaired of.

The figure feels like a penitent, almost a ghost. It's as if the Rapture has just happened: Everyone has vanished or left, leaving the figure alone. Except for a few mystic visions, Botticelli spent his last years in unproductive emotional exile. He lived to see his own Early Renaissance style subsumed by the big three of the High Renaissance: Michelangelo, Leonardo, and Raphael. Botticelli was all but forgotten until the nineteenth century, when the Pre-Raphaelites reclaimed him. From the vantage of today, his life might look like a righteous tragedy—the story of a noble artist defeated by the forces of repressive belief. But they repressed him, too, and oppressed him. Savonarola may have been burned, but his judgment hung over Botticelli nevertheless.

I find myself dwelling on the painting's only detail, a small wooden double door with ironwork atop it in a shallow, narrow hallway. This door is important, I know. The only visual respite in the painting—a patch of blue sky—appears just over that door. I am wondering, urgently, what's beyond that door when a strange question pops into my head: Will the door ever open?

Now I see it: an absence on the door that finally unlocks the painting. I always knew it, but never noticed it before: There is no doorknob, no handle, latch, or lever.

Though some scholars believe that the painting depicts Mordecai from the Book of Esther, I see the figure as Botticelli himself. He could be in hell; there are no gates, so I can't say. Instead, I surmise that he is outside the closed Gates of Paradise. The door before him may be opened only from the inside, by Saint Peter, who weighs one's sins, deeds, and life. However wrong it may have been, Botticelli was condemned because of his own beliefs and actions, and he knows it. This is not hell. This is a terrible purgatory of knowing grief. A constant cry comes from this little picture. It is not Sartre's existential smirk, "Hell is other people," but rather what I now hear every day from people reaching out from their seclusion: *Hell is no other people.*

(2020)

How Caravaggio Destroyed
(and Saved) Painting

A gain and again during these days, unable to actually see art in person, I have time-traveled within myself for sustenance—with the help of the internet, of course. Viewing art online flattens the contextual experience: It is just as easy, or just as difficult, to call up a Renaissance masterpiece as a contemporary painting, and each appears on my computer screen in precisely the same way, shorn of the trappings of art historical importance (gilded frames, museum lighting, grand settings) or contemporary novelty (the vacuum-quiet space of a blue-chip gallery, the buzz of hype).

In these sessions of inner priestcraft, I invariably arrive in the past—always the distant past, often the Renaissance. Lately, I've been traveling to Rome in 1600, when, at the age of twenty-eight, Michelangelo Caravaggio triggered a thermonuclear artistic explosion with his first two paintings of Saint Matthew. From the moment they were installed, in a newly built Roman chapel, everyone knew that something shocking had happened. Caravaggio's fellow painters were said to "[look] upon his works as miracles." Those who counted themselves his rivals groused that "this monster of genius" had wrought the "end of painting." The artists of the time had spent the previous fifty years revering Raphael, Leonardo, and Michelangelo—so much so that ersatz Renaissance paintings had become a cottage industry among worshipful painters and princes wanting to show they had the same taste as popes and potentates—much like current monkey-see-monkey-do collectors of contemporary art. Yet there were also brilliant Mannerists like Pontormo and Bronzino, who were estranged from this type of classicizing but found ways around it by wildly exaggerating certain aspects of Renaissance paintings: elongating necks, fingers, and torsos to the point that their bodies took on the appearance of paranormal apparitions, in order to express strained emotions in ethereal spaces. In one fell swoop, Caravaggio shattered both the Renaissance ideals of wholeness, clarity, recessional space, and unity *and* the Mannerists' aristocratic affectations, anxious self-consciousness, and abstruse optical effects. (I adore Mannerism for all of this.)

Caravaggio's work seems to unleash new human forces into art: whirling, corkscrewing space; shafts of light and shadow; theatricality; and, above all, a new, colossal, un-ideal naturalism, a kind of pure painting from life. He creates an almost modern psychological interiority that pointed directly toward geniuses like Rembrandt and Velázquez (who dispense with theatrics for miracles of sensual inwardness), Vermeer and Bernini, and, in English literature, to John Milton's warning that "Blood, death, and deathful deeds are in that noise, Ruin, destruction at the utmost point." All of this is why Caravaggio's follower Nicolas Poussin praised him for coming "into the world to destroy painting."

Caravaggio would be dead within ten years, but he changed art history. He arrived in Rome in his early twenties, destitute and often in trouble, but was soon taken in by a Medici family associate. A habitual brawler, he was arrested numerous times, imprisoned, convicted of murder, and sentenced to beheading, though he escaped to the south and never returned to Rome. (He himself may have been murdered while trying to get back.) Nevertheless, in his short life he became a pop culture superstar: beloved by the people, controversial among the clergy. Caravaggio's titanic new style was the Baroque, and it transformed painting, sculpture, architecture, music, literature, fountains, cities, religion—everything. The Baroque feels vital now, for its refusal to accept a simple world of surfaces, rule-bound art theory, and overly contrived compositions, instead probing deep into the core of lived experience.

The commission for Caravaggio's Matthew cycle came in July 1599, thanks to his Medici connection. For the unruly, unconventional painter, it paved his way to stardom; for the new Contarelli Chapel, within the San Luigi dei Francesi church in Rome, it was an opportunity to take a chance on a new artist. A lot rode on this commission; plus, the pope might even see it. The cycle was painted in a tear; he must have been on fire. The last painting of the story, *The Martyrdom of Saint Matthew*, was begun first. It is the greatest depiction ever made of what Shakespeare—writing concurrently in *Hamlet*—calls "murder most foul." Two large figures center the painting. One of them is a young man, nearly naked, torso twisting, with a pointed rapier in his right hand. He is grimacing in fury, standing over an older man sprawled on the ground between his legs, whom he has just murdered. Blood spurts from the mortal wound. The murdered man is Matthew; this is his martyrdom; he is already dying. The slayer stands in dominion over Matthew the way Muhammad Ali stood over the knocked-out Sonny Liston. This is the exact second before death, an instant of action and pain never before or since rendered this realistically, horrifically, or beautifully. We are stunned, repelled, frightened, fascinated, and mesmerized by the power of Caravaggio's realism, of his undeniable vision.

According to some accounts, Matthew was martyred in Ethiopia after saying Mass. This is why he wears vestments here and seems to be on the steps of an altar. The surrounding figures, in various states of nakedness, suggest baptisms. All the dress is contemporary to Caravaggio's time; the executioner appears to have been painted from life and may have been a friend of the artist. Predator and prey form this riveting, still center of the pandemonium around them. The geometry is a kind of swirling, chambered-nautilus spiral. There may be thirteen figures here, but it's hard to make them all out; it's like a portrait of some deep-sea vent.

Our eyes search for anything anchored—some place of stability among the chaos. There it is: Above Matthew, visible only to him, is a beautiful winged angel who twists and bends to offer the palm of martyrdom to the dying disciple. Beneath him, an altar boy in white robes screams and flees. His right arm mimics Matthew's; his trunk turns the opposite direction from the murderer's. Caravaggio often works this way—his figures echoing, opposing, mirroring one another. In the darkness over the swordsman's right forearm, we see the artist, large-boned, brooding, staring, and intense.

As maximal as the *Martyrdom* is, Caravaggio's *Calling of Saint Matthew* is minimal. This is the scene where Christ calls Matthew as his disciple. The entire top of this picture is almost empty. That's radical! Whole areas are nothing more than fields of blackness. In a dim room, five figures sit around a table. Matthew was a Jewish tax collector; in this image he's the richly dressed patrician with a coin in his hat, his right hand near a pile of money. Around him are a man apparently paying his taxes; an associate; and two thuggish young buccaneers, one with a sword—typical figures of Caravaggio's time, when Rome was overrun with crime, unemployed soldiers, mercenaries, gangs, and local Mafia-like warlords.

On the right are the figures of Jesus and Peter. Jesus is raising his arm and pointing toward the table—a gesture that intentionally echoes Michelangelo's Adam extending his left hand to be touched by God. This is an artist saying *There's a new game in town.* (Challenging Michelangelo so directly, on both artistic and religious grounds, took amazing guts.) Above Jesus, a beam of light dawns across the room. It shines on Matthew, who instinctively raises his left hand as if to ask, *Who, me?* In the Bible, Jesus beckons to Matthew: "'Follow me' . . . And Matthew got up and followed him." Some have suggested that Matthew is gesturing toward the man at his right, as if saying, *Who, him?* Yet this man is looking down; he has no idea what's going on around him. Now examine Matthew's legs and feet. They unconsciously turn toward Jesus. This is Matthew in the act of leaving one life and joining another. In body and soul, Matthew is being called. Caravaggio is mind-blowing this way.

The final painting Caravaggio completed in the cycle, *The Inspiration of Saint Matthew,* shows Matthew writing his Gospel. He has just arrived at a table—there's an open book on it waiting for him—and dipped his pen into an inkwell. He's so taken by something that he hasn't even sat down; he is turning on one knee even while still standing. (The stool is perched on a ledge, about to fall off.) I've never seen anyone painted this way, before or since—but I know this pose in my bones. I've run to my desk in the grip of imagined inspiration like this, possessed. Yet Matthew isn't looking at the page; instead he looks above, at the same seraph we see in the *Martyr-dom*. This angel gestures with his fingers, as if by counting—one, two, three, this, then that, then the next—he is establishing the narrative of the life of Jesus that Matthew means to set down. It is a moment of patient, angelic support for an author trying to *get this right*.

I've seen these paintings three times; each ranks among the best days of my life. On this, my 188th day of quarantine—a period spent away from galleries and museums, fixated almost entirely on the chaos around us—something in these paintings called to me. A mystery of some kind beckons; a skeleton key that wants turning. I can't stop thinking of that angel showing Matthew how to write, the same angel who reaches quietly downward, extending its palm, as Matthew's arm rises upward. But what are these gestures telling us? Then, *bam*, after ten days, I see it. Amid all the action, the sharp observation, the intense dramatics, a paradox opens. What these paintings capture is *slowness*—the slowness of Matthew wondering, not quite knowing, what is happening. It is there, in all three paintings: a slowness that makes him one with me, with you, with all of us. A slowness that is also humanness.

In the painting of Matthew writing, I see an author at a loss for words to suit the subject, trying, hoping, perhaps failing, waiting for a ghost of inspiration to appear. This is a slowness and desperation that all writers and artists know. The *Martyrdom* is a man looking away from his killer, knowing that another presence is here; not knowing what that presence might be; coming to terms with something; allowing his hand to reach in wonder toward this otherness he feels above him. None of this comes with a lightning bolt of revelation; it is more like the gradual, almost glacial, reckonings I have been feeling these days, as we all gaze at the world from afar, watching it lurch in starts. Matthew's hand extends not in protest or terror, but in a gradual, final acceptance of grace, of knowing something new. In these frozen moments of painting, time eases into the slow pace of dawn. And, finally, this allows me to let go, too. I give up on knowing how Caravaggio created this quietude of balm within clamorous space. Instead, I just savor it.

(2020)

Jasper and Me

One night in 1986, while lingering at the top ramp of a Guggenheim Museum opening as an art world wannabe, peering down at a social universe that seemed distant and magical to me, I found myself standing next to an older man. He seemed to be doing the same thing. We were both in our own worlds. After a while, he turned to me and said, "Hello, Jerry." I was surprised. I looked at him blankly. After a pause, I said, "I am sorry. What is your name?" He said, "My name is Jasper Johns." It was a perfect picture of my unchecked self-involvement and his imperturbability, modesty, and honesty. And he answered exactly what I asked. In that moment, it felt like proof of something I'd sensed before: that Johns was already seen as an outmoded artist from another era. He was only fifty-six.

Jasper Johns made his mark not as a throwback but as a genuine revolutionary—one of the biggest in American art history. For a full century before, beginning with the Impressionists, cresting with Picasso, and reaching a sort of end point with the Abstract Expressionists, most of whom were a few decades older than Johns, the making of art was ruled by the principle of purity and the vision of the artist as a history-bending shamanic genius. Johns initiated a new century, still ongoing, in which works could be purposefully impure, imperfect, and connected to the things of the world, while also being serious philosophical machines. In this, he had predecessors, like Marcel Duchamp and Yves Klein, and successors, like Andy Warhol, Gerhard Richter, and even Jean-Michel Basquiat. But the real track-jump happened, or began, with Johns—in part because, in rejecting the self-consciously iconic grandiosity of many of his peers, he produced what ironically became one of the most iconic works in all of art history. This is why Ed Ruscha called Johns "the atomic bomb of my education."

IN THE FALL OF 1954, the twenty-four-year-old Johns, who had been laboring away at muddy, vaguely Abstract Expressionist–influenced paintings, effectively burned his artistic ships, destroying all of his previous work. "I decided to stop becoming, and to be an artist," he said. "If you avoid everything you can avoid, then you do what you can't avoid doing. . . . You do what is helpless, and unavoidable." That word, *helpless*, is a key to his work.

Not long after destroying his art, he woke up one morning with a vision. "I dreamed that I painted a large American flag," he recalled. "The next morning, I got up and I went out and bought the materials to begin it." The result is *Flag*, the most iconic, transgressive object/amulet in late-twentieth-century American art. At first he used an enamel house paint, but when he found it "wouldn't dry quickly enough," he switched to encaustic, an ancient technique used in Egyptian Fayum portraits and Roman painting, and this became key to the look of all his art. Encaustic is a fast-drying mix of heated beeswax and pigment that preserves every brushstroke in creamy, streaky, sensuous pentimento. The artist Mel Bochner has commented on "the 'dark side' of Eros" in Johns's work, and this is where it lies. In Johns's surfaces, you register every mark and touch, each instance of over- and underpainting, every moment of decision, addition, and erasure. The medium marbleizes and congeals as you look at it, seemingly retracing and preserving the artist's moves. Johns becomes a scribe incising clay, making his own abstract cuneiform tablets. Viewing it, you are almost transported into his body, witnessing the morphological development of a work of art. The effect is spooky, somnambulant, lulling, hallucinogenic, and pleasurable—what Richard Serra meant when he noted that one looks at Johns's art "millimeter by millimeter, second by second." Johns is helping us to see time.

Johns remarked that *Flag* took "a long time" to paint. He has also called it "a very rotten painting—physically." What he means is that the different paints were applied to an unstable surface. Since his mind was helpless to slow down his thinking and seeing to the speed of enamel, he had to speed up the paint. *Flag* is a triptych of panels; it doesn't match the official proportions of an American flag. The work's surface is built in layers, collaged from newspapers, headlines, bits of print, ads, and the like. The writing that's visible through the translucent encaustic has "no significance to me," Johns said. View *Flag* as a paradox: something in which contradictory truths are revealed. It is iconic and ironic; a real thing and a fake; painterly and awkward; visually blistering and psychically cocooned; patriotic and subversive; a new form of beauty made of old forms; drop-dead obvious and forever at a distance.

I think that Johns's dream was partly inspired by "the first person I knew who was a real artist." This was Robert Rauschenberg, whom he met in 1954. The two became lovers. The Texan described Johns as "soft, beautiful, lean and poetic." To Rauschenberg, Johns was "always an intellectual," a lover who read to him from the poetry of Hart Crane. Rauschenberg brought Johns into his world of artists, including Josef and Anni Albers, Cy Twombly, Buckminster Fuller, Franz Kline, Dorothea Rockburne, Willem and Elaine de Kooning, and the dancer Merce Cunningham ("my favorite artist in any field," Johns has said) and Cunningham's partner, John Cage. (Cage, in return, referred to Rauschenberg and Johns, the couple, as "the Southern Renaissance.") It is no exaggeration to say that this circle totally remade American culture at its very mid-century peak. The artists of the previous generation, many of whom had escaped Europe for America, were serious and committed to the project of Modernism—championing art as a cause with a zeal that was tantamount to war. By 1954, that war no longer mattered to the upcoming generation.

While almost all the Abstract Expressionists were straight white men (de Kooning called himself "cunt-crazy"), the younger artists included more women and a lot of gay men. Of course, they were still extremely white.

Johns has always acknowledged Rauschenberg as the nuclear furnace of it all. "I learned more about painting from Bob than I learned from any other artist or teacher." One critic remembered Johns calling Rauschenberg "the man who in this century had invented the most since Picasso." He was right: Rauschenberg is the American Picasso. Or, at least, the art world's Gertrude Stein—which would make Johns, effectively, our Hemingway. Rauschenberg said that he and Johns "started every day by having to move out from the almost overpowering influence of Abstract Expressionism." If Abstract Expressionist art was big, existential, emotional, serious, and about the "sublime," their work would be smaller, figurative, vernacular, more ironic, profane, made from everyday materials, made from life. It was as if they were renaming every animal in the natural world.

On the night of March 8, 1957, for all intents and purposes, Modernism ended and contemporary art began. On that evening, the composer Morton Feldman brought husband-and-wife gallerists Leo Castelli and Ileana Sonnabend (then Castelli) to Rauschenberg's studio. The two immigrants, in their forties, were about to become the deans of a new American avant-garde. They already loved Rauschenberg's work. That night, Castelli mentioned that he had just seen a green painting of a target in a group show. (This was Johns's *Green Target.*) Rauschenberg told them that the artist lived downstairs. "I must meet him," said Castelli. Rauschenberg returned with Johns a few minutes later, and the two dealers headed off to Johns's studio.

In the studio, they saw an array of paintings: flags, targets, numbers, letters, and more. Sonnabend bought *Figure I*, a numbers painting, on the spot. Castelli told the best chronicler of the period, Calvin Tomkins, that the first time he saw *Green Target* he was "thunderstruck . . . I saw evidence of the most incredible genius." Seeing the painting, he said, was like wanting to "get married." Castelli offered Johns a show at his new gallery on

East Seventy-Seventh Street. In the moment, Rauschenberg seemed excited for Johns. Several days later, however, "in a state of near despair," Rauschenberg visited the gallery and asked if he was going to get a show. His own upcoming exhibition was scheduled for two months after Johns's. American art history was about to jump the tracks.

The month that Johns's first solo show opened, the best art magazine of the time, *ARTnews*, featured his *Target with Four Faces* on the cover of its January 1958 issue—an unheard-of honor for a brand-new, unexhibited young artist. On January 20, Johns's debut solo show opened at Castelli's gallery. Five days later, Alfred Barr, MoMA's director of museum collections, viewed the show with MoMA curator Dorothy Miller. By day's end, they had arranged for MoMA to purchase *Green Target* and *Flag* (for $1,000 each), *Target with Four Faces* ($700), and *White Numbers* ($450). *Flag* was acquired as a promised gift by Philip Johnson, because the curators feared that museum trustees would reject the work as communistic and unpatriotic.

Johns's show at Castelli was a sellout. By contrast, Rauschenberg's show saw just two sales—including *Bed*, which Castelli bought for $1,200. In 1989, he gave this absolute masterpiece to MoMA; by then, it was valued at as much as $10 million. (The other work was returned.)

JOHNS MAKES HIS ART, he has said, from "things the mind already knows" and "things which suggest the world," things "seen and not looked at, not examined." For Johns, this has meant everything from flags, flagstone patterns, silverware, cast body parts, sign language, and images of the *Mona Lisa* to systems like maps, numbers, and the alphabet. He lets us see these things while simultaneously allowing us to see how such things "can be one thing at one time and something else at another time," or "one thing working different ways at different times." (In his words I hear echoes of Wallace Stevens's "Nothing that is not there and the nothing that is.")

By 1968, though, Johns had changed his work several times, each time radically. The year after his debut, he began creating garish abstract paintings, some with sticks attached that seem to have been used by the artist to inscribe a circle—paintings that showed their own making. He stenciled the names of certain colors atop fields of a different color, forcing the mind to toggle between seeing and thinking. He attached a thermometer to another piece of work, then painted numbers around it. In 1960, Johns heard that de Kooning was so steamed about Castelli's new gallery, and all of Johns's sales there, that he sniped: "You could give that son of a bitch two beer cans and he could sell them." Johns thought, "What a wonderful idea for a sculpture," and made a painted bronze of two cans of Ballantine Ale. This was Pop Art before it existed, Warhol's Brillo boxes years before the fact. The simple geometric seriality and oneness of *Painted Bronze (Ale Cans)* also triggers minimalism, not to say conceptualism. It's an American version of Méret Oppenheim's fur-lined teacup. Soon Johns had attached a broom, a tin can, and a spoon to different works. By the 1970s, he was making huge paintings using chairs, wax hands and feet, hangers, wire, painted flagstone patterns, even other paintings affixed facedown on the canvas.

In the mid-seventies, Johns stopped making art out of "things the mind already knows" and began making a more inward, arcane, convoluted art—"things my mind already knows," you could say. Tracings of paintings he liked, patterns that caught his eye, prints of his own body and genitals, illustrations of insects, favorite pieces of pottery, and much else. From about 1981 onward, you see his art in parts, not all at once: details; shapes within shapes; the eye changing focus, moving about a work, never centering, never knowing what one is seeing.

Johns has always worked alone; he keeps changing, taking steps forward and back. His career, too, is a paradox. While artists everywhere were setting up huge studios with assistants making their work to meet mounting demand for similar-looking product, he retreated to his own cryptic island: a foundational but castaway artist, living and working almost on another planet. He got off the art historical train of isms. For me, this only expanded his art. For the art world, however, it was a sign that the hull of his artistic integrity had collapsed. He was seen as an eccentric, an artist lost on his own island. This gave his career an arc of atavism and abnegating tragedy, the impression of a willful artist hopelessly at the mercy of his obsessions.

Jasper Johns: Mind/Mirror is the largest retrospective ever devoted to this ur-artist at the center of the late-twentieth-century art labyrinth. Split between the Whitney Museum of American Art and the Philadelphia Museum of Art, the show contains more than five hundred works. The show shines for not being your parents' Jasper Johns show. Rather than the typical art-for-rich-people show, a predictable march of masterpieces, or a belly button–gazing exegesis and interpretive study of all his images, *Mind/Mirror* is a much-needed, experimental new geography of this artist, who created his own private cork-lined bedroom and orchidology of art. It gives us a deeper, more complex artist, who is so committed to his materials that we see—in the words of one of Oscar Wilde's characters—a "mind expressing itself under the conditions of matter." As Johns put it, "The medium expresses itself to you by what it is," free of language that makes your mind work in different ways, and allows you to see things in multiple ways. I advise viewers to surrender to it.

It sounds like an evasion, and maybe it is. In his introduction to the show, Scott Rothkopf writes that Johns "has been considered an important—if not the most important—living artist for more than sixty years." (I left the show thinking, He is.) Yet his critical reception hasn't been a walk in the park. When Johns was still in his thirties, the artist-critic Sidney Tillim opined that he was already in "decline," calling him "a facile technician" who'd "become a little seedy." Tillim is referring to the way Johns's work breaks up into parts, how it features elements that don't add up, things that are impure, that are no longer singular—partial objects, like maps, targets, numbers, and so on. Mark Rothko complained, "We worked for years to get rid of all that," referring to the objects in Johns's art that have struck some as un-serious. (Johns's art was not drawn from dark nights of the artistic soul.) The critic Leo Steinberg, who has emerged over time as one of Johns's greatest apostles, wrote that at first the artist's work "looked to me like the death of painting, a rude stop, the end of the track." One prominent abstract painter attending his first show raged, "If this is painting, I might as well give up." That was the impact Johns had on his peers. As Richard Serra observed, "There was an abrupt shift. It was sort of like the Beatles kicking out Elvis."

THE FIRST JOHNS SHOW I ever saw in the flesh was his Leo Castelli exhibition of 1984. In that show, I witnessed an artist being reborn. Here were crosshatch paintings begun in the seventies, now seemingly put through an abstract blast furnace that produced compression ruptures and expansion cracks across what looked like broken ice sheets. The crosshatch pattern came from a car he saw while driving: "I only saw it for a second, but knew immediately that I was going to use it. . . . [It had] literalness, repetitiveness, an obsessive quality, order with dumbness and the possibility of complete lack of meaning." While this "dumbness" recalls Warhol, in Johns it comes from a more eccentric, personal, unknown, unknowable place. The embrace of these more feral artistic values opened a huge window for me.

By the early eighties, emerging artists were using Warhol, Gerhard Richter, and Donald Judd—not Jasper Johns—as starting points. The theory-heavy approach of Post-Modernism ruled the art roost. (I didn't understand this stuff either; even today, I'm still playing catch-up.) It was a time of smugly cool art-about-art, of slick execution, of self-conscious statements on other self-conscious statements, discourses about photography and mechanical reproduction. Meanwhile, Johns was almost embalmed, shrouded in pious criticism that could find no wrong in him.

In the nineties, the critical roof fell in. After paying tribute to the artist in his review of MoMA's 1996 Johns retrospective, the then–chief art critic for *The New York Times*, Michael Kimmelman, dismissed his work as "self-mythologizing . . . preening obscurantism . . . rambling [and] sanctimonious." By then, Johns was relying less on encaustic; his surfaces had grown flatter, duller, less sensual. His imagery was multiplying as he recycled and branched out at the same time. The work had grown more deeply encoded, which set off countless wild-goose chases looking for the meaning behind it all. My good pal the critic Peter Schjeldahl called a 2005 gallery show "arch . . . self-imitative . . . undernourished and overthought." Clement Greenberg once wrote that his "experience of Johns" included "nothing that justifies the term *major*." It is true. These works are no longer even about "majorness." They are personal workings, explorations, platforms for ideas, occasions for experience, fleeting, silent. I see his silence as a force; I'm reminded of John Currin's words, "Major genius is inaccessible."

All this critical dismissal reminds me of the "contemporary Christian music" of that era—music that brooked no ambiguity, that was relentlessly clear, declarative, and unironic. I hear a pitch of viciousness and grievance in the criticism. Or maybe I'm just a priggish keeper of the Johns flame.

I KNOW JOHNS A BIT, mostly secondhand, through friends. Roberta and I have dined with Johns twice in his Connecticut home. Both lunches were cooked by him and were fantastic. At the first meal, Roberta shattered him into laughter by describing a lyrical loopy shape in one late de Kooning painting as "the Flying Nun." I spent much of my time noodling around in his house, exploring and studying the art he owned. (I seem to recall Diane Arbus's *Identical Twins*, from 1967.) The second time we had lunch, he and Roberta entered a space-time warp talking about "God"— not the entity, but the 1917 ready-made sculpture by that name, a twisted configuration of plumbing by the American artist Morton Schamberg. The two of them spent an hour and a half parsing the work, including their belief that it should be co-attributed to the Baroness Elsa Hildegard von Freytag-Loringhoven (1874–1927). (This attribution, once debated, is now officially recognized.) I watched the two seem to pick artistic nits with each other, drilling with pleasure into the minutiae of this period. Listening to these obsessives was like hearing the ocean waves of an art history lesson that has helped my work ever since.

I've also had scores of small dinners with Johns in other people's homes. Each time I'm around him, I feel a kind of tidal force. Each time I've met him again, he was much taller, larger, than I remembered. He is witty, articulate, patient, curious, thinks of things in almost microscopic detail, is generous with information, is a great teller of stories and jokes. He is interested in everything: nature, politics, poetry, ceramics, plants, plays, history, movies, dance, cooking, whatever comes up. I don't think I have ever heard him swear. The only time he has ever asked me not to talk about something was ten years ago, when someone asked me to talk about my time on a reality-TV show about art. He turned to me and simply said, "Please, Jerry. Don't." I didn't. He exudes dignity, magnanimity, poise, circumspection, and inwardness, and he doesn't bear fools well. He's often described as cryptic, difficult, taciturn, or distant, but I've seen little evidence of this. Some say he can be sharp, painting him as a cloistered, Scrooge-like sphinx who's spent the last thirty years living hermit-like in his Connecticut home. This is flat-out wrong. He goes out often, drives himself everywhere, and has one of the best senses of humor and irony I've ever witnessed—and the best blasting laugh, like an eruption of joy released. (He is also capable of blacker moods: When he learned that an assistant had been stealing and selling his art, I remember the cloud of remorse that descended around him after he had to let this person go. Betrayal, for him, seems to elicit powerful feelings.)

He is the most precise speaker I have ever heard. Any question put to him, no matter how trivial, vain, or bizarre, elicits a pause. You feel him slowly turning over your words in his mind, seeing exactly what you asked in different ways, thinking, weighing the emotional tenor of his answer and the information to be given. In these pauses, I've seen the air go out of dinner parties as the table falls silent. I've heard my own heart pounding in those silences. Then he always answers with a short, very specific, direct response. In these responses, I almost always recognize aspects of the question that I'd failed to notice myself. The way a question is worded will change his answer altogether. An acquaintance told me he once rang the doorbell at Johns's Connecticut home and asked, "Is this Jasper Johns's home? May I come in?" Without missing a beat, Johns replied, "Yes, it is, and no, you may not." Recently, I asked, "How are your knees?" After a moment of thinking, he said, "Much as they were yesterday." This isn't to say that sometimes he doesn't come off as a perverse Zen master.

Then, too, I've seen him withdraw at a dinner, disappear for long moments. When he's ready to go, he simply will stand up and say, "Thank you. Please don't get up. It is time for me to leave." He has the best manners I've ever seen, never failing to thank his host. Being around him in such settings conjures a Proustian world where personages become great, small talk reveals large things, social faux pas become apparent, and everything seems to have both lightness of being and a real gravitas.

The reports that Johns is "difficult" stem, I think, from his being asked the same set of questions for more than a half-century. "Why did you paint this?" "What does so-and-so mean?" "Where does this image come from?" "Can you talk about being gay?" "How did you come to paint *Flag*?" "Tell me about your breakup with Rauschenberg." "What's that green-angel shape in all those paintings?" It reminds me of what the Who's drummer, Keith Moon, said about always being asked about the band's rock opera, *Tommy*: "I'm fed up with talking about it; I'm certainly not fed up with playing it."

I HAVE A FEW JOHNS ANECDOTES. The first is the worst. I'm one of the writers who has asked a stupid *Flag* question, and I'm still mortified by it. In 2003, while studying the painting at MoMA, I had a mini-revelation. Near the lower left-hand star, I saw something I'd never seen before, something I couldn't recall anyone ever writing about. There, stenciled, are the words "United States" in the star field. I went home, studied other flag paintings and prints. Sure enough, the same words or outlined shape are there every time. I was electric.

The next time I saw him, I couldn't wait to get him alone. Finally, over cocktails, I heard these horrific words come out of my mouth: "Why did you paint the words 'United States' on *Flag*?" He stopped for a moment. I thought I spied a look in his eyes that said, *Jerry!* But then I saw a crick of a smile at the corners of his lips that told me it was okay, as if he'd taken a trip into himself, then emerged to let me know I hadn't been abandoned, that he was actually thinking of this himself. In that moment, I was granted the momentary delusion that we had merged. Then he said, "Well, those words must have been there, so I left them there." They were the manufacturer's stitched or printed letters that were on the flag. Obviously, he'd rendered what was there, no more and no less. Had I thought about it a little more, he seemed to imply—had I paid more attention to the work and to his work in general—I would have found the answer myself. I knew, too, on a deeper level, that the reason I hadn't figured it out myself was that I wanted to seem special to him, to strike him as smart, to impress him with a detail so that I could dine out on my brilliant *Flag* story for years to come. Johns's work makes you come to terms with your own lazy angels.

I have never seen anyone look at art as closely as he does. At a 1993 Pace Gallery de Kooning–Dubuffet exhibition, I got off the second-floor elevator and spied him across the room studying one de Kooning painting. He didn't see me. We were alone in the gallery. I won't disturb him, I thought. I'll walk around the opposite direction, superslow, and show him how hard I look at art. I assumed we'd bump into each other naturally; I'd feign my surprise, then fall into discussing the artists. I moved slower than I ever had in my life. I never glanced back at him. After an hour, I had made it all the way around the gallery. Prepared to look up and see him, I turned around and saw him—still studying the same painting. He hadn't budged an inch. It was mystifying, stupendous. This may be why he sees shapes, patterns, configurations, figures, fragments, visual coincidences, contiguities, details, and geometries in ways others never have. Or perhaps he has an extradimensional frontal lobe.

I have seen Johns look at things this way many times. One time, he visited Roberta and me at a large rustic nineteenth-century mountain camp we'd rented. The place had no running water or electricity, and was lit by oil lamps. All the original furnishings were still in place; the rugs were mildewed, the wainscotted walls were still pasted over with paper to keep out the cold. As we toured the house, he looked at every single piece of furniture, fixture, detail, old picture, magazine from the period, plate, rug—even the "tasteful" wildflower bouquets I'd placed nonchalantly about the house. Rather than the usual ten-minute house-proud tour, this one took two hours. Finally, I handed him off to Roberta; the two of them joined the rest of us for lunch long after we began eating. No one batted an eye. We'd all seen him do this before. Much later, a friend told me he thought that Johns had returned alone when we weren't there. He speculated that this ghostly house may have reminded Johns of where he was born in Georgia, abandoned by his divorced mother and father (an alcoholic farmer), sent to live in South Carolina with a paternal grandfather, then with an aunt, then with his mother and a stepfather. (Johns has said of his childhood that it "wasn't specially cheerful.")

What else? In 2010, at the MoMA preview of *Abstract Expressionist New York*, I spotted him looking at the show—very, very slowly—with one of MoMA's chief curators, Ann Temkin. After he left, I approached Temkin. "Ann, can you tell me what he thought?" I asked. She laughed, looked at me incredulously, and gave me the best answer I've ever heard for such a ridiculous question: "You cannot possibly think that I have any idea what he was thinking."

I did once hear him snap at someone. As I looked on, intimidated by his intensity, he had spent forty-five minutes anatomizing an infinitesimal point about one small aspect of a printmaking process. He was relentless, insistent. He placed so much faith in tools, technique, processes, materials, and mediums that this was no trivial issue for him. He showed no quarter. This great quasi-conceptualist, who changed the course of art with work that ruptured its definition, is now one of art's most devoted living craftsmen. The ideas that drove his work, that were once so pointed and iconoclastic, have much more to do with how things are made, what materials do, what touch is, how color works—all of it in service of a bizarre array of images that "the mind" knows.

Johns has said that he wanted to be an artist since the age of five. "It meant," he said, "that I would be in a situation different than the one that

I was in." After a few semesters of state university art classes and a semester of art school, in 1953 he attended one day of classes at Hunter College before going home, where he fainted and stayed in bed for a week. "That ended my career in higher education," he says. All of which is to say that, like most great artists, Johns is self-taught; he makes it up as he goes, out of himself.

That became vivid to me as I glimpsed this eternal, driven "helpless" quality he refers to. Once, at a dinner of about twelve people, I heard the painter Cecily Brown talking to him about the pain she felt around making art, how she felt like she didn't know what she was doing: her anguish and fear. I saw Johns blanch, plumb a place inside himself, give a slight laugh of recognition, and say, "I never think that I know what I am doing, or that I know how to paint." I was floored. Here was the most known artist of my lifetime—an eighty-seven-year-old who'd already outlived his peers, changed art history—saying that, even now, he didn't know what he was doing. I felt this in my bones: the morbid, dispossessed foulness I have felt for years, even after becoming known as a critic, after winning prizes—that all of these are pretty vestments, cloaking devices. It is the feeling of being a commodity who is known for what it does but still does not know what that is precisely, who still feels lost at the beginning of every piece, sick at the thought that maybe any success was a fluke, a deception, a series of lucky bounces and good timing—and that, despite my incomprehensible doubt, I have to go on.

In that moment, a mystery about art opened for me: Perhaps none of us ever really knows exactly what we're doing. Maybe we only know how to do it. We just do it because we're helpless to do otherwise.

JUST TEN DAYS before the Leo Castelli exhibition in 1984, in a Paula Cooper group show, I saw a single Johns painting that changed my life: 1982's *Usuyuki*. It was a giant phosphorescent abstract, a layered atoll of cascading, siliceous marks resembling finger paintings made in a cave, or a prisoner making counting strokes and notations on a wall. In this painting, made when he was over fifty, Johns embarked on a whole new artistic journey. It was here that I grasped that the largest waves don't come at the beginning of a storm.

The *Usuyuki* series began in 1977. The word, which Johns discovered in a Kabuki play, means "thin or light snow" in Japanese. In this series, we see what he meant when he wrote in his sketchbook notes, "Make something . . . which as it changes or falls apart (dies as it were) or increases in its parts (grows as it were) offers no clue as to what its state or form or nature was." This is *Usuyuki* to me.

Like *Flag*, *Usuyuki* is a horizontal triptych. It is a large abstract grid of twenty-seven vertical rectangles of equal size. It looks like a geranium field of iridescent red, flickering green, aqueous blue, filmy oranges, and violet. Succulent, voluptuous, it's covered in individual painted encaustic brushstrokes—as if the paint had been applied by fingers or a stick, one stroke at a time. It's as much an opaque stained-glass window, mosaic floor, or mossy Persian carpet as a painting. Each of the twenty-seven vertical boxes sports a configuration of these marks. Sometimes the boxes match up at the edges; sometimes they overlap or break off. It's an assembling, dissembling abstract map, kaleidoscopic camouflage, palm-frond wallpaper, and an unknown neural network. All this as the painting seems to oscillate colors like an octopus.

Somehow, in viewing the triptych, you glean that—while all these patterns have been invented by Johns—nevertheless the whole is based on a structure "the mind already knows." Everything you see conforms to some complex, correlated, schematic unitary whole. Study the painting, drift over it, and soon you will sense a series of repeating shapes, configurations, and patterns—each order presenting itself in turn, one then another, never all at once. The same way we can never see both versions of an optical illusion at once.

Johns deploys a series of different configurations that repeat in different orders in different parts of the paintings. It's a form of counting or ordered design. You sense that these configurations are repeating in integral orders; you know there's an intrinsic template here, a guide or an odd algorithm. This, then, is how this vision machine spoke to me. I saw counting: not a simple matter of 1-2-3, 1-2-3, or any other obvious pattern, but it's there nevertheless, like algebra or multiplication tables, longitudinal-wave patterns, strange rhyme schemes or musical rhythms. I pick one, a pattern with a little teepee or triangle shape at its center, that occupies the lowest left-hand panel. I scan the image, looking closely and not looking at all, trying to use my body to see. Then I see it again, the same but in dif-ferent colors—this time on the right-hand side of the middle row of the middle panel. (I told you, it's a weird order.) At that point I knew, some-how, that it would appear again somewhere in the top row of the right-hand painting, that this one pattern was traveling up and down the painting diagonally. I thought I saw sand dunes forming and dissolving, solar flares. *Usuyuki* brings the possible and the necessary together; it can make you the pattern-recognition machine you're capable of becoming.

Look longer still, and you'll see how all the colors in the triptych move in very distinct repeating ways. This isn't random. They all move accord-ing to the light waves and particles ordered in accordance to the spectrum—always in alternating orders of red, orange, yellow, green, blue, indigo, and violet, the familiar ROY G BIV we all learned in art class. They flicker left to right, top to bottom, reverse, change orders, while always following the order of nature. An orthomorphic door opens—a portal to another kind of world that lives within us, alongside, visible, intuited, and invisible around us. Johns's numbers paintings work the same way: Placing the ge-neric stenciled numerals 0 to 9 in individual boxes on a regular grid, he triggers the impression of an abstract painting, overlaid with absolutely unexpected orders. The numbers never line up the same way twice; some-times they pile on top of one another, as if they're adding themselves to-gether, or collapsing into one über-number. Each of the rows can be read as one long number, counting up in integers that are there but impossible to predict, in unexpected visual patterns and zigzags. Be it with the marks in *Usuyuki*, with his maps, flags, and targets, and with much else in his art, each of Johns's systems has an infinite quality; every single thing in his work seems to contain a universe. Viewing them, you see that these orders are part of yourself; you come to know them on an organic, cellular, even cosmic level. These are invisible strings of the universe made briefly visible. As Johns has said, all these are "taken . . . not mine."

AT TIMES, looking at Johns's work, I no longer feel like a person. In the instants between synapses of looking, knowing, then not knowing again, I wonder if I might have died. I step outside myself, become more than one person, seeing in different ways. His work imparts a beautiful, bewildering sense of being in touch with things much bigger than yourself, outside yourself, where everything and nothing is fixed. This was the atomic bomb he set off so many years ago with *Flag*.

Usuyuki is now as much a part of myself and as real as *The Iliad*; Beethoven's *Eroica* Symphony; the light, time, space, and color in Stanley Kubrick's *Barry Lyndon*; Bob Dylan's play-by-play psalm of love and loss, "Tangled Up in Blue"; the sum-of-all-things sight of John and Yoko walking on Madison Avenue; hearing Howlin' Wolf sing "Smokestack Lightning" in a Chicago blues bar; the photograph of Muhammad Ali standing over the body of Sonny Liston shouting, "Get up and fight, sucker"; and the most primordial picture of human suffering and cosmic pain I have ever seen: Rogier van der Weyden's *Descent from the Cross*. It is as vivid and implacable to me as the night I met my wife; the Sunday morning when my father told me that my mother had committed suicide; the bedroom I grew up in; the shortcuts I took to school; the out-of-body experience I felt in Berlin's Tiergarten, where I felt I was astral projecting across the universe; the taste of cinnamon; or the smell of fresh bread made every morning in a now-destroyed SoHo bakery. Jasper Johns's work leaves me helpless.

(2021)

Acknowledgments

For a three- or four-time loser, who somehow survived a turn as an undegreed failed artist, followed by a fifteen-year self-imposed exile as a long-distance truck driver, delivery man, limousine driver, gallery attendant, and museum guard, living in an Avenue B dump, who didn't start writing until I was thirty-nine, having never written a word in my life till that moment, I'm still amazed to look back on the point of no return when I realized that anything—no matter how humiliating and hard—would be better than the stalled-stunted life of envy, resentment, procrastination, and imperious delusion I'd fallen into. At that moment, I started to write. I secured a reprieve from my self-imposed solitary confinement; I allowed myself to become radically vulnerable in my work. I know what an enormous role privilege and luck play in this kind of roll of the dice. I spend part of every day thinking about how lucky I am.

I was also incredibly lucky to have a public position, on a weekly/daily deadline, to witness and record a period I consider among the most important, dynamic, and world-changing in all of art history. In my writing career, I have stayed up late with so many art world national treasures and wraiths, sacred cows, sacrificial lambs, hangers-on, passersby, false idols, real geniuses, and bodhisattvas of inspiration. This is my family, the only thing that stands between me and a return to the hell of truck driving, sheetrocking, stealing supplies from galleries where I worked, and seething my way through every day.

I sometimes think that everything I write takes everything I have, every time I do it. That's just the way I write. There's nothing I won't draw on, to try to touch (or at least glimpse) bottom before telling the world what it is that I think I saw. I write what I think of as a criticism of permission, an approach that grants that each of us creates the world every day. This radical subjectivity is a kind of spiritual and aesthetic lifeblood. This criticism of permission has two mottos. The first is Bob Dylan's: "You do what you must do and you do it well." The other is mine, scrawled on a Post-it on my computer: "Don't fuck it up this time."

For me there is no writing; there is only rewriting. In 1998, the editor and writer Vince Aletti called to offer me one of the top spots in the art world mainframe: chief art critic at *The Village Voice*. At the time I had never been edited, not really. My writing output was limited to short reviews and long essays like "A Year in the Life of Painting," in which I reviewed something like two hundred painting shows at once. "No," I told Vince, "I'm not ready." I wasn't. But everyone in the art world is learning on the job. Then, realizing I'd feel sick to my stomach every week reading the person who *was* brave enough to step into the light, I called Vince back and begged for the job. He created the first half-life of my work as a weekly critic.

Nine years later, I repeated that mistake when Adam Moss called to offer me the same position at *New York* magazine. (Luckily, the job was still open when I begged again.) By then I knew what I really wanted. I did not want to write mainly for the art world. I wanted to address a much wider world, one that was filled with others like me, who came to art by accident or through the back door, and who felt intimidated or didn't know how to start. I wanted to be a sort of Sister Wendy or Bob Ross, opening art up, helping people to see how powerful their own impressions could be. It was like discovering a new planet.

In my first years at *New York*, I had the kindest, fastest, funniest editor I'd ever had in Christopher Bonanos. Then, during a 2015 restructuring, I was assigned to the best editor I've ever had in my life: David Wallace-Wells. He pushed me, my paranoias, my fears, my ideas, until they seemed to herniate into exciting (for me), wildly unexpected new territories of thought. David forced me to reach deeper into myself and the art world, to expose parts of me and of that complicated world. He made me a much better writer than I actually am. Some of the ideas I like best in my work derive from him. I always told the powers-that-be at *New York* that if Wallace-Wells ever left I'd leave, too. Then, after not seeing each other in the flesh for more than a year because of the pandemic, we finally met for coffee—and he told me he was going to *The New York Times*. I never felt a farewell like that in my life. I hope I never do again.

Fate moved when Calvert Morgan, an executive editor at Riverhead Books, reached out to me about doing a book together. The first time I came to see him in the offices of Penguin Random House, in a midtown skyscraper, I was in shock; I'd thought he was with some little press, that he must be working out of a little rented space in a dive. As soon as we started talking I felt I was in beneficent, patient, pushy hands. He was like some kind of editor-doge to me, someone who wore his hat of words so well that I fell into line. I've never met anyone who better understands the inner life of the writer. Our first project together was *How to Be an Artist*, an expansion of a cover story I'd done for *New York*. Then, during lockdown, we settled in to work on this book. I'd never thought that twenty years of work could be turned into a coherent single volume, but Cal helped me do it with *Art Is Life*. Throughout the process, he has been my light up ahead—so much so that, for this book, we should really have a twin byline.

Beyond these solar systems is the wellspring of my life, love, and criticism, my wife, Roberta. She is my muse, moonlight shadow, anchor, new reality daily, tempest and ocean roll, warbling bird, maker and destroyer of worlds.

Beyond that is you. I can't write if writing is without you. Without listeners or readers, I have no *music* except the echoing sounds of my own voice. You are the group mind I commune with, the immeasurable, phosphorescent million-eyed creature I see when I write, and that I hope sees me, too. You give my work whatever *soul* it might have. This is the *otherness* of art, writing, reading, and looking.

All of you make me grateful for it all.

Index

Index

Index

Index